P9-DNR-602

Reluctant Capitalists

Reluctant Capitalists

Bookselling and the Culture of Consumption

Laura J. Miller

The University of Chicago Press • Chicago and London

Laura J. Miller is assistant professor of sociology at Brandeis University.

The University of Chicago Press, Chicago 60637
The University of Chicago Press, Ltd., London
© 2006 by The Univesity of Chicago
All rights reserved. Published 2006
Printed in the United States of America

15 14 13 12 11 10 09 08 07 06   5 4 3

ISBN (cloth): 0-226-52590-2

Library of Congress Cataloging-in-Publication Data
Miller, Laura J.
    Reluctant capitalists : bookselling and the culture of consumption / Laura J. Miller.
      p.   cm.
    Includes bibliographical references and index.
    ISBN 0-226-52590-2 (cloth; alk. paper)
    1. Booksellers and bookselling—United States.   2. Bookstores—United States.
  3. Books—Purchasing—United States.   4. Books and reading—United States.
  5. Consumption (Economics)—Social aspects—United States.   6. Consumer behavior—United States.   I. Title.
  Z471.M64   2006
  381'.45002'0973—dc22

                                    2005024219

To all the kids —
Noemi, Mahats, Elias, Zach, Darshana, and Sohana —
who have given me such hope in the next generation

Contents

This book has been a long time in the making, and has turned into something very different from what I expected when I first started doing research on the book industry. Through its evolution, many people have given me intellectual, practical, and moral support. At the University of California, San Diego, I was privileged to have had the assistance and guidance of Chandra Mukerji, Michael Schudson, Dick Madsen, Dan Schiller, and George Lipsitz. Together, they encompass a tremendous range of perspectives and depth of knowledge about culture, and each is represented here.

Thanks to those others who gave support and advice during the initial incarnation of this project: Cindy Baur, Berit Dencker, Ana Devic, Cristina Escobar, Greg Mann, MaryRose Mueller, Margaret Ovenden, Anna Szemere, and Linda Vo. A very special thanks to Sharon Hays, who has shown unwavering faith in my abilities as a sociologist, and who has influenced my thinking in more ways than I can count.

During the second phase of this project, Michael Schudson continued to provide advice, comments, and suggestions. I am especially grateful for his reading of the full manuscript as I was nearing completion. Thanks also to Kathy Coll, Kim DaCosta, Emilie Hardman, Bill Hoynes, Keir Keightley, Daniel Robinson, and George Ross for comments on various sections of the book or equally valuable conversations that helped me work through the ideas here. While not named individually, I also want to acknowledge the assistance I received from other coworkers, staff, teachers, and students at U.C. San Diego, Brandeis University, the University of Western Ontario, and Vassar College.

At the University of Chicago Press, I have benefited from the enthusiasm, skill, and patience of Doug Mitchell and Tim McGovern. Working with publishers is not at all the same as writing about them, and the crew at Chicago eased this process considerably.

My family kept reminding me that there is more to life than academics; at the same time, they maintained interest in this project throughout its entirety. Thanks to Art Miller, Sylvia Miller, Matt Miller, Devra Miller, Vyvyan Tenorio, Roberto Johansson, Noemi Johansson-Miller, Mahats Miller, Elias Johansson-Miller, Zach Tenorio-Miller, and M. Punithakumar.

Many thanks to those who opened up their homes to me and provided generous hospitality during my research travels: Joe and Marilyn Stone, Daniele Rossdeutscher and family, and Lin Neumann and Rebecca Neumann. In addition, I could not have conducted the research without all those individuals who provided me with contacts in the book industry. I am also grateful to the two bookstores that allowed me to interview their customers, and to all the book professionals who took the time to talk to me. Though they may not agree with everything I have to say here, I hope they recognize the deep respect I have for their labors in this industry.

CHAPTER 1

Commercial Culture and Its Discontents

In the early 1960s, Edward Shils wrote an essay examining "the bookshop in America." Shils praised the bookseller, a special kind of person who willingly forgoes a lucrative salary simply to be around books. The bookseller, he noted, performs an important public service, running an enterprise with a unique role in the reproduction and distribution of culture:

> A good bookshop blows the breeze of contemporaneity on one; it puts one "in touch"; it permits first contacts and offers prospects of greater intensity. It is a place for intellectual conviviality, and it has the same value as conversation, not as a "civilized art" but as a necessary part of the habitat of a lively intelligence in touch with the world.[1]

Yet, despite the bookshop's value for American society, Shils believed that the retail book trade was in a very sorry state, and its future looked only worse. The problem, he argued, was that Americans showed little interest in reading, and publishers often bypassed bookstores to sell directly to the public — a set of conditions that only compounded the already unprofitable character of bookselling. As a result, most bookshops specialized in bestsellers and other popular titles and few carried a satisfactory and varied selection — not a good thing, as Shils warned:

It may well be that we live in an epoch in which the bookshop is an institution suspended between "the dying old society" and the "society struggling to be born." It has few defenders. Its protagonists are feeble fellows rubbing their eyes dreamily and perplexedly at the entrance to their caves. Those who benefit from their existence (the publishers on the one hand, and readers and potential readers on the other) are hard at work intentionally and unintentionally scuttling them. Perhaps the bookshop belongs to the good things of the bourgeois epoch, like the rule of law, representative institutions, public liberties, and the right of *habeas corpus,* things from which there is a general benefit but which have been so much taken for granted that their beneficiaries have grown careless about their well-being.[2]

It might be fairly easy to dismiss Shils's ruminations as mere nostalgia on the part of a sociologist distressed by the challenges then being posed to many institutions, including an institution seen as an important source of "good" (i.e., elite) culture. But such a dismissal would be a mistake. The sentiments expressed by Shils about the bookshop echoed those heard decades earlier, and similar complaints can still be heard today. They combine reverence for this retail enterprise with alarm that the qualities that make it so valuable are endangered. The persistence of such sentiments suggests that it is worth asking whether Shils's fears have come to pass. Has a new social order truly vanquished the conditions that kept the old-fashioned bookshop alive? And why is there such regret about the perceived loss of both the bookstore and the kind of individuals who supposedly sustained it? These questions can be clarified by looking at a more recent manifestation of the issues that Shils was engaging.

In May of 1990, Crown Books, then the third largest chain of bookstores in the United States, opened its first "Super Crown" in a strip mall in Alexandria, Virginia. The new Super Crown was distinguished by the fact that it carried 30–40,000 different titles — three or four times as many as the typical Crown store.[3] Similar developments could be seen in the other national bookstore chains. Earlier that year, Waldenbooks had announced that it was converting some of its outlets to a "superstore" format with a greatly expanded selection of titles.[4] And in September, Barnes & Noble launched its version of the superstore in Roseville, Minnesota, a suburb of St. Paul. The new store, located in a mall that housed several large discount stores, outdid its competitors in terms of size, boasting an impressive 15,000 square feet and 100,000 titles.[5]

Of course, huge bookshops were nothing all that new in the United States. Especially since the 1980s, several such stores had dotted the American landscape. But the move by Barnes & Noble, Crown, and Waldenbooks marked a significant shift from the chains' previous strategy of establishing small, standardized outlets specializing in bestsellers and other quick-turnover titles, frequently in areas underserved by other bookstores. Observers were now curious to see how the chains would combine their technological sophistication, marketing savvy, and policies on discounting with the large-store format.

At first, press accounts of the superstore phenomenon were relatively enthusiastic. "They Look Like Libraries!" proclaimed an admiring editorial headline in a major magazine for librarians.[6] "After years of maligning the chains for stocking too few titles, book lovers cautiously salute them for broadening their mix," noted another report in a business journal.[7] Reporters remarked not only on the large number of titles being sold, but also on the decor of the new stores. In contrast to the bright, contemporary interiors of the chains' smaller outlets, the superstores included soft lighting, classical music, and comfortable chairs. These stores were trying to communicate the message that they were designed with the serious booklover in mind.

However, within a year, journalists were acknowledging that not everyone in the book world applauded these developments. Antagonists raised many of the same concerns identified by Shils three decades earlier. But the context in which these issues were discussed had changed in the intervening years. The debate that accompanied the building of the superstores marked the latest battle in an ongoing war between independent booksellers and the national chain bookstores. Although the roots of this conflict go back over a century to disagreements over the bookselling practices of department stores, the controversy took on its present tone with the development of the modern chain bookstore in the early 1960s. After a period of escalation, there appeared to be a lull in the hostilities during the late 1980s, as the chains and the independent bookstores claimed different public images and often appealed to different audiences. But the rise of the superstores ended any talk of rapprochement in the book wars. Questions were now being raised as to whether this new kind of chain posed a lethal threat to independent booksellers, and what that threat might mean for books and readers in the United States.

Independent booksellers accused the chains of harboring monopolist designs, and of engaging in unfair competition to achieve those goals. Pointing to the chains' corporate owners, critics claimed that the superstores' actions were guided more by profit-and-loss statements than by literary considerations. While supporters continued to marvel over the superstores' breadth of selection, detractors insisted that book buyers were simply being treated to more of the same safe, standardized fare found in the smaller chain outlets. And while some congratulated the chains for building the kind of store that could make book buying almost as popular as renting a video, others scoffed that the superstores were better at promoting coffee drinking than an interest in ideas and the intellect. These debates over their impact grew more heated as the superstores began to account for an increasing proportion of the nation's book sales, and as greater numbers of independents succumbed to their competition.

The hostility to the superstores, as well as to their smaller, mall-based predecessors, struck some observers as rather curious considering that the chains were in many ways answering criticisms that had been leveled at booksellers for years. For most of the previous century, book professionals had despaired over the archaic and inefficient systems in place for joining a book with the individual who might want to read it. Many bemoaned the small number of outlets for the purchase of books, the lengthy delays in the delivery of books from publisher to retailer, lackadaisical attitudes on the part of booksellers, ignorance of the book-buying market, and the inability of stores to stock the books customers wanted when they wanted them. Consistently, there were calls for the entire book distribution system to get itself more in step with contemporary business practices.

In the last four decades of the twentieth century, economic, technological, and cultural changes finally pushed the book trade to become more rationalized, that is, to calculate the most efficient means to sell books and then develop the organizational forms and procedures necessary to that task. The growth of the chain bookstore was certainly an important development along these lines, as the chains opened outlets in towns that never before had bookstores, as they invested in sophisticated computer systems that carefully tracked the market for books, and as they worked with wholesalers and publishers to move books more rapidly to where they were needed. However, as the debate over the superstores illustrates, such trends have not been welcomed as absolute progress by everyone in the book world. What Shils called bewilderment felt by those peering at the world beyond their "caves" might be better seen as a wide-eyed yet stubborn refusal to accept the techniques and philosophies that characterize the distribution of other consumer goods. In bookselling, one hears repeatedly, there are grave consequences to a single-minded devotion to efficiency and the bottom line.

The debate over the future of the bookstore is certainly not an isolated event in the history of the U.S. book industry. It is reminiscent of other controversies that have counterpoised dedication to the dissemination of books against crass commercialism. The tension it speaks to was also apparent in the outcries over the tide of publisher mergers and acquisitions in the 1970s and '80s, in criticisms of the new book clubs of the 1920s, and in turn-of-the-twentieth-century protests over the use of agents to negotiate authors' contracts. With each of these issues, some members of the book industry charged that hucksterism, greed, ruthless competition, and obsequence to the "mass" market should simply not be associated with something as valuable to society as are books. As the potential for profit making in bookselling has expanded, it is therefore not surprising that this sector has become a focal point for debates about commercialism.

However, conflict over the style and techniques of the book chains goes well beyond concerns about literary culture. It also points to a certain degree of distress over the very familiar process of rationalization in the sphere of commerce more generally. Ever since the end of the Civil War, there have been periodic outbreaks of opposition to large commercial organizations, including large retailers, which have played an ever more prominent role in American society. Beginning in the 1860s with the Great Atlantic & Pacific Tea Company (A&P), chain stores achieved popularity and profitability by pursuing economies of scale, by emphasizing self-service, and by offering their goods at reduced prices.[8] But some condemned these stores for destroying the independent, owner-operated shop, thus threatening monopoly and removing retail business from personalized, community control. Antichain sentiment has waxed and waned over time, with relatively little organized antichain activity taking place since the 1930s. However, with the growth of the so-called big-box retailers, such as the book superstore, opposition to chains has been reinvigorated. This movement not only revives older concerns about the undue power of giant retailers, but also condemns such stores for depersonalizing relations between seller and customer and standardizing the landscape of the nation's (and increasingly, the world's) communities.

The current controversy over bookselling is thus notable in that it combines abiding ambivalence toward business values in the world of books with ambivalence toward rationalization in the sphere of retailing. My purpose in this book is to explore that double ambivalence in order to address the following questions: Why do efforts to rationalize book retailing promote large amounts of controversy? And what is the significance of efforts to check the power of large retailers such as the book chains? Through these questions, I intend to examine a broader set of issues having to do with the extension of the market and processes of rationalization, the meaning of retailing and consumption in American culture, and the place of books in American society.

While these considerations will entail some examination of bookselling in the nineteenth and early twentieth centuries, as well as of some parallel developments in the wholesaling sector, the primary focus here will be on the development of the contemporary book chains and the resulting conflict with independent booksellers. This conflict not only includes a struggle for market share, but also an attempt to win a moral judgment on the appropriate organizational form for booksellers, and the appropriate conduct of booksellers and consumers alike. The competition between chains and independents gets played out, for example, in retailers' approaches to selecting the books for a store's displays and in the various methods used to market both individual books and the bookstore itself. But beyond these merchandising maneuvers, the conflict described here has also become explicitly politicized, with independent booksellers getting on their soapboxes and taking their cause to the courts, to legislative bodies, and to the public. The bookstore wars demonstrate that retailing is more than just a competitive field in which the economically powerful and agile survive, it is also the site of conflicting visions of how both individual and collective life benefit from the circulation of material goods.

The Culture of Commerce

Both within academic analysis and the popular imagination, there exists an assumption that the economy is in some way at odds with culture. This is reflected in popular images of the business world as a place where cultural niceties fall before Darwinian instincts, and in scholarly debates about whether structure or culture has the greatest social impact. Yet the business of books presents one of the best cases for seeing the importance of joining together an economic and cultural analysis.

Sociological or social historical work that examines book publishing in the twentieth century has been relatively sparse, with an even greater lack of empirical research on bookselling.[9] Many of the available accounts of the contemporary book industry come in the form of memoirs, admiring biographies of editors or publishers, and practical reports aimed at professionals; consequently, this body of work tends to lack a critical edge. But whether historians, sociologists, practitioners, or journalists, almost all those writing about the book world have acknowledged the persistence of debates over commercialization. Such debates have most commonly been understood in terms of a tension between the pressures of the market and a commitment to "good" books. This tension is frequently expressed as an opposition between culture and commerce.[10] As Coser, Kadushin, and Powell describe it,

> The industry remains perilously poised between the requirements and restraints of commerce and the responsibilities and obligations that it must bear

as a prime guardian of the symbolic culture of the nation. Although the tensions between the claims of commerce and culture seem to us always to have been with book publishing, they have become more acute and salient in the last twenty years.[11]

For Coser and his colleagues (as for others who have adopted the culture/commerce dichotomy), this tension describes the "quest for profit and the demands of excellence [that] have all too often refused to go hand in hand."[12] While Coser, Kadushin, and Powell help to refute any conclusion that this tension is new to American society, they leave unexamined various assumptions about the transparency of those demands of excellence. The distinction between the meritorious and the unworthy, between serious and trashy books, is simply taken as a given.[13]

Much scholarship on popular culture in recent years has taught us that such a notion of literary merit needs to be made more problematic; one cannot assume that literary merit is both transparent and commercially unprofitable. Rather, the process by which a book gets defined as "serious" is a social and political one.[14] This is not to say that the culture-commerce tension is not salient. But instead of conceiving of culture as a shorthand for high culture, it is more useful, following Raymond Williams, to think about how intellectual and artistic life are related to a wide range of existing cultural meanings and practices.[15] This can help us see how the very notion of artistic creativity has come to be in part defined by a sense of standing outside the logic of commerce.

A more critical perspective on the culture-commerce tension has explored how commercialization affects the status and power of cultural authorities. For instance, Elizabeth Long argues that longstanding fears of commercialization in publishing are based in changes to the cultural hierarchy that threaten an elite's cultural authority. Especially when the reading public expands, along with the institutions that cater to them, a cultural elite fears that its literary values (i.e., high culture) are in danger of being degraded by the unrefined tastes of the new readers.[16]

A similar argument is contained in Janice Radway's research on the Book-of-the-Month Club.[17] Radway discusses one of the more vociferous debates in the history of the American book trade, one with many parallels to today's controversy over the chains. When the Book-of-the-Month Club formed in the 1920s, bookstores not only feared the new competition, but detractors warned that this innovation would result in literary standardization as consumers allowed the club to dictate their choice of reading material. Similar to the chain stores of today, the Book-of-the-Month Club and its imitators were feared because of their price-cutting practices, because of the preferential treatment they received from publishers, and because of their national reach and, thus, the cultural power they might wield. But Radway argues that there was actually a deeper meaning to the controversies surrounding the book clubs. Like other critics of mass culture theory, she argues that the specter of standardization was primarily a cover for the discomfort of cultural elites who saw their authority challenged by upstart entrepreneurs.[18] These rival cultural authorities appeared especially menacing as they were attempting to lead a huge new mass audience that threatened to overwhelm the Brahmins of the literary world. Such fears were played out in accusations that the Book-of-the-Month Club was a centralized, institutional authority that shamelessly mixed high with low culture, and the purity of culture with the profanity of commerce.[19]

Radway's analysis of the book club disputes is helpful for understanding the current bookstore wars, as well as more general concerns about the commercialization of books. After all, the phenomenal success of the mall-based chain bookstores was in part due to their ability to attract people who found the old-fashioned bookstore elitist and intimidating. And fear that centralized organizations oriented to the mass market will preclude the independent judgment of the free individual remains a component of the contemporary distrust of commercialization. But, as I will argue, ideas about cultural authority have changed considerably in recent decades. A perspective that casts critics of the chains as defenders of elite prerogatives cannot account for the fact that at present both independents and chains are struggling to claim the mantle of populism.

Furthermore, the culture-commerce framework, as it has been elaborated by scholars, is inadequate for explaining the bookstore wars because of the way in which the "commerce" part of the equation has been ignored. We need to recognize that the sphere of commerce is more complex than it first appears to be. Of course, certain aspects of commerce under capitalism can be taken for granted. The market is governed by the imperative that participants compete with one another for relative advantage. Producers against consumers, employers against workers, capitalists against capitalists — each group has material interests that are opposed to those of the other. For this reason, the entrepreneur must continuously innovate; he must find new ways to increase productivity or find new markets, or else his competitors will put him out of business.[20] The constraints placed on members of the book industry by virtue of their being involved in a capitalist enterprise are therefore very real, and people are often compelled to act in ways they find distasteful or that undermine the reasons they entered the book business in the first place. As even the most idealistic bookseller soon discovers, the overall logic of the capitalist system is mainly about making a profit in a competitive environment.

Nevertheless, none of this negates an argument that commerce is culturally marked: the way it is understood and practiced depends on specific historical and cultural contexts. In the first place, as Polanyi has shown, the market economy has a history; humans have not always paid homage to the motive of achieving maximum material gain.[21] Moreover, even within capitalist economies, commercial activity is not reducible to the quest to secure material advantage efficiently. The new economic sociology that has developed since the 1980s has challenged neoclassical economic thought regarding the predictability of individual and organizational behavior in situations of exchange, along with assumptions about the autonomy of the economy from the state and other institutions. Abstract models predicated on a vision of atomized individuals single-mindedly seeking to optimize material interests have been shown not to hold up very well when applied to actual cases in the real world. The alternative approaches to understanding economic behavior that have developed provide an important corrective to assertions that the triumph of enterprises such as the chains is inevitable, or that consumers who favor the lower prices of the chains are simply following human nature.

One highly influential contribution to economic sociology comes from Mark Granovetter, who has elaborated the concept of embeddedness, the idea that economic behavior and economic institutions are embedded in networks of social relations. Differing with rational actor theorists as well as with those who assume that embeddedness does not apply to market societies, Granovetter claims that the pursuit of economic goals in modern society is accompanied by other considerations, such as the quest for sociability, reputation, or power, that arise from individuals and firms being part of social networks. These social networks make orderly economic exchange possible, by providing the foundation for trust, for example, but they also can lead to behavior that is not strictly rational from the economist's perspective.[22]

A number of sociologists have built on the notion of embeddedness to provide an account of economic action that is more attuned to cultural influences. Sharon Zukin and Paul DiMaggio have extended Granovetter's argument to claim multiple kinds of embeddedness that constrain economic action. Among these they include cultural embeddedness, which they define as "the role of shared collective understandings in shaping economic strategies and goals." According to their definition, "culture has a dual effect on economic institutions. On the one hand, it constitutes the structures in which economic self-interest is played out; on the other, it constrains the free play of market forces."[23]

In practice, at least within the United States, it is the constraining rather than the constitutive role of culture that has been most studied. Here culture is examined as a variable factor that influences economic action, and in some circumstances, modifies the extent to which a rational calculation of gains and losses becomes the basis for action. Patricia Thornton, for instance, describes how culture affects decision making in higher education publishing firms. She uses the concept of institutional logic to explain a historical shift in the types of problems and solutions that receive the attention of decision makers. As higher education publishing went from an "editorial" to a "market" logic, she argues, publishers became less intent on gaining prestige for a house and more intent on securing their firms' competitive positions, more likely to engage in acquisitions rather than promote the organic growth of their companies, and more inclined to see the marketing of titles instead of the nurturing of authors and editors as the path to success.[24]

Part of Thornton's aim is to "tease apart the influence of culture from those of social and economic structures."[25] However, this assumes a firmer division between culture and economics than may be warranted. As Don Slater says, "economic and cultural categories are logically and practically interdependent: neither can be reduced to or separated from the other." As he notes, this is a stronger claim than the idea of embeddedness.[26] It is not that economic action is modified by culture; rather, it is in part constituted by culture. And in turn, the organization of the economy affects the development of cultural ideas that extend well beyond the economic sphere to influence all realms of society.

The stress on how culture constitutes economic relations, more typical of European than American sociologists, is a perspective to which I am sympathetic.[27] It is possible that the American theorizing that has taken place has been colored by the fact that we live in an era when the ruthlessness and reach of the capitalist market appears overwhelming. Thus, capitalist relations become the usual starting point for thinking about the economy. But the production, circulation, and consumption of goods can be organized in many ways, and even in the modern world, noncapitalist forms exist, sometimes temporarily, sometimes as a pale memory of earlier organizational types, but nonetheless, not that difficult to find. An approach that examines how culture and commerce are mutually constitutive reminds us that economic activity should not be conflated with capitalism. Similarly, it leads us to question how the ends of economic behavior (including consumer behavior) get determined. In part because so many studies describe seemingly self-contained worlds of the firm or the industry, the goals of economic activity appear self-evident. Yet these economic institutions are in actuality not neatly cut off from the rest of society. As a result, some of the same considerations and concerns that affect how people carry out their roles as family members, as citizens, and as devotees of leisure pursuits such as reading shape the style and substance of the economic activities of work, trade, and consumption.

In this study, I address the question of how book professionals position themselves in relation to some general principles of capitalism, including competition, profitability, growth, efficiency, and impersonality. And though I do pay attention to the day-to-day routines of booksellers, I am less interested in specifying the mechanisms that shape how their decisions about carrying out their work get made than in showing how such decisions help to shape the ways in which consumers relate to those same capitalist principles. My aim is to describe not simply a belated event in the historical accommodation to capitalism, but an ongoing process whereby different cultural models of retailing and consumption continue to compete with one another, even during periods of advanced, seemingly seamless capitalism.

In the following chapters, I intend to explore the culture of commerce, and more specifically, the culture of retailing and consumption. I argue that the debate over bookselling is not a trivial or isolated event, but reflects the centrality of retailing in communal life, and a common belief that shopping plays a central role in individual fulfillment. In this way, the chain controversy can be understood as reflecting certain dissatisfactions with individual and communal well-being. American commerce has seen numerous changes that are associated with greater profitability in retailing, but that have also altered how retail work and consumption are experienced. These changes include the growth of large organizations with the capacity to wield unmitigated power, the spread of impersonal social relations, the standardization of commercial shopping districts, and at least potentially, the tendency for a more homogenous assortment of commodities to be purchased. The critique of the chains, and the moral superiority claimed by independents, represent resentment of how these developments appear to banish idiosyncrasy and sentiment from retail work. This sense of loss is especially acute in bookselling because the consumer goods at issue are items that have long been treated with special respect and even reverence.

At the same time, other historical and cultural developments have shaped the ways in which booksellers understand and respond to the changes affecting their industry. Among the most important was a decline, during the post–World War II era, in booksellers' former identification with a genteel culture and a social elite. This led, on the one hand, to a greater willingness by independents to shrug off conservative respectability and engage in politicized actions to defend the model of retailing they esteem. In their attempts to enlist public support for this activism, they have asked consumers to recognize a collective interest in opposing the usual workings of the free market. But on the other hand, the decline of cultural elitism also contributed to a valorization of consumer sovereignty, and the sense that consumers will and should pursue their individual interests in the marketplace. When defined in stark economic terms, these interests are indeed opposed to those of the independents. Thus, the case of the bookstore wars highlights competing cultural frameworks used to define consumer motivation and consumer responsibility.

Rationalized Retailing

According to Weber, the modern world is characterized by the triumph of instrumental rationality, a way of orienting oneself to one's environment and other people whereby they become means to reach a given end. Rational action has no place for emotion or tradition; rather, individuals or organizations consistently, systematically, and efficiently adjust available means to reach their ends. The economic sphere exemplifies this kind of rationality. The surest way to profit is to refrain from making deals based on personal attachments, or showing mercy for the personal plight of others, or allowing sentiment or sympathy to influence decisions; after all, another's loss may well be one's own gain. These various tendencies are reinforced by the dominance of formal rationality in modern life, the application of calculation in order to achieve predictable outcomes. As Weber's examples of the bureaucracy and the scientific method show so well, calculable procedures and rules applied to all situations and all persons will produce consistent results. Yet despite the technical superiority of rational action, Weber saw the ultimate consequences of rationalization as extremely grim. The vanquishing of irrationality — of emotion and mystery — results in a deadening routinization of everyday life, and the inability of people to find overall meaning in their existence.[28]

While the work of independent booksellers has also been affected by these processes, the chains have rationalized bookselling most deliberately and most thoroughly. The bureaucratic structure of the chains makes it possible for a multitude of far-flung outlets to be administered from a central headquarters. Bureaucratic organization also encourages specialization of tasks, resulting in a more efficient division of labor, and making it easier to train workers and deploy personnel where needed. As uniform procedures produce consistent, predictable results, the chains have favored standardized methods and a standardized style across all outlets. This allows distant managers to be assured that each outlet is offering a relatively uniform bookstore experience, one that is in keeping with the image the company is trying to project. Furthermore, the chains are able to achieve significant economies of scale by centralizing and standardizing many key activities. From selection, ordering, and advertising, to decisions about pricing, store decor, and the placement of sections and displays — to one degree or another, these functions are performed in a central office. New technology has contributed greatly to the rationalization process, especially the application of computerized systems for calculating future sales. Decisions about what titles to stock, recommend, or return to a publisher are now based on rational techniques of analyzing past sales. Certainly, these various initiatives have helped to bring a level of profitability to bookselling unimaginable just a few decades ago.[29] Yet there are other consequences to rationalization about which there is less agreement.

Many scholars have sought to show how the processes of rationalization, and its unintended consequences, are concretely realized in contemporary society. Indeed, what has occurred in bookselling bears some resemblance to aspects of what George Ritzer has called the McDonaldization of society.[30] For instance, his analysis of the negative effects of increasing rationalization within the service sector includes the homogenization of experience and the dehumanization of employees and customers alike, as interactions between them are minimized and those that remain are governed by uniform scripts.[31] However, while Ritzer assumes that the gratifications consumers get from "McDonaldized" retailers are largely illusory, and that consumers' and workers' essential humanity is being violated, an explanation of the conflicting responses to the effects of rationalization in retailing needs to be more thoroughly grounded in both history and culture.

Criticisms of rationalization in bookselling have focused on the perceived ill effects of impersonality, standardization, and bigness. Independent booksellers hold themselves up as guardians of local solidarity, local character, and local interests, while the large, corporate, standardized chain bookstore is seen as fostering impersonal social relations, effacing the distinctiveness of local communities, and using its clout to crush its competitors.

The critique of impersonality reflects the loneliness that some feel as a result of spending so much of their time in large, anonymous organizations.[32] But beyond this, many in the industry are also mourning a way of life that has had a great deal of meaning for those who have pursued it.

People who choose to run an independent bookstore are generally deeply committed to their enterprises; except in the rarest of cases, there is little money to be made, and long hours and tremendous uncertainties are the norm. Independent booksellers consistently describe their work as more than just a way to make a living, and more than just a means of escaping the constraints that come from working for somebody else. These booksellers see themselves as bettering society by making books available. And they get a great deal of satisfaction from the personal relationships they establish with their customers. In this sense, customers are perceived as neighbors, not merely as sources of one's own or distant shareholders' profit. Whether or not many customers experience the independent retailer in this way is a different question. But for booksellers, the rationalization of bookselling has clearly threatened this orientation to their work.

Additionally, rationalization is opposed for the way that it threatens standardization. Whereas standardization in the book industry was once seen primarily in terms of its danger to individuality and its inducing of conformity, the emphasis has changed in the last few decades to the problem of standardized communities as well as homogenous culture. This concern has included an aesthetic critique, with the chains' standardized style denounced for contributing to a loss of community identity. At the same time, centralized and rationalized selection and recommendation techniques are said to threaten the diversity of books and hence the exchange of multiple opinions necessary for the functioning of a democracy. Independents and their supporters claim that by removing the idiosyncratic, personal judgments of numerous individual booksellers, and substituting for them the judgments of a small number of chain employees who use rational techniques to maximize sales, the quirky or critical book that might have only a small audience will be overlooked in favor of the standardized bestseller.

Related to this, the critique of chain retailing continues an American tradition of suspicion toward bigness. In the early part of the twentieth century, this antagonism to bigness found expression in a dislike of large cities, which appeared to inspire corruption and to depersonalize social interaction. It also came out in a distrust of large bureaucratic organizations, which threatened to crush the individual with amoral indifference. Critics claimed that these organizations undermined such American values as self-sufficiency, equality, and the decentralization of economic and political power. In small-scale enterprises, which could evoke if not exactly replicate the small community, lay the hope for maintaining a virtuous and free citizenry.[33] Many of these ideas about the social implications of size have persisted into the present. Indeed, the sense that large organizations are less likely to care about the welfare of employees, customers, and the cultural value of books is not only apparent in criticisms of the chains, but in the alienation expressed by employees of some large independent bookstores.

In short, retailing in general and book retailing more specifically have been transformed in profound ways as they have been subject to increased rationalization. And some people have experienced the myriad effects of this transformation as adding to the harshness and coercion of contemporary life. However, the movement toward increased rationalization is not confined to developments within retail organizations. Consumption itself has also become rationalized, and consumers have come to resemble rational actors more than ever before.

The Meanings of Consumption

Although no one was sure that the chain book superstore would pay off when it was first established, it took only a few years for any doubts about its viability to be swept away. That this kind of store has thrived is testimony to the key role that consumerism plays in Americans' lives today. Historians have shown that a culture of consumption is far from a new phenomenon, but it has consolidated over the last half century as a population with more discretionary income than in the past has been confronted with a surfeit of consumption opportunities. While most scholars have addressed the symbolic meanings attached to commodities, or the ways in which more and more aspects of life become commodified, a somewhat smaller group of researchers has paid attention to the experience of shopping itself.[34] As they demonstrate, shopping has become an important leisure pursuit in contemporary society. However, there is no agreement on what shopping means to consumers.

Much recent sociological work on shopping strikes a celebratory tone, with consumption described as an important arena for individual self-determination. For instance, Rob Shields argues that contemporary shopping is marked by new, postmodern spatial forms that combine leisure with commercial activities. He claims that this results in a breakdown of the separation of value spheres, referring to Weber's ideas about the way that different logics apply to the different dimensions of social life — political, economic, religious, and so on.[35] However, Shields overlooks important continuities with the past; after all, the turn-of-the-century department store, the preeminent modern retail institution, was notable for making shopping into a diversion and entertaining spectacle. Like shopping in general, bookselling has indeed changed over the last century, but in ways that are as much about the consolidation of modernist capitalist principles (such as the rationalization of mass distribution and dominance by large, public corporations) as about a "postmodern" stress on image and theatricality (such as with the increased attention to marketing and store design).

Furthermore, the emphasis that many scholars place on fantasy and playfulness in their conceptualizations of shopping shows just how firmly they, as well as the public, continue to believe that consumption represents a retreat from society. While Shields claims that consumers appropriate private shopping centers for use as spaces to engage in public sociability as well as to experiment with style and identity, this still reinforces the idea that the primary meaning of shopping for individuals is to provide them with an escape from the responsibilities of everyday life.[36] Yet this association of shopping with leisure, an association so easily taken for granted today, obscures the ways in which consumption can also be understood as producing outcomes with a public and political impact.

One suggestive line of analysis comes from a 1954 study by Gregory Stone. Stone was interested in the ways in which urbanites could be more tightly bound to their communities through the relationships they established with the personnel of retail stores. He identified a fourfold typology to describe different consumers and orientations to shopping. The economic consumer was sensitive to price, quality, and assortment of merchandise, and viewed clerks as "merely the instruments of her purchase of goods." The personalizing consumer viewed shopping as an interpersonal experience, and considered the formation of close relationships between customer and sales personnel as important. The ethical consumer viewed shopping in the light of a larger set of values, and perceived a "moral obligation to patronize specific types of stores." Finally, the apathetic consumer had no interest in shopping, and made little or no differentiation between stores and store personnel.[37]

Stone's typology is useful for thinking about the different orientations to shopping found within American culture. Yet these orientations have certainly changed since the mid-twentieth century, and I would like to propose some other ways of conceptualizing the consumer, which are suggested by an examination of bookselling. It is likely that fewer Americans today than in the 1950s look for and expect to form personal relationships with store personnel, but the consumer guided by sentiment has not vanished altogether. However, as much as booksellers try to cultivate the loyalty and affective ties of the sentimental consumer, they increasingly acknowledge the rights of the sovereign consumer whose tastes and choices are to take priority over any judgments on the part of the retailer. Related to this, with customers expecting shopping to be not just painless, but actually fun, re-tailers provide refreshments and diversions in order to satisfy the enter-tained consumer. On the other hand, as retail techniques and styles have become similar across the country, the standardized consumer who expects predictability in the retail experience raises bookseller hopes of finding the formula for producing predictable sales.

These different visions of the consumer coexist within American culture and underlie many of the strategies of both independent and chain retailers. Nevertheless, it is probably the rational consumer, out to obtain desired goods at the lowest possible cost, who has come to dominate Americans' as-sumptions about what motivates consumer behavior. This is a highly in-strumental understanding of consumption, and one that encourages a view of humans as fundamentally capitalist in nature.

Each of these models describes a consumer who is motivated by private interests, however defined. But there is an additional orientation that has emerged at various times in American history, that of the citizen consumer who acts on behalf of a perceived common good and who consciously turns consumption into a political act. This latter orientation is one that relatively few Americans currently adopt, and one that many find peculiar or even of-fensive. Yet the campaign by independent booksellers has, however incon-sistently, contributed to pushing this vision of consumption somewhat more into public consciousness.

In contrast to Stone's typology, I do not claim that these contemporary models describe different individuals; instead they should be viewed as cul-tural orientations that the same individual may draw on at different times. Therefore, rather than seeing these orientations as qualities of persons, I am interested in what circumstances push one or the other to the fore. In par-ticular, by discussing the day-to-day tasks that booksellers face, I aim to show how business practices reflect and create particular models of consumption. This is not to say that retailers are solely or even primarily responsible for such consumption models; they derive from a complex mix of social and cultural factors. Moreover, the public neither automatically accepts these models, nor approaches consumption in a uniform fashion. Consumers are involved in their own search for meaning, and whether it be reinforcing an identity, engaging in sociality, achieving the upper hand in a transaction, or collectively determining the conditions for the buying and selling of com-modities, consumption aspirations may not necessarily coincide with what retailers are offering. Nevertheless, business practices do have an impact in that once they become ubiquitous, it is difficult for individuals to approach consumption in alternative ways. And as our historical memory of alternative ways of approaching consumption fades, we become convinced of the inevitability of those models that now dominate.

The techniques retailers use to select, display, and market the products of print culture deserve scrutiny, for they are highly influential in determining which books are likely to be purchased and read. But as I have been arguing, beyond the issue of how booksellers act as gatekeepers is the question of which consumer visions are being promoted. Those competing orientations to consumption in large part define the bookstore wars, but they also have significance beyond the market share won or lost by different retailers. They help shape governmental decisions about economic development within communities. And they represent how we incorporate the market into our day-to-day lives.

The struggle of independent booksellers thus raises questions about the desirability of a truly free market and about the desirability of capitalist-minded consumers. It perhaps seems odd to consider that retailers could be critics of capitalism. Indeed, as David Monod points out, historians and social scientists have generally treated independent shopkeepers as a reactionary anachronism: viewed as incapable of adapting to social change, they are said to possess an irrational fear of progress and modernity that makes them susceptible to xenophobia and fascism.[38] Marx was one of the first to indict the conservative nature of the petty bourgeoisie, claiming that they can only look backward to a time when their property rights were more secure.[39] No more complimentary, Daniel Boorstin describes the anti–chain store movement of the 1920s and '30s as a "rear-guard action" that expressed "bewilderment" at the changes affecting local communities.[40] And for C. Wright Mills, small businesspeople are the "baffled defenders" of an ideology of utopian capitalism that merely serves to legitimate a system in which corporate capitalism actually dominates.[41] Yet this characterization of the petit bourgeois retailer, while partly accurate, does not fully describe the position of the contemporary independent bookseller.

The antichain rhetoric vocalized by the independent booksellers is a curious mixture of conservative nostalgia for communal harmony and the small-scale, a liberal championing of the individual's right to free expression and free choice in the marketplace of ideas, and a sometimes radical critique of free market competition and the power of economic elites. I am not arguing here that independent booksellers are virtuous heroes who will save Americans from the excesses of capitalism. Indeed, as I will describe, many of their actions are indistinguishable from those of their rivals. Rather, I want to show, first, how their arguments about chain retailing highlight ways of understanding the rationalization of everyday life. And second, I intend to show how the collective action these booksellers have undertaken exhibits an unintentional challenge to assumptions about the inevitability of consumer behavior and free market competition.

Finally, it is no accident that the fiercest debates about chain retailing, and the ones that most stir public opinion, are now taking place in the field of bookselling. Throughout the twentieth and into the twenty-first century, there has been a consistent belief in the distinctiveness of the book, an uneasiness with viewing books as "products" to be bought and sold like any other commodity. As Viviana Zelizer has argued, any enterprise that transgresses the boundary between the incommensurable sacred and the marketable profane must cope with structural ambivalence.[42] Books, as storehouses of ideas and as a perceived means to human betterment, have long been viewed as a kind of "sacred product." Contemporary merchandising techniques that aggressively stress the product over the sacred have thus caused considerable unease. Bookselling is not actually fundamentally different from the selling of hardware or office supplies or pharmaceuticals. And the organizations that constitute the book industry are not unique among for-profit enterprises in situating economic processes in social and cultural considerations. But what *is* unusual is that in the book industry, ambivalence to prevailing ways of organizing commerce tends to be made quite explicit. Therefore, by looking more closely at the unique world of the book industry, one can gain a better understanding of processes that apply to retailing and consumption more generally.

Methodological Notes

To explore the various issues outlined here, I make use of data I gathered from a wide variety of sources. I had numerous informal conversations and conducted forty-four semistructured interviews with members of the book industry; most of the formal interviews took place between 1993 and 1995. I spoke with booksellers, wholesalers, editors, publishers' sales and marketing personnel, consultants, and others. Subjects came from large publishing houses and small presses, and from both independent and chain bookstores. In a few cases, I cold contacted key individuals to whom I especially wanted to speak. However, snowball sampling was usually the preferred method to gain my pool of informants, since it brought me into contact with more of the rank and file of the book industry, and also because my chances of convincing a busy professional to talk to me were greatly enhanced when I had a referral. Although I make no claim to representativeness here, I do believe

I encountered a good cross-section of people in and views about the book industry.

Once I obtained an interview, informants were almost always gracious and patient with my wide-ranging questions. I was also impressed by what an articulate group of people this was. This was a function, no doubt, of their operating in a milieu that is immersed in language and that values verbal expression. But in addition, I believe, it reflected the passion with which so many spoke about their work and the world of books. The topics covered in our conversations held great meaning for my informants, and I was frequently moved by their comments and reflections. The time at which the interviews took place also, perhaps, contributed to greater introspection. Most of these interviews were conducted at a significant transition period in the history of American bookselling, a time when superstores were just taking off, yet were new enough that they were not yet taken for granted. People were still mulling over what to think of these enterprises, while the mall chains were far from forgotten. Consequently, there was the sense that one era was coming to a close, but no one had yet developed absolute certainties about the future. As Ann Swidler has noted, in such "unsettled periods," cultural meanings tend to be more explicitly articulated.[43]

I also conducted much briefer interviews with twenty customers of a chain and seventeen customers of an independent bookstore. These interviews were aimed at gaining some information on book buyers' views of the bookstore experience, and also at allowing some comparison between the imagined reader of the book trade and real book buyers. In addition, I made use of a broad range of written material. This included trade literature on the book industry from the past century, promotional material of publishers and distributors, annual reports and investment analyses, financial statements filed with the Securities and Exchange Commission, legal documents from various court cases and the Federal Trade Commission, and archival material pertaining to price maintenance campaigns. I also attended and observed a small number of relevant meetings and conferences, including the annual convention of the American Booksellers Association. And I subscribed to several Internet discussion and news lists concerned with book industry matters. Finally, like most academics, I spent a good deal of time in bookstores, though, unlike most academics, I often spent more time observing the workers and customers than perusing the books. At a later date, these observations became more systematic when three colleagues and I conducted a study of customer behavior at Canadian bookstores.[44] When they can be applied to the American situation, these observations have informed my conclusions here.

My focus here is on the retailing of what are called trade books, that is, those books aimed at the general public. I will not be discussing the sale of children's books, textbooks, scholarly or technical books, used books, audio-books, or multimedia. This is primarily because these other categories usually use different channels of distribution to reach their target audiences.[45] Finally, my scope here is mainly limited to retailing through bookstores. This means my discussion of Internet sites, book clubs, newsstands, supermarkets, warehouse clubs, and other nonbook outlets will be mainly in terms of their impact on bookstores. This is not because these other outlets are not important sources of books — they definitely are important, and are growing more so all the time. Rather, they do not take center stage because part of my intention is to explain the mystique of the physical bookstore — to explain why so many agree with Edward Shils that this institution belongs to the good things of the (fading) bourgeois era.

CHAPTER 2

From Dry Goods Merchant to Internet Mogul: Bookselling through American History

It is striking how frequently people will comment that the book business is just not what it used to be. With great regularity, members of the industry wistfully hearken back to a golden age when individuals entered this line of work because they cared about books, not money; when publishers engaged with writers, not bestseller lists; and when the American public supported the neighborhood bookseller, who worked so hard to make a living. However, if one actually tries to locate this bygone era, it keeps receding further and further into the past. The years that present-day book people look back on so fondly were not seen as particularly golden by those living through them. Instead, for more than a century, members of the book world have worried about compatriots who appear to treat books as interchangeable commodities rather than as unique carriers of ideas. There have certainly been some significant changes in the organization of the industry and in how book professionals experience their work during this time. But the perception of a vocation in danger of losing its moral bearings has remained remarkably consistent.

In this chapter, I examine the historical context for the contemporary debate over the chain bookstore by describing how book retailing, along with the cultural understandings attached to booksellers and bookselling, has evolved since the Civil War. As I will show, during the twentieth century, the retail scene went from one populated by a highly decentralized group of small booksellers, marginal wholesalers, and assorted drug, department, and variety stores to one dominated by large chains and national distributors employing sophisticated managerial and merchandising techniques to rationalize their work. Although I will be paying a good deal of attention here to the activities of specific firms, it would be a mistake to attribute the transformations that have occurred to the genius (whether inspired or misguided), determination, or *chutzpa* of a few individuals or companies. Instead, I intend to emphasize the long-term social, economic, and cultural conditions that made the actions of these firms both possible and probable.

The years before the 1960s, when the modern chain stores arose, exhibit some important differences from the present period. During this earlier era, book distribution seemed to lag behind scores of other industries, which had learned to utilize new techniques for bringing consumer goods to a mass market. Despite widespread agreement that its system of distribution was archaic and inefficient, the book industry remained impervious to attempts to rationalize its distribution sector. Related to this, for most of the country's history, book retailing was extremely decentralized, with books sold primarily by small merchants who had little communication with one another.

Nevertheless, during the century preceding the modern chain, the failure of any single firm to corner a large chunk of the book market did not altogether assuage anxiety about large enterprises making inroads into the industry. This anxiety can best be seen in the massive opposition and moral indignation that greeted the bookselling activities of department stores such as Macy's. Similar to the kinds of criticisms leveled against chain booksellers today, department stores attracted controversy for their marketing methods, their practice of discounting, their presumed attitudes toward the printed word, and for the size and scope of their operations. The debate over the bookselling activities of such nonbook retailers reveals the way in which a professional identity among booksellers developed during this period. Industry leaders articulated certain standards for the way booksellers should approach their work; these included the view that booksellers should be devoted exclusively to books, and that booksellers should align themselves with the tastes of a cultural elite.

Book retailing continued to be a poorly rationalized and economically marginal undertaking into the years following World War II. However, significant social and industry change affected the conditions under which book retailers operated. The postwar baby boom, the tremendous expansion of higher education, and a vision of perpetual economic prosperity held out the promise of a massive new generation of readers, eager and able to purchase their books. On the other hand, these potential book buyers were increasingly located in the suburbs, not a traditional home for bookstores. As department stores set up their own suburban branches, they curtailed their bookselling activities, but competition from another kind of nonbook retailer, the chain variety store, threatened regular booksellers in the 1950s. Meanwhile, the publishing sector was facing tremendous turmoil as mergers, acquisitions, and the issuing of public stock became more commonplace among publishers. All these various changes set the stage for the emergence of the book chains, as well as for an ambivalent turn away from the elitism that booksellers had previously embraced.

The Formation of a Genteel Industry

Historians of the book have noted that following the development of print in the fifteenth century, the European book trade was adept at rationalizing work methods in order to cut costs and enlarge markets. The early book trade was not only at the forefront of efforts to innovate and modernize commerce, but through its work of producing and disseminating standardized copies of texts, it also contributed to the rationalization of other industries, which could now use such texts to systematize and standardize knowledge.[1] This history adds a certain amount of irony to the situation that prevailed in the United States by the nineteenth century, when the book trade was regularly excoriated for being inefficient and backward.

Bookselling in the United States has always been shaped by geography. From the start, those engaged in the book trade had to contend with the vast American territories and uneven patterns of settlement. During the colonial period and the early years of the Republic, the American book trade was a highly unsystematic undertaking. Historians are divided over whether there was any typical organizational form for the publishing, printing, or selling of books. It is most likely that no form predominated, but rather, a large variety of possible arrangements and combinations of these activities existed. Colonial economies were rarely able to support book publishing as an exclusive enterprise. Instead, it was quite common for a single individual to perform the functions of publisher, printer, and bookseller and often to serve as the source of other local printed matter, including newspapers and bills as well as books.

In the colonial and antebellum years, literacy rates, the price of books, transportation difficulties, and poor systems of communication meant that both demand for and access to books were haphazard at best. Beginning a pattern that continued through most of the country's history, the majority of people did not patronize bookstores for their reading material. For instance, the most well read eighteenth-century Americans supplemented the limited offerings of commercial channels by turning to the owners of large private collections, who circulated books among friends and associates. Within the commercial sphere, books were often sold by persons who had little familiarity with the literary scene. In many towns, books were simply carried along with other merchandise by dry-goods shops.

Itinerant book peddlers served as another important resource for the reading public. These forebears of the traveling sales representative usually carried books along with a variety of other goods that a rural or small-town family might desire, though in a few cases — the famed Parson Weems, for example — the peddler did specialize in books. While the peddler hawked books already published, other publishers' agents toured the country seeking subscriptions, that is, advance orders for books not yet published. Subscription publishing was a useful way to finance a book's publication when a publisher was unwilling to take financial risks, as well as being a way to distribute books more thoroughly.[2]

By the Civil War, the book industry was looking more like the one we know today. The combination printer-bookseller was already on its way out by the end of the eighteenth century, to be replaced by a firm separation between publishing, printing, and selling. Along with this, the years following the Civil War saw the development of wholesalers who carried the products of a mix of publishers. Like most other areas of commerce, the book industry was transformed by the development of the transcontinental railroad. The growth of the railroad was crucial for expanding markets, as it allowed for distribution on a national scale as well as a more predictable delivery system. Retailers could invest more in the sale of books since they could count on actually receiving shipments on a regular basis. The railroad also facilitated more regular communication between publishers and retailers. This was embodied in the figure of the traveler, a commissioned salesperson hired by a publisher to visit booksellers around the country.[3]

Along with these organizational changes, the book trade was becoming more self-conscious as an industry. This could be seen in the latter third of the nineteenth century with the formation of publishers' and booksellers' trade associations, which were founded to address issues such as pricing and copyright. Members of the book trade were now worrying about conquering a national market and about assuming their rightful place as cultural leaders. These commercial and cultural considerations, intertwined as they were, became a significant source of tension within the industry.

The cultural ambitions of book professionals were related to concurrent developments in American society. During the latter part of the nineteenth century, when the structure of the modern book industry coalesced, ideals associated with the book drew on notions about culture in general. As Alan Trachtenberg describes it, "The culture of the Gilded Age, we might then say, contained a particular idea of culture as a privileged domain of refinement, aesthetic sensibility, and higher learning."[4] In this view, which was adopted by most leaders of the book industry of the day, books, like other forms of art, serve both the individual and the nation. Books enrich the spirit and refine sensibilities; they crystallize the nation's hopes and embody the finest sentiments of our national life. These qualities were considered particularly important during a period of great social and economic upheaval brought about by industrialization. As society increasingly appeared to be characterized by competition, greed, materialism, and the breakdown of collective responsibility for individual welfare, books beckoned as an enduring means to the perfection of humankind.[5]

This genteel culture of the Gilded Age gave special pride of place to books. But of course, not all books were the same in this regard. Some volumes, far from elevating the human spirit, were accused of appealing to the baser desires of a portion of the population. The obscenity that corrupted the young, the escapist dime novels of the working class, and the romances that inflamed young women's imaginations were condemned most vocally by moral crusaders, but also met the disapproval of the literary establishment for being degrading rather than uplifting. Thus, the redeeming qualities associated with the written word excluded certain classes of books, which just happened to appeal to certain classes of readers — the young, the female, the working class.[6]

As this hierarchy of reading suggests, the extolment of the book during the Gilded Age was more than just an attempt to provide an antidote to the ravages of industrialization. Those involved in promoting a genteel culture had other agendas as well. As Paul DiMaggio has argued, the formation of new cultural categories that occurred in the latter half of the nineteenth century, positing high culture on the one side and popular entertainment on the other, served to more firmly differentiate the elite classes from those further down the social hierarchy.[7] In the areas of music, visual arts, and literature, the line that was being drawn between true art and salacious entertainments reinforced the higher status of those who had the good taste and education to appreciate the former.

The high-culture institutions that DiMaggio describes — the symphony orchestra and fine-arts museum of Boston — were able to maintain their elite status and their claim to be distributing sacred art in large part because they were nonprofit corporations, easily controlled by Boston's supposedly disinterested Brahmins. In contrast, popular culture was *commercial*—produced and distributed on a for-profit basis — with the presumed effect of reducing culture to a profane commodity while emphasizing whatever would appeal to the largest audiences. This divide between commercial and nonprofit undertakings presented some problems to those book professionals who wished to count themselves among the cultural elite. Such members of the book business became involved in an elaborate exercise of explaining how their obviously commercial enterprises were not *really* commercial. The concept of "commercial" then developed a double meaning that reflected this balancing act in which industry personnel were involved. On the one hand, the book industry was recognized as a part of commerce, and so it was expected that members of the book trade would do all they could to increase their businesses. But on the other hand, many claimed to avoid excessive "commercialism," in the sense of catering to a mass market and promoting large sales, in favor of adhering to other criteria such as literary merit or innovation or personal tastes. The markers of despised commercialism became quite varied, having to do with both the form and the content of books, with techniques of distribution and promotion, and with the social characteristics of readers.

Members of the book trade thus sought to carve out an area of culture that expressed the finer sentiments of society not to be found in the sphere of commerce and that distinguished the elite connoisseur of literature from the less refined and less educated devotee of commercialized popular books. At the same time, their hopes for the industry rested on developing a network of thriving publishing and bookselling firms. Not surprisingly, the cultural goals frequently clashed with those measures needed to compete in a not-so-genteel capitalist economy.

The Problem of Distribution

The extent to which commercialism was a corrupting force in industry culture remained a matter of considerable debate. Nevertheless, there was near consensus that the industry's most intractable economic problem was its distribution system. Indeed, the "distribution problem" was considered the bane of the book trade from the late nineteenth century all the way through the twentieth. The task facing the industry was to match the output of published books with the people who would be interested in reading them. Yet, it was charged, the irrationalities of the system prevented this from happening in an efficient manner. In an industry generally known for its inefficiency and lack of business sense, the sector in charge of moving books to a reading public appeared least amenable to rationalization. Meetings, studies, and editorials in trade journals denouncing the book distribution system became a staple of industry life.

The problem of distribution was often described in the most dramatic of tones. In a 1913 *Atlantic Monthly* article, the president of the publishing house Macmillan contended that the reason book sales were not increasing

> is to be found, I think, in the problems of distribution as applied to books; the distribution problem being the greatest of all problems of modern times, and the one which is engaging the attention of all who have to do with the supplying of the needs of the community, whether of staple articles or of those wanted merely for the public's amusement and gratification.[8]

His assessment of the distribution dilemma was reiterated two decades later in even stronger language. In 1931, the primary book trade associations engaged in a rare moment of cooperation and commissioned an investigation into the economic structure of the book business. The resulting *Economic Survey of the Book Industry*—better known as the Cheney Report, after its principal author—was considered a landmark account of the industry's strengths and especially its weaknesses, and is even today referred to as a relevant and authoritative source on the unique problems facing the trade. The tone of Cheney's report is blunt and often contemptuous of the many practices he saw that should shame anyone intent on running a rational and profitable business. But no part of the book industry elicited more despair from Cheney than distribution:

> Chaotic as are the methods of management and control in the publishing function of list-making, they seem to be almost organized compared with the conditions involved in the function of selling. . . . At this point — usually the binder's warehouse — the publisher has books; at that point is the book buyer. Between these two points is the tragedy of the book industry. Between these points are so many gaps, so many confusions, so much utter ignorance of what is being done that unless these gaps are filled and unless every branch of the industry learns to know exactly what it is doing, the industry, as it is today, is threatened with destruction.[9]

While the industry managed not to self-destruct, little in regards to distribution appeared to have changed twenty years later, judging by another report commissioned by the American Book Publishers Council. While using more measured language than heard in the Cheney Report, the new survey's authors outlined a situation where the retail book business was in terrible economic shape and was plagued by gross inefficiencies, and where great discord between booksellers and publishers reigned.[10] Like its predecessor, this report also touched off a flurry of meetings and journal articles discussing how to reform the industry. Yet despite all the resolutions to come together in order to solve the distribution problem, the perceived irrationalities of distribution remained, as did the perennial commentary about it.[11]

Why exactly was distribution condemned as so archaic and inefficient? The substance of the complaints actually changed little over time. At the heart of the problem was the absence of standardization in the book business: the inevitable lack of a standardized product along with the attendant difficulties of merchandising a good that comes in thousands of new variations each year, and the presumably more preventable lack of standardized business methods within the book industry. This absence of standardization contributed to the generally unprofitable nature of running a bookstore, which meant that few shops actually existed to disseminate books, especially in small towns and rural areas. In 1930, according to one survey, there were 4,053 book outlets in the United States, many of which were drugstores, gift shops, and rental libraries (places that rented books to patrons for a few cents a day).[12] In that year, almost half of all cities with a population between five and a hundred thousand, and two-thirds of all counties had no book outlet at all.[13] By the late 1940s, another report estimated that there were 3,041 book outlets (of which only 1,200 could "warrant being called trade book stores"), plus another 5,000 drugstores and variety chain stores, and 60,000 magazine outlets that carried some books.[14] And by 1957, the number of outlets that did a significant proportion of their business in books had grown to only 8,360.[15] For a large portion of the country's population, access to books for purchase remained extremely limited.

As many scholars have argued, rationalization in the retail sphere was largely achieved by the mass retailers who emerged during the late nineteenth and early twentieth centuries: department stores, mail-order houses, supermarkets, and chain stores. These retailers cut costs and grew in size and scope by standardizing procedures across their operations, by buying in bulk from suppliers, by implementing self-service, and by investing heavily in advertising. The result was to produce high-volume sales, often at lower prices than traditional merchants could afford to charge.[16] But with the exception of department stores, mass retailers played a relatively minor role in bookselling during the first half of the twentieth century. As most booksellers were still small and independent, it is not so surprising that they were slow to rationalize their work. Still, this situation exasperated industry leaders. Most bookshops were disparaged by the publishing establishment for being inefficient, ill-informed, and unadventurous in the stock they carried. Outside observers habitually accused booksellers of not having any idea about how to run a business. They frequently characterized retailers as either dreamy booklovers with their heads in the clouds, or ignorant people who could not come up with anything better to do than sell books. R. L. Duffus, the author of a 1930 investigation of the book industry sponsored by the Carnegie Corporation, warned, "The old-fashioned bookstore was a charming place, but charm alone will not solve the problem of modern book distribution. . . . Hard though it may be to face the fact, the bookstore of to-day cannot be primarily a place for those who revere books as things-in-themselves." [17]

One *Publishers Weekly* article of 1930 advised retailers to become better businesspeople by studying the merchandising methods of chain variety stores.[18] For instance, the article's author said, booksellers should consider ridding themselves of the slow-moving stock they keep just to meet the occasional demand. To do this, she continued, booksellers would have to pay more attention to their record keeping, which compared so unfavorably to the detailed accounting systems of chain variety stores. She also praised chain stores for their open feel and for being free of obstructions, in contrast to bookstores' typically cluttered look. While the author assured her readers that bookstores need not give up their personal touch, she made it clear that more rational methods would sell more books.[19] These suggestions would indeed be acted on some decades later by the chain bookstores and would help account for their success. But in the meantime, booksellers by and large seemed to ignore this advice.

For their part, booksellers accused publishers of being behind many of the irrationalities of the distribution system. A major concern for the industry was how to get books from publisher to bookseller in a timely and accurate manner. Even with the development of rail and motor vehicle transportation systems, book delivery took an inordinate amount of time. Part of the problem was that book retailers had to rely on regionally centralized sources for their wares. Most publishers were located on the East Coast, especially in New York, as were their warehouses; publishers declined to establish regional warehouses, and so booksellers in Oregon obtained their books from the same places as did New Jersey stores. Yet publishers, relatively small firms themselves, lacked the capability shown by truly mass producers of other consumer products to distribute their wares across the country efficiently. Book orders could take weeks, or even months, to be filled, and those bookstores in more remote environs had to pay higher shipping costs.

Not only did booksellers receive books in an untimely fashion, but, they charged, publishers displayed supreme incompetence in their shipping and billing practices. This subject elicited great passion on the part of these small proprietors, who were in a business where practically every item they ordered was one-of-a-kind — each separate title that was received had to be checked against invoice and original order, an already time-consuming process made even more frustrating when publishers made mistakes. And mistakes and inefficiencies were plenty: books were poorly packaged and arrived damaged; invoices were sent at different times from the actual books; books were not consolidated, resulting in higher shipping costs; and returns were not credited properly.[20] To make matters worse, each publishing house had its own set of terms concerning discounts — that is, the discount off the list (retail) price offered by the publisher to the retailer — and minimums for orders, returns, and so forth, which made acquiring books exceedingly complicated. Yet despite all the pleas for greater standardization and attention to the fulfillment process, little changed.

Key to the inefficiencies in distribution was that wholesaling did not play a central role in moving books from publisher to retailer. This subsidiary role of book wholesalers was in contrast to trends in American business in general. In the latter third of the nineteenth century, wholesalers became an important link in the distribution of numerous consumer goods. By the early twentieth century, wholesalers were displaced in those industries that developed mass retailers, but remained powerful in other fields. These wholesalers who focused on gathering goods from manufacturers, delivering them to retailers, and extending credit to clients were essential to rationalizing distribution in American commerce.[21] Not so in the book industry. Throughout the first half of the twentieth century, wholesalers, or jobbers as they were generally called then, were a relatively minor force when it came to trade books sold by bookstores. Wholesalers were used by booksellers for special orders and for reorders of a store's backlist, but jobbers could not rely on booksellers for the more lucrative business in new books.[22] Reformers frequently called for the entire distribution function to be given over to wholesalers, but this only happened on a limited scale. Both bookseller and publisher preferred a direct relationship with one another because they disliked the economic penalty of involving a middleperson, and because they felt more out of touch with each other when someone stood between them. Furthermore, booksellers complained that wholesalers did not always carry the books they wanted, and that service was slow.[23] While jobbers were supposed to speed deliveries, they were not really equipped to solve the problems presented by distance; by 1949, only one wholesaler had regional warehouses.[24]

Despite the pleas of reformers, the wholesaler remained rather periph-eral until the 1970s.[25] Significantly, the jobber was seen as marginal in more than a practical sense. His status as somewhat of an outsider was reinforced by his apparent distance from the culture of the book world:

> He is far more strictly a business man than is the publisher, for he does not handle a book because of the prestige that attaches to it or because he preens himself upon being a cultured missionary. He is not sought after by authors. Nobody expects him to give literary teas. One of the most successful and highly esteemed book jobbers in America likes to startle people by declaring that he knows nothing about literature. His business, he says, is for him as purely a business as it would be if he were handling dry goods or hardware.[26]

The jobber was expected to carry the bad with the good book, to be inclu-sive without thought for discrimination. Having no need for contact with either author or reader, the wholesaler could most easily strip away the emotional aura that surrounded books. In the figure of the jobber, the cut-and-dried business of buying and selling books was most clearly revealed. And this could be profoundly unsettling for members of the book world who believed that books were not at all comparable to dry goods or hardware.

Another indication of the wholesalers' distance from the mainstream of the industry was the more active role they played in servicing nonbook retailers. In the first part of the twentieth century, the principal customers for trade book wholesalers were drugstores, stationers, small department stores, public libraries, rental libraries, newsstands, and smaller book-stores.[27] This no doubt diminished the jobber in the eyes of many book pro-fessionals. The distinction that the industry tried to make between "regular" bookshops and other kinds of book outlets was considered quite important at this time. As had been the case since colonial days, most people who wanted to buy books near their own communities would have to do so at a store that did not specialize in books.[28] But standards had changed within the book world, and industry leaders and other public intellectuals now writing about the issue showed a great unwillingness to grant full legitimacy to sales channels that were not unequivocally bookstores. Of course, this stance against nonbook outlets was not universal. Along with wholesalers, there were plenty of publishers who were quite happy to sell to anyone who would take their wares. But most public statements supported the view that books should be sold in stores primarily devoted to the printed word (with perhaps some allowances for traditional items such as stationery), and sold by people who were well acquainted with prominent authors and who knew the difference between the culturally meritorious and the unworthy.

At first glance, it may seem curious that industry leaders disdained news-stands, drugstores and variety stores, and even methods of distribution such as subscription publishing and direct mail, since they helped to create a more efficient distribution system.[29] But these distribution channels were perceived as doing little to further genteel culture. One of the most common reasons for scorning drugstores, stationery stores, and the like was that they stocked a much poorer selection of titles than did bookstores; their stock also tended to be heavily weighted toward the most popular new books, cheap reprints, and titles for juveniles, none of which were very high up in the literary hierarchy. Nonbook retailers were also the outlets for soft-cover books, which were long treated as a thing apart (and inferior) by the publishing establishment.[30] As an undercurrent to the debate over nonbook retailers ran the knowledge that these other outlets catered to a less elite clientele than did the regular bookshops. In 1930, George P. Brett Jr., soon to be head of Macmillan, tried to reassure his fellows:

> The point that I wish to make is that the reprint business has little effect on the trade of the legitimate book dealer. . . . . [O]bviously, it would be as im-possible for a drugstore, a cigar store, a newsstand to carry any assortment of books of non-fiction which would appeal to the educated mind, as it would be for the legitimate book dealer of today to represent all of the fiction which is being published at the present time.[31]

The drugstores, the discount stores, and the newsstands were the outlets geared toward the growing mass of working-class readers. Bookstores, on the other hand, cultivated the "carriage trade"—a more affluent, educated group of patrons. Thus, bookshop owners did little to counter their grow-ing reputation among the public for being intimidating figures with minimal patience for customers who were not appropriately bookish.

Regular bookstores were additionally distinguished from other outlets by their segregation of books from mundane commodities. As part of their efforts to display books in a dignified setting that lacked the trappings of bla-tant commercialism, this helped bookshops to communicate the serious-ness of their undertaking and the sacredness of the product they were sell-ing. In this view, the environment in which books were placed could shape readers' perceptions of those books, as suggested by a journalist's report on the 1909 opening of a new San Francisco bookshop that sold books and art objects:

> Paul Elder & Co.'s new store in Grant Avenue has been designed with the primary idea of providing surroundings in keeping with the merchandise which the firm has for sale. . . . The place produces an old world feeling, and no doubt will be a welcome retreat for people of discrimination who like to associate books with an artistic atmosphere impossible at the bargain counter.[32]

This assessment was in keeping, to use Lawrence Levine's words, with the "sacralization of culture" that took place during the nineteenth century — the establishment of an attitude of reverence by displaying the embodiments of culture in an appropriate setting and by not allowing them to mingle with less pure objects.[33] Or at least this was the way it was supposed to be. Leaders of the book world were greatly troubled when the line between bookstore and nonbook outlet became blurred.[34]

The Department Stores: Merchandising by the Mighty

Drugstores and newsstands were considered inferior book outlets and presented unwelcome competition to booksellers. However, no nonbook retailer inspired more wrath before World War II than did the department store. Although memories of book shopping in department stores may now be dim, not so long ago the department stores were major forces in bookselling. Reliable market-share figures are hard to come by, but there is no doubt that department stores sold a sizeable proportion of the books bought by the general public from the end of the nineteenth century until the 1970s. The 1931 Cheney Report estimated that 29 percent of all retail trade book sales went through department stores.[35] In 1938, a member of the department stores' primary trade organization, the National Retail Dry Goods Association, offered an even higher figure of 40 percent.[36] And by 1951, it was estimated that department stores represented 40 to 60 percent of all retail trade book sales.[37] These numbers were due to a variety of factors, not least because department stores rationalized bookselling (as they did selling in general) to an extent not duplicated elsewhere in book retailing.[38]

Books were not uncommon in dry goods stores, the predecessors of department stores. And one of the key transitional retail establishments, A. T. Stewart's New Store of Manhattan, which opened in 1862, also included some books among its merchandise.[39] But the first modern department store to sell books in a serious fashion was Macy's. This New York emporium began to carry a small selection of titles in December of 1869. By January, Macy's had opened an entirely separate department for books, stocking a large selection of popular titles as well as magazines and stationery. Within a decade, Macy's was one of the largest book outlets in the country, carrying an enormous selection of titles, and offering to special order any book that was not in the store.[40]

Department stores carried books for a number of reasons, some only tangentially related to the money books would bring in. Profit considerations were not entirely irrelevant; especially in their earlier days, book departments could generate large amounts of revenue for the emporiums. For instance, Wanamaker's of Philadelphia began its career in books in 1877 when ten volumes were placed at the end of a stationery counter. The following year, books were given their own counter and soon after, their own department. By 1884, books accounted for 10 percent of the store's business.[41]

But at least before World War II, a more important consideration than immediate cash was the prestige book departments brought to a store, along with the tony customers they attracted. Books aided in the construction of the department store's desired image; they helped demonstrate how these retail giants were palaces of glamour and gentility. Books added a measure of seriousness, of cultivation, and even of civic-mindedness to the store's self-presentation. And a book reader was among the most desirable of customers — she was often educated, refined, leisured, and had money to spend. This ability to attract the most favored kind of shopper to the department store could even offset a book department's inability to make a profit.[42] Indeed, books were frequently used as "loss leaders," items sold below cost in order to bring people into the store where they could be lured to more profitable departments.

Book departments, even if they were not very profitable themselves, could therefore be indirect economic assets to the store. Another frequently discussed aspect of this benefit was the way in which books could help to sell other items. As a manual for the National Retail Dry Goods Association put it in 1938, books are "arguments" for buying other merchandise in the store that pertain to a book's subject. For instance, it was suggested, the popular book *Let's Set the Table* could be displayed in the china, linen, or silver department, along with a table design taken from the book. Both sales of the book and sales of china, linen, and silver would then be encouraged.[43] This kind of cross-merchandising had unlimited possibilities. Not only were department store managers urged to sprinkle books throughout different departments and in store windows, but book departments were told to display merchandise that tied in with particular books, such as luggage with travel titles, cameras with photography books, and so forth. Even fiction could serve this purpose: "A society novel will make every reader wish to dress well."[44] Books were thus heralded as stimulating the consumer's imagination and desires in ways the department store promised to satisfy.

For all these reasons, department stores, especially the larger ones, were fairly enthusiastic about book departments up through World War II. But in spite of their success in bringing books to readers, the emporiums attracted heavy criticism from people in the book industry. Similar to criticisms of other nonbook outlets, department stores were accused of employing clerks who knew little about books and of focusing on bestsellers. For some, "the department-store class of literature" was obviously distinguishable from "works of higher grade" sold by regular booksellers.[45] In actuality, just like the regular bookshops with which they competed, department store book departments were quite varied. On the one hand, it was not at all uncommon for department stores to outdo any local bookshop in terms of selection and service. These stores hired employees who knew books and the book business well, and did not try to let untrained staff from other departments do the job of skilled booksellers. On the other hand, some department stores provided outlets with a mere scattering of titles staffed by people who had little knowledge of books or authors.

Department stores were also castigated by members of the industry for treating books with insufficient respect. Their willingness to mix books with sewing notions, gloves, or other mundane goods appeared to betray literary values. While gift shops and drugstores were also guilty of not segregating books, the emporiums went further by not treating books as ends in themselves. Whether as loss leaders or as elements in a tableware display, books were used as tools to sell other merchandise. For those who believed in the sacred quality of the written word, this was dismaying indeed.

This instrumental attitude toward books certainly drew the contempt of critics in the book world. However, selling titles at cut-rate prices had more immediate consequences than demeaning books. Independent bookshops claimed that price-cutting by department stores would lead to their ruin, as they could not hope to compete with the discounters. There was truth enough in this statement. Profit margins for booksellers were already so thin that to match the department stores' discounts would entail losing money with every sale. Moreover, the department stores were attracting the regular booksellers' prized middle-class customers as well as the working-class readers to whom they had been more indifferent.

During periods of especially aggressive price-cutting, alarmed book-sellers and publishers warned that the department stores were moving toward a monopoly in bookselling. The specter of monopoly was not, of course, limited to the book industry; there was widespread concern in the late nineteenth and early twentieth centuries about numerous newly giant corporations, which appeared to be threatening American society. Yet the fear of monopoly would remain an important current in the book trade even after the 1930s, when antimonopoly sentiment had subsided throughout much of American society. The clash between the book industry and the department stores over price-cutting, and the tradition of antagonism to large organizations that influenced the book world, are topics to which I will return in later chapters. For now, suffice it to say that the struggle against the department stores, which lasted through the 1950s, helped to solidify the regular bookseller's identity as a guardian of genteel culture.

The Postwar Era

When the Walden Book Company, which for many years had operated a chain of rental libraries, opened its first retail outlet in a shopping mall in 1962, the event did not attract a great deal of attention from the book industry. The inauguration did not even garner a notice in *Publishers Weekly*'s regular announcements of new stores. It would be some years yet before Waldenbooks emerged as a major player in the bookselling field or was recognized to be at the center of a veritable revolution in book retailing. In the meantime, the book business was preoccupied with other matters.

The postwar baby boom had spurred a huge expansion of the nation's educational infrastructure, including the construction of new schools and libraries, and the production of an unprecedented number of college graduates. Sharing in Americans' general optimism that economic prosperity would continue indefinitely, members of the book industry saw before them a vast new market of institutional and individual book buyers. As it turned out, the increase in American college graduates failed to produce the hoped-for quantities of new book readers, but there were some qualitative changes within the book-buying population.[46] The movement of so many Americans to suburban areas represented a potentially large market for those organizations that understood how suburbanites' shopping patterns and reading tastes differed from those of the traditional urban bookstore patron. Furthermore, the traditional attitude that cheap editions, such as the paperback, did not belong in the dignified setting of the bookshop was increasingly at odds with the views of not only low-income customers, but of more elite readers who had grown accustomed to paperbacks in school and college courses. And the success that discount variety houses were having in selling books also suggested that contemporary book-buying audiences were not put off by mass-merchandising techniques or settings.

Although they were to remain an important channel of book distribution for some time, department stores began to scale back their book departments following World War II.[47] Controversy over department store price-cutting continued to take place through the 1950s, but increasingly, concern about nonbook retailers was focused on the new versions of variety stores that were gaining prominence. Variety stores had long been part of the American retail mix, ever since Woolworth's was founded in 1879. Also known as five-and-dimes, Woolworth's, S. H. Kress & Company, S. S. Kresge, and similar chains sold an assortment of notions, household goods, hardware, and other low-cost items. Then, in the 1950s, the discount houses came on the scene. By cutting back on store services and ambiance, these retailers made available brand-name merchandise at discounted prices. A leader in this movement was the E. J. Korvette chain, founded in 1948. Most discount houses specialized in one type of good, but Korvette was described as a discount department store because of the wide range of products it carried. And while its selection was still not as complete as that of the traditional department store, goods were discounted more deeply and more consistently. Soon the largest of the old chain variety stores started to experiment with the discounting strategy too. With its success, new discount department store divisions were formed: Woolworth established Woolco, and Kresge established K-mart, both in 1962.[48]

The discount variety stores offered a limited selection of books that were guaranteed to turn over quickly; children's titles, dictionaries, cookbooks, and bestselling adult books constituted their typical stock. Books were not an especially important item to the discounters, as they made only a minor contribution to store revenues. Nevertheless, because of its potential to increase store traffic, the book and magazine section became a standard variety store offering. And these retailers' sales of the most popular books of the day were substantial enough in some cities to threaten regular bookstores. Korvette was among the most aggressive in selling discounted books, often using them as loss leaders, and so inciting the wrath of booksellers.[49]

Adding to the competition, supermarkets also began to carry some books following World War II. The types of titles they carried were similar to those found in the variety stores: fast-moving children's books and adult paperbacks. In addition, the supermarkets were sources for encyclopedias, as grocers found they could appeal to a mother's concerns for her child's educational and nutritional needs simultaneously.[50] But the significance of both the supermarket and the discount variety store is less to be found in the predictable selection of books they carried, and more in how they demonstrated that Americans were quite willing to forego the bookstore's dignified and knowledgeable presentation of books in favor of outlets that emphasized self-service and that sold books out of bins. The success of these outlets led some to worry that desperate bookshops were now looking to the nonbook retailers as models for their own ventures. One observer caustically noted in 1954 that

> the ordinary book outlet must now compete with everything from delicatessens to whore houses. As a by-product of this development the outlet becomes increasingly less a bookstore and more of a five-and-dime affair for the sale of notions, toys, greeting cards and perhaps, as the bookmen awaken to wider and wider possibilities, suppositories and condoms. Correspondingly as less and less attention is devoted to the selling of books, in these places, less and less books will be sold, and there will be fewer bookstores, as the term is usually understood.[51]

In other words, not even traditional booksellers were necessarily keeping to traditional ideas about the proper environment for the sale of books.

Corporatization Comes to the Book Business

At the same time as the book world wondered about the fate of the bookshop, industry personnel were alternately left enthusiastic or uneasy by the growing trend of mergers and stock offerings among formerly family-owned publishing houses. Following the end of World War II, Wall Street discovered and embraced publishing, causing profound changes in the organizational structure of the industry. The publicly owned publishing house was not a completely unknown entity before the war. However, most houses maintained their autonomy until the 1950s, when the national education boom began to create a large market for textbooks. In order to meet the demand, many publishers sought to expand existing educational divisions or to found new ones. Their need for fresh capital, coinciding with the desire of numerous aging heads of publishing houses to protect their heirs from inheritance taxes, made issuing public stock an attractive proposition. And with publishing apparently poised for growth, investors were happy to oblige.

Issuing public stock was one way to raise funds. Another was by engaging in a merger or selling the firm to a larger company. Mergers between firms had always been a fact of life in publishing, as houses sought to bail themselves out of financial straits or perceived opportunities to expand by joining forces with another press. But during the 1960s, mergers and acquisitions proceeded at a breathtaking pace, often enveloping even those publishers who had gone public just a few years earlier. There have been several successive waves of merger and acquisition activity in the postwar publishing industry — first in the 1960s, then again in the mid-1970s, a renewed surge in the late 1980s, and another beginning in the mid-1990s.

The first wave was characterized by the acquisition of publishing houses by corporations whose lines of business were very distant from books. Although some magazine and newspaper publishers were involved in acquiring book firms, more common purchasers were electronics companies, which sought "synergy" between their technology and managerial expertise and publishers' content and prestige. But despite their initial optimism, the new parent companies' enthusiasm for publishing did not last. By the 1980s, IBM, Xerox, and the others who had had visions of the computerized classroom were starting to dump their publishing properties. The reasons were to be found in a contraction of the book-buying market as well as a realization that instead of synergy, conflict between publishers and a corporation's other divisions was the norm.

Yet while electronics firms were starting to sour on the publishing field, other corporations saw opportunities there. The mid-1970s, when a new wave of mergers and acquisitions took place, was not a period of prosperity for publishing. But in times of economic hardship, publishers became easy takeover targets or, in other cases, attempted to reduce competition by merging with rival presses. Numerically less common than publisher-publisher mergers, but of no small consequence, multimedia firms also began to add publishing to their repertoire. These years saw the formation of conglomerates such as Warner Communications and Gulf & Western, with holdings in film, broadcasting, music, newspapers, or magazine publishing as well as books. Like their electronics predecessors, these corporations saw prospects for synergy, hoping that content could be reproduced across a variety of media, and that cross-promotional strategies could be employed.

The third wave of merger and acquisition activity that occurred in the late 1980s was similar to the events of the previous decade, in that it was primarily publishing or other media firms doing the acquiring. What was notable about this period, though, was that foreign companies were so often involved. These firms helped to inject a more global perspective into their American subsidiaries, especially in terms of cultivating international markets. Merger activity slowed in the beginning of the 1990s, but it had picked up again by the middle of the decade. The pattern since has been for a handful of integrated entertainment and information conglomerates to acquire independent presses, and to trade already-owned imprints among one another. Still, the promise of great profit in bookselling has yet to be realized, and therefore the industry has been a source of shareholder frustration. In the 1990s, parent companies' hopes centered on the role that publishers were expected to play in the exploitation of the Internet and other digital delivery systems. The financial uncertainties and disappointments accompanying these technologies simply added to the pace at which publishers changed hands, as the conglomerates' investment strategies were rapidly revamped and retrenched.[52]

Publisher mergers and acquisitions have become a taken-for-granted component of the book world. However, until the 1970s, it was not widely assumed that bookselling could follow this pattern. Indeed, the idea of bookselling operations with the growth and profit potential to interest investors contradicted most prior experience. For even though chain bookstores had been present throughout the twentieth century, they remained a constant minority among booksellers. According to U.S. government figures, there were thirty groups of bookstore chains in 1929. Between them, they owned 349 of the country's 2,647 bookstores, and accounted for 31.6 percent of bookstore sales. Three decades later, those numbers had barely changed. In 1963, there were fifty firms with three or more establishments, which, between them, ran 244 bookstores. An additional hundred firms owned two establishments each, but they were still dwarfed by the 2,719 single-bookstore firms that held onto 67.9 percent of bookstore sales.[53]

Perhaps more important, even the largest book chains had only a handful of outlets. The biggest national bookstore chains before the 1960s were Brentano's and Doubleday. In 1910, the publishing house Doubleday opened a bookshop; in just a little more than a decade, Doubleday had eight stores, and for the next half century, remained one of the leading booksellers of the country.[54] Similarly, Brentano's had operated a number of stores in several states since beginning expansion in the 1920s.[55] These national chains, along with a few regional chain bookstores such as Chicago's Kroch's & Brentano's and New York's Womrath, constituted an important presence in bookselling for decades.[56] Yet the scope of these chains was relatively modest. In 1960, Doubleday could boast only thirty-three outlets, while Brentano's had but fourteen stores to its name.[57] Consequently, their impact was far more muted than that of the next generation of chains.

While few had visions of building a bookstore empire, many people did believe the early 1960s to be an auspicious time to enter the bookselling business. In response to this optimism, a record number of new bookshops or book departments opened in 1961 — more than 121 of them.[58] Among these were some new innovations in bookselling, including new approaches to selling paperbacks. During the 1940s and '50s, with college stores leading the way, bookstores had experimented with stocking paperbacks, shelved in their own sections. By the early 1960s, many general bookstores were expanding their paperback sections, though the stores usually preferred the larger-format "quality" variety over the rack-sized mass-market books. Paperbacks also made a big leap in visibility with the establishment of all-paperback bookstores, the first of which appeared in the mid-1950s.

The paperback store, like the items it sold, signaled informality and an absence of elitism. The paperbacks' cheap bindings meant that they were disposable; these were books that could be casually read, not collected as status symbols. Unlike the regular bookshop, the paperback stores emphasized self-service, permitting customers to evade the intimidating queries of the bookseller. And the eclectic mix of classics, scholarly works, potboilers, and everything in between to be found in paperback stores and in the paperback sections of regular bookshops invited an equally heterogenous audience to peruse the shelves. One proponent argued for the transformative effects of paperbacks in terms that emphasized their populist character:

> [N]ew customers who rarely buy regular books will be attracted by paperbacks. Some of these buyers are students, some like the convenience of the smaller format, some do not wish to spend too much money for a book, and some are interested in titles that are available only in paperbacks. This author firmly believes that there is another reason, a psychological one. He feels that the paper cover alone makes the scholarly book less forbidding to the buyer and that if the books were issued solely in cloth at the same price, they would not sell nearly as well as the paperback editions do.[59]

The paperback shops proved to be highly popular. One of the best known, Paperback Booksmith, even grew into a chain of seventy-five (mostly franchised) stores before going bankrupt in 1978.[60] The all-paperback store suited the cultural climate of the times, as its antiestablishment image appealed to those readers who scorned the class pretensions of the traditional bookshop. And since the customers of the paperback stores were often the most avid and adventurous of readers, they could not be dismissed in the same way as the variety store patron was.

During this time, it was not only book readers who were exhibiting new cultural sensibilities. People entering bookselling were often coming from social worlds formerly quite distant from the bookshop business. Some new booksellers — Roy Kepler, for example, whose paperback store was founded in 1955 — were involved in the social movements of the era.[61] Paperback Booksmith, which opened in 1961, exemplified a related trend, in that its founder, Marshall Smith, was a disaffected securities analyst. This period produced a number of people with business degrees or experience in the corporate world who were looking for more personally or socially meaningful lines of work. Some of them found bookselling. Both those with backgrounds as activists and those with backgrounds as corporate capitalists would help to transform how booksellers thought about themselves and their work in the years to come.

Sorting Out the Lineage: The Modern Chain Grows Up

It is perhaps indicative of the extent of the changes that have occurred in bookselling in recent decades that so many accounts of bookstores that started in the 1960s and '70s attribute their founders with being the first to engage in practices such as mass merchandising or discounting.[62] As the history presented here shows, such techniques had been utilized in bookselling long before, though generally by nonbook retailers. What did change in the 1960s and '70s, though, was the extent to which these techniques were implemented in the regular bookstore. The changes came about through a convergence of two different elements in the bookselling world. On the one hand, a number of bookstore entrepreneurs were willing to adopt the methods of the once-denigrated department store, discount store, and drugstore. And on the other hand, there was a corresponding interest on the part of such nonbook retailers in owning and running regular bookstores.

The result over the next few decades was the establishment of huge bookstore chains that would come to dominate the bookselling arena. These chains captured a major portion of the retail book market, modernized bookselling to an extent few would have thought possible when they first appeared, and developed organizational structures and strategies meant to please the investors to whom they sold shares. In the process, the chains gained a considerable amount of power within the book world, from the offices of publishing houses to the habits of consumers.[63]

Two chains formed in the 1960s were particularly influential: Waldenbooks and B. Dalton, Bookseller. There were other bookstore chains that also emerged in these years, several of which would play an important role in the bookselling scene later on. But throughout the 1970s and early '80s, the term "chain" was virtually synonymous with B. Dalton and Walden.

Their standing derived from their imposing size and reach: these chains built hundreds of stores that dotted shopping centers and malls all across the United States. Together, they spearheaded a trend that saw a decreasing number of chains capture an increasingly bigger share of the market. In 1963, the five existing chains with eleven or more establishments accounted for only 7.9 percent of bookstore sales. By 1972, the four chains with over fifty branches apiece accounted for 11.6 percent of such sales. And by 1982, Waldenbooks and B. Dalton alone accounted for approximately 24 percent of all bookstore sales.[64]

The family that founded Waldenbooks, the oldest of these chains, was no stranger to the book industry. The Walden Book Company was founded in 1933 as a chain of leased rental libraries in department stores. When rental libraries began to wane in popularity during the postwar years, founder Lawrence Hoyt and his son decided to shift the focus of their enterprise to book retailing. Noting new population patterns, they determined that suburban shopping centers rather than traditional urban downtown sites were the most promising locations for their stores. In 1962, Walden Book Store opened its first retail outlet in a suburban Pittsburgh mall. This original store included both a sales and a rental library component, but as the Hoyts opened additional branches, they concentrated more on retailing, and by 1964 they had phased out rental libraries completely.

By 1969, Walden had fifty-nine stores in nineteen states and was clearly proving that bookselling on a mass scale could be quite profitable. Still, observers were surprised when Waldenbooks was sold that year to Broadway Hale Stores, a California chain of department stores. The acquisition was quite a risk for Broadway Hale, as Walden represented its only retail holding that was not a department or clothing store. However, Broadway Hale believed that there were substantial opportunities to improve its bottom line through introducing bookstores to the shopping centers that were springing up all over the country. With Broadway Hale's capital at its disposal, Walden then embarked on an aggressive expansion program. By the early 1980s, Walden was opening eighty to ninety stores a year; in 1981, with 704 branches, it became the first bookstore chain to have outlets in all fifty states.

In 1983, Waldenbooks acquired Brentano's, which had been having financial difficulties for a number of years, and which had been reduced to only three stores. The following year, with 862 outlets and reported annual profits of $27 million, Walden itself was again the object of acquisition. As part of a strategy to avert a hostile takeover bid from Limited Inc., Carter Hawley Hale decided to dispose of the bookstore chain.[65] Walden's newest owner was Kmart, the contemporary incarnation of the discount variety store. Kmart had a number of motives for purchasing Walden. In the first place, it coveted the leases that Walden held for many choice mall locations, spots into which Kmart could strategically shuffle its various subsidiaries. Additionally, the retailer hoped to use Waldenbooks to improve bookselling efforts in Kmart's own stores. Finally, though not least, Kmart claimed that the acquisition fit into its diversification strategy, which was to purchase relatively trouble-free moneymakers with good growth potential. Consequently, Kmart continued Walden's course of expansion. Waldenbooks was helped along in this with another acquisition in 1987, when it bought the fifty U.S. stores of Coles, a large Canadian chain. Walden was clearly trying to consolidate its position as the biggest seller of books in the country.[66]

In this competition, Waldenbooks' principal rival was B. Dalton. The 1966 inauguration of B. Dalton, Bookseller, attracted a good deal more attention than Walden's original opening had. Perhaps this was because B. Dalton was founded by a nonbook retailer (three years before Broadway Hale acquired Walden), and one with immediate ambitions to create a major bookstore chain. B. Dalton's parent was the Dayton Company, a Minneapolis-based department store firm.[67] Although a highly unusual move for this kind of company, Dayton did not start Dalton simply on a whim. The firm conducted studies that indicated unmet market potential in the book field. Dayton originally conceived of a chain of fine bookshops to be based in both suburban shopping centers and downtown locations. According to the company's original announcement, it planned to construct quality bookstores, which would stress service, including the provision of special orders, monogramming, and free delivery of books. The name B. Dalton was selected because it sounded English and connoted "quality, dependability and authority." The first outlet opened with great fanfare in August 1966 in Edina, Minnesota, a suburb of Dayton's home territory. The next store opened the following February in a St. Louis suburb, and by the end of its second year, there were a dozen B. Daltons selling books. Despite Dayton's original intention to open stores in downtown locations as well as in suburban areas, just about all of these first stores were situated in suburban shopping centers, and it was indeed there that B. Dalton found a key to success.

In 1968, Dayton acquired Pickwick Book Shops, a seven-store regional chain based in southern California. After that, Dayton concentrated on building new B. Dalton outlets rapidly. By 1981, the chain could claim 526 branches, and while still below Walden in number of outlets, B. Dalton matched its rival in terms of revenue.[68] Nevertheless, in 1986, following a difficult year when discounting by competitors caused B. Dalton's profits to fall, Dayton Hudson decided to sell the chain. B. Dalton's new parent was a group composed of Barnes & Noble, a large regional bookstore chain, and Barnes & Noble's principal owners, Leonard Riggio and Vendamerica, the American subsidiary of the Dutch corporation, Vendex International.

Barnes & Noble had a very long history in the book industry, though it was only in the prior decade that it had achieved the stature of a major chain itself. The firm traced its roots back to 1874, when Charles Montgomery Barnes began to sell used books in Wheaton, Illinois. In 1917, Barnes's son William moved to New York and entered into a partnership with George Clifford Noble, who had formerly been involved in publishing and retailing through the firms Hinds & Noble and Noble & Noble. After initially acting as a jobber that supplied educational books to schools and libraries, Barnes & Noble added retail space, and eventually concentrated on textbook retailing, with some publishing on the side.

The company stayed in the Barnes family's hands for many years. But in 1969, when John Barnes died, Barnes & Noble was sold to Amtel, a Providence, Rhode Island, company with diverse manufacturing and retailing holdings. Then, in 1971, Amtel sold Barnes & Noble to Leonard Riggio, a bookseller who operated several college bookstores.[69] Riggio turned the New York City Barnes & Noble, already a large store, into one of the biggest sources of books in the country. He also began, in 1975, to selectively engage in the controversial practice of discounting. By the late 1970s, Riggio had begun to expand the business in earnest. In addition to managing a growing number of college bookstores, establishing trade bookstores in the Northeast, and operating the flagship Barnes & Noble in Manhattan, the company ventured into a number of other book-related businesses. These included publishing, textbook wholesaling, the distribution of books to supermarkets, and with the 1979 acquisition of a firm called Marboro, the mail-order book business as well.

At the time of the B. Dalton acquisition, Barnes & Noble operated 37 trade bookstores and 142 college bookstores. However, the addition of B. Dalton easily turned the company into the largest American bookstore chain. Renamed the BDB Corporation, the chain continued to expand both B. Dalton and Barnes & Noble stores, while making some additional acquisitions. They included two other "majors" of American bookselling: the 1989 acquisition of the Scribner's Bookstore name, plus one Scribner's bookstore, and the purchase of Doubleday Book Shops in 1990. Under the BDB umbrella, the different sets of stores maintained their separate identities, with each meant to appeal to a differently located (both socially and geographically) type of consumer, and to the needs of different shopping mall landlords. As Barnes & Noble explained,

> In 1989 and 1990, respectively, the Company acquired the Scribner's Bookstores tradename and 42 Doubleday bookstores to complement its B. Dalton mall retailing strategy with an upscale alternative to the traditional B. Dalton format for mall developers.[70]

But going into the 1990s, it was still the ubiquitous B. Dalton that was the company's most visible and profitable chain of stores.[71]

As I will describe in following chapters, the design, merchandising strategies, and management of both B. Dalton and Waldenbooks were quite distinct from that of most existing independent stores. In part, these differences stemmed from the influence of the organizational cultures and management expertise of their parent department and discount store firms. Two other major book chains of the 1970s and '80s were similarly shaped by another nonbook competitor of the bookshop, the drugstore. In 1984, the Rite Aid Corporation, a discount drugstore chain, acquired Encore Books, a regional book chain. Rite Aid kept Encore Books for ten years; it was then sold to the Lauriat's chain. Lauriat's, which also included the Royal Discount and Book Corner stores, went out of business in 1999.

A second chain with drugstore ties, Crown Books, also did not last, but was highly influential in the book business, as it made discounting a standard feature among the chains. Crown was started by Robert Haft, the son of Washington, D.C., real estate and drugstore tycoon Herbert Haft. The senior Haft made his fortune by pioneering the concept of the discount drugstore; the first Dart Drug opened in 1954, immediately earning the wrath of pharmacists, who, like booksellers of the day, contended that price-cutting was unfair competition. With the aid of his wife, two sons, and daughter, Herbert Haft then took his Dart Group into a number of other retail fields and commercial real estate.[72]

While attending Harvard Business School, Robert Haft wrote a thesis describing a chain of discount bookstores. After rejoining his father's business, he set about making his proposal a reality. With the backing of Herbert's capital, Robert Haft opened the first Crown Books in September 1977 in a Washington suburb. In a little over a year, he opened ten additional outlets, all practicing the same discount philosophy. By mid-1982, with eighty-one stores, Crown jumped to third place among bookstore chains in terms of outlets, and fourth in terms of revenue. Then in 1983, Crown became the first major bookstore chain to go public. This event signaled to anyone still in doubt that the bookstore business was capable of generating the profits and management style to sustain Wall Street's attention.

Over the next decade, Crown continued to grow. But its pursuit of the two bigger chains came to a screeching halt in 1993 when internal feuding among the Haft family wracked their various business enterprises. The Hafts' involvement with Crown came to an end two and a half years after the initial blow-up, when all family members were removed from Crown's management and had their voting rights taken away. Although corporate officers tried to bring the company out of chaos, Crown was not able to recover, and saw its earnings and stock price fall. In 1998, Dart was acquired by Richfood Holdings, a wholesale food distributor. Richfood announced that it would divest Crown, but when no buyer could be found, the troubled book chain was forced into bankruptcy. Crown did reorganize and emerge from bankruptcy in 1999, but it was no longer able to compete effectively against its rivals. Like Lauriat's, Crown had fallen too far behind in the race to construct superstores. In 2001, Crown declared bankruptcy for a second time, and then was liquidated. Crown's assets were sold off, with a number of its outlets purchased by Books-A-Million, a bookstore chain based in the southeast that was now the third largest in the country. Crown may have come to an inglorious end, but its legacy of discounting lived on among the remaining chains.[73]

From Mall Store to Superstore to Internet Store

By the end of the 1980s, the chains' formula was a familiar one: small stores in shopping centers or malls that emphasized popular titles, minimal service, and heavily advertised discounts. But a closer look showed that all was not well with the old mall strategy, and that the chains had been taking quite an interest in other styles of bookselling that had developed during the previous decade. Already by the early 1980s, there had been a slowdown in the construction of new malls, and this only grew more pronounced as the decade progressed. Not only were there fewer new mall locations to move into, but it seemed that many of the smaller and less glamorous malls were losing their appeal for consumers, while the best mall locations were becoming ever more expensive. Meanwhile, independent bookstores and regional chains, which had lost tremendous ground with the emergence of the major chains, had started to make a comeback by offering more service and a bigger (or at least different) selection than the national chains did. These local booksellers thus seemed to have found a niche that the big chains had no desire to occupy.

But then in 1990, the superstores were unveiled. Superstore was the name given to a new format of chain bookstore, one with several times the number of titles and the amount of floor space found in the typical chain outlet. Rolled out with great fanfare, the superstores were big to begin with, and as time went on, they grew even bigger. Observers were very surprised by the first Super Crown stores, which were 6,000 to 8,000 square feet and carried 30–40,000 titles. They were even more impressed with the first Barnes & Noble superstore, which went well beyond Crown at 15,000 square feet and a stock of 100,000 titles. But within a few years, the original Super Crown would not even qualify as a superstore, and the original Barnes & Noble superstore would be on the low end for size. By 1995, the average superstore was 35,500 square feet and typically carried 125,000 titles, plus a lot of other media items. While sometimes based in malls, the size of the superstores often necessitated their location in strip centers or as freestanding stores. These were clearly no ordinary chain bookstores.[74]

Although it may have seemed as if they came out of nowhere, there were actually a number of precedents for the superstores, and the major chains had been experimenting with variations on them during the previous several years. Superstores were a hybrid of the large independent bookstores that developed in the 1980s, in part as a reaction to the competition presented by the chains, and the large specialty stores, or "category killers," that had developed in several other consumer good fields, the prototype being Toys "R" Us. But there were also a couple other booksellers who managed to turn the large-store format into medium-scale chains during the '80s. One of these was the Texas chain Bookstop, founded by Gary Hoover in 1982. Consciously modeled after the Toys "R" Us format, Bookstop outlets combined discounting with very wide selection, careful attention to display, and a reliance on sophisticated information systems in order to build a chain that would appeal to affluent, educated readers. By 1989, Bookstop had grown to twenty-two stores in Texas, California, Florida, and Louisiana. It had clearly caught the attention of others in the book industry, as that year, both Crown Books and BDB (Barnes & Noble) bought large stakes in the company. After a year and a half of legal and boardroom tussles, Barnes & Noble was finally able to achieve full control of Bookstop, and Crown sold back its share of the company. Bookstop and Bookstar (the name used in some states because of trademark conflicts) then became a key part of Barnes & Noble's early superstore effort.[75]

Another model for a large-store book chain was provided by the Michigan bookseller Borders. The Borders brothers, Louis and Thomas, went from selling antiquarian books to running a general bookshop in Ann Arbor in

1973. Originally catering to a college audience, they created a well-respected store with an extensive selection and a reputation for a deep love of books. In 1985, a second store was added and the chain slowly began to grow, though decision-making was kept relatively decentralized. In 1989, a new manager, Robert DiRomualdo, was hired to modernize and expand the chain, and there was a new emphasis on marketing and centralized management. Then in 1992, with nineteen stores in fourteen states, Borders was acquired by Kmart, which hoped to give its own superstore efforts a boost. Waldenbooks had been experimenting with a large-store format since 1986, when it had started Waldenbooks & More, outlets about three times the size of the usual Walden. In early 1992, Waldenbooks and More was discontinued, and instead, a new version of the superstore called Basset Book Shops was launched. But when Borders became available a few months later, Kmart seized the opportunity to acquire a ready-made chain of successful superstores. Eventually, Basset was folded into Borders, and DiRomualdo was put in charge of the new Borders-Walden Group.[76]

Beginning in 1990, and strengthened by their various acquisitions, the major chains promulgated a dual strategy — the continuation of mall stores and a separate emphasis on superstores. But within a very short time, the superstores started to overshadow the once-invincible mall stores. The chains invested tremendous resources in building new superstores wherever they could find the space, while unprofitable mall stores were suddenly being closed right and left. Reflecting the new dominance of the superstores, in 1991 the BDB Corporation had changed its name to Barnes & Noble Inc. and Borders-Walden was renamed the Borders Group in 1994. The frenzied construction of new superstores was extremely expensive, and in order to raise more capital for its expansion, Barnes & Noble went public in 1993. Meanwhile, Kmart was also considering issuing public stock in Borders, though its motivations were a bit more complicated. Kmart was experiencing financial difficulties of its own, and as problems at its main discount stores intensified, shareholders loudly expressed their unhappiness. Finally, in 1995, Kmart decided to raise money by selling three of its subsidiaries, and by the end of the year, it had spun off Borders completely.[77] Borders had joined its rival chains in becoming a publicly traded corporation.

The effect of the superstore strategy was to give the chains decisive dominance in the bookstore market. Even following the successes of the mall chains, independent bookstores still sold more books. But this pattern was reversed in the early 1990s. In 1991, bookstore chains were responsible for 22 percent of adult books sold, while independents had a 32.5 percent share. By 1997, the chains' share of such sales had risen to 25 percent, while independents' market share plummeted to 17 percent.[78] At that point, the two largest companies by themselves controlled nearly half of the bookstore market: in 1997, Barnes & Noble and the Borders Group accounted for 43.3 percent of bookstore sales.[79] Large numbers of independents were forced out of business, including some of the country's most well known stores. This decline was reflected in the bookstore failure rate, which rose sharply during the 1990s.[80]

In these years, one other retailer became a major player in bookselling, initiating a new direction for chains and independents alike. Amazon.com was perhaps the most visible and talked-about of the early consumer e-commerce businesses. The company was started in 1995 by Jeff Bezos, a Wall Street financier who left his job at a hedge fund to begin an Internet business. Books were a logical choice for an e-commerce experiment. Decades of mail-order sales showed that readers would buy books without first handling them, and that books were small and uniform enough to be packed and shipped for a modest cost. Furthermore, Amazon was easily able to exploit book buyers' preferences for large selections by simply adopting the standard reference, *Books in Print,* as its catalog. Amazon thus offered consumers both the convenience of mail order and the convenience of consulting an electronic version of *Books in Print* from the book buyer's own home.

When Amazon went public in 1997, it became a stock market wonder, attracting investors' enthusiasm even though the company showed no signs of making a profit. Eager to ride the e-commerce momentum, the major chain booksellers, independents, and e-tailers with no prior bookselling experience quickly established online bookstores of their own. Within a few years, there were myriad sites selling books both new and used; there were sites that specialized in specific categories and others that claimed to sell any title in print. Still, all of these Internet booksellers found it difficult to make their enterprises profitable as they confronted the same problems of supply, distribution, and marketing that bricks-and-mortar book retailers routinely faced. Initially, Amazon relied on wholesalers and publishers to fulfill orders. But once sales increased, this became a slow and complicated method for delivering books to customers. Amazon then invested in building a distribution infrastructure to match what its principal competitors, the major chain booksellers, already had in place. Although the company did not need physical storefronts, it discovered that it did require physical warehouses.

As profits continued to elude online bookselling, a number of Internet bookstores closed down while others combined forces. In an alliance that joined a major publisher with a major bookseller, Bertelsmann (owner of Random House) acquired a 50 percent stake in Barnes & Noble's online arm.[81] And after heavy losses on its Internet site, Borders decided, in effect, to give up on e-commerce by making a deal with Amazon to have the Internet leader manage Borders' site.[82]

The Borders-Amazon alliance occurred in 2001, when the dot-com bubble burst. Reflecting a more sober outlook on the possibility of reaping online riches by selling books, Internet booksellers scaled back in a number of ways over the next couple years. Barnes & Noble reacquired Bertelsmann's share as well as outstanding stock of Barnesandnoble.com, ending the online dealer's short life as a separate, public company. Amazon closed some distribution centers, Barnesandnoble.com eliminated some nonbook items it had been selling, and both booksellers cut sales and marketing costs. These costs had been extremely high; Amazon spent as much as 10 percent of sales in its quest to make its name synonymous with Internet shopping.[83] While Amazon decided to move well beyond book retailing by turning into a multi-product Internet "bazaar," chain and independent booksellers integrated the Internet into a more comprehensive strategy for marketing and distributing books through physical stores as well as online. Internet bookselling, which represented 5.8 percent of books purchased in 2001, had not replaced bricks-and-mortar stores.[84] Instead, as I will suggest, the methods of online bookselling were much more similar to those of the physical bookstore than awed observers assumed. And far from the Internet resulting in a more decentralized bookselling environment, the shakeout among online booksellers contributed to the growing concentration of the book retail market.

The End of a Genteel Industry

By the beginning of the twenty-first century, bookselling in the United States looked considerably different from the industry that had once been so marginal to modern capital. In place of a small number of independent shopkeepers, department stores, and drugstores thinly scattered across the country, the American retail landscape was now blanketed by bookstores, most of which bore the same few corporate names. In sharp contrast to a time when booksellers had little knowledge of the universe of published books or the tastes of the book-buying public, rationalized methods, from the collection of data on books and customers to the utilization of carefully planned marketing campaigns, were now being employed by chain retailers in an attempt to make the bookselling process more predictable, and thus to sell more books. In this effort, the chains were aided by new technology and by changes in the retail culture that accustomed consumers to expect informality, convenience, discounted prices, and a barrage of marketing messages at every turn. With their assurance that purchasing a book required little investment of effort or money, and their informality communicating the message that book shopping need not be considered a special occasion, the chains contributed to a growing ownership culture in which people expect that the goods they use should be privately owned. This was no doubt reinforced by the declining fortunes of the public library; fewer Americans now thought to look to public institutions for their reading material.[85]

The success of the chains also turned an uncomfortable spotlight on traditional ways of bookselling. The chains achieved a populist image, which made the book trade's longstanding contempt for certain genres of books and certain kinds of book readers appear all the more elitist. The chains' efficiency and ability to move huge numbers of books into readers' hands reinforced suspicions that people with little business sense were the cause of book retailing's woes. With the chains leading the way, the "distribution problem" of the book business thus looked like it was finally being solved.

However, the chains' ever-increasing control of market share, publishers' attention, and the public's assumptions of what shopping for books was all about was not accepted with equanimity by everyone in the book industry. This new generation of bookstore chains may have been more efficient and sold more books than any other bookstore that had come before. But far from being grounds for congratulations, these were exactly the features that were frequently condemned and presented as a threat to the integrity of the book industry. Concerns were voiced about the clout being wielded by a small number of companies. The chains' early ownership by firms whose primary business was not in books, and their later organization as public corporations, raised questions about whether they were accountable to the traditions of book culture or to investors' demands for profitability. The chains' willingness to engage in mass marketing and to create standardized stores resulted in controversies over the degrading effects of rationalization. And their competitive strategies that decimated so many independent bookstores provoked reactions against the brutal indifference of the marketplace.

The chains not only led or institutionalized significant changes within the book industry, but they helped to alter Americans' perceptions of bookstores and book buying. In the following chapters, I examine in more detail the various elements that contributed to the spectacular growth of the chains, the debate over the effects of these developments, and the corresponding responses of independent booksellers. This analysis will serve to highlight the ways in which various cultural understandings of consumption are embedded in the rhetoric and practices of booksellers.

CHAPTER 3

Providing for the Sovereign Consumer: Selecting and Recommending Books

How do readers decide what books to purchase? There are various ways to approach this question; one can investigate psychological factors that help to determine individual tastes, as well as more social factors such as literacy levels, income, and the influence of reference groups and trusted advisors. One can also take account of the institutional factors that determine which books people are aware of and have access to. Surely, most observers would concur that all these different factors matter to one degree or another. But if the question is rephrased to ask how *should* readers decide what books to purchase, the answers that emerge would be much more selective and would also vary depending on the prevailing values of the time.

How this normative question gets addressed has important implications for the work of booksellers, for decisions about stocking the store shelves are not simply a product of space considerations, and responses to customer inquiries are not solely a matter of staff knowledge. These activities are also influenced by how the bookseller conceives of her proper relationship to her customers. More specifically, a bookseller's judgments about what books to carry and sell are shaped by the extent to which she sees herself as rightfully taking an active role in guiding the reading of her customers. This conception of the appropriate relationship between bookseller and customer has changed over the last century. Within the book trade, an earlier notion that readers benefit from the guidance of informed advisors such as the bookseller has largely, though not entirely, been replaced by a set of ideals that uphold the importance of each (adult) individual freely choosing his or her reading material without interference from others. Yet at the same time as this cultural change has taken place, the number of published books has grown far beyond the capacity of any single store to carry them all, or of any individual reader to monitor all the choices that are available.

In this chapter, I begin to examine some of the industry-related factors that help determine what books readers purchase. I start by looking at the bookseller's job of selecting and recommending books, key tasks that have changed in important ways since the 1960s. These changes are related to various developments in transportation and information technology, as well as to a more conscious integration of marketing into all aspects of retailing. But the ways in which selection and recommendation have evolved are also related to the decline of the bookseller's educational mission, and the concomitant rise of an ideology that acclaims the sovereignty of the consumer.[1] Whereas in the past, booksellers were eager to claim the status of cultural authorities, today they are more likely to demur. Similarly, a prior assumption that booksellers should steer the public toward "quality" reading material has been eclipsed by a vision of the consumer as having the right to freely choose cultural goods without interference from cultural elites.

These cultural changes were under way well before the chains came on the scene. Indeed, the case of the all-paperback store, described in chapter 2, was one manifestation of a reaction against paternalism in bookselling. Nonetheless, the mall-based bookstore chains that developed in the 1960s were unrivaled in the degree to which they both capitalized on and helped to further this strand of antielitism. The chains recognized that they could reach an expanded reading public by focusing on the most popular titles, by carrying inexpensive formats such as the paperback, and by emphasizing the customer autonomy that came with self-service. The resulting successes of the chains pushed independents to rethink their own styles of selling books. In response, some independents demonstrated a newfound commitment to the ideal of reader choice by creating stores that offered a far greater selection than the chain outlets did, though these independents also tended to retain their upmarket orientation. Then, with the advent of the superstore, the chains combined their reputation for nonjudgmental bookselling with the large-store format to construct an image of unparalleled choice.

However, the concept of consumer choice is not as straightforward as this image implies. Book retailers, whether chain, independent, or nonbook, continue to select the books that readers browse, since the need to judiciously stock the store has not disappeared. If anything, booksellers have had to become more selective over the past several decades as the number of new titles produced each year has risen dramatically. In 1941, 9,337 new titles and 1,775 new editions were published in the United States. In 2001, there were approximately 167,000 new titles and editions published. When combined with older titles still available, that meant that there were approximately 1.7 million different books in print in the United States.[2] Even the most massive of superstores can carry only a fraction of available titles.

In addition to the fact that customers will encounter a limited portion of published titles in the bookstore, readers' choices are shaped by bookseller recommendations as well as by more indirect marketing efforts. Booksellers offer recommendations in part because of a genuine enthusiasm for particular books, but also because there exist financial incentives to steer readers to a circumscribed number of titles. And despite an ideology of consumer sovereignty, customers often solicit advice on what books will appeal to them or those for whom they are buying a gift.

So by necessity and design, the bookseller makes it more likely that some books rather than others will reach readers. The process through which this happens differs to some degree between independent and chain stores, though independents are increasingly adopting the techniques of the chains. Still, it is the chain superstore that best exemplifies the technocratic answer to how to reconcile the need to select and recommend with the sovereignty of the consumer. The belief that readers' individual preferences should override booksellers' tastes has been enshrined in the use of rationalized systems for making decisions about selection and recommendation. This process of rationalization has been achieved primarily through the application of technology such as computerized inventory control systems, database marketing, and online tracking and recommendation features. However, as I will show, these systems have simply substituted a less visible form of guidance for the more personalized judgments and advice that were formerly the prerogative of the bookseller.

From Mind Doctor to Conduit for Consumer Satisfaction

As part of their desire to spread a genteel culture, the regular bookseller of the early twentieth century took pride in improving people's lives by introducing them to "good" books. Practices and attitudes varied, but booksellers tended to earn the respect of their peers when their store selections went beyond the popular novels so much in demand, and when they became a guiding force in their customers' reading habits. Complementing this vision of the educative bookseller, members of the book industry assumed that readers needed and welcomed help in choosing their books. As a trade publication from 1914 put it:

> Wherever the bookseller is located, in small towns or large cities, he is an intellectual center that works for the benefit of the community. He is generally the guide and counsel to others as to their reading, their study and improvement. The good he does can not be estimated. Any community without a bookstore is nearly as badly off as without a church or school.[3]

The book trade was perhaps overoptimistic about the actual influence of the bookseller, but what is noteworthy here is the ideal that was being held up as a standard against which book outlets were measured. The bookstore was supposed to be an institution that worked to educate and uplift the population, and thus the bookseller had an explicitly moral role to play in American society. This perspective was also adopted by those department stores that aspired to build significant book departments. In 1938 the manager of the book department at Joseph Horne of Pittsburgh offered the following advice:

> [T]he book salesman [is] in the coveted position of "Mind Doctor" for his or her community. When you or I want spiritual comfort, we converse with a teacher of religion; when we need medical advice, we consult with our physician, and if we need guidance about the law we call upon a lawyer — so why not train and elevate the salesmen of your book department to function in the same spirit of counsel and advice, teaching them to give sound and intelligent information about books for self-improvement and enjoyment?[4]

The responsibility of the bookseller to act as an intellectual advisor included discouraging people from reading salacious material. But most important, the bookseller was to use his personal familiarity and influence with his customers to encourage them to read, and so learn to prefer, the stuff deemed most nourishing. The bookseller would thus use his knowledge and authority to help mold the tastes of his clientele in a way that was both socially and personally beneficial.

Like most ideologies, this ideal of the didactic bookseller was neither absolute in its application nor entirely consistent in its logic. For instance, as Janice Radway has shown, the Book-of-the-Month Club was attacked in the 1920s and '30s by the literary establishment, including much of the book industry, precisely for presuming to select the reader's books for him. But the Book-of-the-Month Club differed in some important respects from the regular bookstore. The club was condemned because it utilized impersonal marketing methods to reach readers across the entire country. Rather than drawing on personal familiarity with a customer to advocate a program of good reading, such as the regular bookseller was thought to do, the Book-of-the-Month Club marketed the same handful of books to all its anonymous mass membership, and thus, critics charged, threatened standardization of the nation's literary fare.[5] This was not the bookselling equivalent of the community pastor, but rather, resembled a remote celebrity prophet.

While the distinction between the harmful authority of the book club and the benevolent guidance of the bookseller seemed clear enough during the Book-of-the-Month Club's early years, by midcentury, there were increased signs of doubt about even the regular bookseller's position as a cultural authority. For instance, at a 1946 panel, a telling exchange took place between a former sales manager at Doubleday and the former manager of Macy's book department:

> Mr. Crowell asked whether it is the function of the bookseller or the publisher to elevate the public taste, and if so, he asked, "Who sets that taste, God, the book buyer or who?" Miss Byrnes replied that she thought it was the function of the bookseller to supply good books, and to show customers books other than the best sellers.[6]

As the century progressed, booksellers with attitudes similar to that of Miss Byrnes, the Macy's manager, would be more hard pressed to defend their views. Thus, in 1960, a guide to bookselling did not even present this issue as one to be debated:

> It is not the bookseller's job to tell the prospective reader what he must read. To do that is to reinforce the trend towards standardization and conformity, which we already have too much of in our daily routine. But it is the bookseller's task to see that the *right* book is sold to the *right* person. It is his primary goal to see that the readers he encounters find the books they are seeking and need.[7]

By the 1980s, this sentiment was largely taken for granted.

The shift in understandings of the bookseller's role had occurred for several reasons, some connected to the particularities of the book industry, some to cultural politics more generally. In part, old attitudes changed because of a general decline in the perceived legitimacy of cultural elites. As Michael Kammen has argued, during the post–World War II years, cultural authority gave way to more indirect cultural power, especially that exercised by the corporate mass media. Those organizations determined which aesthetic and entertainment artifacts were disseminated, but did not necessarily command the respect of the population.[8] Related to this decline of cultural authority, a new generation of booksellers entered the profession. Many were influenced by the antielitism of the postwar era, and many had a genuine regard for popular culture. They were less interested than booksellers of the past in telling customers what books were or were not good for them.

But this greater deference toward the tastes that customers walked in the door with was not just spontaneously offered. It was also a result of independent booksellers coming to terms with the competition of the chains, the success of which was in part due to the chains' populist stance. The chains communicated their rejection of cultural elitism through their outlets' design and placement in shopping centers and malls (see chapter 4). The mall-based chains also indicated that they were not interested in "elevating" or otherwise changing consumer tastes through their selections, which were largely made up of the most popular new books, and through their emphasis on self-service, which allowed customers to bypass the opinions and judgments of the bookseller. At Waldenbooks, for instance, customers could discover a prominently displayed selection of romance novels, a genre that independent booksellers might carry grudgingly, if at all. Bestsellers were also given pride of place in the chains, suggesting that the stores were eager to supply customers with the books endorsed by their peers.

This emphasis on the most popular books was not so apparent in the chains' early days. B. Dalton, in particular, was originally intent on gaining a reputation as a highbrow bookstore with a superior selection. As one profile of an employee suggested, Dalton booksellers had similar views to those of independents concerning their mission: "Baxter was a Dalton buyer of the old school, who saw it as his job to bring literature to the public. He believed that the growing chain could be a vehicle for putting important books before a large segment of readers."[9] But with time, central headquarters took over more of the selection decisions from local managers, and titles that did not sell very well were eliminated. And as mall rents steadily increased, the size of the average chain outlet decreased.[10] With less space available for a wide selection, the chains put more emphasis on the frontlist (new books), and the shelf life for any given title declined. If a book did not do well within a few months, it was sent back to the publisher in order to make way for new titles.

The chains' preference for quick-turnover titles that entered the market with a big splash and sold in large quantities was one factor that contributed to their populist image. These were not stores that tried to push the books favored by literary critics and other elites, but rather, they carried titles that appealed to a wide range of individuals, including the occasional reader and those with less education and lower incomes than had typically frequented bookstores in the past. Of course, there were some differences between the chains in this regard. Crown was considered the most aggressive in pursuing a mass-merchandising strategy, Dalton the least.[11] But with each of them, it was clear that profitability was dependent on the distribution of a limited number of titles to an extremely large number of people.

Equally important for courting a less elite audience, the chains provided an atmosphere that was distinctly unintimidating. By emphasizing friendliness over scholarliness among staff, the chains broke through the common image of booksellers as snooty guardians of high culture. As the manager of a Crown outlet in Berkeley told a reporter in 1982, his staff eschewed the judgmental attitudes to be found in independents:

> "[Cody's owner] Ross says the people working in the chain stores are all just clerks," the manager continues. "But we have degrees. We're not morons. Sure, they've got some pretty sharp guys in Cody's. But they're the kind of people that, if you ask them for 'Gone with the Wind,' they'll laugh at you."[12]

Those independent booksellers who did not reform their assumptions about appropriate reading behavior and tastes found it increasingly difficult to compete against the friendly chains. And indeed, many such bookstores went out of business in the 1970s and '80s.

Today, the notion that the bookseller should not interfere with consumers' legitimate right to enjoy any book that suits their tastes is widespread. This is not to say that the earlier ideal of the bookseller as guide to genteel culture has vanished altogether. Those working in the book business (publishers and distributors as well as booksellers) continue to view themselves as people with a special regard for ideas and words, and a desire to discover and promote notable writers. The hope of contributing to a deeper understanding of the human condition, the idea that books are good for people (as well as a lingering sense that some books are better for readers than others), and a concomitant belief in the uplifting effects of reading continue to underlie the enthusiasm of a great many members of the book business for the work that they do. Just as there remains a connection between book reading and other high-culture pursuits, so there remains a sense that reading or working with books is a way to cultivate the finer qualities in humans. One wholesaler I interviewed spoke of his work as fulfilling for just that reason:

> You have this unique ability to match individuals up with the information that they want to enhance themselves one way or another. . . . I really like doing that. And it's probably one of many reasons why I like being in the business. It's because, well, I believe in the perfectibility of man. And woman. And one of the ways people can do that is to read.

Although this speaker half apologetically described his perspective as "old-fashioned," he was by no means unique among the people I interviewed.

Still, there are important differences between this sentiment and earlier views. What is being commended here is the encouragement of reading in general, not the ability to convert readers to an appreciation of the "best" books. And as this wholesaler suggests, there is a belief that serving the customer by helping her find the material that suits her tastes is an honorable endeavor. Moreover, when book professionals do describe themselves as taking on an active cultural role, they tend to define cultural leadership as adding to the existing diversity of literary voices. This is then less a matter of fulfilling an educational mission, of teaching readers to distinguish between absolute standards of good and bad, than a matter of widening the choices given to consumers.

The erosion of a belief that readers need to be taught the skills of discrimination can be seen in replies to the abstract question of whether the job of the publishing industry should be primarily to supply people with the books they want or to help introduce people to good books. Almost all industry respondents answered that it should be both; for many, these roles are not mutually exclusive:

> Independent bookstore owner: They can do both. I don't think there's any particular limitation. I mean, in terms of commercial viability or anything else. I mean, I think that there's an insatiable need that people have to want to better themselves and/or to entertain themselves. You know, you can do both. And books provide that window of opportunity. So I don't think they're exclusive.

> Chain bookstore manager: Both. Introducing them to good books is very important. Because there's a lot out there, that they're not aware of. There is always something more, in any part of life and I think literature is a great area to become more involved in because there is so much out there. We carry such a wide variety of titles, when our store's remodeled, it'll probably be

300,000 titles. That's a lot of books for someone to think a whole lot about when they [usually] don't. So that's why recommendations do come and play a major part in this business.

As the second bookseller makes clear, the bookseller's power to do good comes from the ability to expose people to new ideas. But what this bookseller refrains from doing is specifying which of those ideas are more deserving than others.

Similarly, bookstore customers only occasionally look to the bookseller for instruction on how to evaluate cultural material. While customers of the past may not have been the disciples that booksellers would have liked, this was generally not because readers assumed booksellers to be ignorant about literary matters. But my interviews with and observations of bookstore patrons indicate that readers today have extremely limited expectations for bookstore employees' knowledge about books, much less the world of ideas in general. When asked what makes for a good salesperson at a bookstore, the majority of respondents cited friendliness or the simple ability to direct customers to the right location to find a title:

> They have to know where all the books are in the bookstore, because it's nothing more infuriating than asking somebody and they don't know where it is. So that's number one. Friendly, helpful, when you want to be helped, you know, when you go and ask for it, rather than being pushy.

> Well, their personality for one thing. If they don't treat you like the book itself, so to speak. Treat you like a human being. And, like I say, knowledgeable and helpful. It's a big thing with me.

> Someone who's nice, who knows where everything is, can help you quickly. You know, who is friendly.

Rarely was familiarity with books in general the first consideration when describing a good salesperson. While the most common attribute cited was being "knowledgeable," by this, customers tended to mean someone who knows his own store's stock, or else someone who can identify the specific book or author a customer is referring to.

> I would say probably the key is just, you know, knowledge, just a good knowledge and being able to be helpful instead of like, "I've never heard of that and I don't know," and so [laughs], that doesn't help. I mean I would say,

for the most part, the bookstores I've been into, the people have been very friendly, very helpful. And if they can't find it, they pursue trying to find it. I mean, they don't just drop it and say, "Well, it's not here so we don't have it."

Someone who knows their stock.

Someone who's friendly and who can assist me in finding or locating the book in the bookstore. Who doesn't mind doing that, or if I have just a topic, this is what I'm looking for, they can either go to their computer or direct me to the section where I can find a book.

About one-sixth of the customers I interviewed did mention the ability to recommend a book as a characteristic of a good salesperson. But in most cases, there was not the expectation that the customer would develop a trusted advisory relationship with a wise, experienced bookseller. As the following comments suggest, the value of bookseller recommendations comes from an ability to discern and remember the tastes of the customer or an awareness of the tastes of the customer's cultural peers:

Be able to help you recommend what you're looking for. If you need a recommendation on a type of book.

Really knowledgeable about books. The perfect salesperson at a bookstore was this guy at this bookstore by Arizona State, he owned the place. And he could talk, he would just talk to you, he wouldn't bother you. But if you started talking to him he could recommend books. He read a lot and he was pretty good at knowing what their tastes were and things. And also he remembered you, so when you came in, he'd say, "Oh we have a new book, you know, you might be interested in." So it was that kind of thing. I really haven't encountered a good — I would say that's probably the biggest flaw with [a local independent bookstore] is that I don't feel like the people there are really book people. But there must be some book people, because there's these little cards with recommended books, but I've never struck up a conversation with them about books.

I think that especially like college students seek out jobs that they particularly like. And usually they're well read, then they'll give you a recommendation on a book or what's real exciting and, you know, that you might have missed.

I think if they show any interest in what you're looking for. If they try to find it on the computer and guide you to it, that's about all. Sometimes they can give you some input as to how a book is doing, how interesting other people find it.

In even more cases, though, customers simply wanted a clerk:

Leaving you alone and letting you browse. Because I have walked out of more bookstores when they kept saying, "May we help you, may we help you, may we help you." You don't have time to look at what you want. If you want help, then you can go to them rather than them — Like at Nordstrom's, you know, they'll leave you alone, if you need them, they're there. You know what I mean?

Just somebody who rings up the cash . . . works behind a cash register. That's all.

Someone who doesn't ask any questions, doesn't get in my way.

I think in a bookstore, [a] salesperson is not necessary, because they are not going to tell me what I should read [*laughs*]. I don't think they are necessary. Cashiers are necessary. And people who reshelve the books and put the books back on the shelves, they are necessary. I don't think a salesperson is necessary.

As C. Wright Mills outlined several decades ago, in a society dominated by bureaucratic enterprises and commercial transactions between strangers, personality replaces skill or experience as the primary requirement of the good salesperson.[13] The chains, with their emphasis on self-service and their high turnover among staff, helped to further this expectation among bookstore customers over the last few decades. Yet, while the chains' reputation for employing skilled clerks is poor, they have a decided advantage in the public relations arena when it comes to personality. Since their early days, their commitment to friendly service to patrons of all ranks has served them well, and has also contributed to customers' assumptions of what a good bookstore experience is. Most customers do not want the bookseller to offer advice unless it is clearly sought out. And booksellers have also come to believe that the consumer should decide for herself what to read.

Similar to what Radway found when studying the selection procedures at the Book-of-the-Month Club in the 1980s, the contemporary understanding of the relationship between bookseller and consumer represents a movement from a didactic to a service role.[14] Of course, an emphasis on service, while enjoying a resurgence in the last couple decades, is far from new in retailing; William Leach has described how service became strongly connected to the notion of consumption that was coming into being in the early twentieth century. As he explains, turn-of-the-century merchants, especially department store and hotel magnates, developed an understanding of service that entailed the provision of comfort and pleasure.[15] While this ideal may have affected the activities of department store booksellers at this time, making the customer feel pampered and well-liked was not something that regular booksellers typically tried to do until the last third of the twentieth century, when chain competition loomed over them.

The move away from an educational mission to a service orientation among booksellers also reflects a more democratic, pluralistic approach to ideas and expression within the book industry. The belief that a wide range of tastes and uses of books can and should peacefully coexist was typical among those I interviewed. Along with respecting and rejoicing in differences in tastes, many within the industry now condemn the pretensions of cultural elites, agreeing with the argument that both individual fulfillment and the world of books are enhanced by cultural democracy.[16] And so, instead of asking, "How can I stop them from reading such trash?" book professionals today are more likely to say, "Who am I to judge what gives people pleasure?"

Those working in the industry usually have well-defined tastes of their own, but do not try to impose them on others.

Wholesaler: I order a lot of different things, there are many of which I find personally repugnant. But I'm not there to pass judgment on other people's tastes by saying, "No, I don't like these things." That's not for me to do.

Chain bookstore manager: I think my job is about making books available to people, period. I'm not an arbiter of tastes. That's not the job that I've chosen. I like it when people do ask my opinion about books, and in part, this store will have my sense of taste in books in it because I've been reordering. But that's as much of an influence as I can really have. To make some available and then [I] still have to work with the parameters of what will sell. I might want to have nothing but a section on Italo Calvino, for instance, but my corporate headquarters isn't going to think too fondly of that if it's not selling. And so I've got those parameters to work with.

By virtue of company policy and personal proclivity, the book professional is primarily there to make customers happy. In this perspective, an ideology of consumer sovereignty exists as both an ideal and a description of how readers actually select their books. The consumer is perceived as sovereign in that her judgments are believed to be independent of and superior to the judgments of those selling to or, more euphemistically, serving her. Following from this, only the individual can really know what book is most suitable for her own needs; for the book professional to presume otherwise is paternalistic and an imposition of his own arbitrary values. Similar to the preferences expressed in the realm of love and religion, the choice of reading material is now viewed as a private matter, the outcome of which stems from individual idiosyncrasies rather than community judgment. In short, if tastes are best understood as private possessions, free from external control or interference, the exercise of free choice to satisfy those tastes then becomes the empowering moment of consumption.[17]

Despite its democratic impulse, this ideology of consumer sovereignty merits skepticism. It overlooks the ways in which consumer choice is first, far from independent, and second, a rather thin basis of power. By presuming that consumer choice is made by autonomous individuals free of external forces, it ignores how individuals' preferences are shaped by their social milieus so that, as Bourdieu argues, those who share similar conditions of existence develop similar cultural tastes.[18] This ideology further presumes a situation in which consumers are not touched by efforts at persuasion, and in which they exist in that theoretical market where all possible choices are laid out before them. It forgets that book readers do not occupy a marketing vacuum and ignores the actual organization of the industry that ends up making a large number of books generally unavailable and therefore almost impossible to choose. The ideology of consumer sovereignty additionally assumes that consumer desires are not only a matter of free will, but transparent to the retailer. But as should become clear below, booksellers' sincere efforts to serve their customers are necessarily based on interpreting imperfect data about an amorphous audience of regular and potential readers.

The idea that consumers can exercise power through their choices of what items to buy is not an empty platitude, as any retailer who has experienced a boycott will testify. Yet the notion of disconnected consumers controlling the literary landscape through the sum of their isolated purchases disregards the vast institutional structure that creates not only the end products from which readers choose, but also the conditions of those books' production and reception. Through the act of exchanging their dollars for specific books, consumers can express their likes and dislikes of the choices before them. But they are not invited to weigh in on other aspects of the book world, such as the ownership structure of publishers, distributors, and booksellers, or labor conditions within the industry, or the resources devoted to marketing books, or the integration of the book industry into a larger media system. To even suggest a role for readers in these processes would appear outlandish to most, defying the division of labor that leaves the power to make such determinations in the hands of professionals. Yet these organizational arrangements, largely invisible to most Americans, have a considerable impact on what books get published, publicized, purchased, and read.

At the level of book retailing, consumer choices are still being managed. However, the ways in which choice is controlled look different from processes of the past. The control of choice now occurs less through personal interactions with paternalistic elites, and more through rationalized, impersonal techniques, which preserve the appearance of upholding consumer sovereignty.

Selecting Books for the Reader to Choose

When consumer choice is seen as a categorical good, it becomes all the more important to offer consumers a large selection of books. And this expansion has certainly been the trend among chain and independent bookstores since 1990. But it bears repeating that no store can come close to carrying all books in print, and as a consequence, booksellers devote enormous care to the selection process. Book industry personnel make a distinction between the backlist — older titles that continue to sell year after year — and the frontlist, meaning the year's (or season's) new books. While it is the backlist that often distinguishes one shop from another, much of the store buyer's time is devoted to making decisions about the frontlist. Determinations about keeping an older title in stock can be made largely by assessing prior sales, though the bookseller's personal commitment to a book also matters. But new titles are untested; their appeal can be estimated, but only with careful deliberation. The frontlist also tends to generate an excitement that comes from the prospect of new discoveries. Furthermore, since it is mostly the new books that have the promotional machine behind them, they are the ones that have the potential for turning into blockbusters. A backlist may be a store's bread and butter, but the frontlist can bring in some highly desirable windfalls.

On the surface, the process for selecting new books appears straightforward. Publishers send catalogs to booksellers well in advance of a book's publication. This mailing is usually followed up with a visit or phone call from a publisher's sales representative, who provides the buyer with additional information. Other news about a title or author may be gathered through trade publications, wholesaler information, conventions and meetings, or simply via the grapevine. The bookseller might also read reviews, both before and after a book's publication. Using all the information at hand, the bookseller places an initial order before the publication date, and then obtains additional copies as needed.

While the mechanics of selection are simple in outline, in practice the process is highly complex. The buyer has a very short time in which to evaluate a large number of different factors, of which only some are related to the book's content. For every new title, booksellers consider past sales of the author's previous works, the current popularity of the book's genre, the publisher's promotional budget and plans, whether the author will be touring or making any media appearances, the sales rep's or editor's enthusiasm and recommendations, the ease of ordering and receiving from the book's supplier, the terms at which the book is being made available (discount, shipping costs, payment and returns policies), the book's list price, production quality and cover design, the book's topicality, the store buyer's understanding of local tastes and habits, the buyer's personal tastes, and finally, the various indications of a book's quality. The ways in which all these factors are combined and weighed affect both the chances that any particular book will be stocked and the chances that the titles of particular publishers will be selected.

This framework for store selection has been in place for much of the last century. But in recent decades, the process has become rationalized, with new technologies and organizational arrangements employed in an attempt to remove inefficiencies and better predict how customers will respond to available titles. Although not consistently the case, these moves toward rationalization have given a certain advantage to the chains.

The book industry is somewhat unique in that tens of thousands of new products (books) come onto the market each year. Not only does the retailer need to discover that those items exist and then make determinations about their fit with his store, but he has to determine how easily he can obtain those books from their suppliers. In this, the bookseller often depends on wholesalers. And indeed, one contribution to the rationalization process was the transformation of the wholesale sector in the latter part of the twentieth century. Beginning in the 1960s, book wholesalers began to become more central to the distribution process. This occurred as regular booksellers became interested in carrying nontraditional formats, in particular, the paperback, as well as the books of nontraditional publishers, especially the multitude of small presses that were established in these years. Wholesalers also became more attractive for booksellers as the former adopted new technologies that allowed them to process orders far more rapidly and reliably than in the past, and as improvements in transportation and delivery allowed them to quickly move books from their warehouses to the retailers' premises. A number of regional and specialized distributors emerged to serve book retailers. But two national wholesalers, Ingram Book Company and Baker & Taylor, grew to become the dominant players in book distribution.[19]

Wholesalers are now almost always faster and more efficient than publishers in moving books; that is, after all, what wholesalers are set up to do, whereas book fulfillment is only a subsidiary part of the publishing process. The wholesaler's speed and reliability rationalized book distribution by enabling booksellers to implement a "just-in-time" strategy, whereby they place conservative initial orders for a title with the publisher and then use wholesalers to restock as needed. Instead of using valuable space to store large numbers of a single title, the bookseller has the room to keep a broader range of books on hand, knowing that a title can be replenished quickly when all copies have been sold. At least theoretically, this should also lessen the number of book returns, since retailers need not overorder.

For similar reasons, wholesalers have been key to the success of Internet bookselling. Online booksellers, including those affiliated with bricks-and-mortar bookstores, typically give consumers access to a far greater selection than can be held in any physical store. Those online retailers who want to offer the most comprehensive selection may simply tap into the *Books in Print* database. But because of additional services the wholesaler offers, many others use Ingram's database. No matter the source of the information on available books, online booksellers rely on wholesalers to speedily get to consumers those items not carried in the retailer's store or warehouse, since getting an item direct from a publisher is just as slow for Internet booksellers as it is for others. In some cases, online booksellers rely exclusively on a wholesaler such as Ingram to fill all orders.

It is not just their ability to act as surrogate warehouses that make wholesalers so valuable to booksellers. Wholesalers are also essential for alleviating the need for retailers to deal with an excess of suppliers. All booksellers, whether independent or chain, online or physical, must contend with the fact that there are potentially tens of thousands of sources for books. There are hosts of established and occasional publishers, organizations irregularly spinning off books, and one-person enterprises operating out of a living room or garage. The 2001–2002 edition of *Books in Print* reports 69,210 publishers in the United States, most of them small. While this represents a rich pool of printed matter, booksellers do not want to juggle countless suppliers in order to stock their shelves. One independent bookseller explained the difficulties:

> Whenever I talk to people trying to sell me a book from a small publisher, especially if it's something that I want, I really try and encourage them to get it to a distributor. Because if they get it to a distributor, I can get it right away. Because I have an account with the distributor. But I don't want to open an account with a small publisher, because I'm taking a chance. I mean if these books don't sell, I have this credit from this publisher that I probably don't want anything else from. And also a lot of them starting out, frankly, don't even know about distributors. They have no idea how things work, they just think to call up every bookstore and try and get them to open account with you. So a lot of times I'm able to hook them up with someone, and they get in right away, and we get the book right away, and then, everybody's happy. [Small presses do call me.] In fact, a lot of this whole big stupid phone system we have is to protect me from these people [*laughs*]. Because all day, I get calls from authors and from publishers, you know, all the time. And it's not that I don't want to sell books. I mean it's just that I simply cannot buy books one at a time. And talk to you for twenty minutes about your book. I absolutely don't have enough time to do that.

From the bookseller's perspective, the fewer vendors she deals with, the less paperwork, the less time spent on unpacking arrivals and packing up returns, and the better terms that accrue from buying in bulk. As a result, most booksellers limit the number of suppliers they use. Some booksellers claim that they will special order any book in print. But many independents, as well as the major chains, will only order books that can be obtained from a given subset of all existing publishers, wholesalers, and distributors.

The growth in the prominence of the wholesale sector has had mixed effects on power dynamics within the industry. On the one hand, it has been an important factor in the small press revolution. Despite all the mergers and acquisitions that have taken place, it is not the case that there are fewer publishers than before; on the contrary, there has been a tremendous increase in small presses during the last four decades. From a total U.S. publisher population of 2,350 in 1958, the number jumped to 6,113 in 1972, to 10,803 in 1978, to about 22,500 in 1987, to approximately 49,500 in 1994, and to approximately 69,210 in 2001.[20] Many people in the book industry believe small presses to be the major source of innovation and excitement within publishing.[21] As one consultant said, "I think that's where the dynamism is in book publishing." And a sales rep agreed:

> I think the small presses today are the exciting presses, personally. Because they're publishing the first-time authors that at one time a company like Knopf would have done, or Scribner's would have done. But now with the large conglomerates that publishing has become, the first-time authors, the smaller authors, they're not getting that break by the big houses. And some of the smaller houses take chances.

Most small presses actually engage in nonfiction niche publishing, specializing in business, spirituality, how-to, and other circumscribed areas. But while these presses may be admired for filling (or creating) a need among readers, it is the presses that engage in literary fiction, poetry, and serious political and social commentary that inspire so many small press advocates. Small presses are seen as more willing to take risks, whether out of conviction or simple inexperience in predicting sales.

On the other hand, the period in which numerous, diverse distributors flourished was relatively brief. Beginning in the early 1990s, many wholesalers and distributors failed or were acquired by others.[22] Competition took its toll, as well as the instability caused by the chain superstores, which would place huge orders to fill their new expanses of shelf space and then, at a later date, return huge quantities of unsold books. A wholesaler spoke of how new ways of managing orders had transformed the industry:

> I think what has changed with distribution is that the whole market structure has changed — with the superstores and with the high competition, and the need for more efficiency. Because if you're dealing with superstores, they cannot be dealing with a whole bunch of little vendors. So they're doing a lot more consolidation. And with consolidation, they also want to be able to work or partner with companies that can also hook up with them electronically. So I think it is difficult now for somebody to break in to the wholesale business because, unlike where I started, in the back of my truck and very primitive doing things, I could get away with it because people were not computerized at that point, and they were dealing with small vendors. And so it made it possible for me to break into this with no capital. And now, it is a lot more difficult because you're going to need to have a seventy-five-thousand-, hundred-thousand-dollar computer system to even be able to compete. You can get into it, but you're going to need capital.

At this writing, there are still many regional and specialized wholesalers. Nonetheless, the effect of wholesaler consolidation has been to increase the dependence of small presses and retailers alike on relatively few distributors, most notably, Ingram.

As the wholesaler quoted above observes, the ability to process orders electronically is an important element of book distribution today. And certainly, automation has been a linchpin of the rationalization process. When B. Dalton was launched in 1966, it was the country's first bookseller to be fully computerized. Dalton continued to maintain a reputation for staying at the forefront of new technology, but none of the other major chains was far behind, and unlike owner-operated bookstores, they all had the capital to invest in sophisticated systems. For instance, in 1979, years before they were common in bookstores, Waldenbooks started to experiment with POS (point-of-sale) cash registers. These electronic cash registers could immediately update inventory records as a sale was rung up. They also allowed for rapid centralization of information — each night, the chain's central computer would "poll" the computers of individual outlets to gain data on the day's sales and current stock figures.[23]

As the cost of computer technology went down, independent stores also gradually became automated in the 1980s and '90s. Industry leaders urged booksellers to modernize in this way, so that timely and accurate information could be more systematically utilized in the management of store operations. Computers in the bookstore have mainly been used for inventory control, that is, keeping track of titles in stock and books sold. The computer can alert the bookseller when it is time to restock, thus preventing the loss of future sales. Additionally, computers can produce reports based on past sales that are used to guide decisions on when to return a title or how many copies of a new book to order. By knowing which titles, authors, and genres have sold in what numbers, at what times of year, and in many cases, to whom, booksellers can make predictions about how similar titles, authors, and genres are likely to sell.

While most industry members marvel at the difference automated inventory control makes, some point out certain dangers in becoming a slave to the computer. One independent bookseller put it this way:

> The mind has a certain capacity for forgetting things, for growing bored with things, or just getting sick of certain titles. And the buyer's mind sort of works the same way as the customer's mind. Seeing the same title out on the table or whatever, after a while you're just sick of it. So is the customer. But with the computer, each title on a computer system has exactly the same

value or relevance to the store. And in your mind, they don't. And so the computer tends to help reorder again and again and again the same books that have been selling. So you tend never to get rid of titles that are, you know, they may be selling but they're not selling quite fast enough, or you're just sick of them. And you need a new look, you know, you need a new thing. And so I think that inventory tends to become a little stagnant, and there's less experimenting.

In other words, rationalizing the selection process eliminates the unpredictability and the subjective value judgments that can make for a more interesting store. It can also lessen a bookseller's inclination to take risks on books that analyses of prior sales predict will do poorly. Computer-guided selection decisions can thus make tomorrow's bookstore look like yesterday's store — only more so.

Along with keeping in stock the titles that are most likely to achieve predictable sales, computerization has rationalized the returns process by ensuring that titles that do not sell within a given period of time will be promptly returned to the publisher. Regularly scheduled reports can be generated to inform the bookseller that a book's shelf life has now expired, and it is time to pull it down to make room for something else. This is not simply a matter of removing books that are not selling at all. Rather, depending on the store, titles that are selling slowly, or in fewer numbers than expected, may be weeded. With the demand that a book must find its audience fast if it is to find one at all, those titles that do not have promotional muscle behind them, or that appeal to an audience less attuned to new releases, or that have the potential for steady but slow sales, are prematurely deemed failures and disappear.

Because of its ability to track sales so precisely, computerization appears to have contributed to shortening the average shelf life of books among many stores. The type of store most ruthless in enforcing a short shelf life policy is the warehouse club. For instance, in 2002, the average shelf life of a book at Costco was six weeks. And about a quarter of the approximately three hundred titles carried by Sam's Club would change weekly in 2001.[24] The mall-based chains also tend to move books in and out quickly; during the 1990s, the typical shelf life at a Waldenbooks, B. Dalton, or Crown was three to six months. The chain superstores during this period averaged six to twelve months, though in some cases, titles were allowed to linger for longer. Independent stores vary greatly of course, ranging from those that aim at fast turnover to others that let favorite titles with few sales remain on the shelves for years.

A bookstore of any size can rely on computer analyses to determine stocking, thus eliminating human discretion in what is chosen for the shelves. But the efficiencies in using automation for selection increase as the organization grows. When selection decisions need to be made for hundreds of outlets, a centralized computer system will be far more cost effective than hiring multiple skilled human buyers for each store.

It is this form of centralized selection that has drawn so much criticism to the chains. Neither the practice nor the disapproval is especially new. For instance, Doubleday, one of the oldest bookstore chains, employed centralized buying for its branch stores long before the arrival of the mall chains.[25] And in 1963, both Brentano's and Doubleday were criticized for focusing on fast-moving titles, and for not maintaining enough variety among their different branches:

> Indeed one of the chains' major failings is that they vary hardly at all except for the differences made necessary by the physical size of the branches. From the point of view of the chains, this is a virtue for reasons of control, efficient operation, training of personnel, central buying and store image. But as a result, they all tend to have a cold, impersonal atmosphere.[26]

But new technology has allowed for the scale of operations to increase so that a central headquarters can oversee the buying for hundreds of outlets that serve diverse populations. Reorders for books are automatically generated when an outlet sells out of titles that the system has determined should be kept in stock. And a centralized system can perform analyses of differences between outlets in order to customize individual store selection with little input from the outlet's employees.

Borders has been especially active in applying technology and management innovations to a centralized selection process. During the 1990s, Borders developed a system that combined artificial intelligence with past sales and inventory information to forecast future sales at both the corporate and individual store level. And in 2002, Borders began to implement a category management program modeled after techniques used by the grocery industry. With this, Borders partnered with publishers (who paid fees to be part of the program) to conduct market research. The information obtained from consumer surveys was then used to define book categories (e.g., romance or cooking), and to make decisions about selection and display. The impetus was once again to rationalize book merchandising by using relevant data about past sales and customer preferences, as well as considering which books distinguished Borders from its competitors, in order to achieve predictable future sales.[27] Defending itself against critics who contended that category management would favor the books of large publishers who could afford the program, Borders claimed that the system was in actuality customer driven, a way to more precisely give customers what they want.

It should be noted that exact methods of selection vary from chain to chain, and because these are not static organizations, methods can change from one year to the next. So saying, some trends can be identified. Certainly, the vast majority of selection decisions for chain outlets are made from a central headquarters, and if anything, centralized control has increased over time. During the 1990s, superstore employees reported to me that 70 to 75 percent of a store's stock was the result of centralized decisions; the rest came from decisions made by the local store's managers. At the other extreme were mall stores with as much as 95 percent of an outlet's books the result of decision making by the home office. Local discretion for superstores has lessened as computer systems have grown more sophisticated; according to Barnes & Noble in 2002, centralized selection accounted for 80 percent of a store's stock.[28]

Centralized decisions are made by groups of buyers who, like their independent counterparts, meet with sales reps and consult all relevant information about available titles. Chain buyers often have a good deal of interaction with publishers' sales reps and editors, but they will know about their own local stores primarily through the sales reports that are sent to them on a regular basis. Speaking with some disdain, a superstore outlet manager spelled out the shortcomings of the purchasing process:

> In this company, we have buyers that purchase our books from different publishers and different distributors in the United States. Those people [the buyers] I hardly ever, as a manager, will hardly ever come in contact with. They think that they know what is good for my store or for an area.

The organizational outcomes that this manager disliked are precisely what the chain is trying to achieve. With individual store autonomy decreased, the centralized buying system allows headquarters to maintain tight control over selection operations and adds to the chain's profitability by creating economies of scale. Furthermore, it contributes to the view that selection has been turned into an objective response to consumer preferences.

A centralized ordering process is also, of course, quite efficient for publishers, who no longer need to call on all the individual outlets of a chain. But it has made the clout of the chains very tangible. Because the chains represent such a large portion of publishers' business, publishers pay careful attention to chains' intentions toward a title. At least as early as 1973, B. Dalton offered, as a "service" to publishers, "expert advice on a title's potential to sell *before* it is accepted for publication." The company's president made Dalton's intentions quite clear: "We want to help publishers be more selective in what they publish, and encourage them to check with us on titles they are not sure about." [29] The result, as Walter Powell noted a decade later, is that publishers who take advantage of this kind of opportunity may be less interested in publishing a title that chains indicate has little sales potential in their stores. [30] The practice of publishers' running titles by chain buyers in the early stages of acquisition has continued into the present. Rumors circulate of books cancelled after chain buyers inform publishers that their stores will pass on a title. From a publisher's perspective, sales that could be made outside chain avenues may not be worth the trouble, cost, and risk of printing a book.

While chains' assessments of how well a title will do in their stores may occasionally result in a book not being published, more commonly this information is used in other ways. As a publisher remarked, his house will frequently talk to "key customers, and get their feeling about what they might order" to help determine how many copies of a book to print. This is certainly a logical thing to do when setting a print run. But since the number of copies printed also determines a publisher's stake in and commitment to a title, and with that, how much sales and marketing effort is put into a book, those key accounts are having a big say in a book's future. Such influence is troubling to many book professionals, as one wholesaler's comments suggest:

> I think you have five buyers in this country, maybe ten, to determine how many of a book is going to be printed and maybe even whether it's going to get printed. I think that's too much power for individuals whom I have watched through the years and may know no different than you and me. I mean they might know more about books in certain ways and things like that, but they're normal human beings.

For others in the industry, this power is a reasonable tradeoff for the wide exposure that the chains bring to so many books. In this view, one need only look to the massive size of the superstores and the huge number of titles they carry. In 2002, Borders stores carried between 62,000 and 209,000 titles each, with an average of 110,000. That same year, the selection at Barnes & Noble stores ranged from 60,000 to 200,000 titles. [31] The current generation of superstores easily dwarfs most independents as well as the mall-based chain outlets. Furthermore, it would be incorrect to assume that the various outlets in a chain are identical to one another. For instance, Barnes & Noble claimed that approximately 50,000 titles were common to all of its superstores while "the balance is crafted to reflect the lifestyles and interests of each store's customers." Similarly, about 50 percent of the titles at Borders were the same from one store to another.[32] So simply in terms of sheer number of titles, the superstores have brought great choice to the reading public. However, it is far from the case that all books sell equally. According to one 2000 study, about 20 percent of frontlist revenue at Barnes & Noble comes from 100 titles, while about 20 percent of backlist revenue comes from 500 titles. The great majority of titles carried in the superstores sell fewer than two copies a year.[33]

People in the industry came to describe the superstores' selection of small press and more esoteric titles as "wallpaper," books that contributed to the desired ambiance but were not actively pushed or expected to sell well. One small publisher had no illusions:

> My own feeling is that the chain buyer for Barnes & Noble buys our books with greater intelligence than anybody that I've ever seen. And I think that the net result of the chains is that they're probably selling more books. And we're getting them out in places where we'd never get them out. . . . On one level, in terms of simple numbers, the chains coming in and the superstores coming have been [good]. In terms of the long-range things, it gets scary. And it gets scary because ultimately the chains don't give a damn about me at all. And once the independents are gone — I mean, to some extent we're interior decorating for [the chains]. They're going to have a whole lot of our books around to give them depth, to give them breadth, to compete with the independents, to make themselves complete. But that's not where they're making their money.

The superstores can also be too much of a good thing for small presses. When chains place large initial orders, a press seeing the prospect of boom times invests a good deal of capital in printing the requisite number of copies. But if the books do not sell well, and a chain decides to discontinue the title, returns can flood back to the unsuspecting press a year after the books went out the door. The press must then give the chain credit for the returns and is left with piles of unwanted, perhaps even damaged books. As a result, some presses have been forced out of business.

An ideology of consumer sovereignty would suggest that autonomous, decisive consumers freely pick and choose from the books arrayed before them. But as book professionals know quite well, just placing a volume on the shelf does not guarantee that it will sell. In most cases, it needs some additional push to land in the hands of a reader.

Recommending a Good Read

In keeping with their diffidence about acting as cultural authorities, booksellers today are careful not to impose their advice on readers. However, independents in particular do proudly note their ability to "handsell" a book, that is, to convince customers to try the bookseller's personal favorites. As one industry journalist commented, the popularity of the term "handselling" coincided with the rise of the chains.[34] Independents looking for a new competitive strategy found that they could distinguish themselves by offering personalized, enthusiastic recommendations of lesser-known books, and by getting to know their customers well enough to be able to suggest books to fit their tastes.

As one consultant I interviewed explained, one of the things that gives the book professional's work great meaning is the chance to be an advocate for those books he feels are genuinely deserving:

> One of the nice things about publishing, I think, and bookselling, is that it is possible — it does happen fairly often — that an editor or a bookseller will fall in love with a book. And when that happens, the force of that emotion and commitment will make the book work much better than it would otherwise work. It's nice to be in an industry where just passion for something has a force, it has an effect.

But as a commitment to consumer sovereignty has grown, the nature of bookseller recommendations has also changed. The difference between contemporary handselling and recommendation practices of the past is that today's booksellers are unlikely to urge customers to read a book because it will bring moral improvement and make them better people. Rather, booksellers tell customers that a book will bring enjoyment; it will make readers, at least temporarily, happier people. Moreover, as differences in tastes are seen as deserving respect, handselling is supposed to be tailored to the individual. The bookseller's ability to match the right book with the right customer is thus a highly prized skill. Yet like other aspects of the bookseller's work, this process has also become rationalized as technology has been joined to efforts to analyze and systematize readers' preferences.

Most automated inventory control systems now include functions for collecting and collating customer information to help the bookseller engage in what is called database or relationship marketing. Booksellers compile databases of customer profiles that include demographic information, sales histories, and preferences. Thanks to POS systems and the membership cards that many bookstores issue to their customers, detailed information about items sold can be recorded with every transaction. This information is then used to customize promotional communication, for instance, informing readers about specific author appearances or sending frequent customers discount coupons. Advocates of relationship marketing describe it as a way to hand power to the consumer. Booksellers are encouraged to build a "personal" relationship with their customers in which marketing is conceived as a dialogue where customers tell booksellers what their needs are. Demonstrating the way in which database marketing tries to merge sales with the appearance of intimacy, one expert advised using research questionnaires:

> Smart booksellers create these to obtain significant data about their customers to simplify future efforts at finding people who fit their customer profile and to help them form warm, caring human bonds. It's ironic how technology, considered cold and impersonal, lets you get so cozy and snuggly with your customers.[35]

In this view, booksellers become concerned facilitators of meaningful consumption rather than, as a different perspective might suggest, merchants performing the hard sell.[36]

The development of Internet book retailers, and the bricks-and-mortar bookstore's incorporation of online services, allowed for additional innovation in the automation of "personalized" recommendations. While most attention has been paid to the Internet in terms of its ability to augment the choices consumers have, its impact on bookselling is actually as great in the area of marketing as it is in selection. Online booksellers, it turns out, are persistent and persuasive recommenders of books.

There are, of course, the customer reviews that Amazon and some other online booksellers allow individuals to append to the information on a book. Enthusiasts of online bookstores often praise this feature as evidence that the Internet has democratized recommendation. However, such reviews are not as representative of the nation's readers as customers might assume. A small number of people have become such popular and prolific reviewers, contributing hundreds or thousands of reviews to Amazon, that they are courted by authors and publishers who send them free advance copies much like what professional review outlets receive. Furthermore, the option of submitting a review anonymously has opened the door to authors, and their friends and relations, lavishing praise on their own books in the guise of disinterested readers.[37]

Customer reviews do appear to have some impact on sales. More important, though, are the recommendations generated by the online booksellers themselves. All of the major Internet booksellers include prominently placed lists of recommended print and nonbook items. These recommendations tend to be for those titles with the publisher's publicity machine behind them, and they are thus equivalent to the physical bookstore's display of books anticipated to generate high sales. Other recommendations are more targeted. At Amazon, for instance, repeat customers are immediately greeted with the message "Hello [Your Name Here], we have recommendations for you." One set of recommendations is a customized list based on analyses of prior sales to the user; this list displays titles in a similar vein or by the same author as previous purchases. Other recommendations are also based on the customer's prior purchases, but using a technology called collaborative filtering, the recommended list is derived from books purchased by other customers with similar buying histories. Although the title base upon which they are drawing is broad, such recommendation features are still selective and not entirely neutral; they tend to steer customers to those books that are most frequently purchased. While customers may be flattered by the seemingly personal attention and deference to their tastes and desires, the effect of automated recommendations is to replace idiosyncratic bookseller passion with a dispassionate polling of the like-minded, and to increase sales of those books already in the public eye.

Diversity and Homogenization

One might well ask why it matters whether readers choose to read more or fewer of the same books as one another. For some, widespread familiarity with the books of the day should be understood as a social good. Indeed, one bookstore patron, a native of England, told me disapprovingly that the English are not great scholars because they do not read bestsellers; instead "they'll read just anything." In contrast, she noted, Americans are better readers because everyone reads the bestsellers. However, diversity is a taken-for-granted good among people working in the book industry. Diversity is valued in part because it represents greater choice for consumers. But diversity also has extra significance in this context because it is a book rather than some other product that is being sold. When it comes to this particular commodity, diversity assumes certain moral qualities.

Industry members believe that through diverse sampling of books, readers are encouraged to expand their minds and develop new insights. And a diversity of books is believed to contribute to an informed citizenry capable of debating ideas and social policy. Reflecting a culture that values independent thought and individual action, the uninhibited circulation of diverse ideas is supposed to help stave off tyranny and foster the possibility of new solutions to social problems. In this light, one wholesaler suggests, books are essential to democracy:

> What bookstores are dealing with is ideas. And I believe that restricting the free flow of ideas and information in our society is a negative thing. We can certainly point to any number of countries that have tried to take a tough stance on what information is available to the people that are in their society and in a lot of cases you can point to the negative ramifications of that. And certainly our First Amendment, which is one of the rights that a lot of us hold dear to our heart, is something that we feel America would be much worse off if we didn't have the ability to speak freely and to exchange ideas freely.

For those involved in the book business, furthering diversity is a form of social responsibility. And as the publisher of one small press suggested to me, viewing diversity as a commendable goal permits book professionals to engage in the individual self-expression that makes their work meaningful:

> I guess I kind of feel that if you're going to be doing something, you ought to do something that is in one way or another unique. It doesn't simply repeat what was there before. And how do people want what they don't yet know about. I mean they want more of the same. You had Ben & Jerry's fudge chunk chocolate, and you liked it, and that's what you want. But when they come out with a new flavor, then maybe you say, "Oh, I haven't heard of that, maybe I'll try it." Maybe that's not the way to financial success in publishing, but I think that's the way to satisfaction, personal satisfaction. Because we don't make a lot of money anyway, we may as well be happy. And often doing something that's new or, like I say, pushes the conversation a little bit further, is I think what keeps most people in publishing.

But during the last couple decades, a debate has taken place over whether the chains have stifled diversity. According to independent booksellers, centralization of selection should be feared because it leads to a homogenization of the reading material available to people. Independents claim that because they themselves are members of the communities they serve, they can know community needs much better than any distantly administered chain can. The homegrown bookstore, it is said, is more attuned to local tastes and also has the flexibility to respond to community variations. Argued one independent,

> They need to be a part of their community. You can't just drop a bookstore that's the best plan somewhere else in the country in the middle of somewhere and expect it to be a *good* bookstore. It may get its share of the market if it's the only game around or if it has enough special deals that it undercuts everyone's prices. It may get a certain percentage of business. But I wouldn't call it a good bookstore in the sense that it's really meeting the needs of the community.

When asked how booksellers get to know their communities, he replied, "You live here. You talk to community groups, you invite community groups in — you just ought to know the territory." In contrast to the bookseller who knows a locale by being intimately involved with it, the chain, it is alleged, is simply not able to comprehend the subtle differences that exist between communities. The idea that the chains represent a standardized, mass culture trampling on local distinctiveness is key to the independent bookseller's critique. In this view, centralized buyers must be faulted for foregoing the face-to-face interactions that provide a real understanding of local tastes.

This argument is not only about adequately serving local audiences. There is a related concern that centralized buying systems oriented toward achieving profitability will result in the overall homogenization of the nation's culture:

> I mean, everybody's extremely depressed. And the things we're depressed about, culturally, is people really feel that if the new attitude is just going to be simply bottom-line money, that that's the most important yardstick to judge everything by from now on, then diversity is going to narrow down. . . . And I don't mean to be an alarmist, because I know we're only really talking about the fringes. It's the stuff that there wasn't a huge demand for anyway. This stuff won't be supported by the chains, and if there aren't any more independent bookstores, it's not going to be supported by anyone. *But* I truly believe that culture happens on the fringes.

In this scenario sketched by an independent bookseller, the loss of the independents hurts not only the individual reader in quest of new ideas, but the general culture. The fear is that instead of making a place for deserving books that have a limited audience, book industry executives stick to the safe formulas that attract predictable sales.

Booksellers readily agree that as businesspeople, their selection decisions have to correspond to what will sell. But because the items being sold are *books*, carriers of ideas and embodiments of culture, there is more than just economics at stake. Perhaps more than any other consumer good, the differences between books are seen to have a moral, political, and aesthetic nature. Selection thus has both economic and moral implications. Despite their commitment to the consumer's right to choice, booksellers have a difficult time treating books as interchangeable commodities, and treating their work as mere merchandising.

While the notion of the book as a special kind of product has existed for over a century, the emphasis on preserving diversity has taken on much greater importance in recent decades. As the chains' antielitist image earned them tremendous success, independent booksellers gradually realized that their assumed position as cultural authorities was as much a liability as an asset. The independents then turned to a theme that was always in the background of the book industry and elevated it to new prominence. Diversity became a key feature said to distinguish the independents from chain booksellers. The independents' claim to preserve diversity of reading material is a democratic message that combines the promise to offer extensive choice to the consumer with the promise to uphold the citizen's right to freedom of thought. In this view, the autonomy and privileges of the individual consumer-citizen are best realized in the marketplace of ideas where expression is unregulated by church, government, or other institution, and where people are free to buy or ignore whichever ideas they choose.

Of course, such claims by the independents raise the question of how the selection of the chains in actuality differs from that of independents. To this, I cannot give any definitive answers. In order to resolve this question, it would be necessary to compare stock lists for such variables as subject, author, publisher, and date of publication. Such a project would require the cooperation of each of the major chains as well as a large cross-section of independent stores. This type of cooperation is extremely unlikely within an industry notorious for collecting little reliable statistical information on itself. But without making any claims to certainty, an impressionistic analysis suggests that in terms of book choices, the superstores' selection (in contrast to that of the chain mall stores) does not tend toward homogeneity. Although it is illusory to think that their selection is truly representative of all books in print, and though there are many presses whose books never make it into the superstores, these retailers do make available a great number of diverse titles. However, selection by itself is not sufficient to ensure that diverse books get read. And because of the ways in which bookstores, especially the chains, *market* books, people are more likely to purchase the same titles as one another. Recommendations are one important means booksellers have to make a book stand out from the crowd, but as I will describe in later chapters, marketing takes many other forms as well.

In the same way that the chains have joined independents in lauding the importance of diversity in the bookstore, independents have come to sound more like the chains in their praise of the sovereign consumer. Yet it is worth questioning the belief that deference to consumer choice is an unqualified good. Critics of this perspective, such as Christopher Lasch, point out that the pluralist notion of choice is based on the assumption that there are no real consequences to choices made, and that any attempt to apply moral judgments to consumer preferences is an intolerable interference with freedom.[38] Unlike an older philosophy that book selection should be carried out bearing in mind the moral consequences for the character of individuals and the refinement of culture, booksellers today are more inclined to maintain that reading choices are primarily a matter of personal style or taste, and that the bookseller's responsibility is to broaden choice. This transformation is hardly cause for indictment. There is good reason not to regret the passing of the moralistic bookseller or the elitism of the past. But the worship of consumer satisfaction, the idea that the consumer knows best and the consumer should be made happy, has consequences that go beyond the downfall of a moralistic elitism. It elevates individuals' personal predilections and judgments over other considerations; it creates the belief that politics do not belong in the realm of consumption. But as I intend to argue, consumption should be understood as deeply political, with effects that go well beyond individual satisfaction.

Of course, the book industry, like the larger society of which it is a part, is not entirely consistent in its belief systems. Just as book professionals habitually deplore the prominence of bestsellers, but at the same time continuously chase after the next blockbuster that can bring them quick riches, they valorize the adventurous reader while simultaneously encouraging people to act as a mass audience that is predictable and easily marketed to. At the same time as homage is being paid to consumer sovereignty, the consumer is being made more manageable by accustoming him to standardization.

CHAPTER 4

Designing the Bookstore for the Standardized Consumer

The history of retailing in the United States has shown that standardization is fundamental to a mass merchandising strategy. The larger the organization, the greater the benefits to be had from standardizing methods and materials, since the costs of decision making and acquiring product and supplies can be spread out over a larger number of units. Mass merchandisers will aver there is no need to duplicate the expense of designing a store interior or developing training material for employees when it can be done once and applied to all outlets. Standardization can also help rationalize demand. Just as the manufacturers who developed national brands at the turn-of-the-century taught consumers to associate a product's brand name with predictable (ostensibly high) standards,[1] mass merchandisers taught the American public to expect and welcome a predictable level of service, decor, and selection from any outlet bearing their company's name. While other types of merchants have followed suit, it is the chain store that has long been the leader in pioneering and implementing standardization, as this 1922 management guide for chain stores indicates:

> The independent retailer makes a success by personal supervision and by personal service. But the chain store is more impersonal. Its policies, like its store fronts, must be standardized. And this principle pervades the whole chain structure. Appearance, arrangement of stock, price, wages, everything is standardized. Instead of personal

service, there is standard service. Human nature cannot be standardized, but almost everything else can.[2]

When these words were written, standardized techniques were being utilized for the selling of groceries, drugs, tobacco, and various other goods. But few then thought it possible that the selling of books could be done in this way. It was not until half a century later that Waldenbooks, B. Dalton, and similar organizations definitively showed that these principles could indeed be applied to bookselling.

In this chapter, I examine how standardization has been an important aspect of the chains' efforts to rationalize bookselling, and a key element in their success. In contrast to earlier models of bookselling, this retail strategy reflects a vision of consumers as patrons of the mass market, behaving in similar ways and subject to similar desires around the country and even the globe. To explore these themes, I will be discussing the economic and cultural significance of bookstore design, as well as the creation of book displays. The construction of identical book outlets, located in suburban strip centers, shopping malls, or big-box power centers, benefited the chains by making available economies of scale, and by contributing to the chains' populist image. The chains deliberately attempted to make their outlets look as familiar and nonthreatening as any other store in the mall. In so doing, the chains managed to make bookstore browsing a regular activity for a whole new class of readers. Even the superstores, which strive for a grander feel than the mall outlets, blunt a message of exclusivity through their familiar, standardized appearance.

The chains have also achieved lower costs, higher sales, and a less elite clientele through the construction of displays that employ mass-market techniques, which had formerly been unusual (and subject to disapproval) within bookselling. Many such marketing techniques were borrowed from supermarkets and other unrelated retailers, including displays that stack up, and thus sell, large numbers of a single title, or the practice of inviting a publisher to promote a title across all outlets by paying for prime display space. These sorts of standardized promotions help to draw local communities of readers into a more unified national book market.

But while the spread of standardized stores across far-flung and diverse communities has been a hallmark of the chains' success, it has also been a focal point for their critics. Independent booksellers in particular claim that the chains' standardized look is of a piece with their allegedly homogenous selection. And, it is charged, the impersonal, bland experience of shopping at a chain is alienating for customers and demeaning for books.

The disparagement of standardization in bookselling was not much heard until the 1960s, but it is rooted in a long history of general antichain sentiment in the United States. For more than a century, chain opposition has drawn on a populist tradition of antagonism toward large organizations that appear to have too much power. More recently, opponents of chains have accused them of fostering impersonal social relations and effacing the distinctiveness of local communities. Chain critics juxtapose the large, national, corporate retailer and an image of the small, independent business, which is celebrated for championing the small scale, for an orientation to community rather than the global arena, for reflecting local character rather than homogenized mass culture, and for embodying tradition in its look and methods. In arguing for the moral superiority of the owner-operator, the small businessperson and her supporters invoke longstanding themes in American culture, including the value of individuality and nostalgia for a mythical past of communal harmony among small property-holders. The independents' request for recognition and support is thus based on appealing to certain symbols that resonate with many Americans.[3]

The changes that have affected bookselling, and the perception that these changes are not entirely for the good, are thus continuous with trends affecting retailing in general. Like their counterparts in other retail fields, opponents of the book chains are objecting to a way of life and style of business represented by the mass merchandisers. However, these changes came relatively late to bookselling, startling those who assumed that bookshops could continue to be bastions of personalism, smallness, and uniqueness. The strong dismay generated by the sense that such changes were not supposed to happen in bookselling throws into relief the logic of chaining, as well as various questions about why these developments might matter.

Bookselling Goes to the Mall

Among the important changes that came with the post–World War II suburban boom were new patterns of shopping. Before midcentury, cities were the unrivaled commercial centers of the country. Small towns were limited in their shopping opportunities, though the offerings of local stores were supplemented by goods available from national mail-order houses. On the other hand, the suburbs that grew up early in the twentieth century were generally built with the assumption that residents would do their major shopping in the city. Suburban women would take periodic shopping trips to the city, and commuting men would pick up items on their way home from work. Some suburbanites minded the inconvenience, especially those who saw the city as a place of iniquity and danger. But though there were some suburban shopping centers built in the years preceding World War II, it was not until the 1950s that developers of suburbia routinely constructed shopping districts that made trips to the city unnecessary.

These shopping areas differed significantly from urban central business districts or the main streets of smaller cities and towns. Corresponding to the automobile orientation of the new suburbs, stores were designed to be easily accessible from major thoroughfares. Thus, there developed the low-density strips that grew up along arterials on the outskirts of town, with retail buildings connected to parking lots and often sporting garish signs to catch the attention of the drivers zipping by.[4] Following the war, there was tremendous growth of shopping centers (also called strip malls) comprising several businesses that shared a parking lot. And, of course, the shopping mall, which became an emblem of suburban living, made its appearance. Shopping malls thrived because they accommodated (and encouraged) the automobile dependency of suburbanites, and because they created controlled environments that kept out both inclement weather and socially marginal people.[5] Shopping centers and malls gained the enthusiastic approval of suburbanites, and in these sites, chain outlets found fertile ground. Mall owners paid careful attention to the retail mix included on their properties, and chain outlets were, and continue to be, especially favored as tenants. The chains could pay higher rents than could independents, could afford to lose money in a single location until establishing a customer base, and were almost guaranteed not to go out of business, no matter how slow mall traffic was. Independent stores still have a much more difficult time winning a mall lease, and once in the mall, have a harder time staying in business.[6]

The population shift and recentering of shopping to the suburbs was quite apparent as it was happening, and as far back as 1950, *Publishers Weekly* was advising booksellers to consider locating in the suburbs.[7] However, booksellers only gradually acted on this advice. Department stores did establish book departments in suburban branches during the 1950s and '60s, and some adventurous bookshops were also finding homes in this new commercial frontier. For instance, Lauriat's, which later became the fifth largest bookstore chain in the country, long preceded Waldenbooks by opening its first branch store in 1950 in a suburban Boston shopping center.[8] But by and large, bookstores were slow to arrive in the suburbs. Booksellers were accustomed to looking to urban, downtown locations in order to attract both the kind of sophisticated individual who was interested in patronizing a bookstore, and the necessary amount of foot traffic to keep a business going.

In contrast, Waldenbooks and B. Dalton realized that in a changed urban and social landscape, locating where parking facilities were available could be more important than being in the heart of the city. And with large numbers of Americans opting for leisure pursuits close to or in their suburban homes, placing the bookstore nearby was a way to encourage recreational reading. Especially when trying to attract women, who were now better educated than ever before, and who were also now the caretakers of a massive new generation of potential readers, a suburban locale made a good deal of sense. So these chains defied tradition and made the suburbs their base of operations. Walden and Dalton did eventually experiment with establishing stores in urban central business districts, but the vast majority of their outlets remained in suburban areas.

The 1970s saw the mushrooming of enclosed shopping malls, and Waldenbooks and B. Dalton became staple tenants in them. As large, nationally recognized, financially secure organizations, the chains were far more likely than a local book business to win a lease at a new mall, and could negotiate a lower rent than an independent would be required to pay. There is some dispute as to whether the chains settled in areas that lacked a bookstore or targeted areas where a bookstore already existed. But in actuality, both things happened. In following the construction of new shopping malls, the chains did not avoid those communities that already supported one or more independents. On the other hand, especially in their early days, the chains set up shop in communities where the nearest bookstore was miles away. For many people, the establishment of the local Walden or Dalton represented the first time that they had convenient access to a sizeable number of books for purchase. There is no question that the chains contributed significantly to making the bookstore a common retail institution across the United States.

The placement of bookstores in these locations served another important purpose. It lessened the elite aura that had formerly encircled the bookshop by bringing the bookstore down to the level of the supermarket across the parking lot or the teen jeans outlet next door. This association with the other consumer-friendly businesses of the shopping center, strengthened by an architectural design that allowed the bookstore to fit into its surroundings, helped to make the chain bookstore appear as just another place to shop. It was part of a deliberate strategy to attract nontraditional book buyers, who, as Crown Books' market research found, "perceived that bookstores are intimidating."[9]

Along with their suburban locations, the decor and atmosphere inside the book chains were very different from that of the traditional bookstore. The old-fashioned bookshop had gained a reputation for being either patrician and clubby or dark and musty, and often stereotyped as a place of narrow aisles and a confusing jumble of books whose logic was known only to the bookseller. The bookstore was thus assumed to be a serious place for serious or affluent individuals. The modern chain did not immediately eschew this old appeal to class and intellect, at least not entirely. For instance, as we have seen, the reasoning behind the selection of the name B. Dalton, with its "English" sound, indicated that parent Dayton had no intention of abandoning the bookstore's traditional association with high culture and the elite (England, at this time, still signaling unimpeachably high culture). This belief in the value of a classy image extended to the original design of the stores. Initially, Dalton tried to create an atmosphere that combined gentility with accessibility. Stated the architect for the original B. Dalton prototype, "In a bookstore, we strive for a design mixing leisure with excitement, casual warmth with soft elegance, high-brow culture with worn-shoe comfort, and serious study with simple fun." [10] All of the early outlets were replicas of one another, with the same four-room division, parquet floors, gold ceiling, light beige walls, and Williamsburg library desks. This vision of the bookstore intended to communicate the message that books belong to both the intellectual elite and the ordinary American looking for entertainment. However, after two years, a Dalton executive said that the store may have gone overboard in its attempt to set a tone of elegance and would be rethinking the concept. Indeed, a few years later, new stores were decidedly more casual. [11]

Each of the major chains soon renounced elegance and abandoned any suggestion of highbrow culture to settle upon a formula that emphasized a distinctly modern, casual look. They did this by using bright colors, contemporary materials for shelving and counters, bold signage, and above all, good lighting. Aisles were wide and shelves were low to create an open, uncluttered feel. While such design principles were common in other retail fields, they were considered innovative in bookstores in the 1960s. An architect who designed some of the Doubleday outlets compared his approach to what he saw as typical attitudes of the past regarding bookstore design:

> In the old shelf-and-table days most of a store manager's ingenuity seemed to be devoted to seeing how many obstacles he could crowd in the middle of the floor without making the aisles literally impassable. The walls took care of themselves; they were lined with (occasionally adjustable) shelves anyway, and the only option left was how high to build them. The result may have been admirable for browsers. If they found what they were looking for it was a small triumph in itself! Certain it is that books became shopworn (for it was

necessary to paw through them in order to find what one wanted) and cleanliness was difficult to maintain.[12]

In contrast, books in the chain store were organized and signage was clear, so that a customer could avoid asking for help from a bookseller who might disapprove of her taste or ignorance. As a former B. Dalton executive noted, the chains' emphasis on self-service was key to breaking down the carriage-trade image of bookstores.[13] It was an important element of the atmosphere of informality the chains were trying to foster — as well as being a way to save on labor costs.

The chains also communicated that they were informal places welcome to all by standardizing the interiors from one outlet to another. By the early 1970s, Waldenbooks maintained its own construction company to build its similar-looking outlets around the country.[14] And by the early 1980s, Walden had established a visuals department to develop shelving, signs, and furnishings to be installed in each new store. By using the same paint colors for walls and the same typefaces for signs, for instance, a Walden outlet would become "instantly recognizable."[15] Even if far from home, potential customers knew that inside a Waldenbooks was familiar terrain. Among the major chains, it was actually Crown Books that had a reputation for taking standardization to the limit. This not only fit with Crown's emphasis on keeping costs down, but such standardization could also be reassuring to some book buyers. Browsing a Crown anywhere was an easy, predictable experience; consumers need not worry that a display of cultural capital was the price of admission.

Because of a continuing association of books with education and an attendant stratification system, any bookstore is vulnerable to being perceived as an elite enterprise. But the kind of standardization practiced by the chains mitigated some of these class associations. Standardization is precisely not about distinction and exclusivity, but rather about transcending differences. Standardized chains smooth over some of the status markers in consumption by removing any mystery about the style and substance of what might be found inside. Class-based market segmentation thus appears to represent merely minor variations in lifestyle choices rather than separate worlds marked by customs and tastes the outsider can never comprehend.

And so, in part because of their standardization, the book chains were perceived as more accessible than the independents. Of course, the low status of the chain bookstore patron should not be exaggerated. Book purchasers remained well above average in both education and income, and before building a new outlet, market studies were conducted to assure that a region contained a critical mass of the desired segment of the population. The chains were hardly drawing in the poor and least educated. But they did capture a wide range of the middle class, including some of the same clientele who once preferred to patronize drugstores and variety stores for their books. These readers had not been typical *bookstore* patrons before.

Superstores: Mass-Producing Homeyness

The spare, modern look of the mall chains became so much a part of their identity that when the chain superstores appeared, they drew almost as much attention for their decor as for their size. The superstores, which aimed to attract the book aficionado as well as the occasional reader, in many ways went back to B. Dalton's original concept. While keeping the good lights, wide aisles, and clear signage that helped to make the mall stores so easy to navigate, the superstores were designed to project a little more (i.e., higher) class and, in a major departure from the mall outlets, to invite people to linger. To accomplish these goals, Barnes & Noble, for example, claimed to provide "a library-like atmosphere of wood fixtures, antique-style chairs and tables, and ample public space used for sitting and reading." [16] Taking their cue from popular independent bookshops, the superstores aimed to establish an air of homeyness to encourage customers to stay awhile. As Barnes & Noble stated, "store ambiance [is] designed to treat customers like house guests in a relaxed yet exciting environment." [17]

Like the mall outlets, a chain superstore is quite identifiable. Visits to several Barnes & Noble superstores show that the layout may be somewhat different from store to store, but the signage and color scheme are unmistakably familiar. One is struck on the one hand by the combination of classical music and dark bookcases, suggestive of high culture, and on the other by bright lights, signs announcing discounts, and assertive displays, suggestive of a supermarket. Chairs and tables are placed all about the premises and, like the store café, are frequently filled. A similar atmosphere can be found in any Borders. These chains have found tremendous success in this careful mixing of high and popular cultural symbols. As one architect observed, Barnes & Noble manages to express a hip sort of casualness along with the grandeur of a public space. [18]

Not all superstores followed the same design route. Before Crown Books went bankrupt, its Super Crowns were not radically different in style from the chain's smaller outlets, though its first superstore did win admiring reviews for such features as high ceilings and tasteful carpeting. [19] Those chains that were less intent on attracting the traditional customer of the independents were more likely to reject the "old world" or "library-like" touches. Media Play, for instance, developed a high-energy design that utilized bright colors and loud music.[20] And Bookstop/Bookstar, superstores owned by Barnes & Noble, at one time strove for "a high-tech look with metal shelves and much neon lighting."[21] Yet the most successful superstores ended up being those whose ambiance was high culture "lite." In a nod to this, Books-A-Million opened a Books & Company outlet in Birmingham, Alabama, in 2002 that, with its dark wood and soft lighting, resembled a Barnes & Noble or Borders more than the typical Books-A-Million.[22]

Consistent with these design tendencies, the demographic profile of the chain customer has changed since the coming of the superstores, with less representation from low-income households, and more representation from the highest-income households.[23] Indeed, while comprehensive national statistics are not available, one annual survey shows that among those households of heavy purchasers of books, the independents attract more lower-income readers than the chains do, though these differences are minor compared to the differences between bookstores and other types of outlets. Mass merchandisers, supermarkets, drugstores, and mail-order book clubs still cater to a greater percentage of lower-income and lower-education readers than do chain or independent bookstores (with the exception of used bookstores).[24] Of course, the chains are aware that the bourgeois allusions in their superstores might be off-putting to some customers. But Barnes & Noble Inc. and the Borders Group resolve this problem by retaining their mall outlets. Through their different subsidiaries, the chains try to segment the market and appeal to a range of book buyers, as an analysis of mall stores by Barnes & Noble makes clear:

> B. Dalton stores employ merchandising strategies that target the "middle-American" consumer book market, offering a wide range of bestsellers and general-interest titles. Doubleday and Scribner's bookstores utilize a more upscale format aimed at the "carriage trade" in higher-end shopping malls and place a greater emphasis on hardcover and gift books.[25]

For their part, independents learned from the successes of the chains, and over the past few decades, they have made conscious efforts to modify the elitist atmosphere of their shops. Booksellers have done this by paying more attention to creating a decor that projects a friendlier image for their stores. In articles, seminars, manuals, and testimonials on bookstore design, the themes of warmth, lack of intimidation, and user-friendliness are constantly stressed. The 1997 BookExpo America (the primary industry trade show in the United States) even featured two sessions on using feng shui to help stores achieve greater balance and harmony. After continuous urging by book trade leaders, independents came to accept that brighter, cleaner, and less cluttered stores will provide a more welcoming environment for the contemporary consumer. Booksellers generally now agree that the bookstore itself — as well as its staff — must have a winning personality.

Positioning a Book for Success

Standardization is clearly a cost-effective strategy for the building and maintenance of a vast fleet of bookstores. The same principles come into play with advertising and marketing. The pre-superstore chains invested heavily in advertising, both on a national and a regional basis, with ads tending to highlight those books aimed at a mass audience. Crown's advertisements in particular became familiar to consumers, with the ever-present photo of Robert Haft himself — that is, before the Haft family fell apart — and the slogan that defiantly proclaimed Crown's discount philosophy: "If you paid full price, you didn't buy it at Crown." By training their patrons to expect a similar appearance and experience when they entered a chain outlet, the chains were also teaching bookstore users to consider themselves part of a national market and therefore the "natural" targets of geographically broad advertising campaigns. The assumption that book buyers will respond to marketing in the same way no matter where they are located obviously creates huge efficiencies in the creation and deployment of marketing materials. The retailer can reach more people with less effort and expense than if visuals, slogans, humor, and the like need to be customized for every locale.

The book chains did not stop there in adopting the techniques of mass merchandisers. Marketing inside the store was similarly guided by efforts to vigorously promote a relatively small portion of available books (leading to high sales of those titles), and to standardize promotion across all outlets. One of the most important means for in-store marketing was the creation of displays. As William Leach has shown, new approaches to retail store display at the turn of the twentieth century were notable for dramatizing commodities and the places that sold them, and for fueling consumer desire for goods.[26] Display still serves those functions in retailing. In the bookstore, the ways in which books are displayed both help to set the tone for the shop and influence the sale of particular titles. At the most basic level, the naming and placement of the different sections in a store is a key element in channeling customers' attention. Shoppers' browsing behavior is partly a consequence of their gravitating to those categories in which they have some prior interest. Similarly, decisions about where to shelve individual titles influence which readers will pick up a book. While one title could conceivably be classified as either "self-help" or "religion," the corresponding sections will be browsed by different groups of people (with some overlap, of course), and thus the simple act of classification may predetermine a book's audience.

Aside from classification considerations, the physical arrangement of books has a large impact on browsers' likelihood of making a purchase. Books displayed face out, rather than spine out, are more likely to be noticed, as are displays with multiple copies of the same title. The mall-based chains were diligent about putting these rules of merchandising into effect — and consequently attracted much criticism for their willingness to stack volumes up in huge piles as if they were so many cans of soup. In defending their style of marketing, the chains claimed that the well-being of the book industry depended on casting aside sentimental inhibitions about treating books like any other commodity. As Barnes & Noble and B. Dalton head Len Riggio stated, "I disagree with the elitists who say we can't sell books like we sell toothpaste. I think what we should be looking to do is sell more books than toothpaste." [27] From this perspective, adopting modern merchandising techniques is the means to sell more books, hence increasing profits for the companies involved, and furthering the book-reading habit among the public. In this scenario, everyone wins.

Yet the toothpaste analogy remains a highly discomfiting one for a large portion of the book world. To sell books like toothpaste appears to reduce what books represent — the life of the mind — to something as generic and purely utilitarian as toothpaste. Of course, largely thanks to marketing, even toothpaste is not a purely utilitarian item. But the sex appeal or other symbolic traits associated with using one or another brand of toothpaste are usually recognized as byproducts of more mundane purposes. For those who see books as different from other commodities, reading effects a transformation of the mind that is thoroughly intangible, unpredictable, and ethereal — and there lies its great value. The independent bookseller who commented, "We don't stack them twenty-five or fifty like some chain might do. To me, it somehow diminishes the book rather than makes it look better," appears to believe that the "pile 'em high and watch 'em fly" style (as another independent put it) is an attack on the dignity of the book, and by extension, an attack on the dignity of the humanity represented within the book's pages. In contrast, the bookstore that displays books more like gallery objects than prosaic commodities compels the browser into an attitude of thoughtful contemplation. The distaste for mass marketing exhibited here thus reiterates the independent bookseller's stand against a mass society dominated by standardized mass culture. By recognizing each book's singularity, the book professional tries, as indicated by the bookseller quoted above, to uphold a world that is distinctive, not homogenous.

Less controversial, at least in principle, is the use of special themed displays. The *New York Times* bestseller wall is one example of this; also common are tables or racks in prime locations containing new titles, recommended books, books tied to some event or subject, or bargain books. Books displayed so prominently are far more likely to be sold than if they merely sat on a shelf. However, since these kinds of displays also take up valuable space, they tend to be reserved for a select number of titles.[28]

The location of displays, along with a store's floor scheme, also makes a difference for book sales. As a rule, sections at the front of a store receive much more traffic than those at the back. Some booksellers try to lure their customers through the length of a store by putting the destination sections, such as bestsellers, toward the rear. More commonly though, booksellers place the sections likely to produce high sales at the front. Waldenbooks' vice president of marketing explained how Walden combined several of these display principles during the early 1980s:

> One of our first moves was to make our 800 stores visually exciting. We dedicated the first 20 to 25 feet of our stores to the display of bestsellers, magazines, computer software, audiovisual cassettes, and classic titles. This strategic positioning, coupled with different storefront themes which change every two weeks (for example, signage and featured titles for Mother's Day, Summer Sports, and Baby and Child Care) gave our stores a fresh look on a regular basis. About two dozen books which relate to the ongoing themes are discounted during these promotions.[29]

As well as the front of the store, the best locations for generating sales are at the intersections of main aisles.[30] An especially prime spot is the endcap, a display area that faces the aisle, placed at the end of a wall of shelves. "You usually get three to four times the normal rate of sale when they're featured on the endcap," noted one bookseller. Also conducive to generating sales are areas near the cash register, called point-of-purchase displays. While nonbook items (cards, bookmarks, etc.) do very well here, books that lend themselves to impulse buys are also favored for this spot.

From the customer's perspective, these various types of displays are visually appealing; they break up the imposing monotony of walls of books, stir interest, and enhance the shopping experience. Yet special displays also, if unobtrusively, communicate the message that some books are more worthy than others. One may then wonder whether the range of titles selected for such displays reflects the bookseller's professed commitment to promoting diversity. Although some independents pride themselves on their unique choices for displays, the general pattern is to showcase new books and best-sellers. This may seem only logical; after all, readers appear to desire what is new and popular, and the bookseller can maximize sales by capitalizing on whatever buzz the publisher has created. Yet this also reinforces the divide between the relatively few books currently in fashion and the vast majority of titles. The result of current practices is that few backlist books or new titles with little publicity behind them get prominently displayed — and therefore, their lower sales are assured.

Another consideration goes into which books are displayed in the prime spots. In the chain stores, and to a much smaller extent in independent stores, these locations are actually purchased by publishers, as one chain bookseller explained:

> Mostly, our promotions devolve around some kind of an endcap and/or front-of-store kind of promotion. . . . Endcaps, we sell those to the publishers out of co-op — co-op advertising dollars. And same with front-of-store displays. . . . And all of that is co-op with the publisher. And we also have the best-seller wall. We have usually the top fifty on either the left- or the right-hand side of the store when you first walk in. So those are also promotion vehicles. And at Christmastime, we also use that as a vehicle to generate co-op dollars from the publishers. Top tier, second tier, bottom, and they're all featured on the walls for a price.

Co-op, or cooperative advertising dollars, refers to the funds publishers make available to retailers to share in advertising and promoting specific books. Co-op can contribute substantially to a bookstore's budget for advertising and promotion, and as marketing has taken on an increased profile in the book business, the quest for co-op dollars has become a greater concern. Each publisher has a different formula for distributing co-op, but the amount is usually either a percentage of all sales for a given period (used to promote any book on the publisher's list), or a percentage of sales of a specific book (used to promote just that title). Co-op is channeled into a great variety of promotional activities, planned and executed by booksellers with the publisher's agreement. They range from newspaper advertisements to store newsletters, from giveaway t-shirts and bookmarks to special in-store events. And, of course, co-op is used for window and prominent in-store displays, or as it is sometimes cynically called, the sale of real estate.

These sorts of payments preceded the superstores. For example, in the mid-1980s, Waldenbooks developed a promotional vehicle called Walden-books Recommends. The program featured a single title, chosen each week, and given a prominent place in racks in front of each store's cash register. While Walden selected the title, the promotion was conditional on the book's publisher paying as much as $3,000.[31]

However, in the 1990s, the level of such activity, as well as the stakes involved, were ratcheted up considerably. In 1990 (the year the superstore was born), Barnes & Noble inaugurated its Discover Great New Writers program, which devoted special displays and a review in a special brochure to the book of a new author — whose publisher paid a fee. By 1996, the cost to publishers for participation in this program was $1,500. Other options offered by the chain were pricier. In 1996, Barnes & Noble charged publishers $3,000 a month for a title to be displayed in an endcap, or $10,000 a month to occupy the entire endcap. A dump, a cardboard display rack, placed at the front of a store also cost $10,000 a month. Rival Borders charged publishers between $7,760 and $7,900 a month for a children's endcap, and its Original Voices program (similar to Barnes & Noble's Discover Great New Writers) cost $1,500 to $2,500 a month for a title.[32] Books-A-Million was perhaps the most entrepreneurial about pursuing such payments. Like the other chains, Books-A-Million makes available endcaps and its "New and Notable" sections. But in the mid-1990s, Books-A-Million additionally offered periodic "management seminars" for its employees for which publishers paid thousands of dollars to attend in order to promote their books at booths, meals, and meetings (all separately priced). And perhaps most creatively, the chain provided publishers the opportunity to purchase promotional spots on its trucks, shopping bags, café coffee cups, and welcome mats.[33]

In general, only the major publishers regularly participate in these programs. The prices are high enough to effectively exclude the struggling small press. As one such publisher pointed out, "It's not outrageously expensive considering what you get. But it's certainly more than what a small publisher can do. . . . That [amount] might be the whole promotion I do for a single title." Certainly, even the publishers who can afford it are not always happy about participating in the chains' promotions:

> Theoretically, there's going to be a special table, or [something]. But [when] you've actually surveyed, often they don't do anything. Or the individual stores aren't, you know, they get this list from Chairman Ed that says Mother's Day promotion, the following titles are being hot. And whether the person actually gets it together to put them all together on May 1st when they're

supposed to, you know, if it's any percent amount of time. . . . And we've done surveys where we've gone into stores and actually looked. So — but it's a bribe, it's a bribe, it's just out and out. If you're buying to have the display space, you're paying for them to take more copies. And so anyway, we've done it because, of course, we want to stay in business too.

The major publishers appear unwilling to risk the consequences of refusing to go along with these promotions. Not only do publishers covet the prime displays, but they fear that a chain may suddenly lose interest in carrying many of their books if they decline a promotional opportunity. And because the chains now command so much of the market, this could be devastating to those publishers whose high costs demand high sales.

While a chain may not gain much from any single promotion, book after book, month after month, these payments add up. And with so much money available to them, the chains' own promotional expenses are greatly reduced. Barnes & Noble at one time stated that it generally limits its mall store promotional programs to the amount it receives in co-op.[34] This means that it did not have to divert funds to promotion at a time when resources were being poured into building up the superstores. Moreover, the chains can even make a profit from co-op. Selling store display space is one way this happens. Another practice is to include the books of several different publishers in one advertisement. By charging each publisher a set fee, the chain can recoup far more than the actual cost of the ad.[35]

The soliciting of publisher payments extends to the large online booksellers as well. In 1998, Amazon began to use co-op money as a way to charge publishers for the prominent display of titles on its Web site. Prices varied from approximately $5,000 to $10,000 for a spot on Amazon's home page, or under an Amazon "New and Notable" or "Destined for Greatness" or "What We're Reading" heading, or to be part of its e-mail alerts to customers, or for an author profile. After *New York Times* reporter Doreen Carvajal broke this story, customers who had believed that these were purely editorial decisions (and who had little understanding of the economics of large-scale bookselling) voiced their feelings of betrayal. Amazon responded by including co-op disclosure information on its site.[36] In its explanation of "sponsored" or "supported placements," Amazon insisted, "We accept co-op advertising to keep our costs low and discounts to customers high. However, we don't sell our reviews — and we don't say a book is good just because it's a publisher-supported title."[37] Amazon has also run programs (e.g., Sponsored Links; Buy X, Get Y) that allow publishers or authors to benefit from the popularity of other works by paying for their book to be promoted alongside another title.[38]

In contrast, independent booksellers cannot reap the same promotional awards from publishers. The problem for independents is that the requirements for obtaining co-op money can be complex and burdensome; the paperwork is cumbersome, and the publisher has to approve how the money will be spent. If a retailer orders books through a wholesaler, it is even more difficult to get co-op credit from the publisher. The chains (and Amazon), who have regular and continuous contact with publisher representatives, clearly have an advantage in this regard. But more significantly, since a chain buys far more books than an independent does, the amount of co-op available to the chain far exceeds what an independent can draw on. The chains can then use this vast pool of money for promotions that would be out of an independent's reach. For instance, B. Dalton and Waldenbooks ran television advertising campaigns in the mid-1980s, heavily subsidized by publishers, that cost millions of dollars.[39] Such a campaign would be inconceivable for an independent.

As I will discuss in more detail in chapter 7, the contention that co-op practices favor the chains was one aspect of an antitrust suit brought by the American Booksellers Association in 1994 and 1996 against six publishers. In the final settlements, each publisher agreed that its promotional allowances should be proportionately equal for all retailers, and that it needed to allow for alternatives when retailers did not earn enough co-op to pay for highly expensive promotions, such as national advertising. However, payments for displays are still considered legal (as long as all retailers have a crack at them), and in certain circumstances, retailers can still legally collect from publishers more than the actual cost of a promotion.[40] While independent booksellers may now find it somewhat easier to collect their share of co-op, the chains' formidable purchasing power ensures not only that they can convince publishers to make lots of co-op available, but that the chains will get the bulk of it.

Independents remain angry about the unequal treatment of booksellers by publishers they say co-op practices reveal. Consequently, they have organized to try to secure more of these payments for themselves. In one such effort, the American Booksellers Association developed an initiative to help booksellers who participated in its e-commerce program, Booksense.com, to collect co-op funds in return for posting on their Web sites prepared content related to promoted titles, and featuring those titles in in-store displays.[41]

On the other hand, some independents and their supporters see co-op practices as yet more evidence that the chains place profit considerations above a true devotion to books. In the mid-1990s, the director of the American Booksellers Association warned,

The idea of being paid money to simply display certain books in one's store in a certain way or in a certain place is anathema to many booksellers. Selling bookstore space may be perceived to be dangerously close to "selling out." Some idealism may be lost from independent bookselling; indeed, booksellers may begin to appear to prostitute their independence of thought and judgment for money. They might be accused by customers of misrepresenting the books they are touting or, worse, promoting an inferior book over a superior one merely for being paid a fee.[42]

From the perspective of many independents, accepting payments for displays is equivalent to stating that the intrinsic merit and unique qualities of each individual book are irrelevant. Payments imply that one book is as good as another. And they deny the bookseller's (as well as the reader's) right to make personal judgments about a title. One independent bookseller articulated how indifference to a book's unique qualities is related to the effacement of a store's distinctiveness:

> Now, you know, people who are really into marketing, I mean, that's their goal. You know, if you go into one drugstore and it's part of a chain, you ought to be able to find the toothpaste in the same place in the other drugstore. It helps them enormously. And I think that chain bookstores operate on that same principle. But it's in some way demeaning in terms of respect for the intelligence of their clientele. They're trying to create an artificial world that is in no way distinctive. And whatever the commercial prospects are for a particular book, that's what's being promoted. So that the books you see in the window of a chain store, publishers tend to pay to put them in the window. The book you see in the front counter, the publishers paid money to have it out in the front counter. There is no real selection being made in terms of the particular buyer for that store, in terms of the community, etc., etc., etc. It's just a question of money. And, we're an anachronism along those lines because we're not interested in whatever the publishers are grooming for the bestseller list. You know, unless it's what's called a crossover book. It's something that has merit as well. And fortunately there are some. But most of the books promoted, it's just somebody's — I don't know, it's somehow an elaborate scam.

In this view, mass marketing and standardization represent a form of centralized control put in place purely for the sake of profit. Booksellers who submit to this regimen are then seen as selling out their own autonomy and the individual characteristics of their communities in return for financial gain. Of course, bookstores are hardly alone in accepting payments for promotional

space. These booksellers are simply imitating a practice common to other retailing sectors, from supermarkets to recorded music stores. But for critics,
this is precisely part of the problem. This kind of practice takes bookselling
further down the path of mass merchandising and erodes the notion that the
selling of books is different from other kinds of retailing.

The Critique of Standardization

Concerns about standardization in bookselling encompass several different
issues, often discussed in relation to one another. Critics of standardization
focus on how the work of the industry gets carried out, the products that are
sold, and the look and experience of retail outlets. There are also a variety
of social ills that have been connected to standardization, ranging from the
deadening of people's individuality to the disproportionate accumulation
of power. Although such concerns take on a special cast in the book world,
they draw on a long history of opposition to standardization in American
economic and cultural life.

One can look to early theorists of industrial capitalism for explanations of
how standardization is a key aspect of rationalization. Thorstein Veblen, for
instance, described how the industrial process requires standardization of
materials, methods, and measures, and in turn produces standardized products. All this then encourages the growth of ever-larger organizations engaging in industrial activity.[43] Even more, Veblen argued, standardization results
in a "disciplinary effect" upon the very habits of thought of those who work
in industry; it creates a tendency toward regularity and precision, and an orientation to knowledge based on impersonal cause and effect rather than on
custom or authority.[44] Standardization in modern society has thus been associated with the large-scale, with impersonality, and with the uniform rhythms
and products of the machine.

But American society has long exhibited contradictory stances toward
large-scale, impersonal enterprises. While the regulatory environment has
facilitated the growth of large organizations, Americans have habitually expressed anxiety about big business, big government, and other big institutions. Hostility toward big business was especially strong at the turn of the
twentieth century and in the 1930s; during these years, concerns about manufacturing, transportation, and financial trusts or monopolies were also extended to the department and chain stores that were becoming a fixture of
economic life. Consumers were clearly choosing to shop in these stores, but
at the same time, public discourse was filled with condemnation of big

retailers. The chain stores in particular were viewed as exhibiting monopolistic tendencies. In answer to the question of what is wrong with the chain store, one critic in 1931 framed his answer in terms of equity and freedom:

> Because it produces great accumulations of wealth under the management and control of impersonal corporations whose sole aim is MONEY for the power of money. . . . Because the economic power represented by this money is a monopolistic power and, after the nature of monopoly will become tyrannical.[45]

Like the railroad trusts or Standard Oil, it was charged, a retail monopoly would combine wealth with power and therefore create injustices in commercial life.

Further, the chain store was believed to threaten individual autonomy and the independence of local communities. Numerous commentators drew attention to the machinelike efficiency of the large chain retailer, noting that it fit with the machinery of the industrial age and, if not checked, would turn American citizens into mere automatons as well. For such critics, the standardization at the heart of chain store economics would act to standardize the human beings who worked and shopped there:

> To find mass outlet through chain distribution a product must be standardized. As a result, almost everything associated with living is becoming highly standardized — our homes, our dress, our food, our amusements, our reading, our beliefs, even our thoughts — and, as a result, our actions. Are we really behaving like individual human beings? Or are we placing the chain around our own necks?[46]

Contained in the notion of a standardized population and the human machine was the fear that free will and basic humanity were being destroyed by the impersonal sameness of consumer goods and practices. And as Daniel Boorstin has put it, the anti–chain store movement also protested the loss of local communities, with their personalized relations, to larger, national "consumption communities," where people were connected through their use of similar consumer goods.[47]

Within book retailing, such concerns over standardization were rarely heard, since chain bookstores still played a minor role at this time. But as Janice Radway has documented, an important exception was the Book-of-the-Month Club in the 1920s, which inspired similar arguments to those put forth in regards to chain stores. By creating a "selling machine," the

Book-of-the-Month Club was seen as driving Americans to read the same works, perpetuating literary standardization, and sapping the population's individuality.[48]

Still, the view that standardization was necessarily negative was not universally held in these decades. For some, standardization was to be applauded for bringing a more rational outlook to the production and selling of goods. Chain store defenders recognized that standardization was feared by the public; they took pains to qualify the kind of standardization that occurred in these stores. They insisted that standardized methods or goods are not equivalent to standardized people.[49]

Significantly, the critique made against chain store standardization in the first half of the twentieth century was not an aesthetic argument. That is, while concern was voiced that standardized products and standardized methods could lead to standardized individuals, there was little dismay over a standardized look spreading across the shops of the United States. On the contrary, supporters of chain stores drew attention to their modern, clean appearance as a community asset. For instance, a 1940 book on chains argued that competitors were imitating the chain store style to the benefit of all: "Today, therefore, all local stores are brighter, cleaner, better arranged, more convenient, more sanitary, with fresher and better stocks."[50] Indeed, as Daniel Bluestone has shown, at least in the case of roadside development, some reformers in the 1920s and '30s looked to chains to tame the chaotic architecture they saw as a blight on the landscape. Standardization was actually embraced as an antidote to the commercialism of local retail enterprises. Chain architecture was seen as bringing a high-minded order in contrast to the unruly, overtly commercial independent businesses that lined the roads servicing automobile travelers, and as creating a look that was less urban and more suggestive of a peaceful, rural (soon to be suburban) life.[51]

With the end of the Depression, antimonopoly fervor dissipated across the country, and hostility to chain retailers became much more muted. But although it would be many years before a movement against chain monopoly developed again, concerns about standardization did not disappear. Instead, around the middle of the century, the opposition to standardization in retailing moved from a primary concern with standardized individuals to a more elaborated concern about standardized communities. This included a critique of the ways in which chain stores were contributing to a uniformity of appearance and experience of communities throughout the country.

The new focus on the connection between chain retailers and standardized communities came about for several reasons, some only indirectly related to the chains. In the first place, the post–World War II years were marked by an extraordinary suburban construction boom. Where open land once existed, new housing subdivisions were soon to be found. And in contrast to earlier periods in American history, when there was significant regional variation, the styles of the houses now being built were similar across the country.[52] Levittown became the symbol of a new kind of community, filled with look-alike homes and, reputedly, conformist residents to go with them. While the population's conformity could be disputed, what Levittown did do was demonstrate the viability of mass-produced housing. And while many Americans welcomed the affordability of these houses, the uniformity of the mass-produced suburbs promoted a sensitivity to standardization in the built environment, as is clear in the comments of one architect and planning consultant in 1961:

> Due to the large scale of our enterprises — whether we consider the manufacturing industry, business operations, or housing developments — monotony is the bane of our contemporary existence. In the factory, it means a repetition of the same small task throughout the working day. In the city it means miles of identical streets. But we are, in general, complex creatures, ill-suited to the strait jacket of endless repetition — either in our activities or in our visual environment.[53]

Suburbanites may have taken pride in their individual homes, but one finds much less evidence of enthusiasm for the uniformity that characterized the housing developments.

At the same time that the suburbs were sprouting tract housing, the cities were also being transformed. Government-sponsored urban renewal programs tore down older housing and commercial areas, sometimes replacing them with multistory housing projects, in other cases, erecting office towers or freeways. By the mid-1960s, there was considerable opposition to these programs, which had destroyed neighborhoods, displaced residents, and built massive structures that were considered ugly and alienating. Jane Jacobs, probably the best-known critic of urban renewal, excoriated city planners for what they had created:

> Low-income projects that become worse centers of delinquency, vandalism and general social hopelessness than the slums they were supposed to replace. Middle-income housing projects which are truly marvels of dullness and regimentation . . . Cultural centers that are unable to support a good bookstore . . . Commercial centers that are lackluster imitations of standardized suburban chain-store shopping.[54]

Urban renewal thus raised awareness about problems associated with destroying older urban forms and building large-scale uniform structures in their place. Like the suburban housing developments, it helped to crystallize an association between standardized forms and deadening experience, and thus to catalyze sentiment against the disappearance of unique commercial businesses.

For commercial enterprises were also increasingly standardized in these years, both in terms of their appearance, through the construction of shopping centers and malls, and in terms of their ownership, through the spread of chaining. One important development in the postwar years was the growth of a very visible type of chain, the franchised restaurant. Such restaurants first populated the strip centers that grew up on the outskirts of towns, and then in the 1960s, made inroads in urban areas. Part of what made them so successful was their strict standardization — of method, product, and appearance.[55] The franchises, with their distinctive signs meant to capture the attention of passing motorists, were clearly bringing a common commercial element to communities across the country.

By the 1970s, criticism of the uniformity of shopping centers was often combined with opposition to the chains that filled them. Americans' regard for the small businessperson was being revived, but now with an emphasis on the retailer's role in preserving a certain quality of community experience. These associations between small businesses, an architectural aesthetic, and a valued way of life were amplified by historic preservationists. The historic preservation movement grew up in the United States in the early twentieth century as an effort to preserve sites of historical importance, as well as buildings considered to have particular architectural significance.[56] But until the 1970s, this movement, led by the National Trust for Historic Preservation, did not concern itself with commercial structures. In 1977, the newfound attention to retailing was marked by the formation of the National Trust's Main Street Project, which aimed to preserve and revitalize the main streets that were deteriorating in the face of shopping mall competition.[57] The National Trust brought its political, financial, and communicative resources to promoting the preservation of older commercial architecture; as time went on, this campaign became more explicitly antichain. Around the same time, in 1976, a smaller organization, the Society for Commercial Archeology, was founded to document and preserve "significant structures and symbols of the commercial built environment."[58] These efforts were very much about preserving history, or at least a particular segment of the nation's heritage. But they also included a denunciation of standardization in social life. As a 1973 National Trust report said, "Historic preservation is a qualitative factor for instilling a feeling of place and time in a rootless, mobile and standardized society."[59] Since the 1990s, the National Trust's campaign against a standardized commercial landscape has intensified, in large part because of the proliferation of chain superstores and the spread of big-box architecture.

The reaction against standardization in commercial enterprises therefore came about during a period of significant change in the American landscape. But this does not entirely answer the question of why so many people object to standardization. Some scholars might charge that such opposition simply reflects a class bias. For analysts such as Herbert Gans, critics of cultural standardization not only miss the true variety that exists in cultural life, but also show intolerance for the cultural tastes of a less elite public, unfairly denigrating those people who enjoy mass-marketed culture as misguided or manipulated.[60] However, the politics of commercial aesthetics cannot be so easily reduced to class conflict. Indeed, it is not always the case that independent stores are associated with a bourgeois aesthetic while standardized chains are favored by a working or lower-middle class. A number of gentrification battles provide evidence of this, such as the campaign by local officials in Myrtle Beach, South Carolina, to rein in the idiosyncratic, "tacky" visuals put up by local merchants catering to a working-class clientele in favor of a more sedate, standardized, and upscale look. Reminiscent of the roadside reformers of the 1920s, officials and tourism boosters have imposed ever-tougher regulations on the look of independent retailers while encouraging the development and patronage of shopping complexes that contain many familiar chain tenants.[61] Further complicating the issue of commercial aesthetics, those Americans who express regret about the passing of distinctive neighborhoods are often the same individuals who patronize chain stores. How then, can we reconcile the desire for the familiar chain store with the condemnation of commercial uniformity? To answer this, one needs to inquire about what other dissatisfactions in contemporary society are represented by the critique of a standardized look and experience in community life.

In part, one can refer to the cultural climate that prevailed when this critique emerged. After all, the focus on commercial standardization in the 1970s followed a period when there was considerable weight placed on the value of social diversity and individual expression. Thus, the reaction against standardization picked up on a cultural current of distaste for too much order and regulation.[62] Indeed, one influential architectural statement published in 1972, *Learning from Las Vegas,* argued that the seemingly chaotic Las Vegas Strip should be praised for being a richly communicative environment. In the authors' view, the strip's vitality came from being inclusive of uses and images in contrast to "the deadness that results from too great a preoccupa-tion with tastefulness and total design."[63]

But it is also worth considering a more general relationship between stan-dardization, identity, and alienation. Edward Relph has described the rela-tionship between community and place, the ways in which a communal identity is strongly connected to a particular landscape. Along with this, ac-cording to Relph, one's personal identity and sense of one's relation to the world are also tied to places. Places are *specific;* they have a specific appear-ance and are the locations of specific people and experiences. Placelessness, on the other hand, is characterized by synthetic landscapes created for other people (such as tourists) not working or living there, by giant-scale develop-ment, and by standardization. Relph describes the placelessness of the other-directed, commercialized suburb or "subtopia":

> [T]he effects are much the same everywhere — it becomes virtually impos-sible to tell one locality from another, for they all look alike and feel alike; there is little spatial ordering that can be experienced directly (except perhaps from a car), for subtopia has been developed not on the basis of direct expe-rience but in an *ad hoc* way from the remote and abstract perspective of maps and plans.[64]

What this suggests is that standardized communities are experienced as alien-ating because they preclude the experience of knowing one's place, that is, of maintaining one's bearings and sense of identity through identification with a particular place. And watching the standardization of one's community may lead to a kind of internal displacement similar to, though certainly far less intense than, that experienced by refugees forced to leave their homes.

Of course, this is not to deny that our local chain store can make us feel at home; it becomes meaningful by virtue of being incorporated into our daily routines. But nonetheless, it does not root us in a particular locale that is more than just a repository of our own personal histories. What is impor-tant about one-of-a-kind stores is that they contain a social narrative about a place. We cannot necessarily unlock that history simply by looking at a shop, but we know it is there.

The critique of the standardized book chain draws on these sentiments about the effects of large-scale chaining. Bigness, impersonality, and the uni-formity of mass merchandising are associated with the obliteration of unique communities and also, significantly, with unique books. Independents and their supporters are scornful of the chains' standardized stores, which make shopping in Montana the same experience as shopping in Manhattan. It's

"Barnes & McNoble," one bookseller quipped.[65] Another independent described the chains in this way:

> I mean I know that that's part of their appeal, it's like the tourist in Paris who goes to eat at McDonald's because they recognize it, and it's comfortable to them. So I know that that's a lot of the reason why people would go into Barnes & Noble. Because it's something that they're used to. But there are other people who don't like that, who don't [go] for that very reason. And I don't know, a more individualistic kind of person. A person with broader tastes. A person who hates evil mega-corporations — I don't know.

In this view, the independents offer a shopping experience that is unique, and therefore more interesting and stimulating than the interminable sameness that is said to characterize the chains. Similar to their critique of chain stores' selection, the independents consider the chains' standardized look as another step toward the homogenization of the nation's culture.

The chains are clearly sensitive to such accusations and make an effort to distance themselves from an image of dull uniformity. For example, Borders told its shareholders in 1996, "Although some may say 116 stores constitutes a 'chain,' we have, to the credit of our people, kept our stores 'un-chainlike.' Each features excellent design values and an individual flavor all its own."[66] Six years later, the company was delivering a similar message: "Each store is distinctive in appearance and architecture and is designed to complement its local surroundings, although Borders utilizes certain standardized specifications to increase the speed and lower the cost of new store openings."[67] As this suggests, the standardized bookstore experience is not a sure sell to the public.

It is important to note that there is an additional economic argument to be made against big chains. Chains are said to hurt communities by driving up commercial rental costs: they have deep pockets and are willing to sign long-term leases (and are favored by developers and commercial landlords for that reason), making it harder for remaining local businesses to stay solvent. And while sales taxes from a branch outlet may benefit an area, the profits that are generated do not stay within the community. They are either distributed to the company's shareholders or used to build up the enterprise. In the words of one independent bookseller, "It's . . . a social issue in the fact that you have local businesses versus national businesses, businesses that don't really care that much about the particular community, and they're really not putting anything into it. This money is going into the pockets of someone who lives elsewhere." Moreover, smaller firms that do not have geographically dispersed outlets tend to do more business close to home; by spending and banking their money at a local level, the local economy benefits instead of distant suppliers.[68]

The various criticisms of chain standardization thus combine distress over the loss of distinctive places with concerns about the accumulation and exercise of power — the ability to control the look, experience, and economic well-being of a community from afar, and the ability to use standardization as a technique to amass such influence. When chains dominate an area, it is clear that neighborhood control and neighborhood aesthetics do not rest in the hands of those who live and work in the community. However, as independent entrepreneurs gain better access to far-flung suppliers, vendors of specialized services, and sources of information about profitable retailing strategies, residents may find that standardization can affect independents too.

The Retreat of Geography

The chain bookstore successfully used standardization in its quest to realize large-scale retailing. But during the late 1990s, the meaning of "large-scale" took a new turn as the chains began to see the limits of national expansion. Borders, for one, tried to become borderless, setting up shop in a number of countries around the world. Starting with its first Singapore outlet in 1997, Borders soon spread to Australia, New Zealand, the United Kingdom, and Puerto Rico. A different method of store replication was initially tried in 2004 when the company entered into an agreement with a Malaysian group to open the first Borders franchise.[69] As this latter deal suggests, the impact of the chains is not necessarily limited to those stores they actually own. Indeed, going well beyond that, the chains have contributed to a globalized style of retailing by providing a model that is adopted by indigenous developers who build domestic versions of the superstore. The markers of this style include bigness, informality, and a blending of shopping with entertainment. And it is premised on providing a standardized and predictable shopping experience.

Canada perhaps provides the best example of this. Canadian book chains, some of which resembled the American mall-based chain, had long been a fixture in that country. But the bookselling scene changed dramatically during the mid-1990s. In 1995, Borders made a bid to enter the Canadian market. However, it was turned down by the government agency Investment Canada, which listened to arguments that the presence of Borders would devastate independent booksellers, and that Borders could stock stores from U.S. sources and so take away sales from Canadian publishers who distributed American books.[70] The government's decision to stop Borders was grounded in the special consideration given to the cultural industries in Canada, as well as an assumption that Canadian-controlled organizations are most likely to showcase Canadian authors or books about Canada. But the government did not try to assess whether the basic model of retailing embodied by Borders — the superstore — was appropriate or not for Canada. On the contrary, regulatory agencies have encouraged the development of superstores, both in bookselling and many other fields.[71] And indeed, two Canadian book chains modeled on the American book superstore emerged around the time of the failed Borders bid.

In the case of the first to be established, Chapters, the ties to the United States were multifaceted. To begin with, Barnes & Noble was for a time a minority investor in Chapters. Along with the financial links, some of Chapters' original top executives were former employees of Barnes & Noble. And in 1999, Chapters' college bookstore division bought a controlling interest in the Canadian division of Barnes & Noble College Stores, further cementing the relationship between the American and Canadian chains.[72]

While Chapters denied that Barnes & Noble ever interfered with company operations, the resemblance between the two chains was unmistakable. Like just about any chain book superstore, Chapters featured classical music playing in the background, comfortable chairs and tables scattered about the premises, and a vast selection of books and periodicals. But beyond those features, the dark wood, shelving, and even signage at Chapters was quite similar to that used at Barnes & Noble. Additionally, both Barnes & Noble and Chapters had arrangements with Starbucks to serve its coffee products in the bookstore cafés. Altogether, the look, the service, and the merchandising strategies of Chapters closely matched those of the American book superstores. This was not lost on the Canadian public. A 1999 poll conducted by Chapters found that 40 to 50 percent of its customers either did not know that Chapters was a Canadian company or believed that Chapters originated in the United States. This misconception was difficult for the company to combat. As one customer told a journalist, "It's from the U.S. . . . It just looks like one of those big U.S. institutions."[73] The other Canadian book chain established in the 1990s, Indigo Books, was also in the mold of the American superstore, though it did not resemble any specific American store in the same way Chapters did. The two chains grew quickly, with Chapters alone controlling about 50 percent of the bookselling market by 2000.[74] But Chapters appeared to have overreached. After it ran into financial trouble, Indigo initiated a hostile takeover, and the two companies merged in 2001.

The diffusion of the superstore style of bookselling around the world is making geography less important for defining the experience of shopping. The increasing irrelevance of geographic boundaries is even more apparent with the growth of Internet bookselling. One indication is that Amazon has itself become a global entity; by 2004, it had operations in the United Kingdom, Germany, France, Japan, and Canada, and had acquired a Chinese online retailer, Joyo.com.[75] Even more important, consumers can now easily purchase books from different online booksellers scattered all across the globe. Despite copyright laws that place restrictions on the selling of books outside of designated territories, plenty of retailers are willing to serve foreign online shoppers who are rarely even aware of such restrictions. But there is an additional sense in which geography matters little when shopping online. Electronic commerce has evolved in such a way that the experience of visiting one online bookseller tends to be very much like visiting another.

Initially, Internet bookstores, like all early e-tailers, were highly idiosyncratic. But within a fairly short period of time, Web bookstores began to resemble one another more closely. Online booksellers found it beneficial to include standardized features in order to attract users who were not technically proficient or adventuresome. But the economics of designing and running a Web site also resulted in greater standardization. A few companies emerged to offer booksellers a packaged Internet site, a real boon to small retailers who could not afford to design one from scratch. Similar to the American Bookseller Association's BookSense.com, companies such as BookSite and SeekBooks provided booksellers with a template, searchable database, and order-processing capabilities, among other services.[76] Most such systems did allow for some customized content, though some, including BookSense, also required the inclusion of prepared content.

Tellingly, it is the biggest American booksellers — Amazon, Borders (whose site is managed by Amazon), Barnes & Noble, as well as the BookSense network of independent booksellers — whose online stores look most alike. The home pages typically have three columns going down, along with a bar across the top with familiar buttons and tabs, search boxes, and shopping cart. One can usually count on finding a bestseller list, along with descriptions and jacket photos of books being promoted. Shoppers at Barnesandnoble.com and Amazon.com will see links to bargain books and information about television-sponsored book clubs. Those who want more information on a book will find the publisher's description, a *Publishers Weekly* review, and customer reviews if available. As discussed in chapter 3, the two online giants also make available customized recommendation features. Ironically, the development of sophisticated technologies — and the fierce competition not to be left behind in using those technologies — have created Internet book retailers with very little variation between them.

The case of Internet bookselling shows that within the space of a few years, consumers can learn new routines and develop new expectations. This is surely gratifying for those booksellers whose plans for expansion necessitate the cultivation of diverse customers scattered across the country or even the globe. The online book buyer is perhaps the most extreme example of the faceless, interchangeable customer (after all, the "greeting" one receives depends on one's password, not one's face). But the rationalized, large-scale bookselling that happens in physical bookstores is also premised on finding (and producing) customers who know the territory and behave in regular, predictable ways.

As consumers are increasingly drawn into a mass market, there appears to be less and less that differentiates book buyers based thousands of miles apart. But this is a vision of book consumption to which many independents strenuously object. Independent booksellers claim to continue to be bastions of personal relations, of smallness, and of uniqueness. This allows them to differentiate themselves from the chains (and from Amazon), and to position themselves as the true representatives of the populace. For booksellers, the question of whether it is the chains or the independents who are truly populist matters because both moral and competitive arguments for supporting one or the other rest on claims to be nonelite. In the campaign for public sympathy as well as for the public's dollars, booksellers found it necessary to distance themselves from an elitist past. While the chains' stylistic innovations gave them an early advantage in this contest, the independents responded in the 1970s by emphasizing a different side of their stores. Stressing their local ties and contributions to the common good, the independents began to describe the bookstore as not simply a place in which to purchase books, but as a community center that provides meaningful services and enjoyable diversions. The independents reinvented themselves and in the process transformed Americans' ideas of what a bookstore is all about.

CHAPTER 5

Serving the Entertained Consumer:
The Multifunction Bookstore

In 1995, Barnes & Noble described the concept of the superstore in the following manner:

> Barnes & Noble has led the way in inventing this friendly, stress-free entertainment center — "an amusement park for the mind" if you will. . . . The result is a new concept that feels remarkably familiar: comfortable and welcoming. We have become a place where families can spend evenings, a spot where friends meet, a point where intellectual pursuit and joyful escapism intersect.[1]

A similar image of the superstore was provided by the president of Borders Stores, who, in the months following September 11, 2001, explained to a journalist her view of the role that Borders outlets play in their communities:

> It's really important for people to kick back and relax right now, and our job is to provide a fun, welcoming atmosphere for our customers. . . . This is an information-hungry period, and people are also looking for diversion. . . . Bookstores are a great resource, and a great environment to get away from the world, so we're hoping that maybe we can provide people with a bright moment in a dark time.[2]

These statements may reflect the exaggerated assessment of a company's importance that typifies public relations, but the overall image of the superstore as a place providing amusement and sociability is one that most Americans would recognize today. Indeed, these attributes are not limited to the two major chains, but could be applied to book shopping in general, for by the end of the twentieth century, the bookstore had become a center of entertainment and a popular recreational spot for the American middle class. This image is somewhat startling when counterposed to the bookshop's prior reputation for being a stuffy place for the serious-minded. And contemporary booksellers' pride in creating an environment that attracts people out to have a good time stands in sharp contrast to the efforts of book professionals a century ago. As I have recounted, industry leaders, along with other cultural elites, previously tried to draw a firm line between meritorious culture and crass entertainment, with regular bookshops scorning the latter. The question then is, how have we gone from a situation in which bookstore shopping was considered to be so staid, to one in which it is so hip?

In this chapter, I examine the circumstances, within the book trade and within American society more generally, that produced this phenomenon. And I consider how it both reflects and reinforces a vision of the consumer who equates shopping with leisure, fun, and diversion. Reacting to the standardization and impersonality of the chains discussed in chapter 4, independent booksellers in the 1970s began to stress the extra, personalized services they could provide. During the 1980s, independents were describing their stores' unique atmosphere and personalism as helping to build community solidarity. And by the 1990s, with the superstores now on the scene, both independents and chains tried to market the bookstore as far more than a place that houses books, but as a multifunction community center offering food and drink, educational events, and a much needed public space. Though this concept was pioneered by independents, the superstores were able to implement it on a grander scale and quickly became associated in the public mind with cafés, author events, and comfortable reading and gathering spaces. Consistent with their drive toward rationalization, the chains developed a formula for the creation of such community institutions. And consistent with more general trends in retail and the mass media, they put greater emphasis on the entertainment function that the bookstore can serve.

The ways in which so many bookstores now combine retail and entertainment space can be seen in their interior design, which includes comfortable furniture and room for socializing. The talks given by authors and other themed events lend a festive air to the book-buying experience, while the attached cafés invite customers to people-watch over a latte. Indeed, by the end of the twentieth century, shopping for books had become one of the quintessential expressions of consumption as a leisure activity. In the process, the bookstore has helped to create a new equation between books and fun.

Shopping for Community

Despite other ways in which they appealed to so many Americans, the small, standardized, mall-based chain bookstores were not places that invited lingering. The fast-food analogy frequently made by critics was apt, in that B. Dalton, Waldenbooks, and Crown were designed to allow consumers to find the books they wanted quickly, with minimal interaction with staff, and then quickly get out. This convenience was one of the strengths of the chains, but it also presented independents with a way to distinguish themselves and better compete. It is perhaps no surprise that independents began to stress their unique features, depth of selection, and willingness to provide personalized services. But what was not so predictable was that independents soon framed these business strategies in the language of community.

By the early 1970s, when it was becoming clear that chain competition could put other booksellers out of business, some enterprising independents started to tout the various services they provided to customers. Gift-wrapping, charge accounts, personalized attention, and author autographing parties were among those features meant to distinguish them from the self-service chains. But by the 1980s, these extras were being described as more than mere retail services; they were often presented as evidence of the independents' commitment to their communities. By the 1990s, the appeal to community became a key device for talking about the importance of the independent bookseller and the corresponding deficiencies of the chains.

Community is, of course, a notoriously vague term, one that can have a wide assortment of definitions and connotations. As Joseph Gusfield notes, it is sometimes used in a territorial sense, to refer to a geographic locality. But it is also commonly used to describe a particular quality of human relationships.[3] Frequently, these two meanings get melded together to describe a physical place and set of ideals juxtaposed to the world in which most Americans now live. Community connotes the small social realm, such as a rural area, small town, or neighborhood, as against large, anonymous urban spaces. Community implies social bonds based on affective ties and mutual support in contrast to instrumental social relations directed primarily by the market. And community evokes a past steeped in tradition as opposed to a constantly changing present.[4]

The notion that the bookstore can be a center of community life in the United States is not an altogether new one. The early American bookseller frequently acted as the local printer and publisher, and sometimes even as-sumed the duties of postmaster. His establishment was therefore often a center of news and a local gathering spot. However, as its function became more specialized, the bookstore also grew more marginal to public life. The idea that strong community ties are important never vanished entirely from the bookseller's consciousness. But for much of the twentieth century, com-munity involvement by the bookseller tended to be cast in terms of the busi-nessperson's civic responsibility, rather than of the bookstore as an indige-nous organization that fosters communal solidarity.[5] This began to change after the ascendance of the chain stores. Now, when an independent book-seller speaks about serving her community, she is in part pointing to a fairly concrete entity — a bounded locality, whether neighborhood or town. But she is also conjuring up a vision of that locale that draws on other idealized qualities. Maintaining that no large corporation can be truly sensitive to lo-cal needs and traditions, the independent bookseller purports to stand as a bulwark against the total destruction of meaningful community life.

The independent argues that this happens in large part through person-alized relations that develop between a caring, homegrown staff and cus-tomers. Instead of settling for a situation in which two strangers carry out an instrumental transaction, the good bookseller is said to cultivate a warm acquaintanceship with the people who regularly shop at the store, getting to know them as individuals rather than as generic consumers. In the book-store, at least, money changing hands can perhaps be given greater meaning:

> I mean this is a small store. . . . So I *see* everyone who comes in the store. And because it's a neighborhood bookstore, you see the same people come in over and over again. So you talk to them. And so you ask her periodically, "Well how's your sister and how she's doing," and various things like that. I think that's really important. People come in here on a Monday night and they see my son and they'll come in the store a few days later and say, "Oh, your son's working here now." I think people, not everyone, a lot of people like know-ing who they're giving their money to. . . . [Customers say], "The nice lady over at the [bookshop], she'll order whatever you want, and she'll wrap it, and she'll send it for you, and she's nice." They like that. I like that too.

For some independents, size matters for the ability of a store to provide personalized relations. Many small booksellers equate the bigness of a super-store outlet, as well as the chains' bureaucratic organization, with impersonal-ity. As one independent said, "I mean, for me, I prefer going into a smaller bookstore where you have a sense of community as opposed to walking into somewhere and feeling like you're in a Safeway." Another small independent remarked, "I think we've probably felt some impact [from a nearby super-store]. . . . Although we really noticed some of our older customers coming back again. Because they're so relieved to come in somewhere where some-one knows them and knows what they're talking about." For these inde-pendents, their small size was a significant source of virtue.

Still, size is not the only way in which independents differentiate their abilities to create a communal environment from those of the chains. Larger independents also stress their connections to community, usually empha-sizing their embeddedness in and commitment to a locale. And indepen-dents tend to argue that the chains' drive to maximize profits will invariably interfere with the existence of any genuine sympathy between bookseller and customer. Emphasizing the emotional bond between bookseller and community that is supposed to result from the independent's local roots, the president of the American Booksellers Association reinforced this sense that the chains lack something essential:

> The need to go to the place where "everybody knows your name" will drive people to certain stores, and the bookshop of the future will have that nur-turing, almost spiritual, sense about it. People will go there not because they can buy a book but because of how they feel when they are there. And here is the salvation for independent bookselling. . . . The bookseller will, in fact, have to know the name of each customer as well as each customer's children. The bookseller will wrap their clientele in a blanket of comfort which will satisfy both their emotional and retail needs. Their stores will be interwoven into the fabric of the community as only a local retailer can be. They will support the institutions of the community because they will be a part of that community.[6]

In this perspective, retailing is a labor of love as much as it is a profit-making enterprise.

There is certainly a heavy dose of hyperbole (along with sentimentality) contained in the ABA president's statement. Nonetheless, these sentiments do reflect a cultural model of customer-retailer relations that, especially in the past, was far from exotic. As Gregory Stone argued in the 1950s, some consumers develop emotional connections to store personnel, and these attachments can be important in binding residents to their communities.[7] This kind of relationship may be less available today than it was in prior decades. But for the independent bookseller, that is exactly the point; the independent is promising to maintain a style of retailing that Americans at least profess to miss.

Along with personalized relations, independents claim that the right kind of business, nourished by its vital connections to a locality, can rise above profit considerations to provide community service as well as customer service. And so some shops open up their spaces for local organizations to use for meetings. Others donate a percentage of their proceeds to community groups, schools, or charities. Reflecting on such activities, a small press publisher commented on a local independent bookstore:

> One of the really most interesting bookstores in that way is Gaia. [They're saying,] "People who come into our store, we're all a community of one sort or another, because we're interested in the same kinds of issues. You wouldn't come into the store if you weren't interested in this goddess or nature stuff. So let's try to find ways to come together more and more, and see how we can take some of the ideas that are inside the books in here, and bring them out into the world." But using the store as the center for doing that. So they've got food drives at holiday time, and they've done forums on homelessness. I think that's fabulous. You know, I would encourage that kind of bookstore to do that more. To sort of take the natural interests of the people who are coming into the store, and then trying to help us all create community.[8]

These sorts of gestures solidify the ties between retailer and a community's residents. They give added meaning to the bookselling endeavor and, as independents themselves point out, by creating goodwill among the local population, these gestures are good for business.

Independent booksellers also claim to support community life by offering a much-needed public space. Customers are encouraged to use the bookstore as a site for socializing: a place to gather with friends or engage in interactions with strangers. This function is often facilitated by the presence of a café. During the 1970s, bookstores such as Kramerbooks & Afterwards of Washington, D.C., and the Upstart Crow of San Francisco popularized the concept of the bookstore-café. Booksellers found that a café not only could increase traffic into the store, but contributed to the kind of atmosphere independents were trying to create — one of conviviality, relaxation, and receptivity to the printed word.[9]

The ability of the bookstore to promote itself in this way is related to the decline and privatization of public space. That is, there has been a shrinking of spaces that are open to all residents of a locale, spaces where strangers expect to mingle and where individuals are allowed to loiter in public.[10] While the privately owned bookstore is not a genuinely public space, it does claim to provide at least some of the functions of a town square, public park, or public library. As long as their conduct does not violate expectations of orderliness, bookstore patrons can linger undisturbed for hours, perhaps engaging in discussion sparked by the books and periodicals surrounding them. As one industry consultant remarked, "Because what's browsing other than sanctioned hanging out?" Independents have worked to shed their exclusionary reputations of the past and present themselves as places, if not exactly for the masses, then for a broad sector of the middle class frustrated by so few opportunities for public sociability.

As the statements I have reproduced here show, community is now a common referent for independent booksellers. But the rhetoric of community service and community embeddedness not only permeates independents' talk, it is also consciously incorporated into marketing ideas and materials. Exhorted one management consultant,

> As an independent bookseller, you have the clear advantage over the corporate competition when it comes to community awareness and involvement. Across the country, more and more of our national conversation is about finding and building community. Perhaps your customers are only beginning to realize their hunger for connection matches their thirst for trendy coffee. To create a sense of community within and without your store, you needn't build a cappuccino bar. If you emphasize your community connections to your customers, garner publicity for your involvement, and invite your customers to join in your efforts, you might just be able to effect some value migration of your own.[11]

Trade associations and industry literature are full of suggestions for how booksellers can integrate the concept of community into their activities. Underscoring the centrality of the community angle, for two years running (1995 and 1996), the American Booksellers Association made "Building Community Foundations" the theme of its National Independent Bookstore Week, a promotional event meant to highlight the importance and unique qualities of independent booksellers. Utilizing the expertise of a public relations firm, the ABA made available posters, sample advertisements and press releases, and detailed case studies to help booksellers increase public awareness of their community ties.

In an odd alliance between the commercial and the cooperative, community has thus become both a promotional slogan used to woo the public and a sincerely felt aspect of what it means to be an independent bookseller. But like any marketing concept, the community handle can be appropriated by the competition. And indeed, the rhetoric of community, along with the

corresponding actions, were smoothly lifted by national, corporate booksellers in the 1990s, evidenced, for example, by Borders' 1995 annual report
to its shareholders:

> [Our employees] were responsible for opening 41 new Borders stores in 1995,
> all of which fit comfortably into and are important additions to their respec-
> tive communities. . . . [T]he management of each Borders location is com-
> mitted to making its store a community center, entertainment resource and
> social gathering place.[12]

Barnes & Noble made similar claims in its annual report:

> Throughout his tenure as America's Poet Laureate, Robert Hass met with
> business and civic leaders across the country. "Capitalism makes networks,"
> Hass reminded them; "imagination makes communities." At Barnes & No-
> ble, both forces are in effect. As entrepreneurs, we are compelled to deliver
> appropriate returns on invested capital; as booksellers, we are driven to con-
> tribute to the intellectual life of the communities we serve. . . . Like the vil-
> lage tavern, the town square, the corner café, Barnes & Noble bookstores are
> places where people gather.[13]

The contemporary idea of the bookstore as community center may have
been pioneered by independents trying to distinguish themselves from the
mall chains, but the chain superstores have taken the concept and run with it.
With their greater resources, the chains have been able to construct more
spacious facilities, produce more elaborate events, and sponsor more high-
profile charitable efforts. These actions have definitely paid off for them. By
the mid-1990s, the nation was abuzz about this seemingly new form of publicly accessible private space. Bookstore patrons now tend to assume that the
chains are the places to go when looking for a setting in which to relax over a
cappuccino or a meeting space for a reading group. But in their enthusiasm,
patrons seem little inclined to recognize the irony of community, an ideal
whose essence is public and cooperative, being reconceptualized as an alien-
able experience, produced by private organizations, and sold to individual
consumers.

From Community Center to Entertainment Center

Of course, some aspects of the community ideal have been easier for the
chains to reproduce than others. With their large size and rapid turnover of

staff, the superstores found it difficult to provide personalized relations. Furthermore, the payoff for implementing various community-oriented efforts is not uniform across the board. For instance, building community goodwill is a more indirect and harder-to-measure method for increasing sales than is developing regular attractions or special promotions that produce immediate store traffic. It is perhaps for such reasons that first Borders, and then Barnes & Noble, cut or reorganized staff who previously had been devoted to community relations. Until 2001, each Borders superstore had a community relations coordinator to arrange for store events and other aspects of community outreach. These coordinators were replaced with area marketing managers who were responsible for coordinating store events on a regional basis. Barnes & Noble started on a similar path in 2003 when it cut a quarter of its community relations managers, individuals who organized store events and acted as liaisons to community groups.[14]

An emphasis on the marketing of events rather than the superstore's civic image was indicative of the way in which the chains were increasingly stressing the possibilities for fun and diversion to be found in their outlets. During the 1990s, the chains promoted the superstore as a site that offers a unique shopping experience; an important element of this was defining the superstore as a destination for those seeking entertainment. The mall chains paved the way for today's entertaining bookstore by emphasizing a casual environment and a nonjudgmental attitude toward readers and their tastes. But the superstores went much further by outfitting their stores with the accoutrements of fun: the food and drink, the wide aisles and tables and chairs that encourage sociability, and the author performances that turn the bookstore into a stage.

Just as the independents' emphasis on community influenced the chains, the superstores' stress on providing entertainment had the effect of encouraging independents to make similar efforts. While large numbers of independent booksellers were driven out of business in the 1990s, those remaining tended to redouble their efforts to make the bookstore into more than just a place that houses books. The fierce competition between bookstores led independent and chain bookseller alike to put considerable resources into marketing the enjoyments that can be had from visiting the bookstore.

The design of the bookstore, as I described in the previous chapter, is central to creating an atmosphere that puts customers at ease and encourages them to stay awhile. Common to many bookstores are the tables and chairs that are scattered about the premises. With these, customers are invited to settle in for a good read or a chat with friends. However, booksellers monitor the use of this furniture rather carefully. While the superstores are often commended for producing a space that customers treat like a living room, there are occasional reminders that homeyness has its limits. Barnes & Noble outlets in New York City, for instance, attracted attention when they replaced some of their comfortable chairs with hard wooden seats. Evidently, people had been planting themselves for extended periods of time, but not making the transition from guest to customer.[15]

The café, on the other hand, ensures that sitting will be accompanied by at least a purchase of coffee. Cafés have been one of the most important elements in making the bookstore into an entertainment center, and they are tremendously popular among the public. Today, all the chain superstores have an adjacent café, as do many independents. Barnes & Noble opened its first bookstore café in Bryn Mawr in 1992.[16] By the following year, coffee bars became a standard feature in the company's superstores, installed, as Barnes & Noble said, "To further the image of the superstore as a meeting place."[17] In an alliance with another controversial chain, Barnes & Noble formed an agreement with Seattle-based Starbucks to serve its coffee products exclusively. While Borders previously used a variety of coffee vendors, in 2002, Starbucks moved closer to dominating the chain-bookstore coffee business when it began operating the cafés for Borders' British outlets. Two years later, Borders signed an agreement with Seattle's Best Coffee, also owned by Starbucks, to operate cafés in most of Borders' American stores.

Some stores have experimented with taking the café concept beyond the provision of caffeine and snacks. For instance, when the Book Cellar of Chicago opened in 2004, wine was carried along with the usual fare in its café.[18] And in a 2002 partnership with Cosi Café, one of Borders' Michigan outlets began serving alcoholic drinks in the evenings. Additionally, first Borders, and then Barnes & Noble, installed wireless Internet service (Wi-Fi) in their cafés, further expanding the entertainment options of those visiting their outlets.[19] Through these enhancements, the bookstore-café solidifies the association between book buying and pleasurable experiences.

Both the café and the furniture in the bookstore proper have encouraged the use of the bookstore as a social center. Observations show that socializing takes place at all hours, but is most intense in the evenings and on weekends. Families with children, couples, and groups of friends chat with one another or read side by side. The wide aisles typical of newer stores also allow for companions to wander the shelves together; here too they sometimes plant themselves for extended conversation.[20] The bookstore has not only become an appropriate destination for a Saturday night date, but at least in some communities, is known as a place where singles might meet others looking for romance beyond the pages of a book. Not withstanding the claim to serve the entire community, patrons know that much of the bookstore's clientele consists of people fairly similar in terms of education, race, and class. And while retail stores are not traditionally associated with singles scenes, the bookstore may be attractive to some because it is a regulated environment without the apparent dangers of less constrained arenas such as bars. Moreover, books hide their commodity status better than other products; in the bookstore, customers can forget that they are in an establishment whose primary purpose is to engage them in rather unromantic market transactions. Yet, this soft-sell atmosphere is cultivated precisely to put customers in the mood to make a purchase. In other words, the bookstore's self-presentation as a place that facilitates human connection — and does not charge for doing so — is a form of marketing.

The atmosphere, the cafés, the spaces for socializing — all these help to project the promise of the bookstore as a good time. But it is in the steady stream of the events that bookstores host that the complete merging of marketing and entertainment can best be seen. The musical performances, author readings, workshops, poetry slams, literary theme parties, and storytelling hours help to associate the bookstore with entertainment. And perhaps with the exception of the music, all these events are directly tied to specific books for sale. In some cases, an entrance fee or book purchase is required for admission. But more often than not, these events are free, with the bookseller confident that once inside, people will freely spend.

Events are a significant cornerstone of the superstore strategy. For instance, in 1998, there were about six thousand events booked by the national office of Barnes & Noble, and about eighteen thousand events booked locally by its five hundred superstore outlets.[21] Author appearances remain the most common form of event, with many stores attempting to keep a regular schedule of readings and signings by literary figures. Some stores like to emphasize their community ties by inviting local authors in to speak. But those are not generally the writers who draw the large crowds and media attention. Instead, it is the authors on the bestseller lists who can sell stacks of books in a single evening and leave customers thinking that the bookstore is a happening place. As a result, fierce competition has developed between stores to host the biggest names. The chains have created separate corporate divisions devoted to working with publishers to schedule author appearances; some of the larger independents also designate a full- or part-time employee to coordinate author events. Along with managing local publicity, these employees have the job of convincing publishers to include the store in an author's tour. Celebrity authors may have to be booked a year in advance, and stores are required to demonstrate a track record in producing successful events. As the competition for big-name authors has accelerated, accusations of favoritism toward the chains are bitterly made against large and small publishers. The problem is not only that independents may be left off an author's schedule, but even when included, they are given fewer opportunities to debut famous authors in their towns.

Author events are not a new phenomenon. The department store Marshall Field's of Chicago pioneered the practice of autographing parties, as they were then called, in the second decade of the twentieth century.[22] While such parties were seen as innovative and glamorous in their early days, they had lost their luster by midcentury. Before the independents revived them in the 1970s, book and author gatherings, in the words of the trade magazine *Publishers Weekly,* were "thought to be an old-fashioned means of merchandising to ladies who lunch."[23]

Bookstore events have come full circle in a number of ways. In its heyday, Marshall Field's was known for its flashy promotions. The department store brought in performing dogs to advertise dog books, "stalking Indians" to advertise Indian books, clowns to promote circus books, and once, a live elephant to help sell a children's book.[24] Such carnivalesque merchandising raised eyebrows among those who believed that books deserve a more dignified presentation.

Today, carnivalesque events earn the admiration of fellow booksellers, as they add extra fun to the book-shopping experience. For instance, many bookstores hosted costume and slumber parties the nights before the release of the later Harry Potter books. In another case, Rainy Day Books of Kansas City sponsored an Anne Rice appearance that also included a magician, tarot card readers, a costume contest, and a fake graveyard to give the appropriate ambiance. Nearly two thousand people turned out for this event.[25] And in an example reminiscent of Marshall Field's, Book Works of Albuquerque promoted dog books at a Canine Christmas event. The store invited customers to enter their pets in a best-dressed pooch parade, as well as giving them the opportunity to adopt one of the dogs being shown by ten different animal rescue groups.[26] Booksellers have demonstrated that any type of book can become the basis for an event. Fiction or nonfiction, highbrow or commercial, newly released or backlist — all can be utilized effectively. As the annual Bloomsday events honoring Joyce's *Ulysses* show, even difficult-to-read classics can be used to create a festive occasion.

Retailing as an Entertainment Industry

Bookstore events have the purpose of selling more books; this is why book-sellers refer to them as promotions. Yet they are surely experienced by customers as entertaining. They exemplify a process that has become quite prevalent during the last century, whereby commercial entrepreneurs turn an experience into something one can purchase, and turn the act of purchasing into an experience itself. The bookstore's transformation into an entertainment center should therefore not be seen as a singular phenomenon, but parallels trends in other areas of retailing.

The turn-of-the-century department store and amusement park were probably the most important institutions for popularizing and innovating techniques for the commodification of experience. The major department stores pioneered the notion that a retail establishment could be a total entertainment center. These stores typically included tea rooms and restaurants, reading rooms with newspapers and writing materials, art galleries and exhibits, live music, lectures, cooking, embroidery, and child care classes, meeting rooms for women's organizations, and sometimes even hot baths. As several historians have shown, the department store played an important role in defining shopping as a recreational pastime. Whether or not the customer made a purchase, there were sights to dazzle the senses and activities to fill the hours.[27]

Some present-day bookstores, such as the Anchorage store Cyrano's, which includes an art gallery, cinema, and nonprofit live theatre in addition to the usual café, or the Marin County store Book Passage, which offers scores of classes, workshops, and conferences, are reminiscent of the early department store model of retailing.[28] Similarly, the legacy of the amusement park can be seen in many bookselling efforts. This goes beyond the creation of carnivalesque events. John F. Kasson has argued that an important reason for turn-of-the-century Coney Island's appeal was that the audience for its amusements was not simply a group of spectators, but participated in and became part of the spectacle.[29] In its promotion of opportunities for people-watching and participatory events, the entertaining bookstore picks up on this strategy. One bookstore took to its logical extreme the principle that customers themselves are part of the show. During the 1999 holiday season, Canterbury Booksellers of Madison used its customers as live window display models. After putting out a request for volunteers, scores of people agreed to sit in the store window for a couple hours, along with whatever props they liked, while reading a book. The promotion was a big hit with customers both inside and outside the window.[30] As this demonstrates, marketing and entertainment can fit together seamlessly.

In the post–World War II era, the department store was replaced by shopping centers and malls, and the ailing amusement park was pushed aside by the theme park. Not long after the establishment of these new retail and entertainment forms, they drew closer together. Facilities for entertainment have been an increasingly important component of shopping malls since the 1960s, with malls often deliberately borrowing techniques from theme parks.[31] This finds its most extreme expression in Minnesota's Mall of America and Alberta's West Edmonton Mall, famous for their roller coasters, lagoons, and multiple restaurants and movie theatres. Many stand-alone stores have also incorporated entertainment activities, such as rock climbing at outdoor-wear stores or food tasting at warehouse clubs. Even a trip to Costco can thus be experienced as a fun outing. In this context, it seems less odd that a company like Barnes & Noble would hire as president of its bookstore operations a former Disneyland executive who had been responsible for developing the theme park–inflected mall, Downtown Disney.[32]

The notion that the bookstore could act as an entertainment center is also made more comprehensible when one considers how shopping has become an increasingly important form of leisure in the United States. A trip to the mall, a weekend of antiquing, or a Sunday at the flea market provides the hope of finding diversion and novelty. Compared to other stand-alone stores, the bookstore is well suited to deliver on these expectations since its inventory is constantly being renewed by the steady supply of titles being published; a customer never knows what she will discover from one trip to the next. The bookstore additionally offers the possibility of a more social and less segregated shopping experience than do other specialty stores. Retail shops have long provided Americans (primarily women) with opportunities for public sociability; in this, the bookstore is simply following in the footsteps of the country general store or the urban department store. But the contemporary bookstore differs from its retail predecessors, and many of its contemporaries, in the way that it has successfully sold the bookstore experience to people of different genders and ages. The bookstore provides a venue for men and women to socialize in the context of shopping, and it is seen as fun for both families and singles.

These various developments in retailing speak to the way that fun has become a key measure for evaluating a successful shopping experience. Indeed, American culture in general now puts a tremendous premium on fun.[33] One can find expressions of this in all realms of social life, from the family (the notion that parents and children should spend quality time together is certainly not about performing domestic labor) to education (hence, the assumption that students should not be subjected to dry and boring teaching styles) to politics (witness the expectation that protests should be occasions for festivity and self-expression). The flipside of a population seemingly mired in epidemics of depression and boredom is a nation obsessed with the quest for happiness and entertainment. Commercial entrepreneurs have long been at the forefront of articulating the need for fun and the means to achieve it, so it is no surprise that consumption is now often deemed a disappointment unless it is entertaining.

The competition that has taken place between independent and chain booksellers has been in part over the public's perception of which kind of store provides more important benefits to the community. Despite the independents' claim that an enterprise that is not of the community cannot be for the community — that it cannot cultivate the personal relationships that create bonds of loyalty and sympathy between residents and retailer — the chain superstores have managed to gain an enthusiastic clientele for the entertainments they provide. This suggests that Americans have come to understand the notion of a vital community life (at least as it is manifested in retailing) more in terms of communal fun than in terms of affective ties between community members.

In sum, the bookstore's foray into the provision of entertaining experiences is of a piece with much of consumer culture. However, to understand why the bookstore has so successfully adopted entertainment retail, one also needs to take account of how books, specifically, have been incorporated into a culture of entertainment. The widespread use of books as building blocks of entertaining experiences represents the culmination of a process first seen so clearly in the early amusement park. Kasson claims that Coney Island represented a cultural revolt against genteel expectations that leisure should be connected to moral improvement; instead, the amusement park promoted novelty, excitement, and a release of inhibition.[34] As I have shown, book professionals have long wrestled with a tension between a view of books as morally uplifting and one that sees them as a source of pure enjoyment. The entertaining bookstore is an indication that the cultural revolt described by Kasson has truly reached deep into the book world, with transformative results.

An important aspect of this transformation has to do with the book's status as a medium of mass communication. The development of the entertaining bookstore reflects the almost complete integration of books into an interlocking entertainment industry. On the one hand, the integration of books into the entertainment industry has been organizational. Beginning in the 1970s, book publishers were acquired by corporations with holdings in film, broadcasting, music, newspapers, and magazines. Today, almost all the major American book publishers are owned by such diversified media conglomerates as Bertelsmann, Time Warner, and Viacom.[35] Although antitrust regulations prevent the major bookstores from being owned by those same companies, formal and informal partnerships are made, such as Bertelsmann's partial ownership of Barnesandnoble.com (which it divested in 2003).

Related to the organizational ties between publishers and the entertainment industry is the trend toward convergence of different media, including books. To use a buzzword of the 1990s, media companies try to create synergy — to bring together different areas of mass communication in order to create new products and new marketing strategies. Behind the idea of synergy is the notion that content is not bound to form, but is transportable across a large variety of media. This concept is not new, but it was given heightened emphasis with the growth of the entertainment conglomerates, and with the growth of new technologies that depend on content originally developed for other media. Synergy goes in multiple directions. Thus, we find books that are the basis for film scripts, as well as the novelization of films and television shows. Synergy is perhaps most fully realized within children's publishing, where licensing deals have become a significant source of revenue. In this arrangement, books based on television, movie, sport, toy, comic strip, or advertising characters are created, such as the *Sesame Street* line, or, as in the case of *The Magic School Bus,* the book comes first. Each product helps to cross-promote tie-in items, and marketing campaigns for the different media are carefully coordinated.

With the general enthusiasm for synergy, it is no surprise that many booksellers developed high hopes for the revenue and crowd-drawing possibilities of multimedia sidelines. Although some booksellers continued to worry about diminishing the book by giving too much space to nonbook items, the tough financial climate and greater openness to innovation pushed others to introduce new products into their stores. While traditionally stationery was the most common sideline carried, the decline of letter writing and the growth of office supply superstores mostly eliminated the once-popular writing materials from the bookstore. In their place came the food and drink sold in cafés, some gift items, as well as other media products such as magazines, music, videos, and DVDs. The importance that the chains placed on becoming multimedia retailers in the 1990s was reflected in Borders' 1994 purchase of CD Superstore, a small music chain, and Barnes & Noble's 1999 purchase of Babbage's Etc. (later renamed GameStop), a video game and entertainment software retail chain principally owned by Barnes & Noble's chairman, Len Riggio.[36]

However, bookstores have not found it so easy to profitably diversify their entertainment products. In this they are not alone; a number of retail ventures based on the concept of selling a mix of media products failed in the early 2000s, including Zany Brainy and the Viacom Entertainment Store, while others, such as Media Play and Hastings Entertainment, were surviving, but not without problems. For booksellers, differences between books and other media with regard to supply channels, methods of marketing, and staff expertise proved to be much more difficult to reconcile than expected; evidently media content was not so free-floating after all. As a result, the major chains began to cut back on some sidelines, especially music. Like other retailers, the book chains saw music sales decline, and so Borders, Barnes & Noble, and Books-A-Million all reduced their CD offerings. Another retreat from the multimedia strategy occurred in 2004, when Barnes & Noble spun off GameStop.[37] By 2003, nonbook items represented 20 to 30 percent of chain sales, a not insignificant amount, but still clearly keeping such items to the side of the books taking center stage.[38] Average independent sales in sidelines were probably somewhat lower, as independents were less likely to have the resources to put into learning how to select and market different product lines. Thus, it appeared that bookstores would remain primarily in the business of selling books.

While the difficulties in merchandising multimedia products show some limits to bookstore efforts to become total entertainment centers, booksellers have benefited from more successful ways in which books have been integrated into the entertainment industry. One important manifestation of this is the growing prominence of books and authors on television and radio programs. While direct advertising to readers is thought to do little to stimulate book sales, media publicity, especially when it involves celebrity figures, is a different matter. Publishers assiduously court media attention for specific books by sending out review copies, press releases, and other promotional material, and by faxing or phoning journalists, reviewers, and radio and television producers. Author appearances on talk shows have been common since the 1970s, with National Public Radio offering the most extensive book coverage. But in the 1990s, a wider range of broadcast media discovered that audiences like to hear about books and authors. In the mid-1990s, several television programs devoted exclusively to books and publishing appeared, such as C-Span's *Booknotes* and *About Books,* while other television shows featured book-related segments. Perhaps the best-known broadcast segment on the printed word was Oprah Winfrey's Book Club, which rates among the most effective promotional vehicles for books ever invented. Publishers would routinely print an extra 750,000 copies of a title when it was selected for the televised book club. This not only reflected the great influence of Winfrey on her viewers, but it was also testament to the way in which book talk was now perceived as accessible entertainment. Indeed, after Winfrey shut down her book club in 2002 (as it turned out, only temporarily), other book clubs sponsored by various print and broadcast outlets sprung up, including NBC's *Today Show* and *Live with Regis and Kelly,* and ABC's *Good Morning America.*

Similarly, the Internet presented new opportunities for promoting books in the context of providing entertainment. Borders, Barnes & Noble, and Books-A-Million each contracted with outside companies to provide Internet-based programming, such as book excerpts and author interviews and lectures.[39] This was a way to bring the type of popular events based in the physical outlets to the scattered customers of the virtual stores. At the same time, the online bookstores, including Amazon, were becoming more cluttered with various features meant to amuse browsers and keep them on site for a longer period of time. Links to bestseller charts, book-related news, book club picks, and other options helped transform the earlier image of Internet stores as places for goal-oriented consumers who desire a quick, efficient transaction.

The intricate ways through which so many different media now cross-promote one another provide the context for consumers' willingness to attend to book-marketing messages. As Susan Davis argues with regard to the theme park, entertainment and advertising can become so thoroughly fused that it is hard to know the difference.[40] In the same vein, book retailers try to make their promotions seem like gifts of entertainment rather than intrusive sales pitches. An event or a newsletter is certainly designed to sell particular books, but it may well be experienced as a "free" service, compliments of the bookseller.

By emphasizing the entertaining qualities of their establishments, both independents and chains are also furthering an association between books and fun. Neil Postman, for one, has argued that the medium of print is oriented toward serious and rational public conversation, whereas the medium of television is intrinsically biased toward entertainment. He accuses television of altering public discourse so that people no longer exchange ideas, but instead try to entertain one another.[41] What his technological determinism overlooks, however, is the importance of social and cultural contexts for shaping what we do with different media as well as our very definitions of entertainment. The meanings attached to the book are themselves variable, and are, in part, connected to how books are produced and distributed.

Developments in the bookstore demonstrate that books can certainly be associated in the public mind with leisure, fun, and diversion.

Similarly, in creating an inviting environment that facilitates social interaction, the bookstore may be encouraging people to associate the act of browsing, and possibly even reading books, with socializing. This challenges the ways in which reading has been understood during much of the twentieth century as an intensely private kind of experience. For instance, Robert Escarpit calls reading "the supreme solitary occupation," as the reader is forced to cut himself off from any social interaction or competing activity.[42] And according to David Riesman, reading is one of the few activities that can promise some privacy, and therefore some escape from the pressures to conform to mass society.[43] But the fact that many individuals choose to spend time reading in a quasi-public, consumption-oriented place such as the bookstore suggests that Americans may see reading as an activity that can be both social and solitary, as much an adjunct to other activities as an escape from them.

The efforts of booksellers to sell the bookstore experience in order to sell more books may therefore be working to teach people to think of books differently. Yet, in this vision, books are as much the backdrop to fun as they are the source of fun. To recall the term used in the industry, books make good "wallpaper" for a setting in which other entertainments occur. Whether people are socializing, drinking coffee, or watching a performance, books provide an agreeable atmosphere as well as a ready way for people to occupy themselves when they need to fill in the spaces of leisure time. In this way, the mere presence of books is sufficient to create the desired experience; the actual contents of them become less relevant.

The perception of books as an entertainment medium and bookstores as an entertainment institution is a significant development. But I am not arguing here that it signals the degradation of books or literary values. Surely it is a good thing when books are perceived as accessible to more than an intellectual elite. And the tremendous number and variety of new books published each year presents evidence against any claim that the serious consideration of ideas no longer takes place in print. Nevertheless, contrary to prognoses by some book professionals that the superstore model of bookselling would be the salvation of the industry, the association of books with entertainment has not led to more reading overall. Per capita book reading, as measured by time-use studies or book acquisition statistics, remained fairly stable for the latter decades of the twentieth century. If anything, at the turn of the twenty-first century, book reading was in decline. During the 1990s, the decade in which the superstore grew up, the total number of trade books (including both adult and juvenile titles) purchased by Americans rose slightly, but the number actually diminished relative to the nation's population growth.[44] One time-use study by the communications industry investment bank Veronis Suhler Stevenson found that the average amount of time adults spent reading books dropped 7 percent between 1997 and 2002, from 116 hours per year to 109.[45] While changes in bookselling may indeed be influencing how Americans think about books, compared to the rest of the world, the United States is still not a country of heavy readers.

Furthermore, the emphasis placed on entertainment has not completely crowded out other ways of conceptualizing books and bookstores. Not all booksellers have embraced the entertaining bookstore model. And despite efforts by the media conglomerates to treat books as just another vessel for content, Americans stop short at viewing books as interchangeable with other cultural products. With only one exception, everyone I interviewed — book professionals and bookstore customers, regular and occasional readers — indicated that books are a worthier medium than other forms of culture, and that reading is a qualitatively different experience than partaking of other cultural entertainments.

It is in comparison to television that people most clearly articulate what they see as the unique value of books. Whereas respondents tended to assert that television requires little imagination and that it controls its audience, they claimed that a book allows the reader to retain more power and be a full participant in the communication process.[46] The remarks of some bookstore patrons I interviewed reinforce this sense of reading as an active, engaged, and independent habit:

> I like reading because you can interpret it the way you want to. It's written descriptively, you can use your imagination in how you interpret that. With movies, television, music videos, it seems that the creators are trying to get across their ideas of what they want you to believe, and in some cases, if you identify with that, that's great. I guess you can say the same for books, but it does leave a little bit to the imagination, that you can picture a character or a location in your own mind as opposed to just having it there.

> Oh, it's very different for me because here I can have my own pace, and television imposes a need to follow the sequence of pictures and the speed of television. And here I can take a break, I can think about it, and I can resume reading again whenever I want, I can read the book, go to another one, come back. So this gives me a lot of freedom in my choice.

If you're looking at casual reading, nothing works better than a human being's imagination. TV is kind of like spoon-fed imagination, and it's actually somebody else's imagination that they're trying to get you to agree to. Same thing with movies. You could probably take the same story line, I bet, and if someone wrote it into a story, you could probably make a pretty good movie out of it in your mind, without having somebody else do all of the special effects and stuff for you. TV is being spoon-fed. Reading a book is — you can make it as good as you want in your imagination.

For some, this freedom granted to the imagination is understood not just in terms of a loose leash from the books' creators, but also in terms of an ability to think differently from other readers. One wholesaler described the sense of having a unique perspective as essential to the act of reading:

I think the solitariness of it and the purely interpretive element of books, personal interpretation is what really sets it apart. I mean you could read a book and I could read a book, we can have two different concepts of what went on and I had different pictures in my own mind that I conjured up due to my own experience. I think media like TV manipulates you, usually manipulates you auditorially, and I think books leave it more to the individual.

Others argued that reading is less fleeting than other entertainments and hence, as another wholesaler remarked, a more enriching activity:

I think that reading is by its very nature a kind of an exercise which has a much more permanent and lasting effect on the individual than watching television. It requires a more overt kind of effort and concentration than watching television or listening to the radio. Even if it's an educational program. I think it's more nourishing, it can be more nourishing depending upon what you've decided to sample.

A bookstore customer used similar language when she said, "On television, you spend a lot of time on things that aren't anything that's going to nourish your soul." For both of these respondents, the greater effort required by the act of reading is intertwined with the likelihood of finding more substantive fare in books than on television. Indeed, what underlies many of the discrepant evaluations given to books versus other cultural products is the book's association with education, both formal and informal. As another bookstore patron said,

> Very different. I can't even really see a resemblance to a book and television. Television is something that you put on which entertains you. A book, you sit down, you read it. It entertains you, but you also are learning at the same time all sorts of different things. So yeah, there's a great difference.

Thus, despite an understanding of books as a legitimate source of entertainment, books continue to be perceived as attached to learning and to the betterment (both moral and intellectual) of individuals. And because they increase self-awareness as well as provide insights into the human condition and natural world, books are believed to have a unique potential for bettering society.

As the last customer quoted above suggests, newer meanings attached to print can exist side by side with the old. Books, more than any other medium of mass communication, are understood as both educational and entertaining, and the bookstore represents a place that offers the opportunity for both communal fun and private reflection. Bookstore customers generally find few contradictions between these various sets of meanings, and why should they? Just as humans can crave both enjoyment and enlightenment, they can create objects and institutions that offer some of both. Yet book professionals may not always be able to support all meanings equally. And what booksellers have found is that entertainment is easier to market than learning or personalized relations.

Marketing is obviously important for selling more goods, and the marketing that takes place in bookstores often, though not always, achieves that purpose. Yet a more significant impact of marketing is the way in which it helps to change how we think about our social relationships, our material culture, and the activities of everyday life. The case of the bookstore provides a prime example. Booksellers have redefined their role and have employed sophisticated marketing techniques to redefine the image of the bookstore. In the process, they may be helping to reshape our ideas about both books and shopping.

The entertaining bookstore has reinforced the equation of shopping with leisure, fun, and diversion. This message of shopping as entertainment is one that both independents and chains now try to communicate. But despite its appeal as a marketing device, this is not the only meaning of consumption that has emerged from the competition between bookstores. Chain booksellers have also encouraged a view of consumption as about bargain hunting and individual economic interests, while independents have tried to articulate an understanding of consumption as tied to personal relations and civic responsibility. This clash of perspectives on consumption is not unique to book retailing. But because of the strong persistence of older views about books, the meanings of book shopping are perhaps more easily contested than those of other consumer goods. The products themselves matter for how we think about consumption.

CHAPTER 6

Bargaining with the Rational Consumer:
Selling the Low-Cost Book

Human beings love a bargain. This piece of popular wisdom may not always hold up to empirical scrutiny, but it does shape how many Americans understand themselves and other people. As one customer at an independent bookstore stated when asked if discounts matter when book shopping, "Always. If I could get the same book at a discount, there's no choice. And I do check discount first. That's my approach to investing, that's my approach to life. [I did] that before it was popular even. That's just me . . . I was born discounted or something, I don't know." This man uses the language of inevitability to describe the allure of discounts; for him, prioritizing the bargain when buying books is simply the extension of a general approach to how one naturally acts in the world. His remarks typify a common assumption among Americans who frequently, if inconsistently, imagine human nature as motivating people to get the most they can for the least financial cost. While this belief can be applied to many spheres of everyday life, it is most clearly realized in the realm of shopping, where monetary prices play such a conspicuous role in the marketing and display of goods, as well as in the transaction between clerk and customer.

Yet, as with other cultural models of consumption, this vision of the self-interested, bargain-hunting consumer has not always existed in its current form. And although this view has grown stronger over time, even today its hold on conceptions of consumption is not absolute. Indeed, the customer quoted above said in his very next answer (to the question of what makes for a good salesperson at a bookstore) that he would "pay a little premium to" those bookstores that voluntarily help him find a book they themselves do not carry. That is, he is willing and able to ignore his compulsion to seek the lowest prices when a bookseller also deviates from the laws of the capitalist marketplace by recommending a competitor who has a desired item. What this response suggests is that the impulse to get the most for one's dollar may not be so deep-seated after all.

Some economists might try to explain away such disinterested behavior as showing that merchants simply capitalize on consumers' willingness to pay for "added value"; in such cases consumers still perceive they are receiving a good deal since they are getting extra services along with the item being purchased. However, the economists' explanation ignores a potential quality of the retailer-customer relationship that is not solely about maneuvering for advantage but may be shaped by loyalty, goodwill, or generosity. Such personal relationships can discourage behavior that is oriented purely toward individual self-interest.

The extent to which personal relations guide economic transactions depends on the structure of the existing market as well as on cultural norms.[1] Thus, in markets based on bargaining, discounting may be connected to a personal relationship. The seller might on a whim decide to reward favored individual customers, while the buyer who has good social skills can get a better price than those who are more remote. Once the fixed-price system emerges, however, discounting becomes rationalized and instituted as part of a seller's policy, so that all customers receive the discount whether or not they are personally known. Frequent customers sometimes do receive a bigger discount, but it is based on an impersonal system of tabulating sales, and is open to any and all buyers who want to join. In this kind of market, the idiosyncratic relationship between retailer and customer remains irrelevant for the terms of the exchange.

The price at which goods are sold is only one aspect of the retail transaction, but it provides an especially important lens for considering the ways in which self-interest does or does not become a component of consumption. An orientation to shopping that stresses price accentuates the competition between buyer and seller, and encourages the consumer to accumulate a greater amount of goods. On the other hand, an orientation to shopping that deemphasizes price places other considerations, such as the personal relations between retailer and customer, above or at least equal to victory in expanding one's purchasing power. An orientation to personal relations can still be found today in the United States, but it is often dismissed as a quaint anachronism. Its allegedly anachronistic status provides some evidence for how the growth of systematic discounting has led to a more single-minded focus by consumers on price and a concomitant cultural understanding of the consumer as a rational actor out to obtain desired goods at the lowest possible cost. The foregrounding of consumer price consciousness has been an especially noticeable development in the book business.

In this chapter, I look more closely at the historical development of the practice and ideology of discounting, as well as at how book professionals have tried to counter the figure of the bargain-hunting consumer. There is probably no issue in bookselling that has been so contentious for so long as discounting. Price-cutting has been practiced ever since American book-selling emerged as a distinct enterprise in the nineteenth century, often to great condemnation by other book professionals. In the first half of the twentieth century, such condemnation was intertwined with other criticisms of nonbook retailers, since the discounting of books occurred primarily in department, drug-, and variety stores. Price-cutting by regular bookstores, on the other hand, did not become widespread until the mall-based chains institutionalized it in the 1970s and '80s. Since that time, price-cutting has contributed to the growth of bookstore chains and other mass merchandisers while contributing to the demise of independents. This is because discounting is usually viable only when a retailer is large enough to benefit from economies of scale; those who cannot afford to discount will then often lose business to their price-cutting competitors.

Much of the debate surrounding price-cutting has been concerned with its economic effects, with supporters commending the efficiencies that discounters achieve, and detractors warning of an ever-downward spiral of profits that will lead to financial distress for publishers and booksellers alike. But underlying these economic considerations are additional concerns about the social and cultural effects of price-cutting. What is especially important here is the highly instrumental understanding of consumption embodied in and encouraged by this practice, one that furthers a view of humans as fundamentally capitalist in nature.

While this view of consumption has come to dominate commonsense assumptions about economic behavior, it did not arise uncontested in American culture. Especially during the 1930s, independent retailers in a variety of fields criticized price-cutting as capitalism run amuck, with cutthroat competition said to result in the unchecked power of large organizations. The philosophical stance against discounting was manifested in the policy struggle over resale price maintenance, the practice whereby the supplier of a good compels those organizations (usually retailers) who resell that good to maintain a minimum, maximum, or fixed price. Publishers in the first half of the twentieth century, under pressure from regular booksellers, thus tried to curtail price-cutting by requiring retailers to sign agreements to maintain minimum prices on their books. Yet booksellers were less vigorous in their efforts to see price maintenance legalized and enforced than were other retailers such as pharmacists or liquor dealers. Because leaders of the book trade were concerned with building an image of professionalism and gentility in these years, they were more reluctant to organize and less inclined to publicly denounce the growing dominance of big business than were many other types of merchants. This limited their effectiveness in making price maintenance widespread, and in stemming the practice of discounting. It was not until the bookstore chains began to engage in regular price-cutting that booksellers became more militant in their actions — even if they were perhaps more moderate in their rhetoric than their counterparts of an earlier era.

Nonbook Retailers and the Discount Evil

Price-cutting has been seen as a serious problem since the earliest days of the modern American book industry. The trade sales of the mid-nineteenth century attracted criticism for selling discounted books directly to the public and therefore undercutting bookshops. Similar complaints were voiced when publishers engaged in mail-order sales, as readers were offered prices at or below the cost that retailers themselves paid. In these years, *The Publishers' Weekly,* the industry's primary trade journal, took a firm stance against what it called the "evil" of discounting. Despite its frequent exhortations to publishers to oppose price-cutting actively, the magazine was not entirely successful in its mission. For instance, in 1892, an editorial in the journal noted that it was highly unlikely that publishers would punish those booksellers who persisted in this practice, though the writer expressed hope that local booksellers would form agreements to refrain from the harmful pricing competition that could spell their mutual ruin.[2]

The situation became even more severe once department stores began to sell books. As we have seen, department stores, along with drugstores and variety stores, liked to use books as loss leaders, items sold below cost in order to bring people into the store where they could be lured to more profitable purchases. During the first half of the twentieth century, the most notorious price-cutter of all was the New York department store Macy's. By discounting popular titles, Macy's was able to attract prime customers, and in the process, sold enormous quantities of books. Macy's and the other department stores invested heavily in newspaper advertisements that triumphantly proclaimed their discounted prices. Not only potential customers, but other booksellers took note of these sales, and periodic price wars would break out.

In keeping with their hopes to reform the various inefficiencies that plagued the book trade, many industry leaders decried the uneconomic nature of price wars. *Publishers Weekly* stated in 1935 that the current situation was a "fool's paradise," where the laws of commerce no longer applied to books.[3] Independent bookshops that could not match the department store discounts would be forced out of business, it was claimed, and publishers would find themselves with even fewer book outlets than the already small number that currently existed. Occasionally, bookstores did find a way to sell discounted books successfully. For instance, in the late 1930s, Barnes & Noble opened the Economy Bookstore, separate from its main store, which it proudly compared to a department store bargain basement (the place where overstock and last season's fashions were sold).[4] However, this was still a different matter from discounting newly published books, which were so important for a bookstore's profitability.

Despite attempts by publishers and booksellers to stem discounting, department store price-cutting continued through the 1950s. During that decade, discount variety houses joined department stores in using books as loss leaders. The discount houses carried an even more limited selection of books than the department stores did, which earned them considerable contempt in the eyes of independent booksellers. But as the executive director of the American Booksellers Association told a Senate subcommittee in 1959, the discount houses had to be taken seriously, since they cut prices on the most popular titles, taking away significant business from bookstores:

> Price cutting is a serious threat to the very existence of the American bookseller. This threat has been redoubled in the last few years with the mushroom growth of large-scale discount houses. These non-book-minded merchants have reached out and skimmed the cream from the new book market. Bestsellers which formerly served to keep the retail bookseller in a reasonably liquid financial condition are now offered by these new discount houses at prices close to cost. . . . Price cutting unless stopped will ultimately eliminate the personal bookstore from the national scene and in turn will have a serious effect on the quality of our national literary production.[5]

Forty years later, nearly identical statements were being made in reference to Wal-Mart, Costco, and the other descendants of the discount houses. But by then, some bookstores had also joined the discount fray.

The Chains Learn to Discount

In the 1960s, the expanding market for books, along with the declining influence of department stores, muted the problem of price-cutting. During these years, B. Dalton and Waldenbooks were becoming established, but discounting was not part of their original strategy. In fact, discounting remained largely the province of nonbook retailers until the mid-1970s. It was only after Crown Books burst on the scene in 1977 that bookstore discounting took off. Even though Barnes & Noble began to discount some bestsellers two years before Crown was founded, Crown's influence was actually much greater in this regard. Its highly aggressive discount policies had a tremendous impact on other booksellers and on consumer expectations around book pricing.

First of all, Crown's discount was big — 35 percent off hardcovers that had made the *New York Times* bestseller list, and somewhat less for other books. Second, Crown claimed that *all* books in its stores were discounted, and its heavy investment in advertising to spread the message suggested to consumers that they need never pay full price for a book again. Of course, as Crown's competitors angrily pointed out, this claim was somewhat disingenuous. Crown actually made the bulk of its sales, not from discounted new books, but from remainders, that is, publishers' overstock, which is always sold at a discount. The layout of a Crown store was designed in such a way that anyone wanting to get to the bestsellers in back had to pass by the shelves of remainders in front. The result was a large number of "impulse buys" of the profitable remainders, sales that subsidized drastic, even money-losing discounts on new books.[6]

For a few years after Crown's birth, the other two major chains resisted price-cutting. But Crown's popularity proved to be too much for them. B. Dalton started by experimenting with discounts on bestsellers in a few of its stores that competed with Crown. Then, in 1982, Dalton launched what was expected to become a whole new chain of outlets called Pickwick Discount Books. Each Pickwick carried about a fifth as many titles as a regular Dalton did, but all of those books were discounted. After a couple of years during which the concept was tested, Pickwick was expanded in 1984. But then in 1986, after Pickwick had grown to thirty-seven stores in four cities (well below the initial projection of over a hundred outlets), Dalton announced that it would close the chain. Contending that Pickwick proved to be unprofitable, executives said that they would instead continue with selective discounting in regular Dalton stores.[7]

Meanwhile, Waldenbooks was even more reluctant to start discounting. Its first attempt was in 1983, when it instituted discounts on bestsellers in its Los Angeles stores in order to compete with Dalton. Then, when Kmart purchased Walden in 1984, there were widespread fears that Kmart would spread its own discount habit to its new acquisition. And sure enough, by the end of that year, Walden began testing a new chain of discount outlets called Reader's Market. But like Dalton, Walden found it difficult to duplicate Crown's success and make a profit from an all-discount chain. Before long, Reader's Market was taken out of Walden's domain and integrated into regular Kmart stores.[8]

These short-lived ventures showed that in a business where profit margins were already thin, comprehensive price-cutting was difficult to sustain. But while the two biggest chains did not succeed with an all-discount format, selective discounting, especially of bestsellers, became an integral part of Dalton's and Walden's strategy. When sold in very high volume, a discounted popular title could still reap large profits, and at the same time bring customers into the store where they might make other purchases. And so, leaving their initial reluctance to discount far behind, both Walden and Dalton used their promotional machinery to create an image of being "value" (i.e., low-priced) retailers. By the beginning of the 1990s, it was hard to remember that not long before, price-cutting in the bookstore was highly unusual.

When the chain superstores were unfolded, they continued the mall outlets' practice of selective discounting. Highlighting discounts was an especially important element of the chains' marketing strategy, as it completed the promise that the superstores could deliver it all — elegance, fun, wide selection, and low prices. The actual extent of discounting varied considerably over time with the chains (including Amazon) sometimes engaging in price wars and sometimes pulling back from discounts when they ate too much into profits. At times, a chain would institute a national discount policy; in other years, discounts differed between regions as the company took local conditions and competition into account. But once the superstores were firmly established, the overall trend was to restrict the scope of discounting. For instance, Barnes & Noble had stopped discounting paperbacks by 1994.[9] During the mid-1990s, Barnes & Noble and Borders typically offered 30 percent off of *New York Times* bestsellers and 10 percent off of other hardcover books. But in 1999 and 2000, the two major chains started to limit even their hardcover discounts to a handful of bestsellers and other titles.[10]

Despite the fact that most titles were sold at full price, the perception of providing extensive discounts remained a key part of the chains' appeal.

Book chains were hardly alone in this regard. From sellers of clothes to office supplies to electronics and more, discount chains were growing at much faster rates than traditional retailers. They communicated a message of consumer plenitude: with so many bargains available, there was no reason to do without; vast quantities of goods could be within the grasp of everyone. In the book world, the image of the perpetual bargain was strengthened by Internet bookselling, where the fiercest price wars were carried out, often led by Amazon. Both Amazon and Barnesandnoble.com were willing to lose money on deeply discounted titles in order to gain market share, and their strategy was to publicize special deals extensively. For instance, on one of the biggest books of 2003, *Harry Potter and the Order of the Phoenix,* Amazon only broke even on the 1.4 million copies it sold because of its heavy discounts. Amazon, though, considered this a good investment, as the company gained 250,000 new customers who, it hoped, would now shop regularly at the online dealer.[11]

The Internet also furthered the message that consumers should expect a bargain more often than not by enabling comparative shopping. Various Web sites that allowed consumers to see side-by-side the prices that different retailers charged for an item sprung up in the 1990s. Almost always it appeared that online booksellers offered the best deals. But here too, the low-cost image could be deceptive, as a minimum purchase for discounts or added shipping costs increased the amount consumers paid.

While online discounts did not always amount to much in the way of cost savings, certain nonbook retailers were truly living up to their price-cutting image. Through the 1990s, an increasing assortment of mass merchandisers and warehouse clubs, from Wal-Mart to Costco to Best Buy, were selling books, though they still carried a highly limited selection. Prices were so low at warehouse clubs that nearby independent booksellers would sometimes even purchase their books to resell in the bookstore. Booksellers claimed that the warehouse clubs' retail price was similar to what they would pay a wholesaler or even the publisher for a title.[12] In 2001, warehouse clubs, mass merchandisers, and other discount stores accounted for 14.8 percent of adult trade books sold. This compared to 10 percent a decade earlier.[13] Although discounters had been selling books since the 1950s, the kind of clientele patronizing the warehouse clubs and mass merchandisers had changed significantly by the end of the twentieth century. Highly educated and affluent book buyers were no longer disdainful about these kinds of stores but were enthusiastically doing their book shopping there.[14] The high profile of superstore discounts probably helped lessen the class stigma attached to shopping at the mass merchandisers, as the superstores assured more elite readers that they too are entitled to seek out discounts without fear of losing status.

By 1998, one estimate was that 36 percent of all books in the United States were bought at a discount.[15] Certainly, some independents have also tried to engage in price-cutting. But smaller stores have found it difficult to make discounting work. For one thing, it requires greater capitalization to finance the constant advertising needed to inform consumers of the latest great buy. Furthermore, to see the same profit as selling at full price, a bookseller must increase the number of units sold many times over. In other words, considerable economies of scale are needed to be able to cut prices.

The result has been that full-priced independents have lost customers in droves to the price-cutting chains, online dealers, and warehouse clubs. But part of the problem for independents also has to do with which books are discounted. As department stores discovered a century ago, bestsellers can be used as loss leaders to draw customers into a store where they are likely to purchase full-priced merchandise. The chains have sometimes engaged in price wars and sold books at a loss, though usually the high volume at which they sell bestsellers ensures that these books will earn a profit. Either way, discounted bestsellers help to make the chains the bookstores of choice for many consumers. However, independents feel the loss of bestseller sales quite keenly. These books provide a higher profit margin than backlist volumes because the bookseller can acquire them at a lower cost, and because they turn rapidly, that is, sell quickly and do not take up shelf space for long. New books slated for the bestseller lists also present opportunities to earn cooperative advertising dollars from publishers. Popular sellers were once the bread and butter that supported many independents' less profitable selections. Now that market has largely been lost to the chains and warehouse clubs.

As price-cutting has become widespread in chain bookstores and nonbook retailers, readers have grown to expect discounts and, indeed, may believe that they are being cheated if a store sells at full price. Even if they enjoy browsing the independents, many customers seek out the discounts when it is time to make a purchase:

> I do buy at Price Club because a lot of times they're the same book for a very discounted price. I just came from the largest Crown bookstore. And what I like about that, of course, is the price. I *love* beautiful bookstores like this [independent]. . . . I think that the chain stores can give you a better price. But I think that the independents have more atmosphere. And more eye appeal.

But as the following bookseller explained, such consumers rarely consider how the discounting of one store might endanger the atmosphere of another:

> I mean I have people come into my store all the time who say, "It's so won-derful to have you here." And I know they then walk six blocks away and do their major purchases at Crown. So as much as they want me here, they only have twenty-five dollars to spend on books this month, and they can buy more books for that. And I understand that. I *really* understand that. But I think we need to make some decisions. My best example of what goes on on a certain level is in the [area where] I live . . . people feel very strongly about keeping their neighborhood together. So they're willing to spend more money at Sam's deli than going to the Safeway. Because they want Sam to be there. There's meaning behind that for them. And I think unfortunately where [my store is], people don't have that kind of feeling about small businesspeople. And at the same time they complain that people have gone out of business. I don't think people *get* it that they can't have both. They can't have the nice guy down the street who will do all those last minute things, or order a book for you, or fix your flat tire for only a dollar, and then go to Price Club and buy all their major purchases. It's just not going to work.

What this bookseller points out is that lower monetary prices come at a different kind of cost.

Consumption and the Logic of Self-Interested Acquisition

The sentiments expressed above represent competing philosophies about the practice of consumption. On the one hand, the customer who shops at Price Club suggests that a consumer's rational self-interest compels her to go where she will find the lowest prices. Yet the bookseller suggests that there are circumstances in which people might gain in other ways by paying more for consumer goods. However, it is rare today to hear a case made for why the consumer should turn her back on lower prices. Most people take it for granted that consumers may be fanciful in regard to the different possible pleasures of consumption but are invariably hard-headed when it comes to different prices for equivalent items. But if one goes back in American history to a time when the morality of discounting was a question of public concern, one can find the logic underlying these different philosophies articulated more clearly. Especially during the 1930s, when department and chain stores aggressively discounted a variety of goods, the debate over price-cutting exposed assumptions about the appropriate motivations of the consumer.

Defenders of discounting stressed an individualistic notion of consumption whereby the consumer's foremost obligation was to herself and her family. One 1931 proponent of chain stores tried to lay to rest any doubts about this:

> After all, Mrs. Housewife, doesn't it narrow down to this: your main interest in spending your household budget is to get the most you can for your money? To be sure, you are loyal to your town; you want to see all storekeepers prosper, but your chief duty is to yourself and to your family. You must spend your household allowance where you get the best values. Now if you can make such savings as 19 cents in buying your boy's gloves, save two cents on every loaf of bread, save 30 cents on a double boiler, you are justified in putting aside every single consideration — personal and otherwise — and shopping at chain stores.[16]

But more than this, advocates of discounting claimed that it is irrational not to make cost savings one's main priority; indeed, they implied, only a sucker would pay more than he has to. A 1938 radio address mocked those who wanted to impose extra taxes on chain stores:

> But strange to say, we are faced with a nation-wide attack upon these efficient, low cost distributors as enemies of the common weal. . . . It may seem that their antagonists are appealing to some strange secret desire of the American consumer to get much less than a dollar's worth of goods for every dollar spent. . . . But I cannot convince myself that American housewives and American workers really want to throw away their own money. I honestly believe that our people are just as anxious as any other people to get as much value as possible for every dollar they spend.[17]

As chain store supporters rightly noted, efforts to restrain the chains through special taxes or price maintenance regulations constituted an intervention into the competitive process of the free market system. Chain supporters saw such moves as an outrage, since they believed that economic competition should be applauded, not condemned. In the free market system, competitors could show their true mettle, and both winner and loser deserved their unequal rewards. In a *Reader's Digest* debate over legislation restricting the chains, another chain defender put it bluntly:

> The independent retailer is usually a nice fellow. But is he nice enough to inspire all his fellow citizens to subsidize him out of their own pocketbooks?

> Or shouldn't he — like everybody else — have to prove his value to society in open competition, regardless of sentiment?[18]

The paeans to competition took an especially forceful turn during the cold war years, when opposition to discounting was called "un-American"[19] and, in one case, reminiscent of the Pilgrims' "miserable failure of a communist experiment." The supermarket operator making this charge warned that only when the Pilgrims abandoned their system of dividing up goods equally among themselves and recognized the motivating force of self-interest did they prosper.[20] In this perspective, protecting the retailer from the competition of discounting undermines the social welfare as well as bedrock American values.

For proponents of discounting, the natural workings of the free market and the natural workings of the human spirit fit smoothly together. The view that it is human nature to want more for less was perhaps put forth most clearly by a Macy's vice president testifying before a congressional committee in 1958:

> No one has found a way to force people to ignore the profoundly human trait of shopping for and getting bargains, or to prevent retailers from providing bargains — and since no one can convince the public that this is immoral or illegal, they will do this, on a "bootleg" basis, if necessary.[21]

Speaking at a time when Americans were involved in the biggest consumer splurge in the country's history, a splurge in part fueled by consumer credit, this executive described, not exactly thriftiness, but a calculating acquisitiveness as part of the human condition.

Nonetheless, at least during the early decades of the twentieth century, many did argue against encouraging humans to follow the "laws of the jungle," asserting that there were good reasons for the consumer to pause before hunting for the best bargain. For opponents of discounting, the results, if not the process, of unfettered price competition were immoral. Some noted that price-cutting was often subsidized by manufacturers who were pressured to supply their goods to retailers at low prices. In order to cut their own costs, those manufacturers then hired fewer workers and paid them less. Thus, the American worker was another casualty of discounting.[22] Critics also pointed to the deception that could be involved in price-cutting, claiming that discounters tended to charge higher prices on some items to make up for the low prices on others.[23] But perhaps the worst effect in the eyes of critics was that discounting, practiced by and benefiting the largest retailers, would lead to monopoly. Loss leading and other "predatory" pricing practices, it was claimed, were being instituted in order to eliminate competitors, especially the small merchants who could not afford to discount. In an oft-quoted statement, soon-to-be Supreme Court justice Louis D. Brandeis warned in 1913 that

> Americans should be under no illusions as to the value or effect of price-cutting. It has been the most potent weapon of monopoly — a means of killing the small rival to which the great trusts have resorted most frequently. It is so simple, so effective. Far-seeing organized capital secures by this means the co-operation of the short-sighted unorganized consumer to his own undoing. Thoughtless or weak, he yields to the temptation of trifling immediate gain; and selling his birthright for a mess of pottage, becomes himself an instrument of monopoly.[24]

The fateful outcome of price-cutting, in this view, was to lure the consumer into succumbing to greed, abandoning any personal loyalty to the small retailer, and becoming an accomplice to the accumulation of power.

Antidiscount Activism: Booksellers and Price Maintenance

Booksellers who faced price-cutting, first by department stores and then by discount houses, echoed these concerns about unrestrained competition. A spokesperson for the American Booksellers Association argued in 1952,

> [W]e submit that "free" competition should not give a powerful, wealthy, general merchandise retailer the right to destroy his financially weaker competition, the retail book seller. "The American way" has never been to encourage economic jungle warfare.[25]

Throughout the history of the book trade, price-cutting has been the greatest spur for booksellers to take collective action in defense of their interests. And because they are selling books rather than some other commodity, the issue has been framed somewhat differently than in other industries.

As early as 1900, the instability caused by price-cutting was considered serious enough that the leading publishers formed the American Publishers Association with the goal of compelling all book retailers to maintain prices at a minimum level set by a book's publisher.[26] That same year, the American Booksellers Association was founded to assist in this effort. At its first convention, ABA members passed a resolution stipulating that they would not deal with publishers who did not establish a system of minimum prices, and that any ABA member who violated such a system would be expelled from the organization.[27] In 1901, members of the publishers association asked all book retailers to sign agreements guaranteeing that they would do this. The majority of outlets, including most department stores, did comply. But a significant exception was Macy's, which made low prices a key part of its marketing strategy. Publishers first tried to force the renegade store's hand by refusing to sell books to it. Macy's reacted to the boycott by dispensing undercover agents to buy books from out-of-town wholesalers and retailers. The department store flagrantly defied the publishers, taking out newspaper advertisements that proclaimed discounted prices for books it was not even supposed to have access to. In 1902, Macy's sued the publishers association for restraining competition. A group of publishers then countersued, charging Macy's with destroying the market for their books. The issue went back and forth in the courts for the next ten years. In 1913, the Supreme Court finally ruled in Macy's favor, and the American Publishers Association was subsequently disbanded.[28] After this defeat, American publishers would never again be so united in support of price maintenance.

However, the matter was far from settled. Court decisions pertaining to several different industries had determined that resale price maintenance was a restraint of trade under the Sherman Anti-Trust Act.[29] The Federal Trade Commission, formed in 1915, also opposed price maintenance. But manufacturers and independent retailers in a number of industries continued to lobby for relief from price-cutting department and chain stores. Independent booksellers' sense of urgency was heightened when another round of price wars commenced in the 1930s. With the Depression, price-cutting by department stores and drugstores became fierce, and income for publishers and book retailers consequently went down. Hopes for mandatory price maintenance were raised with the National Recovery Administration's (NRA) trade codes, which instituted rules intended to curb destructive competition and unfair practices. Among the rules governing some seven hundred industries was the retail booksellers code, established in 1934, which prohibited the sale of new books below the publisher's list price.[30] Bookseller satisfaction was cut short, however, when the trade codes were declared unconstitutional in 1935.

Meanwhile, in 1931, California had enacted its own price maintenance law. Called a fair trade act, the measure legalized contracts setting minimum retail prices. Shortly before the end of the NRA codes, several other states also passed fair trade laws, including New York's 1935 Feld-Crawford Act. This was the state law that mattered the most for the book trade, as New York was both the center of publishing and contained the country's most promi-nent booksellers — as well as prominent department stores. Macy's pre-dictably challenged the law in the courts. But the conflict took a new turn in 1937 when Congress passed the Miller-Tydings Act. This legislation permit-ted states to enact fair trade laws that allowed manufacturers (including pub-lishers) to bind retailers with price maintenance contracts. As almost all states soon passed their own fair trade laws, members of the book industry thought price maintenance had finally prevailed. But once again, Macy's proved them wrong, this time by exploiting a loophole in the law that exempted book clubs. Soon Macy's was joined by Bloomingdale's, Gimbel's, and other de-partment stores in running so-called book clubs, which were essentially retail sales with a membership card. This precipitated more lawsuits, and the is-sue was again tied up in the courts for years. Finally, as retailers in other fields were also clamoring for relief from discounters, Congress passed the McGuire Act in 1952, which strengthened fair trade laws by allowing manu-facturers to extend price maintenance even to retailers who refused to sign contracts.[31]

Yet these legislative victories were short lived. During the 1950s, price maintenance rapidly lost support, both within the book industry and within the government. Opponents of price maintenance referred to the practice as price *fixing* and claimed that it represented a restraint on competition. In-creasingly, lawmakers were coming to agree with this assessment. Although the federal McGuire Act permitted the enforcement of fair trade laws, during the 1950s, state courts began to turn against such statutes, ruling that they violated state constitutions. And publishers who had previously supported fair trade stopped issuing price maintenance contracts during the 1950s, as they changed their minds about the benefits of supplying the discounters. Whereas publishers had once been leaders in the fight for price maintenance, the American Book Publishers Council declined to testify at a 1962 congres-sional hearing on a federal price maintenance law because publishers could no longer agree on the issue.[32] This lack of action against the discounters left independent booksellers deeply resentful. They charged publishers with fo-cusing on the short-term gains to be had from selling to the discounters while remaining indifferent to the survival of the independents who formed the backbone of the industry.

When the federal government finally repealed the Miller-Tydings and McGuire Acts in 1975, only thirteen states had fair trade laws with nonsigner clauses (provisions that bound even retailers who would not sign price maintenance agreements), and twenty-three states had fair trade laws with-out nonsigner provisions.[33] But by then, price maintenance was a distant memory for most book professionals. Price-cutting by the chain bookstores, on the other hand, was only just getting started.[34]

Putting a Price on Books

The debate over discounting that took place earlier in the twentieth century has largely faded away as consumer consciousness has increasingly focused on the notion of "value," that is, getting the most for one's money. With the spread of retail discounters of all types, businesses have encouraged an image of the smart consumer as someone (usually female) who helps her family achieve a better standard of living by acquiring more products for her dollar. Considerations such as loyalty or the maintenance of a personal relationship have little place in this image, and those few retailers who ask consumers to put sentiment over savings are routinely scolded for holding unrealistic expectations. Of course, an instrumental approach to consumption makes particular sense for households that no longer have a full-time homemaker who can make errands a meaningful part of her daily routine. Similarly, this approach is understandable in an era when so many retail transactions are carried out with strangers, a condition intensified by an expansion of the geographic range for consumption from neighborhood shops to regional malls to national catalog companies to global Internet commerce. And so, an instrumental orientation to consumption can appear rational and natural today; likewise, the notion that discounting is immoral appears to mix value spheres (to use Max Weber's term) that have nothing to do with one another.[35]

Yet one place where this supposedly nonsensical notion is still occasionally heard is in bookselling. It is not very surprising that the issue of discounts would become a prime focus of booksellers. After all, few things affect a retailer's bottom line so directly as the cost of acquiring her product or the price at which she sells it. However, the discounting issue has taken on much larger significance in the industry, and indeed, it is at the heart of the chain-independent struggle over whose vision of book culture should prevail. For independents, the undiscounted prices at which they sell books to the public represent all those extras — the personalized relations, the commitment to diversity, the sensitivity to local needs — that they believe cannot be reduced to market valuation, and that they insist that no chain can provide. In this view, the chains' discounts destroy the possibility of offering these extras and reduce books to just another interchangeable commodity. For independents, pricing remains very much an issue of morality.

Echoing arguments made earlier in the century, contemporary independent booksellers suggest that something beyond their own livelihood is lost

when they are forced out of business. Thus, for the bookseller quoted earlier who spoke about the lack of loyalty among her customers, maintaining the character of a community depends on retaining its characters, those known individuals whose presence helps define a neighborhood and who are not solely bound by rational procedures judged to be cost effective. This means that while overall prices in an independent store may be higher, the small retailer is willing to do favors such as "fix your flat tire for only a dollar" or, in her case, give change for the bus to people who are not customers.

But in addition to the consumer's discount orientation endangering the small and personal, a threat that affects retailers of all kinds, this bookseller saw the prioritization of price as a threat to the knowledge and respect for books that independent booksellers bring:

> And I think because of the economy, people are concerned with price. I mean why should they buy Updike's new book from me when they can go to Crown and get it for five dollars cheaper. It's the same book. Does it matter that I might be nicer and know more about Updike? To a lot of people, it doesn't make a difference.

Similarly, a consultant sympathized with bookseller frustration over free-rider consumers:

> I think from what I've gathered, [the ones that the superstores] are really hurting the most are some of the juveniles, the children's bookstores. These stores used to pride themselves on a great deal of service to teachers and librarians, making up lists of books and then giving them, you know, a little bit of an extra discount. You opened early to sit down and go through and — and now [customers] are taking the lists and saying, "Oh, but thank you for the list but I can get it at X discount at Barnes & Noble." And now I don't blame them for wanting to shoot the person at that point. I really don't. I think I'd do something very dire to them if they just picked my brain for my expertise and knowledge of these titles and then take the list and plod off elsewhere.

The point I am making here is not that independents are always knowledgeable about books; anyone with extensive book-shopping experience could present evidence to the contrary. Rather, the belief that books ought to be sold by people who are knowledgeable about and devoted to them provides independent booksellers with a logic that acts as a counterforce to the consumer's fixation on price.

Because book professionals view themselves as engaged in an undertaking that brings unique benefits to society, they will often suggest that the anything-goes spirit of capitalism should not apply to bookselling, at least not entirely. The comments of a sales representative are telling in this regard:

> I wish there was something to be done for subsidizing bookstores. Because of the rents. You know, maybe there could be a law that if you're a bookstore, they could only raise your rents so much because the profit margin is only so much. Because it's not like — How many shoe stores do you need on a block? A bookstore goes out of business, it's a loss. To the neighborhood. If a shoe store goes out of business, there are five other shoe stores down the block.

The idea that booksellers should be partially exempt from the forces of the free market demonstrates the way that books continue to be seen as a different kind of commodity. This sense of difference means that booksellers are not offering a full-scale critique of the competitive qualities of the marketplace, but instead are suggesting that consumers restrain their instrumental orientation in this particular sector of the market.

With this, one can hear echoes of book professionals of an earlier era. The owner of a Toronto shop that sells used books keeps prices on his stock high, "not from greed but as a way of reflecting what he sees as their worth as cultural artifacts," thus worrying, like booksellers of the past, about maintaining the dignity of the book.[36] For him, discounts degrade the unique items that he sells. Statements that describe the superior worth of books and the need to shield bookselling from unrestrained competition recall the imagery of jungle predation once so common in attacks on price-cutting. While book professionals are unlikely to use such language today (probably recognizing the racist overtones), some of the ideas expressed by this image — that consumers need to accentuate what is specifically human and "civilized" — persist through the hope that with books, if not with other items, the competitive qualities of human behavior can be suspended. Books continue to be seen as a refining influence.

The notion that books are a privileged kind of commodity has long made booksellers see themselves as more than mere merchants. But while this might provide booksellers with an argument against discounting and unrestrained competition in their field, it has also worked to dilute the effectiveness of their opposition to price-cutting. By carving out book retailing as an arena that deserves special protection, booksellers cede the argument that under normal circumstances, shoppers will naturally evince calculating impulses. Furthermore, in the past, the notion that bookselling was

fundamentally different from other retail ventures lessened booksellers' inclination to make alliances with merchants in similar situations. Indeed, despite their passionate opposition to price-cutting in the first half of the twentieth century, independent booksellers proved to be far less organized and far more timid than many other retailers pressing for price maintenance, most notably the pharmacists who were instrumental in getting the Miller-Tydings law passed. During the 1930s, druggists from around the country sent thousands of telegrams urging President Franklin Delano Roosevelt to stand up to the "chiselers" and protect the small businessman. Other groups that made a concerted lobbying effort for the bill included tire retailers and gasoline dealers. But few members of the book trade did so.[37]

Booksellers' reluctance to engage in aggressive action in favor of price maintenance was in part due to their early court defeats. Once the courts ruled in the Macy's cases that the American Publishers Association had illegally formed a combination to restrain trade, publishers and booksellers alike were hesitant to cooperate in support of price maintenance, fearful that they would be challenged on antitrust grounds.[38] A 1941 Federal Trade Commission report noted that price maintenance had been most extensive in trades where distribution remained primarily in the hands of strongly organized dealers who consistently acted together for the adoption and maintenance of prices.[39] Booksellers were simply not able to achieve this level of organization or solidarity. But fear of legal repercussions was only part of the story. Booksellers' indifference to making common cause with one another was also related to the way in which they self-consciously identified with genteel culture and the carriage trade. Anxious to demonstrate their affiliation with a refined middle class, the conservative bookseller shunned the label of political activist.

As I have outlined in this chapter, there are numerous continuities between book trade discounting of the past and present. Early department store discounters and late-twentieth-century chains alike were attacked as giants who used price-cutting to crush their competitors ruthlessly, and who taught consumers to view books as potential bargains rather than as unique embodiments of culture. However, as chapter 7 will explain, by the time price-cutting in the book business was revived in the 1970s, much had also changed. Publishers were now suspected of actively aiding rather than opposing the discounters. The book trade was becoming more attuned to modern methods of marketing. And despite the continuing conviction that books were a special kind of commodity, booksellers were less likely to identify themselves as part of an elite. The result was a set of very different responses to the perceived injustices of the market.

CHAPTER 7

The Revolt of the Retailers:
Independent Bookseller Activism

In American political culture, the concepts of "business" and "activism" appear to be describing diametrically opposed tendencies. One tendency suggests working with the existing system, while the other suggests working against it; one appears to thrive on stability, while the other is oriented to change; people associated with one seem to form relationships based on the potential for profitable exchange, with the other, on the basis of shared ideology. Of course, Americans well understand that politics and economics are often joined; that reformers agitate for change in the economic realm, while representatives of companies and industries pressure the state to create conditions favorable to their operations. Still, the notion of business interests is often assumed to comprise a unified set of goals; it is less common to consider the competing interests among those actors who represent American capitalism and how the resulting antagonisms can lead to activism. This image of conflict-averse business exists not just within popular discourse, but also among those who consider themselves businesspeople. It is certainly the case that for most of the last century, booksellers in the United States did not expect that political activity would be a component of their jobs. Yet by the end of the twentieth century, large numbers of booksellers were engaged in rhetoric and action they recognized as explicitly political and oriented toward exposing the conflicts of interests within their industry.

Beginning in the 1970s, when competition from the major chains was taking its toll on smaller booksellers, a collective identity among independent booksellers emerged, along with some suggestions that collective action might be necessary to secure their survival. This radicalization of independents, that is to say, the development of a willingness to point to fundamental differences between sectors of the industry and to insist that these differences be addressed, was a gradual and conflicted process. Especially in the first couple decades after the modern chains' establishment, independents who experienced financial difficulties were often told by their confreres that they had only their own inefficiencies to blame. For instance, in 1973, the executive director of the American Booksellers Association chided, "the difference between a successful bookseller and an unsuccessful one is that the former concentrates on his own problems and the other worries about what other people are doing." [1] In this view, time was better spent working on improving internal business operations than whining about the competition. But as Waldenbooks and B. Dalton outlets proliferated around the country, their influence could hardly be ignored, and by the mid-1970s, a vocal contingent of booksellers was asserting that independents were not only facing ruthless competition, but that publishers were abetting the chains' competitive practices. By the end of that decade, these independents were demanding that the industry act to rectify the situation. But while some organized against the chains during the 1970s and '80s, independent booksellers were not by any means in agreement about the best course of action, and many disapproved of the confrontational stance taken by their more activist fellows.

However, during the 1990s, a perceptible change occurred as independent booksellers displayed much greater unity about the need to defend their interests. This newfound unity was a direct result of the growth of the chain superstores. The superstores disrupted the possibility of peaceful coexistence based on a clear differentiation between chains and independents. No longer could independents simply compare their diverse selections and full service to the small, standardized mall chain. Now they were competing against chain stores that resembled some of the most successful independents of the 1980s. Furthermore, while economic stability had always been elusive for many independents, the problem worsened once the superstores came on the scene. The severity of the situation was underscored by the number of venerable and formerly healthy booksellers who rapidly went out of business after a superstore popped up in the neighborhood. These included some very well known, highly regarded stores around the country: the Chicago chain Kroch's & Brentano's, which went out of business in 1995;

St. Paul's Odegard Books, Albuquerque's Salt of the Earth Books, the Dallas-based chain Taylor's, and Shakespeare & Company of New York City's Upper West Side, all of which went under in 1996; and Washington's Sidney Kramer Books and New York's Books & Company, which both failed in 1997. While these once powerful stores represented some of the more notable failures, closings of bookstores of all kinds rose steadily in the 1990s. In 1995, bookstore failures were up 26 percent from the previous year, with 132 firms closing, and in 1996, the failure rate rose another 14 percent, with 151 firms closing. Most of these stores cited superstore competition as a key factor.[2] Indeed, since my research began, several of the booksellers I interviewed or otherwise had contact with had closed their stores.

At the same time as the economic climate of bookselling became harsher, the culture of the book business was also being transformed. With the major publishing houses becoming corporate, and often conglomerate entities, booksellers' hesitation about crossing publishers with whom they had personal ties was replaced by a sense of betrayal by publishers' bureaucratic policies, which appeared to favor similar large organizations while treating the independents as largely irrelevant. By the 1990s, independent booksellers were united in confronting their major suppliers in ways that would have been hard to imagine just fifteen years earlier.

Contributing to this activist stance, a different kind of bookseller than had been typical early in the century now faced the chain problem. Unlike bookshop owners of decades past, the bookseller of the late twentieth century was rarely concerned with maintaining an image of conservative gentility. Instead, a populist style had become a marketing asset, and a populist identity had given the independents moral justification for overtly political rhetoric and activity. Whereas in the past, independent booksellers shunned controversy as they sought to be pillars of their communities, the latter-day independent sought to be a savior of community life by standing up to those powerful organizations that appeared to threaten local autonomy.

Independent booksellers' activism took three related forms. First, independents agitated to make their trade organizations a base from which to organize. Second, they tried to use antitrust laws to equalize the terms publishers and wholesalers grant to chains and independents. Finally, booksellers engaged in educational campaigns aimed at convincing the public to patronize independents. These campaigns mixed the kind of public relations common to any consumer industry with an effort at consciousness-raising and an attempt to politicize the chain-independent issue. These various strategies were often undertaken simultaneously, but there was considerable debate about which was the most appropriate and effective. One of the deepest disagreements had to do with just how adversarial the independents should be. After a brief period in which more confrontational efforts were on the ascent, independents, led by their trade organizations, moved toward favoring marketing as a way to prevail against the chains.

In this chapter, I describe several examples of these different strategies, including the transformation of the American Booksellers Association into a platform for independents, the 1982, 1994, and 1998 lawsuits charging discriminatory publisher practices that favored the chains, and the Book Sense marketing campaign that began in 1999. These various efforts demonstrate the peculiarity of a social movement composed of small businesspeople. Here, one can see an ongoing tension between the drive toward radicalization, as seen in political and litigation activity, and the drive toward professionalization, as seen in attempts to improve business practices and, ironically, to adopt many of the same methods as the chains employ. These different strategies raise two interrelated questions: What is the difference between marketing and political activity? And how do they represent competing understandings of consumers and consumption?

An Independent Identity

For most of this discussion, I have been speaking of chain and independent businesses as two easily identified (and polarized) camps in the book world. People in the book industry do consider it self-evident who qualifies as an independent and who is a chain bookseller. But the boundary between these two types of enterprises is not actually based on any precise, formal definition. This was brought home to me during an interview I conducted with a bookstore customer who startled me when she called a local bookseller with three outlets a chain. Technically, of course, this customer was right. But I had grown accustomed to the heated debates of the book trade, where the terms "independent" and "chain" are now defined as much by reference to scope and to a state of mind as they are by number of outlets or legal status. In effect, the notion of "independent" has come to be defined in opposition to what is represented by the few very largest chains.

Although the concept of the independent bookseller has existed for a long time, "independent," when referring to booksellers, was not always as loaded a term as it is today. In fact, up until the 1970s, the term "personal" bookseller was used interchangeably with "independent" to describe a single, proprietor-owned bookstore. That earlier label conjured up the personal relationship a bookseller might establish with his clientele, as well as the personal stamp he would put on the character of his store. But owing to poor channels of communication and a lack of inclination, the country's personal booksellers paid little attention to considering what tied them together. That changed as an identity of independence, with its corresponding sense of solidarity and its expression of certain values, started to emerge after the establishment of the modern chain bookstores. This identity coalesced as beleaguered booksellers, facing the competition presented by the new chains, struggled to maintain their economic and cultural status.

A few themes consistently emerge when independents distinguish themselves from chains. Independence signifies smallness (even though the independents count among their members some of the largest bookstores in the country), being locally based, and limited in geographic scope. But along with these organizational attributes comes a certain freedom to act idiosyncratically and according to criteria that are not always economic in nature. Booksellers proudly refer to their independence from a single-minded focus on profit; other considerations are allowed to play a role when retailers are not beholden to investors or a parent organization:

> I think we care more. Independent booksellers, I mean by that description, we are independent. We are in this business for various reasons, and a lot of people are very dedicated to getting ideas and thoughts and words out there for people. And I think chains are concerned with making a certain amount of money.

These independents see themselves, in contrast to chains, as devoted to books for their own sake rather than as a means to acquire monetary reward.[3]

Nevertheless, it has not always been entirely clear just who is a chain and who is an independent. For instance, for many years, Chicago's Kroch's & Brentano's was among the nation's top five general bookstores in terms of both number of outlets and revenue. But this chain of stores stayed confined to the region surrounding Chicago and was also still in the hands of the family that founded it. For at least some in the industry, its private ownership and limited geographic range meant that Kroch's & Brentano's did not qualify as a *real* chain. Additionally, self-described independents today are far more likely to have one or more branches than they were twenty years ago. This occasionally generates heated disagreement over a store's true status as an independent.[4] It can also generate such semantic innovations as the "independent chain," as one Maine bookstore group called itself.[5]

While booksellers have been in the forefront of defining an independent identity, they are not the only ones within the book industry involved in this effort. Since the 1970s, it has been common to use the terms "independent press" and "small press" interchangeably to refer to the thousands of publishers who produce small numbers of titles, often on shoestring budgets.[6] The independent presses frequently describe themselves in similar terms to those used by independent booksellers. Independent presses are "in the American spirit of happy, cranky individualism" and provide "the diverse and idiosyncratic voice in publishing."[7] "In little publishers, there's a great deal more love of books," said one such publisher in an interview. Nevertheless, not everyone in the industry agrees on just what an independent or small press is, or whether they are even equivalent to one another. For some, independent refers to size, for others it implies a particular philosophy, and for still others, it simply means that they are not owned by a conglomerate.[8]

Even less well defined is the notion of an independent book wholesaler or distributor. Members of the book trade only occasionally use this designation, apparently to refer to a wholesaler who carries small press books. Again, what appears key is a refusal to cater to the purely commercial, and a demonstrable commitment to support books that are "deserving" but that may have a limited audience. Here, too, independent refers to a personalized, small-scale enterprise, one that services other small-scale organizations. However, maintaining a strict adherence to these principles is not so easy, as few wholesalers can remain financially viable when their customers and suppliers are limited to small organizations. Consequently, the issue of selling out their independence is a touchy one for some distributors. Indeed, there appears to be an implicit hierarchy of independence among wholesalers, with even the less mainstream firms sometimes criticized for carrying books from the large houses or for emphasizing sales to the chains.

The move toward establishing an identity of independence in these different branches of the industry encapsulates much of what is seen as problematic in the growing influence of commercialism in the book trade. Of course, these developments parallel similar movements in other cultural sectors, from the growth of so-called indie music to the semantic evolution from alternative (news) press to independent press.[9] What differentiates booksellers from these other manifestations of the indie phenomenon, however, is that independent booksellers have almost never seen themselves as standing outside the mainstream of their industry. On the contrary, they have been intent on claiming that what they stand for represents longstanding and still-relevant core values of the book business. In this context, it would make little sense to refer to themselves as alternative booksellers. It is rather the chains that are viewed as having brought a different, and less worthy, sensibility to the trade.

Nonetheless, the willingness to assert an independent identity is tied to some changes in the types of people who entered the book industry in the 1970s and '80s, as one San Francisco Bay Area bookseller explained:

> And this business is filled with idiosyncratic, quirky people. The people in their thirties and up, you know, mid-thirties and early forties, all came out of the '60s. And bookselling is one of those professions where you could go and work because you were not of the system. I mean if you look at Bay Area bookselling, if you look around the country, many of the premier bookstores in the country came out of— certainly not all of them — but many of them came out of the antiwar movements. Cody's, Kepler's, those folks came out of the pacifist movement of the early '50s.[10] And if you go around the country, there is this myth that most booksellers are liberals. And it is a myth. There are many very conservative booksellers. But certainly the Bay Area, much of this community came out of the antiwar movement. Even the sales reps, many of the sales reps came in [from] that same movement.

As I have noted in earlier chapters, the individuals who entered bookselling in the latter part of the twentieth century did not identify with a genteel clientele as much as earlier generations of booksellers did. Similarly, many of these younger booksellers had taken part in or sympathized with the social movements of their day, and so did not find the very idea of activism distasteful, as their predecessors might have. But that is not to say these individuals entered the bookselling profession with the intention of becoming crusaders within the industry. Instead, they saw this profession as a refuge of sorts; the book trade seemed to represent a way to live out their ideals while still earning a living. However, circumstances within the industry changed, and with that, the notion of independence became both identity and cause.

Politicizing the Conflict

By the 1970s, booksellers had identified a number of grievances stemming from chain practices and from publisher actions that benefited the chains. Although some of the details changed over time, the general issues remained much the same from the 1970s through the 1990s. For instance, as we saw in chapter 4, the issue of cooperative advertising dollars was one that rankled booksellers. Independents contended that publishers not only made the procedures for obtaining co-op much simpler for the chains, but that they offered to the chains secret, special co-op allowances that were not equally available to independents.[11]

Especially contentious was the issue of publisher discounts to book retailers. In this context, discount refers to the prices at which publishers sell their books to retailers (calculated in terms of the discount off the suggested retail or cover price). As evidence emerged that the chains received better discounts from publishers than did other booksellers, independents challenged publisher policies as discriminatory. Federal antitrust law (the Robinson-Patman Act) allows suppliers to grant better prices to customers in cases where the supplier has a cost savings, which may arise from large-volume orders. And indeed, it is common in most industries for a supplier to sell goods at a lower price when customers order in large quantities. However, independent booksellers pointed to irregularities in this practice. They objected to publishers' granting favorable discounts to chains even when "drop shipping," that is, shipping books ordered centrally to multiple outlets. Independents claimed that the handling and freight costs involved in this practice cancelled out any cost savings from the larger order, though this issue became less salient in the late 1990s as the major chains expanded their own distribution facilities, and therefore minimized drop shipments.[12] More seriously, the chains were accused of violating the law by using their clout to compel discounts that were not advertised or made available to independents. Once the major chains institutionalized price-cutting in the 1980s, the favorable discount terms they received from publishers were believed to make possible the lower prices that chains offered to the public.

Discriminatory practices were not unheard of in the prechain era. In 1959, the New York Area Booksellers Association discussed taking legal action to force mass-market paperback publishers to make public their discount schedules, as booksellers were suspicious that newsstands were receiving favorable treatment. Just one month earlier, the Federal Trade Commission (FTC) had charged five mass-market publishers with paying promotional allowances to a number of newsstand chains without making them available to other retailers. In 1962, the FTC's case came to a close when a large group of publishers signed consent decrees agreeing to not discriminate among competing customers.[13] When complaints about bookstore chains receiving favorable discounts first surfaced in the late 1970s, it was again in regard to mass-market paperback publishers.[14] After that, the practice appeared to become widespread among a broad range of trade publishers.[15]

In addition, independents and the FTC charged that a number of other irregularities persisted. Publishers allowed chains to automatically deduct from their invoices an amount, selected by the chains, to cover shipment mistakes or books that arrived damaged. Unlike independents, chains did not have to provide documentation for such problems or return damaged books.[16] The automatic deduction also meant that there was no delay in receiving credit, greatly improving the chains' cash flow. Another accusation was that publishers' stated rules concerning returns did not apply to the chains, which were allowed to return books without the usual invoice information and without the time restrictions that applied to other booksellers.[17] The cumulative effect of all these various practices was to give the chains a substantial competitive edge, as they could obtain and return books more cheaply and with less hassle than independents could.

In the early years following the establishment of Waldenbooks and B. Dalton, independents realized that the chains were a force to be reckoned with, but they did not define chain advantages as unjust. Instead, independents' attempts to organize themselves were mostly directed at augmenting their own effectiveness as businesspeople. For instance, in 1973, the Independent Booksellers Cooperative was formed to allow small bookstores to consolidate their orders so as to obtain the higher discounts that large chains were getting.[18] The network of regional bookselling associations across the country also provided a base for assisting independents. While technically open to chain outlets, these organizations had few active chain members, and they increasingly took on activities specifically meant to help their independent constituents.[19] Along with sponsoring group insurance plans and hosting seminars on the nuts and bolts of bookselling, these organizations also occasionally engaged in more partisan efforts aimed at encouraging the public to patronize independent over chain outlets. In 1983, for example, the Pacific Northwest Booksellers Association began a campaign to publicize the differences between independent and chain bookstores. Its slogan, "There's more to a bookstore than bestsellers," highlighted independents' pride in their diverse title selections and wide range of services.[20]

Although the vast majority of regional associations remained open to chain branches at this time, a couple fledgling organizations established themselves as distinctly antichain. In 1977, independent booksellers from the southwest met to consider forming a regional trade group that would exclude people associated with chains. By the following year, the resulting Independent Booksellers Association counted fifty member stores from around the country. Similarly, the short-lived Wisconsin Independent Booksellers formed in the late 1970s, and in 1980, the longer-lasting Oklahoma Independent Booksellers Association was founded.[21]

While the various regional organizations offered a forum in which booksellers could talk about mutual problems and offer mutual assistance, these groups lacked the resources and clout of the booksellers' national trade association, the American Booksellers Association. The ABA was a pivotal organization in the book industry: it sponsored the most important industry gathering in the United States each year, it was a central source of information and education for prospective and established booksellers, it acted as a liaison between booksellers and publishers, and it claimed to speak for American bookselling. This latter task was complicated by the fact that, like the regional associations, the ABA counted chain stores as members, though independents were always in the great majority. Once independents perceived the chains to be a serious threat to their existence, it became increasingly difficult to maintain peaceful coexistence within the same organization, and starting in the mid-1970s, a struggle ensued over how the ABA should position itself vis-à-vis the chain-independent conflict. Over the next two decades, booksellers pressured a reluctant ABA to transform itself into an explicitly and aggressively pro-independent organization, a process that illustrates the development of a strong collective identity among American independent booksellers, with interests separate from and often opposed to other members of the book industry.

The attempts to make the ABA into a platform for independents began in earnest in the late 1970s, when a poor economy, combined with the rapid growth of Waldenbooks and B. Dalton, put the survival of many booksellers in doubt. A massive increase in postage rates hit booksellers especially hard, and publishers' seeming indifference about these higher freight costs contributed to the sense that they were content to let independents flounder. In 1978, after numerous complaints from independents, the ABA board of directors authorized its attorney to investigate evidence of inequitable treatment of large and small booksellers, and articles discussing the issue began to appear regularly in *American Bookseller,* the ABA's monthly magazine. But some independents were not satisfied that the association was responsive enough to their concerns, and in 1979, a group of booksellers put forth a dissident slate for the elections to the ABA board. The board, which was composed of member booksellers, was usually constituted by a nominating committee that solicited suggestions and then put its choices before the membership for approval. Among the official nominees that year was Harry Hoffman, the head of Waldenbooks. Claiming that "independent bookstores just are not being represented," and voicing concern about "conglomerate control of the publishing industry," the dissidents displayed their anger at Hoffman's nomination by calling for the exclusion from ABA membership of bookstores that were not owner-operated. The ABA leadership (made up of hired staff and elected officers and directors) criticized the dissidents and their demands, and the slate went down to defeat.[22]

Discontent with the association continued to grow, however. "Policies which favor the chains seem to be the same ones the ABA actively supports," complained one independent.[23] This bookseller, like others, was frustrated by the ABA's refusal to contemplate legal action against publishers engaged in discriminatory pricing policies. Increasingly, booksellers were viewing legal action as the best strategy for countering the power of the chains and what independents saw as publishers' collaboration with them. The following year at the annual membership meeting, a resolution was adopted directing ABA officers and directors to hold meetings with members across the country to discuss the ABA's role in combating discriminatory policies. These meetings, held in the summer of 1980, were sometimes raucous sessions, with booksellers denouncing their association and its passivity. At the Chicago meeting, one independent issued a damning charge: "[T]he ABA is perceived as a weak, impotent, moribund organization incapable of taking any action which could force publishers to address these problems. And this perception is correct."

A statement from the Northern California Booksellers Association started from the same conclusion:

> The American Booksellers Association must recognize the revolutionary transformation which has occurred in retail bookselling over the last ten years. We cannot allow ourselves to be lulled into complacency by self-help bromides and exhortations of positive thinking. We must recognize that the unfair privileges accorded national chains pose a critical threat to the independent bookstore. The only meaningful action which can insure the survival of the independent bookstore is the analysis and reform of the underlying economic structures which have caused the unprecedented concentration of retail bookselling over the last ten years.

In his report on the meetings, the ABA's associate executive director warned the board that booksellers found the ABA badly out of touch with its membership, and that continued inaction could spell the demise of the organization.[24]

Nevertheless, the ABA leadership proceeded with caution, expressing numerous concerns about engaging in litigation, including the cost, the possibility of countersuits, the problem of alienating publishers whose exhibit fees at the ABA's annual convention paid for a substantial part of the association's budget, and the question of charging its own chain members with criminality. Rather than assuming a confrontational stance toward publishers and widening the rift between independents and chains, the leadership tried to stress common ground and the preferability of amicably negotiating better terms for independents. Plenty of booksellers agreed with this position:

> Authors, publishers, and booksellers should be mutually supportive elements in a book creation/delivery system. Differences are bound to arise among the members of the system. Discussion and negotiation are the reasonable ways to resolve differences between dependent entities. . . . Once legal action is initiated, we harden our position toward each other and push into the future, after years of litigation and expense, the solutions that would benefit us now.[25]

A 1982 survey of ABA members found a wide range of opinion on the question of litigation. While 59 percent approved of their dues being used for an antitrust suit (with 33 percent disapproving), 62 percent said they would be unwilling to see their dues raised for this purpose.[26] The ABA leadership cited this survey as further reason to not engage in legal action.

The most controversial issue of this period arose in April 1982, when the Northern California Booksellers Association (NCBA), the most militant of the regional associations, filed its own suit against mass-market publisher Avon Books, a division of the Hearst Corporation. The NCBA charged Avon with giving preferential, unpublicized discounts to chain booksellers (including B. Dalton, Waldenbooks, Crown, Doubleday, and Brentano's), therefore discriminating against independents while helping to fund the chains' growth.[27] Booksellers around the country were highly divided about the wisdom of this move, and a heated debate occurred at the ABA convention held in Anaheim the month after the suit was filed. Led by a California contingent, a group of booksellers took over the agenda of the membership meeting, and called for endorsement of the NCBA lawsuit. After the ABA board refused to give support to the lawsuit, one bookseller introduced a resolution declaring no confidence in the board. The membership voted the resolution down, but by a very narrow margin.[28]

The new president of the ABA, an independent from Boulder, Colorado, deplored the events at the meeting, calling them factionalizing that would dissipate independents' strength:

> The gentle persuasion of the ABA Publisher Planning Committee has contributed, and will continue to contribute, to the improvement of publisher terms. . . . The ABA Board of Directors was encouraged by some of you at

Anaheim to think of the association as a sort of Kamakazi [*sic*] plane which the ABA Board had the right and responsibility to pilot into the nearest battleship. In the name of "simple justice," all real hope for continued improvement was to have been abandoned. I think that the Board acted responsibly by not succumbing to this view.[29]

In response, an NCBA bookseller (and the primary plaintiff in the lawsuit) expressed contempt for those ABA officials who seemed to believe that placating publishers was more important than standing up for the rights of independents:

In [executive director] Roysce Smith's interview in August, *American Bookseller,* he unashamedly admitted to all intents and purposes that the ABA exists in a client relationship to publishers and that this relationship is sacred as long as the convention accounts for 60% of ABA's income. . . . Had [President] Laing shown to us the same open-mindedness and "gentle persuasion" that he is so proud of exercising with publishers, then we feel his desire for unity would have been more fully realized.[30]

Although the ABA board did vote its official support for the lawsuit a few months later, many booksellers remained dissatisfied by its stance against providing financial assistance to the case.

Conflict erupted again in 1984 when a group calling itself the Independent Committee for an Effective ABA echoed earlier efforts by putting up alternative candidates for the ABA board election. Once again, the dissidents rallied against the continuing reluctance of the ABA leadership to combat unfair trade practices aggressively. Denouncing the latest choice of nominees for the board, a group that included representatives of college and department store book departments, the dissidents promoted a platform meant to address independents' particular interests. This included greater ABA support for the NCBA case and a revamped dues structure requiring members with multiple outlets (i.e., chains) to pay more. The ABA leadership criticized the dissidents for bypassing the regular channels for addressing grievances, and for trying to redefine the organization as one that served only independents.

But this time, the dissidents were quite successful, winning four out of five contested seats. At the next membership meeting, the new look to the ABA board did not go unrecognized. A department store bookseller voiced her alarm that neither department stores nor chains were represented. "We who engage in large volume bookselling are made to feel like the enemy," she said.[31] As this bookseller suggested, the ABA was beginning to reflect the position that the differences between large and small booksellers, between owner-operated and chain stores, were greater than their common interests. Some independents were also troubled by this polarization. Wrote a Virginia bookseller,

> The most important issue that I see facing the ABA today is in determining representation of large and small booksellers on the ABA Board of Directors. I don't think there is a perfect solution, but there must be some compromises or the ABA will not be effective in helping all booksellers. . . . I truly believe that we can all work together. After all, we all sell books.[32]

However, the ABA took another step toward aligning itself with the independents' cause soon thereafter, when the new board voted to fund an evaluation of an Avon study that was a cornerstone of the publisher's defense against the lawsuit. The association had finally given material support along with moral support to the NCBA's efforts.[33] In doing so, the ABA was drawing closer to an official recognition that a general desire among retailers to sell books was not necessarily equivalent to unity of purpose, and that different approaches to book retailing could be fundamentally incompatible.

The Legal Front

In the meantime, the NCBA's case was proceeding slowly. Some months after first filing its suit, the NCBA named Bantam Books, the country's largest paperback publisher, as a codefendant. Both Avon and Bantam admitted that the chains received different terms from other booksellers; Avon offered higher discounts, and Bantam offered the chains "incentive payments" for their purchase of Bantam books. But both publishers contended that these deals were cost-justified, that is, it was less expensive to do business with the chains than with other booksellers. Additionally, Avon and Bantam claimed that they were simply meeting the competition presented by other publishers who provided the chains with such discounts.

Finally, late in 1986, a U.S. district court judge ruled that the higher discounts Avon was giving the chains could not be justified on the basis of cost savings to the publisher. Judge Thelton E. Henderson also found that Avon had kept its discount schedule secret, thus making it impossible for independents to take measures to become eligible for the better prices. In his decision, the judge noted that the chains' ability to open and stock new outlets had been markedly facilitated by Avon's policies: "The evidence suggests that the extra revenue provided to the chains by Avon's preferential discount helped the chains increase the number of their retail outlets and dramatically increase the volume of their purchases from Avon."[34] Judge Henderson made it clear that Avon's practices were no aberration, but were common among most of the major paperback publishers. Not surprisingly, Avon decided to appeal the decision.

Throughout the proceedings, the chains themselves remained notably quiet, refusing to comment publicly beyond repeating that they did not engage in illegal practices. But it looked as if they might be pulled more directly into the fray when shortly after Avon filed its appeal, the NCBA requested an injunction prohibiting Walden, Dalton, and Crown from receiving any unpublished discount or payment. The NCBA reasoned that this would be the most expeditious way to gain relief. Upholding its litigious reputation, Crown promptly filed a countersuit, charging the NCBA with conspiring to fix and raise prices. In his statements, Crown president Robert Haft sought to reframe the issue, describing the conflict as not simply a dispute between large chains and small independents, but as an attempt by independents to deprive consumers of the benefits of low-priced books. In this view, readers' interests were tied to those of the chains, while independents were depicted as greedy retailers who wanted to make consumers and large booksellers pay for the independents' own inefficiencies.

But Haft did not have the opportunity to pursue this interpretation of the situation in the courts. After so many years of litigation, both publishers and the NCBA were ready to settle, and the case wound down later that year. Avon, Bantam, and other mass-market publishers announced new discount plans that made it somewhat easier for independents to earn better discounts. Once the publishers signaled that they would finally agree to change their pricing policies, the NCBA and the chains dropped their suits against one another, and a settlement was reached between Avon and the NCBA.[35]

The independents did gain improved terms from mass-market publishers, though they still found most policies less than ideal. But perhaps a more important effect of the lawsuit was to further alter relations within the book industry. The revelations made by Avon and Bantam, along with the district court ruling, helped to convince formerly skeptical independents that publishers truly were engaged in unfair practices. And the reforms finally agreed to by the publishers demonstrated that, contrary to the ABA's initial fears, a legal action could have positive results for independents. Independents thus emerged with a strengthened sense that they were an embattled group in the book world, but that they could successfully fight for their rights.

Despite the changes promised by the mass-market publishers, the question of unequal pricing policies did not end with the NCBA suit. Once the case was resolved, the Federal Trade Commission, which had been monitoring the proceedings, decided to renew its interest in the matter. Following the stormy ABA meetings of 1980, the FTC had opened an investigation into publishers' discounts, but held back from acting until the NCBA case was concluded.[36] After determining that discriminatory pricing practices were still widespread, the commission filed a complaint in 1988 against six of the country's largest publishers: Harper & Row (which later became Harper-Collins), Macmillan, Hearst/William Morrow, Putnam Berkley, Simon & Schuster, and Random House. By including mass-market and trade divisions within its complaint, the FTC broadened scrutiny well beyond the paperback houses to encompass a large section of American book publishing.

The publishers mounted the same defense that had been used in the NCBA case — that the differential treatment was cost-justified, and that they were meeting the competition presented by other publishers. This last point was especially revealing, as it demonstrated the extent to which publishers had become dependent on the chains' good graces. As Harper & Row protested, the publishers didn't see much leeway when it came to pricing:

> In addition, customers promptly inform sellers whenever their prices are not competitive with those of other suppliers. Were Harper & Row to refuse to provide the competitive discounts offered by other publishers, the business would go to the competition. The law does not require that Harper & Row, or any supplier, must commit economic suicide.[37]

In contrast to an earlier era when publishers held the balance of power, a publisher now risked bankruptcy if it did not do what was necessary to induce the chains to buy its books. Indeed, the FTC described examples of times when Dalton and Waldenbooks had temporarily boycotted Bantam and Doubleday until the publishers gave the chains the extra discounts they were seeking.[38]

The entire book industry took a keen interest in the FTC proceedings, with independents hoping that the clout of the federal government would force publishers to equalize their treatment of booksellers. But members of the book business were not the only ones concerned about the FTC action. A piece in *Chain Store Age Executive* expressed alarm at the case, and urged chain retailers of all kinds to lobby the federal government to enact legislation formalizing the right of suppliers to give price breaks to customers who buy in volume. "Otherwise," the author wrote, "chain store retailing that began with A&P 130 years ago, and that withstood congressional interference in the 1930s, may be jeopardized by the Federal Trade Commission."[39] By challenging the influence exercised by major customers, the FTC was threatening to hinder the economies of scale that made mass merchandising possible.

In 1992, the FTC announced that it had reached consent agreements with the six publishers. But there were then several more years of delay. One reason was the addition of a seventh publisher, Bantam Doubleday Dell, to the FTC complaint. But for some time, FTC commissioners were also deadlocked on whether or not to approve the agreements. This was in part related to President Clinton's 1995 appointment of Robert Pitofsky as FTC chair. Pitofsky had been a principal defense counsel for Bantam Doubleday Dell during the FTC investigation and so recused himself from the case, leaving the commission split two to two on accepting the agreements. Then, in 1996, the FTC surprised observers by simply dismissing its complaints against the publishers. Seventeen years after first taking an interest in the matter, the FTC said that it had reached no decision on whether illegal practices had taken place. Instead, it claimed that developments within the book industry, including the ABA suit (see below), limited the adequacy of the consent agreements. "In view of these developments, further investigation, and possibly litigation, by the Commission does not appear to be a necessary or prudent use of scarce public resources," it concluded.[40]

Through their decision, government regulators demonstrated that they were not willing to discourage chain retailing. As an FTC representative told a group of booksellers, the agency was interested in preserving competition within the marketplace, not in creating a level playing field for businesses.[41] The government appeared to be indicating that as long as a monopoly situation did not exist, it would be hesitant to intervene in the marketplace for books. The types of arguments made by independents, such as the importance of local institutions, the idea that as a "different" kind of object, books needed special protection, or the fairness of differential pricing policies, were not consistent with the principles of a free market, and thus had no place in these considerations.

The decision was a disappointment to independents, but the setback was overshadowed by other events that had been occurring in the meantime. While the FTC case was lumbering along, the superstores had come on the scene and significantly changed the economic and cultural climate for booksellers. Startled by the rapidity with which the chains were able to open and stock their warehouse-sized outlets, independents assumed that publisher (and wholesaler) cooperation was again key to the chains' ability to expand. As independents felt renewed urgency about the situation, they again debated the kinds of actions they should take to combat the chains. However, unlike the discussions of the 1980s, there was now little disagreement about the need to take bold measures. Few independents believed that the chains' quest for expansion would leave them unharmed. And with the publishing landscape so changed by all the mergers and acquisitions that had occurred, independent booksellers now felt less affinity with their suppliers, and less compunction about crossing them.

The new unity of purpose among independents could be seen in the movement to close regional bookseller associations to chain outlets. Over a period of a little more than a year, starting with the Northern California Booksellers Association in 1993, four of the ten major regional bookseller associations voted to include "Independent" in their names, and/or to change their bylaws to reinforce their independent status (e.g., by excluding members who did not have headquarters in the region or by denying voting rights to branch stores).[42] In 1996 and 1997, three more of the main regional bookseller organizations followed suit.[43] Additionally, between 1992 and 1995, another nine subregional groups made similar moves (joining the already existing Oklahoma Independent Booksellers Association).[44] These actions represented formal statements that independent and chain booksellers did not share the same interests, and ought not to work together.[45]

Although most of these organizations acted swiftly and with minimal dissention, it initially appeared that the ABA would again refuse to engage in actions that risked alienating other members of the book industry. The 1993 membership meeting was reminiscent of meetings a decade earlier, with members accusing the leadership of not taking the chain threat to independents seriously. Once again, the specific issue most in dispute was whether the association should contemplate legal action. After denouncing the ABA board for being indifferent and ineffective, members introduced and approved a motion directing the board to investigate unfair practices. Also approved was a motion to launch a national public relations campaign stressing the importance of independent bookstores.[46] This latter initiative would prove to be highly significant a few years later.

Although board members decided not to make the information public at the time, they had already been preparing a legal action. On the day preceding the 1994 ABA convention (the most important annual gathering for the entire book industry), the board announced a lawsuit against five publishers for discriminatory practices that favored the chains.[47] The lawsuit caused something of an uproar at the convention, with several publishers criticizing the timing of it and the divisiveness it brought to the book trade. Independent booksellers, on the other hand, appeared jubilant. At least during the ABA membership meetings, not one voice of dissent was heard. One bookseller spoke of how the mood had changed:

> I had a real sense of liberation today that I hadn't experienced before, walking the floor. So many people smiled at me and said, "Go for it." They couldn't say anything because their guys are doing it. But so many of them are behind us.

Booksellers were clearly buoyed by the sense that they had done something very daring in defense of their rights, and that this was also for the greater good of book culture. Another bookseller related to the membership how he had attended Sunday mass at a nearby church. The priest first asked how many booksellers were present, and then asked about publishers. But before giving publishers a chance to respond, the priest admonished that there were probably not many present, but those who were should treat bookstores on an even plane. The booksellers at the membership meeting cheered this story, and one called out, "At least we know God's on our side today." For these booksellers, the act of standing up to the powerful publishing establishment was colored by moral purpose as well as self-interest.[48]

As the suit dragged on over the next two years, bookseller support for the action remained high. Some others in the book industry, however, lamented how differences had become so overtly politicized. *Publishers Weekly* retained its opposition to the lawsuit: "It is clear that we are now beginning to see the true costs of the litigation, above and beyond legal fees; the dispute serves to exaggerate the fault lines already present in the business."[49] For their part, publishers defended themselves by arguing that they were simply following standard business practices. In a motion to dismiss the case, the accused publishers asserted that the lawsuit stemmed from

> a nostalgic longing for less competitive times . . . whatever the virtues of such times past, defendants ought not and cannot be made scapegoats for the difficulties that some booksellers now may be experiencing in the marketplace due to their inability or unwillingness to adjust to a new competitive world.[50]

As the publishers described it, retrograde booksellers could not accept that a new economic order had left them far behind. In this new world where efficiency, innovation, and hard-nosed business acumen were rewarded, the sentimentality exhibited by independents had no place.

Nevertheless, the ABA appeared to have collected enough evidence to convince the publishers to settle. In February 1995, the first settlement was reached with Hugh Lauter Levin. Levin agreed to abide by rules specifying nondiscrimination in pricing, credit, and returns. Houghton Mifflin was the next to settle, also admitting no wrongdoing while agreeing to new terms for discounts and promotional allowances. By the autumn of 1996, settlements had been reached with all of the affected publishers, each agreeing to similar terms.[51] Although booksellers expressed some satisfaction with these results, the sense that independents were under siege had not dissipated. Nor had the belief that, if necessary, booksellers should take their grievances to court. Indeed, the following year, it was discovered that Penguin had been granting "unauthorized" discounts to a couple dozen customers, a practice that had continued even after the consent decree with the ABA had been signed. After an investigation, Penguin agreed to pay the ABA and its members $25 million, the largest settlement in the history of U.S. antitrust discrimination law.[52]

Still, this success did not mark the end of litigation. In March 1998, the ABA, along with twenty-five independent booksellers, filed another lawsuit, this time against Barnes & Noble and Borders. The suit, filed in the U.S. District Court for Northern California (which had been such a favorable setting for the NCBA case), claimed that the two chains violated both the federal Robinson-Patman Act and California unfair trade practices laws. The ABA contended that the chains used their market clout to coerce unlawful preferential terms from a large number of publishers and wholesalers. Publisher reaction was muted, though the head of Random House expressed disappointment in continued legal actions that "poison the industry." On the other hand, Len Riggio, the head of Barnes & Noble, issued an open letter condemning the ABA's campaign against the chain and arguing that Barnes & Noble had broken no laws, but on the contrary had been a positive force by increasing the availability of books in the United States.[53] Independent booksellers were initially optimistic that the case would be another step forward in restraining chain power, but this time, the court proved not to be very sympathetic to the independents' claims. After some unfavorable rulings by the presiding judge, the ABA settled with the chain defendants. The settlement was largely a defeat for the independents, as Barnes & Noble and Borders agreed only to pay the association an amount less than the cost of its legal fees. Just as significantly, the ABA agreed to destroy all documents and depositions obtained during the case, and to refrain from any further litigation for three years.[54]

While these various legal actions consumed the book industry, they did not attract a great deal of attention from the public. By appealing to the courts and regulatory bodies, independents were asking that their claims be legitimated by the public's surrogates, but individual citizens were not being asked to take positive action themselves. However, one other incident illustrates how independent booksellers and their supporters did sometimes challenge the chains on not just legal, but moral grounds as well, and organized opposition to the chains among both government and the public. In late 1998, Barnes & Noble, the country's largest bookseller, proposed the acquisition of Ingram, the nation's largest book wholesaler. The proposed merger created great alarm among many sectors of the book industry as they faced the prospect of a single company controlling a significant portion of book distribution in the United States. Opponents of the merger not only warned that it would result in one organization holding undue power, but also claimed that independent booksellers would be gravely harmed if Ingram, one of their biggest suppliers, was controlled by Barnes & Noble, their biggest competitor. This was because Ingram's knowledge of competitive internal information on independents' finances and buying practices could potentially be transferred to Barnes & Noble.

Independent booksellers, led by the ABA, then organized a campaign calling on the Federal Trade Commission to nix the deal. Going well beyond mere lobbying, booksellers appealed to the public to phone and write letters in opposition to the merger. By placing antimerger petitions in their stores, booksellers collected over 125,000 signatures of bookstore customers to present to the FTC.[55] The support of other organizations and local government was also mobilized; for instance, the City Council of Berkeley, California, passed a resolution in opposition to the merger. Working Assets Long Distance, a socially responsible long-distance telephone company, even picked up the cause, and after it publicized the issue on its phone bills, its customers made 35,000 calls to the FTC.[56] The language of the Working Assets appeal mirrored that of the independents, evoking the specter of a giant corporation amassing great power and squashing competition:

> Barnes & Noble, the nation's leading bookseller, is consolidating its domination of the book industry by buying Ingram Book Group, the largest supplier of books to independent bookstores. Ingram knows which books sell better, as well as the financial condition of almost every bookstore. Having access to such vital information will provide Barnes & Noble with an overwhelming competitive advantage. Call Robert Pitofsky, Chairman of the Federal Trade Commission, at 202/326–2100 and urge him to block the merger of Barnes & Noble and Ingram. (There is no after-hours answering machine.) It is profoundly anti-competitive and might be the death blow to thousands of independent booksellers.[57]

Critics of the merger highlighted the opposing interests of Barnes & Noble and the independents and sought to equate the public interest with the independents' position. Thus, the political nature of the chain-independent conflict was made explicit; the public was being told that rather than just dismiss this as an internecine fight among interchangeable competitors in the marketplace, individuals had a duty to choose sides and then act on that choice. Whether because of public sentiment or simply because of the antitrust issues involved, federal regulators also took a dim view of the merger. When it looked as if the FTC would indeed block the deal, Barnes & Noble and Ingram called it off.[58] This victory for independents and the ABA showed that concerns about bigness in the book industry still had some resonance among Americans.

A sensitivity to bigness also helps explain why, around this time, independents were coming to define Amazon as equivalent to the major chains. Independents were increasingly seeing their interests as being opposed to those of online-only booksellers; as one indication of this, the Northern California Independent Booksellers Association altered its criteria for core member status in 1997 to require a physical storefront location.[59] The loss of customers to Amazon and other online retailers was felt especially keenly by those bookstores in college towns or other areas with a concentration of highly educated individuals, as such people were often early adopters of computer technology as well as steady book buyers. The Internet's ability to lure away these customers caused considerable bitterness, since they had been seen as potentially receptive to the antichain message. But what really put Amazon in the same category as the chains were its competitive strategies, such as its discount policies, and its growing clout in the industry. Similar to the chains, Amazon was perceived as receiving favorable treatment from publishers. One incident that infuriated independents concerned the publication of *Harry Potter and the Goblet of Fire* in 2000. The publisher, Scholastic, agreed to allow Amazon to ship the carefully embargoed book in time for it to reach customers' homes on the official laydown (release) day. Other booksellers had designed their Harry Potter plans to comply with Scholastic's requirement that the book could not leave a secure environment until the laydown date. When the Amazon deal was made public less than three weeks before that date, independents scrambled to get Scholastic to approve their own "secure" plans to ship presold books.[60]

Scholastic insisted that it treated all booksellers equally and that its last-minute policy conditionally allowing early shipment of presold books was not in response to any pressure from Amazon, but was formed in order to be consistent with how *Harry Potter* was being sold in Britain. Nevertheless, independents saw this incident as simply more evidence that the major booksellers had special influence in the trade and were able to obtain privileges that gave them an unfair advantage. The advantages that Amazon could garner were generally similar to those of the chains, but some were unique to Internet retailing. In particular, independents resented how on-line booksellers could usually avoid charging sales tax (thus lowering the price to consumers), and in 1999, the ABA launched an initiative to lobby local and state governments for sales tax equity.[61]

Altogether, the lawsuits, the action against the Barnes & Noble–Ingram merger, the sales tax campaign, and other incidents demonstrated the great breach that existed between the ABA and the chains and Amazon by the late 1990s. In 1997, Barnes & Noble declined to renew its ABA membership, signaling its belief that the association no longer represented bookstores like its own.[62] That same year, the ABA followed the lead of the regional associations by formally redefining itself as an organization meant to serve independents operating physical stores. A new strategic plan setting forth the association's mission opened with a definition of the ABA's primary constituents:

> ABA's core member is the independent bookstore with a store front location which is operated by professional independent booksellers according to sound business principles. Although ABA will provide programs and services to others in the bookselling industry, its primary focus will be on its core members.[63]

After two decades of controversy, the ABA had firmly thrown its weight behind the independent bookseller. But the organization, like its membership, was still not entirely comfortable with an adversarial stance. And indeed, the ABA was starting to rethink the means through which the fortunes of independents could be improved.

From Militance to Marketing

During the years when legal and organizational measures were taken to counter and isolate the chains, independents had also engaged in public relations campaigns to promote the merits of the independent store. These campaigns took the form of advertisements, brochures, bumper stickers, and posters urging customers to support their local independent; public-speaking appearances to get a similar message out; and from 1994 until 1997, a National Independent Booksellers Week coordinated by the American Booksellers

Association. The event, originally designed by a PR firm hired by the ABA, used slogans such as "Celebrating Your Independent" and "Building Community Foundations" to gain extra media attention and, hopefully, extra public sympathy for independent booksellers. The ABA even formed an alliance with the nonprofit Habitat for Humanity to cross-promote each other's causes during the week. The ABA used this partnership with Habitat to further indicate independents' commitment to bettering their communities.[64]

These activities signaled the future of ABA efforts. At the same time that the ABA filed its lawsuit against the chains and led the opposition to the Barnes & Noble–Ingram merger, it also began to move its advocacy efforts in a new direction. In the process, the ABA would again draw back from a confrontational style and instead engage in public relations endeavors that in many ways emulated the sophisticated marketing of its chain opponents. The heightened focus on marketing can be seen in various reorganizational moves that took place within the ABA starting in the late 1990s. In the fall of 1998, the association hired Michael F. Hoynes, whose background was in advertising and marketing, to oversee the ABA's marketing programs. At the same time, the ABA eliminated the position of director of research, an office that for many years had collected statistics and information relevant to the membership. As the ABA stated, its research was now to be more focused on implementing its marketing campaigns.[65] A few years later, another department was subordinated to marketing when the ABA cut the staff positions in charge of membership. An ABA executive stated, "Increasingly in not-for-profits, the trend is to fold membership into marketing. The jobs became irrelevant because recruiting efforts are all done through marketing."[66]

The new marketing initiatives took a variety of forms, but were notable for employing slick methods that independent booksellers had typically not bothered to learn in the past. Indeed, many of these efforts resembled the kinds of strategies that had formerly distinguished the chains. The majority of the ABA's marketing initiatives were brought under the umbrella of a national campaign called Book Sense, which the ABA launched in 1999. Through Book Sense, the ABA hoped to win over consumers with advertisements and promotional materials that could "brand" independents. Using the tagline "Independent Bookstores for Independent Minds," the ABA meant to create in consumer consciousness the association of independent booksellers with a set of characteristics that underlay the independent bookseller's identity, and that market research found would resonate positively among book buyers: knowledge, passion, character, community, and personality.[67]

There were a number of facets to the Book Sense campaign. Booksellers who decided to participate in the program signed a letter of agreement pledging to display Book Sense decals, window stickers, and posters, and to prominently place the Book Sense logo on store bookmarks and shopping bags.[68] A gift certificate program enabled any Book Sense store to redeem gift certificates purchased from a different Book Sense bookstore. The Book Sense Bestseller List, launched in November 1999, was meant to rival other national bestseller lists and bring to independents some of the clout that such lists wield among publishers. The major bestseller lists, especially the one published by the *New York Times,* are among the most powerful marketing tools in the industry, gaining a title media publicity, prominent retail displays, and increased readership.[69] Stores known to report to the *New York Times* list have an easier time getting regular visits from publishers' sales representatives, and booking appearances by sought-after authors on publicity tours, as publishers are keen to boost the sales of their books at reporting stores. The ABA intended for the Book Sense list to also serve this dual function — to sell more books to readers who gravitate to bestsellers, and perhaps more important, by selling large numbers of select titles, to gain the deference of publishers perceived as seeing independents as irrelevant.

One of the original components of Book Sense was the "Book Sense 76" list (renamed "Book Sense Picks" in 2004).[70] Similar to the bestseller list, the Book Sense list was meant to raise sales of books promoted by independents and thus make the independents a selling force to be reckoned with. Rather than reporting books already selling well, the monthly list of seventy-six titles (later reduced to forty) was compiled through recommendations of deserving books by Book Sense booksellers. Booksellers were then encouraged to prominently display and otherwise promote some or all of the titles. The ABA also pursued co-op advertising deals with publishers of Book Sense titles.

The most expensive and difficult Book Sense program to implement was BookSense.com, which provided participating independents with an e-commerce vehicle. After several delays, BookSense.com was launched in November 2000. Booksellers who joined the program (for a fee) had access to Web page templates, which they could customize for their stores, and to a mechanism for processing payments. Orders were actually filled by the wholesaler, Baker & Taylor. With Americans swept up by visions of the Internet as the shopping mall (and the billboards) of the future, the ABA considered BookSense.com an essential component of its marketing campaign. Yet, by late 2002, there were only about 230 bookstores that had signed up with BookSense.com, representing perhaps a fifth of Book Sense members.[71]

One of Book Sense's later initiatives is interesting for the way in which it capitalized on the marketing of other brands. Many companies today enter into alliances to cross-merchandise their products along with apparently unrelated goods. The ABA entered this territory with an alliance with Coca-Cola. Through a program called "Book Cash," customers who sent in a number of proofs-of-purchase from Coca-Cola's Minute Maid brand drinks received a certificate giving them four dollars off the price of a book at participating Book Sense bookstores.[72] Subsequent ABA cross-promotional deals were made with the *New York Times,* Pizza Hut, and Visa, among others.[73] The ABA might have taken the concept too far, though, when it entered into a partnership with Minute Maid to promote both books and Bacardi Mixers to book clubs. A number of booksellers found the drink rather remote from what they believed books represent, and the deal prompted some to express concern about the ABA partnering "with corporate entities." In response to the criticism, the ABA promised to seek out appropriate partners, but still remained committed to doing cross-promotions.[74]

Along with these different initiatives, the ABA took out advertisements promoting Book Sense in the *New York Times,* in national magazines such as the *New Yorker, Smithsonian, Gourmet,* and *Conde Nast Traveler,* and by underwriting programs on National Public Radio.[75] The choice of venues reflected not only the upscale, highly educated audience of readers targeted by independents, but also the desire to reach others in the industry. The campaign was meant to show publishers, agents, and authors that independents count, every bit as much as the chains, as visible, sophisticated merchandisers of books.

The ABA put an enormous amount of resources into the Book Sense campaign. Between 1999 and 2001, the ABA invested approximately $10 million in Book Sense and BookSense.com, contributing to a decline in the organization's net assets.[76] Along with the financial and staff commitment, the ABA devoted much of its communication with its membership to urge booksellers not only to join the campaign, but to do so with the enthusiasm of religious converts. Indeed, the internal marketing campaign to convince independents of the value and importance of Book Sense appeared just as strenuous as the external marketing campaign. Through newsletters, mailings, and meetings, ABA staff and officers exhorted booksellers to push the gift certificates, to display the Book Sense 76 titles, to stamp the Book Sense logo on their newsletters.

The ABA also renamed some of its preexisting programs to bring them into the Book Sense fold. For instance, the American Booksellers Book of the Year (ABBY) award was renamed the Book Sense Book of the Year. This represented another way to get exposure for the Book Sense name and demonstrated the ABA's intent to integrate its activities that promote books or booksellers under the Book Sense umbrella. This also created additional pressure on independents to join Book Sense, as only Book Sense members could submit nominations, and only top titles from the Book Sense 76 list (also chosen by Book Sense members) were eligible for nomination, compared to the old system where any ABA member could nominate a book for an ABBY. Presumably, this system did not meet universal approval, as it was later changed so that any ABA member store could nominate books.[77]

According to the ABA, Book Sense was a real success. The organization proudly pointed to the number of Book Sense titles that made national bestseller lists, though there is no real evidence that being a Book Sense title was the key factor in a book's popularity. And the ABA claimed that Book Sense helped member stores increase sales, though there is no way to quantitatively measure the effectiveness of the campaign.[78] Oddly enough, as of 2004, the ABA did not appear to have conducted any studies evaluating the extent to which Book Sense had gained name recognition among consumers. If such a study had been conducted, it probably would have found little awareness among even regular patrons of independents. Nevertheless, the trade group made the Book Sense brand its primary tool for saving independent bookstores.

The Independent Brand

Branding, of course, became one of the more shopworn buzzwords of the 1990s, as not only private businesses, but a host of public and nonprofit bodies determined that refining their brands was key to achieving their various goals. With branding, an organization attaches a particular image or a set of meanings to its product. Despite its current trendiness, this is not a new approach in retailing. As William Leach notes, the concept of the "central idea," taken from theater, was used in nineteenth-century department stores to bring all elements of decoration, lighting, display, and so on, to create a unified impression.[79] And while they may not have called it branding, numerous retailers throughout the twentieth century sought to carefully control the images associated with their store names.

However, branding has an uneven history in the book industry. Unlike with other manufactured consumer goods, branding rarely works in publishing, since few readers buy a book based on familiarity with or regard for a publisher. Exceptions to this rule do exist, including certain computer book lines and some genre fiction, most notably, romance novels. Indeed, a Harlequin is virtually synonymous with a type of romance novel in popular consciousness. But in general, efforts to brand books have failed. The notion of branding was also rarely applied to bookstores until the chains appeared. But as I have shown, Waldenbooks and B. Dalton achieved their successes in part by exercising strict control over the chain image, especially through standardizing the look and experience of their outlets.

As the chains demonstrate, a consistent and reliable image is key to the branding strategy. Branding thus represents a highly rationalized form of marketing, leaving little about the consumer's impression of a store to chance. Yet it is precisely that standardized experience provided by the chains that is denigrated by the independents, and to which they are trying to provide an alternative. In a rather odd juxtaposition, Book Sense is attempting to communicate that independent bookstores represent a predictably idiosyncratic experience. As the ABA stated,

> The cornerstone of an effort by the American Booksellers Association members to establish a brand identity, Book Sense seeks to build a national identity for independent bookstores while celebrating the unique character of each store — to create awareness of independent booksellers across the country and underscore their collective strength to consumers.[80]

The irony of branding independence has not been entirely lost on the ABA, and part of its efforts have been focused on convincing its membership that a national brand of and for independent minds is not a contradiction in terms. In response to an independent who asked, "Are we independent bookstores becoming a giant chain, with the ABA functioning as our corporate HQ?" Carl Lennertz, the former senior marketing consultant of Book Sense, insisted that was not the case:

> Book Sense is strictly a vehicle, a shorthand message that quickly gets across the positive message about our attributes and says that we are still important, still a force, and still a vital place to buy books despite what the media or sales reports say. . . . Book Sense is a lens: your huge range of efforts, which generally go unnoticed beyond your loyal customers due to the lack of a collective voice, can be "gathered" and shot through the lens almost laser-like to the intended audience — the media, authors, publishers, and the public.[81]

The technique of branding tries to distill the most important aspects of a product into a few easily remembered themes or slogans. What Lennertz is emphasizing here is the efficiency of persuasion when the sellers' messages have been encapsulated in this way.

However, branding involves more than external communications; it also necessarily affects internal operations. Independents are thus asked to do more than just give their assent to the Book Sense concept. In order for Book Sense to be viable, the ABA needed to enroll a critical mass of booksellers. This it was able to do in a relatively short time; by the end of 2000, 1,226 bookstores had joined up (compared to a total ABA membership of 2,461 stores in April 2001).[82] But a more difficult job was to convince a group of businesspeople who were used to running their stores as they saw fit to participate actively in the various programs of Book Sense. Rather than implementing the entire campaign, booksellers appeared to prefer to pick and choose which Book Sense components they applied and how often. Furthermore, Book Sense proponents had to contain some independent dissent over the general strategy. Facing such dissent, Lennertz stressed the seeming inevitability of adopting the contemporary appeals to consumers that the chains use so adeptly:

> Amazon.com and B&N have the brands of the moment. The challenge of getting our huge, sprawling messages into a sound bite was both critical and almost impossible. And yes, it's a shame that we even have to sound bite ourselves, but that's the game today. . . . Could we have used a different word just amongst ourselves, a gentler word? Bonding instead of branding? Or both. The brand is our face to the world, a means towards an end; the bond is what we all feel now with each other. It was and is absolutely critical to the success of Book Sense that the public see that we're linked arm-in-arm, happy to display a book recommended by a bookseller from across the country! Happy to sell a gift certificate good at another store! Very symbolic, very powerful . . . VERY tangible. Independent booksellers can come to work each day, feeling connected to thousands of other independent booksellers! As one bookseller said: Connected strong links, but not to a chain. But we still need that little logo everywhere, especially on your newsletters. That, plus the other aspects of Book Sense, plus your own words about the brand will — hallelujah — help create the bond with more and more customers.[83]

As a marketing text notes, "The brand idea will not take unless *everyone in the company lives the brand.*" [84] Thus, a lack of unity among booksellers could jeopardize the image being projected by Book Sense. In Lennertz's statement, the feel-good solidarity of collective action is harnessed to the task of making the brand ubiquitous, and therefore generating brand loyalty among customers. But whereas booksellers may in principle embrace the need for cooperation, some remain concerned that branding is a device that could destroy their individuality.

There have been some indications that the ABA membership may not be as enthusiastic about Book Sense as is the leadership. For instance, an ABA survey of six strategic goals for the association found that promoting independents through Book Sense ranked below advocating on independents' behalf.[85] And in what appeared to be a concession to those who saw the Book Sense brand crowding out recognition of distinctions among booksellers, the ABA changed the names of its regional bestseller lists so that "Book Sense" no longer preceded the name of the region the list was meant to represent. Said Lennertz: "It's obviously important to have the national list known by the name of our national marketing campaign — Book Sense — but on a local level, maybe it's more important to be, well, local." [86] Still, this compromise does not seem to have portended a return to the 1980s, when independent booksellers fought their association on the grounds that it was unresponsive to their plight. Rather than making a public challenge, booksellers who do not desire the Book Sense brand simply decline to join the program (though this means that they are then excluded from full participation in the ABA). And few booksellers question the general importance of marketing; some simply prefer to market their stores independently.

Certainly, Book Sense has been applauded by numerous publishers and others in the industry, including Larry Kirshbaum, former chairman of AOL Time Warner Book Group:

> [I]f there's one thing that I've hated for the last 15 years, it's the litigious environment that existed between the chains and the independents, which tended to make it seem like there was this huge schism in our business. . . . The thing that has made me excited about Book Sense is that, for the first time, the independents are beginning to think in terms of their marketing as if they were a chain, a federation, if you will, marketing titles on a national scale. And that's what we need.[87]

Nevertheless, once independents begin to think of their activities as more chainlike, their own identity as independent booksellers becomes more muddled. Size of organization is a key factor in distinguishing independents from chains, but it is not the only factor. Also important is the freedom to conduct their businesses in ways that may not always be the most rational or cost-effective, but that may help support the kinds of books a retailer admires, or that help to create more meaningful relationships with customers and others in the neighborhood, or that simply make the bookseller's work more enjoyable. Independents who see their stores as expressions of their own and their communities' personalities may find it a compromise to attach a national logo to store packaging or to give up display space to books that others have selected. And to the extent that independence is meant to incorporate a refusal to embrace "commercialism," the discipline of a branding campaign represents a retreat from an independent position. Furthermore, while consistency in sales efforts may indeed be effective in getting the attention of other book professionals, how it affects bookstore patrons is less clear. Some customers might respond to a familiar pattern of marketing by opening up their wallets. However, the more independents become like chains, the less ground they have for asking the public to treat them as qualitatively different.

Moral and Market Appeals

In looking at the growth of activism among independents in the last quarter of the twentieth century, one can see the development of a collective identity and a willingness to risk alienating other book professionals in order to promote their collective interests. This has sometimes resulted in a critique of the free market system and the unequal power relations it gives rise to. Yet it is important not to exaggerate the radical nature of the independents' actions, and to note the limits to their oppositional stance.

In challenging the fairness of the terms publishers grant to chains, as well as the various strategies the chains use to expand their businesses, independent booksellers have sometimes, though perhaps inadvertently, offered a radical interpretation of the problems they face. Rather than conceding that the strongest and most efficient retailers deserve to prevail, these booksellers have asserted that such an outcome actually shows the deficiencies of the market. While they do not go so far as to condemn the very concept of competition, they do suggest that the rules of the competitive game may be fundamentally flawed, that the game is fixed against independents by automatically favoring large booksellers over small. This kind of argument was heard in the ABA lawsuit against Barnes & Noble and Borders when independent booksellers maintained that fairness demanded that all booksellers be treated the same by publishers, regardless of their size. According to this logic, economies of scale should not matter in setting the terms of sale. Bigness may contribute to efficiency and cost-savings, but it is also equated with an impersonal and alienating world, and with an alarming concentration of power. Therefore, its economic advantages are not recognized as legitimate.

With this, one can hear echoes of the kind of antimonopoly sentiments that were common a century earlier. David Monod has shown that the ideas of community, independence, smallness, and fair competition were part of a "folklore of retailing" that was in place by the late nineteenth century.[88] Today's independent booksellers are thus not unique but can be seen as part of a long tradition of small businesspeople claiming to uphold values important to North Americans. But unlike other retailers, booksellers sell books. And the persistent belief in the different, sacred quality of books gives an added dimension to the campaign for the moral superiority of the independent retailer. Independent booksellers may subscribe to the ideal of the self-made entrepreneur (which according to Monod was a key component of the turn-of-the-century shopkeeper's identity), but this is not the aspect of their work that holds the greatest meaning for them. Interestingly enough, none of the bookstore owners I interviewed mentioned the desire to be his or her own boss as a motivating factor in running a bookstore. What they did consistently speak about, however, was a reverence for the printed word. Combined with the conviction that small, personal, independent retailers are the only ones who treat books and readers with the proper consideration, this gives their movement an added rationale for claiming the support of others.

Indeed, by warning that their demise may be the outcome, independents have precipitated an industry debate about the morality of a system in which efficiency and cost-effectiveness carry the day. A wholesaler got to the heart of the matter:

> Distributors and publishers were giving a certain discount to booksellers and a certain discount to *chain* booksellers and the two didn't match up. And they could justify it based on volume but the fact of the matter is — I guess in a moral sense that it's discriminatory pricing. In a capitalistic sense maybe it isn't. Maybe it's based on volume and strictly as bottom-line companies, a lot of people can justify it.

While this wholesaler recognized that suppliers were simply doing what was necessary to benefit the financial health of their companies, he was clearly troubled by it. A system in which self-interest pushes people to ally themselves with those who are most powerful demonstrates all too clearly that this world is not fair. And particularly for individuals who have chosen their line of work because of a belief in its social value, fairness matters.

Nevertheless, while independent booksellers and their industry supporters have sometimes challenged the logic of market relations, this should not be seen as a full-scale assault on capitalism. Capitalism, after all, is predicated on private property. And although one can occasionally hear the wistful suggestion that it would be nice if books and bookstores were not private property, that the world would be a better place if books and the means to distribute them were available to everyone, this is not a strong theme among independent booksellers. Rather, it is the issue of bigness that is stressed, an emphasis that makes the independents more anticorporate than anticapitalist. Capitalism may fit well with large bureaucratic organizations, as they are an efficient means to centralize power, control labor, and create profit. Nonetheless, capitalism existed prior to the emergence of large corporations, and independents imagine this earlier world as one that would have been more hospitable to retailers such as themselves.

Independent booksellers therefore do support liberal capitalism, as can be seen in their frequent insistence that they "just want a level playing field" on which to compete. The Book Sense marketing campaign is an attempt to create that level playing field by massing the collective weight of independents against the ten-ton gorilla represented by the chains. Yet Book Sense also highlights the limits of bookseller opposition to the system in which they operate.

Whereas judicial and legislative strategies call into question the rules of the competitive game, and hence the social Darwinism that underlies the free market system, through Book Sense, independents are trying to beat the chains at their own game. When attacking the chains for posing unfair competition, independents asserted that market clout should not take precedence over the provision of diverse books and service to local communities, moral undertakings in which the independents claim to excel. But with Book Sense, independents appear willing to trade claims to occupy a moral high ground that stands outside the usual market criteria of efficiency and growth for claims that they offer consumers a better product than their rivals do. These booksellers are then appealing to consumers' preferences for the independent bookstore experience rather than to citizens' agreement that the political nature of the independent-chain conflict requires the social regulation of the market.

These contrasting types of appeals, corresponding to contrasting visions of the consumer, raise the question of the theoretical and practical differences between political and marketing campaigns. Independent booksellers do show that the line between politics and marketing is not always clear in practice and can be easily blurred. After all, whether it is via Book Sense or an antichain petition, independents are still asking the public for increased patronage and support. But there *is* a theoretical difference between these two types of appeals, and this difference does have practical results.

Theories of propaganda maintain that goal-oriented political persuasion and commercial persuasion are fundamentally the same. Whether for purposes of selling a political ideology or a longing for a consumer good, the concept of propaganda holds that individuals are manipulated through the use of distortion and lies to believe something that they otherwise would not. And without vigilant oversight, political and commercial expression is likely to turn into propaganda.[89] This perspective has rightfully been criticized for its conceptualization of communicators as deliberately misleading audiences for self-interested reasons, and of audiences for being passive recipients of such lies. But beyond that, this perspective does not recognize the different stakes involved in propagating and accepting political versus commercial ideas.

An important tradition in political theory, coming from classic theorists such as Aristotle and Rousseau, as well as more recent theorists such as Habermas, relates the realm of politics to the common interest; for some, this has a moral dimension as well.[90] Political persuasion can thus be seen as appealing to a set of moral principles, which by definition have the force of duty and obligation. As Durkheim notes, morality goes beyond the self in a couple different senses. In the first place, behavior directed solely toward personal ends is not moral: "To act morally is to act in terms of the collective interest." And second, since its authority is social, morality is experienced as superior to the individual.[91] Marketing, on the other hand, is about providing a choice that fits individual preferences that themselves can vary according to situation and time. With marketing, self-interest is flattered and assumed to be the most salient consideration in decision making.

This distinction between political persuasion and marketing is not to deny another meaning of the word "political" that pertains to power. Certainly, definitions of morality reflect and reinforce differences in power. And as Nancy Fraser has argued, definitions of the common good are "tainted by the effects of dominance and subordination."[92] Nevertheless, politics employs a different kind of logic from that of marketing as it appeals to collective values rather than individual ones. And in the end, collective values are more powerful and binding. If you can get it, a moral victory is a much more secure basis for public support than winning popularity among consumers in the market, as consumer loyalty is capricious, changing not only with personal economic and lifestyle fluctuations, but across the life course.

Despite the ability of some entrepreneurs to find a small, specialized niche, the structure of the contemporary capitalist market does not favor retailers such as independent booksellers. In the areas of supply, distribution, pricing, real estate — and marketing — chain retailers in many fields have shown that they can conduct their operations more efficiently than independent merchants can. Therefore, once they leave behind the moral high ground, independents may find that their voices are drowned out among the clamor of marketers. Instead, it is on the terrain of politics, where consumption is viewed as a political and ethical problem, that independents can issue their greatest challenge, not just to chains, but to consumers as well. This is an argument I will develop in my eighth and final chapter.

CHAPTER 8

Pursuing the Citizen-Consumer:
Consumption as Politics

As the previous chapters demonstrate, the changes that have taken place within bookselling since the growth of the chains have given rise to debates over rationalization, competition, and the place of small-scale enterprises in the book industry. These debates are often passionate in nature, and show little sign of being resolved anytime soon. But one might be inclined to ask, to what extent are these concerns simply internal to the circle of book professionals, those people whose life work is in books? And does this in-many-ways-atypical corner of private industry have much significance for American society in general?

Considering that frequent book buying is limited to a minority of the American population, one would not expect great familiarity with or interest in those matters that preoccupy booksellers. Similarly, the book business produces few celebrities and generates relatively little in terms of money, power, or glamour, the sorts of attributes that tend to attract media attention. Nevertheless, since the advent of the superstores, the issues outlined here have seeped more into public consciousness. There are, of course, those individuals who are not book professionals who have nevertheless been directly affected by industry developments. They include the bookstore patron who discovers his neighborhood independent has gone out of business, as well as the student who lands a part-time job at a bookstore. But even among the general public, those people who have little direct contact with bookshops, there is some awareness of at least the general contours of the chain-independent conflict. The press not infrequently profiles the struggles of independents to stay alive; this theme has even been addressed by the entertainment media, for example, in the 1998 film *You've Got Mail*. From the mid-1990s through the early 2000s, readers of the *New York Times* were especially likely to find accounts of book industry controversies through the reporting of Doreen Carvajal and David B. Kirkpatrick. And when incidents such as the proposed Barnes & Noble–Ingram merger have arisen, independent booksellers have had particular success at shining a spotlight on their concerns, not just via the mass media, but through smaller-scale information outlets such as their political allies' newsletters or the Internet.

Therefore, while few people may have a detailed understanding of the bookstore wars, many know they exist. This indicates not only that news about these issues gets publicized, but that it sticks in public consciousness. To some degree this occurs because the public is likely to recognize these issues as representative of processes that are happening, not just in bookselling or even retailing in general, but in many other spheres of everyday life. The succumbing of small enterprises to large institutions and the elimination of external competitors, internal inefficiencies, and other barriers to personal or organizational advantage are familiar tendencies in modern society. Yet Americans are probably more cognizant of how these tendencies affect bookselling than they are of similar situations in the fields of toy, hardware, drug, or office supply retailing. Because books are involved, this phenomenon appears to have particular resonance for many individuals. And on occasion, those individuals have acted on their concerns.

In this chapter, I examine how some people outside the ranks of book professionals have taken action against the spread of large-scale, rationalized bookselling. This has generally meant working against chains and in support of independents, but in some cases, large independents have also been targeted. In particular, I look more closely at activism on the part of two groups: low-level workers at bookstores and residents of communities experiencing a changing bookselling environment. While their explicit grievances might differ, both groups have been affected by rationalization and market processes in ways they find undesirable. What appears to be lost with bookselling models that prioritize cost-efficiency and standardization is a sense of being a part of a distinctive enterprise or neighborhood, as well as a forfeiting of control over one's job or one's community to powerful organizations and other less tangible heteronomous forces. The campaigns by both workers and citizens are notable for expressing a belief that bookselling should be something of an oasis from these processes that otherwise seem so unstoppable.

This is seen on the one hand in the clash between bookstore workers' expectations of being involved in a socially worthwhile undertaking and the low pay and heavy-handed control doled out by their employers. In response, some workers have engaged in unionization drives, both at the chains and at a few large independents. These workers have consistently voiced a sense of betrayal that the bookstore is acting just like any other business, treating them as unskilled and easily replaceable. On the other hand, the potential loss of a favored bookstore has spurred local residents and governments to take action in a number of communities. This includes organized efforts of patrons to provide direct material and moral support to struggling stores, as well as initiatives by citizens to restrict the entry of chain bookstores into their communities. In some cases, these citizens employ land-use and taxation policies to deliberately intercede in the free market.

What these various activities reveal is that the low prices and great efficiency of large bookstores come at a cost. Those apparent consumer benefits make it more likely that locally based shops will be replaced by standardized chains, which centralize the selection and marketing of books. Such developments also help change the balance of power in the industry, so that publishers and distributors must tailor prices, policies, and sometimes even products to the demands of their major bookstore customers. Furthermore, the discounts and uniformly entertaining experiences provided by booksellers are made possible in part by bookstore workers' low wages and minimal autonomy. That is to say, the vast quantity of goods consumers can purchase as well as the style of consumption they have come to enjoy are directly related to the working conditions of others. These sorts of issues have been most prominently publicized in regard to overseas sweatshops of clothing and shoe manufacturers, or the labor practices of the biggest retailer in the world, Wal-Mart. But they hold true for all businesses engaged in the production and distribution of consumer goods, including the book business.

It would be an exaggeration to paint the various forms of bookstore-related activism by nonprofessionals as more than tentative movements; most unionization drives have been short-lived, and the chains are hardly under siege in most communities. Yet these activities have significance beyond their immediate impact on the bookselling world. In the first place, while organized collective efforts are the most visible and effective types of actions, they inspire the possibility of individual consumer action as well. Similar to the consciousness-raising efforts of booksellers I have described in previous chapters, such activities encourage individuals to wield what financial power they have by making considered decisions about how to spend their money.

Second, and related to this, the actions of nonprofessionals are important for the understandings of consumption they embody. Together, collective and individual activities in defense of the small bookstore suggest a vision of the consumer as one who acts on behalf of a common good. This is in contrast to the conceptualizations of the consumer described in previous chapters: the sovereign consumer whose freedom from external constraints is celebrated, and whose personal satisfaction is the primary goal of retailing; the standardized consumer who responds in predictable ways to mass marketing, and who trades the distinctive character and history of a locale for the familiarity of standardized environments; the fun-loving consumer who looks for entertainment in the shopping experience; the rational consumer guided by economic self-interest, who shops wherever the bargains are to be found; and even the consumer who seeks out a personal relationship with a shopkeeper, united by bonds of sentiment. Each of these models describes consumers motivated by personal interests, varied as they may be. But it is also possible that consumers can be guided by considerations that give weight to larger group interests. Such an orientation perceives shopping in terms of a set of moral principles held to be important. This approach understands consumption not simply as directed to personal gain, but as tied to public outcomes. While there might not be agreement on just what the common good is, the point is that individuals incorporate some understanding of a social benefit into their consumption habits. Consumers who take this approach thus turn the choice of where to shop and what to buy into a political statement. As I will argue, the consumer and the citizen are in this way joined together.

The View from Behind the Counter

When I have referred to booksellers in this account, I have reflected industry practice by meaning the owners or managers of independent and chain stores, as well as others in managerial capacities at chain headquarters. What this ignores, however, is the large number of people in lower-level staff positions — the clerks at the cash registers, the employees unpacking shipments in the back room, and those who fill the bureaucratic ranks at chain headquarters. There is a definite divide in the book world between the "booksellers," those individuals who make this line of work a career and consequently keep up with the happenings of the industry, and the "staff," those who see their bookstore employment as a temporary job, have few responsibilities, and have very little knowledge of the overall workings of their own stores, much less the book industry in general.

Ever since the chains became a major force, the caliber of their in-store staff has been considered one of their weak points. By defining their workforce needs in terms of people with general retail skills rather than salespeople with book-related knowledge, the chains were assured an inexpensive and abundant labor pool from which to fill their ranks. However, this contributed to a reputation for hiring "mere" clerks whose only qualification, it was presumed, was to know how to run a cash register. Stories about the ignorance of chain employees are commonplace. A 1993 report in *Publishers Weekly* made clear its disapproval of employees who lack the requisite literary education:

> Comedy or tragedy? Overheard at a new Barnes & Noble superstore, one clerk asks another: "A customer wants the 'folder' edition of Shakespeare. What's that?" The second clerk answers, making an illustrative hand movement: "You know, it's like a folder." [1]

The fact that *Publishers Weekly* did not bother to explain the mistake to its readers (presumably, the customer was referring to the Folger Shakespeare books) reveals an assumption that true industry insiders (i.e., readers of *Publishers Weekly*) have a broad knowledge of titles, authors, publishers, and editions.

These kinds of comments disparaging the bookstore staff are reminiscent of criticisms directed at regular (independent) bookshops earlier in the twentieth century. But now, independent booksellers are widely viewed as the ones who are appropriately learned — and it is those independents who most vocally express contempt for the chain employee:

> I think there's probably a different kind of person that continues to shop at an independent. I mean, someone who loves books, someone who cares, someone who wants to talk to someone who knows or reads something. Like I've heard, overheard myself, some chain, someone asks for Hemingway, and they're going now, "Is that science fiction?" [*laughs*]. And like not having any idea where anything is, and that's troublesome to people.

The dichotomy drawn between the ignorant chain clerk and the knowledgeable independent bookseller is meant to convey the more serious moral purpose of the independents. The latter's staff are believed to reflect their truly deep esteem for books, as this comment by another independent implies:

> But I mean I hear story after story about people who will go into a chain bookstore and the help doesn't know anything about books. They have no

idea who George Eliot is. "Who is he?" Well, right. So they're hiring people at the lowest possible wage to sell books.

Observations at chains support the contention that much of the staff is not very well versed in book matters. Partly, this reflects the fact that so many bookstore workers are part-time, temporary, or both. (For instance, in 2002, Borders had approximately 17,000 part-time and 15,000 full-time employees.)[2] And contrary to the way professionals view their work, these workers do not necessarily perceive bookselling as a worthy career goal; indeed, one chain bookstore employee bemoaned it as a waste of talent:

> It's interesting but it's kind of sad interesting seeing exactly how much potential is in that store and nobody's really doing anything with it. Well, they are I guess, they're playing with books and talking with people and stuff like that but in some cases it's a brief stopover. . . . A lot of them have been doing this since the store opened. A lot of them have been there two or three years. And it's kind of sad. I don't want to be a professional retail salesperson, you know. I look at these people and [I'm] thinking, "Wow, man, you're even more educated than I am." . . . That kind of creativity should be totally utilized in a far different manner as opposed to just selling books.

Of course, the line between staff and professional is more fluid than this suggests. Some who take what they think is a temporary position at a bookstore are enchanted enough by the business that they stay with it forever. And especially at independent stores, employees can be given responsibility for selection, meeting with sales reps (an important source of news about the industry), and designing promotional campaigns. But particularly at the chains, employees come and go very rapidly, and their jobs are highly circumscribed. Yet, for precisely these reasons, they have developed unique concerns and perspectives on the issues confronting the industry. These perspectives are relevant for thinking about the chain-independent conflict as well as about how bookstore patrons carry out their roles as consumers.

Bookstore employees have developed a set of grievances common to retail workers in many sectors. It is important to recognize that these grievances are not always limited to chain employment. But there are factors related to the chains' size, centralized structure, and drive to rationalize the business of bookselling that have made work at chain outlets less compelling than it is at other bookstores. In the first place, these factors have led to a greater deskilling of staff. In small independents, by necessity there is no elaborate division of labor; the person who does the buying is also often the one at the cash register. Larger independents, on the other hand, do have a division of labor that can result in a high degree of specialization and, sometimes, accompanying dissatisfaction. Still, these arrangements usually pale next to the formal hierarchy of the chain, where tasks are discrete, important decisions are made in the regional or home office, and managers — who generally *are* familiar with the details of the book world — tend to be administering in back rooms.

One of the more important ways in which deskilling has occurred is with the computerization of the bookstore, which, at least until the end of the twentieth century, was far more advanced in the chains than in most independents. Automation means that it is much less necessary than it was in the past to find staff who are knowledgeable about books. Rather than knowing who George Eliot is, an employee merely has to get the spelling right to look the author up in the database. Indeed, in my superstore observations, just about all customer questions led to the computer, which informs staff where a book is shelved, whether it is in stock, and whether it can be special ordered. The advantages for the bookstore that incorporates this technology are obvious — employees are more easily trained and can be paid relatively little. And so they are. Minimum wage, or close to it, is the norm for people starting out as bookstore clerks, whether in independents or chains.[3]

Some analysts argue that wages, benefits, workplace conditions, and job security are actually worse in small businesses than in large companies.[4] This may well be true for businesses in general, but there are certainly differences from one sector to another — and by these measures, chain bookstore employees are not better off than their independent counterparts. While starting salaries may be similar, the bureaucratized chain with its handbook of formal rules governing employee conduct often contrasts unfavorably with the independents' relatively informal environment (better realized in some places than in others) and more flexible, personalized relations with store owners. This is not to say that a warm, fuzzy feeling exists in all, or even most, independents. But the chains, with their greater resources and familiarity with the latest in management techniques, have been able to institutionalize various controls over employees that are out of the reach of most independents. One example is the chains' increased vigilance in combating "shrinkage" (theft) through scrutinizing their workers. In the late 1980s, B. Dalton led the way by installing video camera systems in its stores to catch employee theft.[5] This kind of action does not help employee morale; neither do the bag searches, drug tests, lie detector tests, rules forbidding dating between employees, and other practices reported at one or another chain. Combined with the poor pay and benefits bookstore clerks receive, it is not surprising that retaining a highly-qualified staff has been a continuing problem for these companies.

There are, of course, distinctions between the different chains. The mall chains, such as B. Dalton and Waldenbooks, appear to have the least skilled staff, as well as the greatest turnover. Indeed, these stores often end up hiring high school students. On the other hand, Borders was for many years a notable exception to the dominant image of chain stores staffed by ignorant, poorly trained clerks. Borders enjoyed a reputation for employing a highly educated workforce, and the chain's written exam that tested prospective employees' knowledge of books and authors was a point of pride for the company.[6] In fact, Borders was the most ambiguously "chainlike" of any of the major booksellers in several respects — from its counterculture origins to its selection, which at least until the late 1990s was highly respected among book professionals. Yet by 1996, it was clear that even Borders was having trouble reconciling its progressive and serious-about-books image with the realities of running a corporation. And whatever family feeling may once have existed between employees and executives was rapidly vanishing. In the face of heavy opposition from management, Borders employees were the first among chain bookstore workers to unionize on a significant scale.[7]

Borders' unionization drive started in Philadelphia with an effort led by the Industrial Workers of the World (IWW). In March of 1996, the Philadelphia store employees voted twenty-five to twenty against unionization. But that was not the end of the matter. That June, Borders fired Miriam Fried, an employee and union organizer at the store, for insubordination. Fried's case soon garnered national attention as the IWW, calling her charges trumped up, publicized her exemplary work record and picketed Borders outlets in twenty cities. Fried received support from labor groups and writers around the country, and even a resolution by the Philadelphia City Council asking Borders to "restore its reputation as a socially responsible company" by rehiring her.

As unwelcome as this attention was to Borders, it was nothing compared to the public relations nightmare that soon followed. Filmmaker and writer Michael Moore, who has made a career out of condemning corporate maltreatment of workers and mocking corporate hypocrisy, was scheduled to appear that September at the Philadelphia store to promote his book *Downsize This!* After finding an IWW picket line when he arrived, Moore sought and received permission from store managers to invite the protesters inside to discuss their case. But following this event, Borders' promotion of Moore's book took some odd turns, and the author's relations with the chain quickly deteriorated. At the New York City Borders a few days later, Moore was told by corporate executives that he would not be speaking as planned, but could only sign books. At a Des Moines talk the next month, only store managers were allowed to work the Borders book table, while unionizing employees resorted to sneaking a note to Moore's staff explaining their situation. Then Moore claimed that a Fort Lauderdale Borders appearance had suddenly been cancelled, though Borders insisted that Moore was never confirmed to speak. All this became quite public when Moore published an article in the *Nation* titled "Banned by Borders." As well as being covered by the *New York Times,* the piece was widely circulated over the Internet. After describing the unionization drive and incidents around his book tour, Moore concluded his piece with this "Note to Borders Executives":

> If, after this column is published, you retaliate by removing my book from your shelves, or hiding it in the "humor" section or underreporting its sales to *The New York Times* list, I will come at you with everything I've got. You sandbagged me in Philly, and the only decent way for you to resolve this is to give Miriam Fried her job back and let the workers form their union without intimidation or harassment.[8]

While the Moore affair received considerable notice, less publicized were the organizing drives taking off in several other Borders stores. A Chicago outlet was the first to unionize, allying with the United Food and Commercial Workers Union (UFCW) in October 1996. By the summer of 1997, a total of four Borders outlets had voted to unionize (all with the UFCW), while three outlets plus a warehouse had voted the union down.[9] While union drives were spreading to additional Borders outlets, organizing efforts were also beginning at Barnes & Noble and Encore bookstores. Several World Wide Web sites sprang up to aid communication between discontented bookstore clerks, along with a newsletter called *Eight Ball,* funded with the help of Michael Moore and dedicated to organizing bookselling employees around the country.

The Borders workers' grievances included the poor pay and lack of benefits that characterize bookstore work in general. But their resentment was fueled by the evolving corporate culture at Borders, which put a premium on satisfying investors by producing high profits, and by the company's ambitious expansion plans directed at capturing market share. Workers noted Borders' rising revenues and executives' hefty compensation packages and asked why none of this cash went toward improving their own

$6.50 average hourly wage and their unaffordable health plan. One worker, a former teacher, made this argument for unionization:

> I did not expect to become rich as a bookseller. My pay is less than a third of what I made teaching. I knew I was trading off money for less emotional involvement and stress. I did not, however, think I'd have to impoverish myself to be a bookseller at Borders. No matter how you do the math, there is a cut in frequency and percentages of raises through the last (almost) four years I've been here. . . . I'm in favor of the union because stockholders own this company and their profits are the bottom line (I'm a big girl, I know this is a business, of course) and it seems that profiting and expanding are done without any consideration or show of fair wages and compensation for the employees who are helping this corporation become so successful.[10]

Workers also saw Borders as betraying its roots by exchanging a devotion to books for a devotion to the bottom line. Pro-union workers at the Philadelphia store made this concern quite explicit; one of their demands was that the title base in the store never dip below 125,000.[11] Employees' attempts to unionize have thus in part been motivated by their sense of what it means to be a good bookseller:

> In the struggle for the soul of Borders, for that elusive, but so often invoked specter, "Borders culture," it's the grubs who will always remain truer to the mission purpose. . . . [T]he grubs are the ones who are still so close to the original reason why they came to work in a bookstore in the first place that they care about that lost space for new university titles, about those pull lists that will delete important works before their time, about keeping the reading groups interesting, about trying to get worthwhile author events, etc., etc. Managers may care about that stuff, but they're too busy distributing those RPL's [return lists] and scheduling and making sure the co-op advertising is displayed precisely as per the tiny print in the Time Warner contract, and just shoveling through the daily sludge that comes sluicing out of Ann Arbor, as it does from any large company, to exert much time or effort to those other concerns — at least, if they want to get on the Borders express track.[12]

The unionization drive among its workers marred Borders' preferred image of a chain bookseller that does not act like a chain. Rather than winning plaudits for nurturing a loyal and learned workforce that mirrored the company's commitment to literary values, Borders now looked like any other retail giant that puts a priority on keeping labor costs low. Employees exhibited skepticism toward the notion that Borders was different from the other chains:

> As it stands now, we are the pawns in the growing bookstore war. It's easy for those at the top to define the battle-lines via "pride in the company" as us vs. the competition (B&N). In reality, this is a battle being played out like all economic conflicts — between those at the top and those at the bottom. When it comes to wages, job security, collective bargaining, and "at-will" clauses, we have everything in common with fellow wage-earners (both at B&N and Borders) and very little indeed with those far fewer making millions from the work we do.[13]

That bookstore unionization was strongest at Borders, where clerks enjoyed somewhat better pay and prestige than at the other chains, suggests that Borders paid the price for hiring employees who were led to believe that they were more than mere clerks.

It is never a simple task to unionize retail workers since they tend to have high turnover and be spread out over a large number of outlets. Bookstore workers are no exception. The four Borders stores that originally voted to unionize lost their union representation within a few years, and for a time, labor organizing at the chain slowed. But in 2002, successful union drives restarted at two different Borders, a Minneapolis outlet and its flagship Ann Arbor store. Worker demands remained similar to those of earlier years, including higher pay (now averaging $7.50 an hour in Minneapolis and $8.20 an hour in Ann Arbor), and the right to be involved in store activities such as "in store promotions, book placement, community relations and establishing attendance policies."[14] Meanwhile, customer service workers had (unsuccessfully) tried to organize at Amazon.com, calling for better pay, job security, and respect for employees.[15] Workers at Barnes & Noble were less active, but also periodically engaged in discussions about unionization. Altogether, it appeared that chain bookstore workers were not a completely happy lot.

Of course, being a bookstore clerk is not now and never has been a highly remunerated job in independent stores either.[16] No matter the ownership structure of the store, there is a definite disjunction between the knowledge and skill envisioned for the ideal bookstore staff, and the low, retail-level wages generally paid. But the poor pay received by the bookstore clerk has traditionally been compensated for in other ways. People usually enter bookstore work because they like books and reading.[17] Such individuals are motivated by the anticipation of having access to so much reading material or being surrounded by people immersed in literary matters. These jobs also appear to carry somewhat more status than the typical retail sales position. Indeed, the cachet of working at some of the nation's best-known independents draws an extremely qualified workforce to stores such as the Tattered Cover in Denver or Cody's in Berkeley — their employees are known for their high levels of education (graduate students are common) and low turnover.

Those instances where independents have experienced labor disputes of their own are telling. Here, too, workers' complaints often include a denunciation of what management practices mean for the store's literary standards as well as for workers' welfare. For instance, in 1998, employees at the famed Portland independent Powell's restarted a unionization drive that had been unsuccessful in the early 1990s. Workers were now not only unhappy about the usual low wages they received, but also with a plan to reorganize job responsibilities. Up until then, Powell's had a system whereby ninety section heads were responsible for and developed expertise in particular subjects. But in order to better serve its growing Internet business, Powell's management determined that shelving needed to occur more quickly, and this would happen if workers had broader job responsibilities. Employees contended that the reorganization would erode one of the store's primary strengths, the knowledge that workers had of their areas of specialization. They also voiced unhappiness about increased employee surveillance carried out in the name of efficiency, including a new system for monitoring and disciplining worker tardiness. One union supporter warned that these changes would only serve to weaken the bookstore:

> Powell's has managed to retain many great employees for whom money is obviously not as important a consideration as flexibility. A company that offers little in the way of compensation or flexibility will test the loyalty of its long-term employees and find it ever harder to find new quality hires. Books are a wonderful thing but this company will soon learn whether books alone will suffice to maintain knowledgeable and committed workforce.[18]

Powell's strongly opposed worker efforts to affiliate with the International Longshore and Warehouse Union, and even after the union was voted in, employee relations with the bookstore remained rancorous, periodically marked by strikes and National Labor Relations Board complaints. But with a second contract ratified in 2004, it looked as if the union was there to stay.[19]

Powell's was one of the largest independents in the country, with several hundred employees and seven outlets in the Portland area. It had also been expanding in recent years, a process that often generates pressures to reallocate resources and contain costs. It is therefore perhaps not so surprising that

Powell's would institute the kind of bureaucratic control measures that workers find so objectionable. But small independents are not entirely immune to labor discord either. In one case, the Concord Bookshop in Massachusetts prompted about a third of its employees to give notice after its owners decided to demote top management and place them under the control of a new general manager. The store's owners contended that a new management structure was needed for the store's financial health. Customers of the store, including several who were prominent authors, publicly voiced their dismay about the loss of staff who "are themselves such thoughtful readers." [20] Here, as in other cases, customer solidarity with worker grievances echoed employees' concerns about the dedication of the bookstore to disseminating a range of worthy books.

Consumers may readily join employees in condemning practices that appear to dilute a store's selection of books. But these same consumers often seem surprised that a bookstore, whether chain or independent, would breed workers discontented with their jobs. Indeed, what this suggests is the way that books, as the objects being sold, act as a kind of cover for unfavorable labor conditions. For the same reason that people have sought out bookstore work, because of a belief that it is different from other retail jobs, customers rarely stop to offer sympathy to the workers serving up books to them. Yet the bookstore that promises speed, efficiency, low prices, and a predictable experience achieves all this by tightly controlling its employees. In this way, bookstore employment is not especially unique.

While customers may overlook many of the similarities between bookstore and other retail jobs, their obliviousness to workplace conditions is also of a piece with contemporary consumer culture. Part of the consumption experience Americans now expect is one where workers are committed to serving them, not coerced into it. [21] The consumption experience is likely to be less carefree and entertaining if one realizes that the people making it possible are miserable in their jobs. And just as advertisers know that television programs depicting social problems make viewers less receptive to the appeals of commercials, [22] retail employers do not want gloomy employees casting a shadow on the consumption fun. Bookstore workers who are required to project an image of an organization that is not only entertaining, but community-minded and cares about books, can be left feeling highly bitter at what they see as the hypocrisy of their employers.

Scholars and other observers who celebrate the possibilities for creativity and self-expression in consumption often forget that shopping involves interacting with people who are engaged in the world of work. Shopping is not simply about an isolated consumer making meaning for himself, for that consumer's experience has an impact on a wide range of people involved in supplying the goods and services offered to him. Bookstore workers who have made their grievances public interrupt the imaginative roamings of the consumer to request that he avoid those stores that do not treat workers decently. Sometimes workers have set up picket lines to make this point more forcefully. Strikes tend to make consumers unhappy, as they are being asked to forego the freedom of choice and convenience that so define contemporary understandings of consumption. But if consumption is viewed as incorporating a moral dimension, then convenience will probably not be the primary criterion for where to shop.

Residents Take a Stand

Bookstore workers are waging an internal battle against the tendencies of large-scale, rationalized bookselling. But outside the store, some citizens have also joined the fray. These activities have generally taken two forms, one having to do with preserving existing independents, and the other with direct opposition to chains. With the first, fundraising appeals to save bookstores in tough economic straits have become increasingly common since the 1990s. These efforts are notable for treating the bookstore more like a nonprofit cultural institution than a for-profit business. Typically, a store in danger of bankruptcy asks customers for donations or holds benefit events. Numerous bookstores have raised thousands of dollars in this way, including Our Story Books of Plainfield, N.J., Panacea Books of Port Chester, N.Y., Chapters Literary Bookstore of Washington, D.C., Black Images Book Bazaar of Dallas, Ruminator Books of St. Paul, Reader's Oasis of Tucson, and Midnight Special of Santa Monica. Women's bookstores, which in some cases have been organized as collectives or not-for-profit organizations, have been especially partial to these kinds of fundraising efforts. Most of the time, the bookseller is the one to organize such fund drives. But occasionally, community members take the initiative. When Cover to Cover Booksellers of San Francisco decided it would have to close, customers were the main organizers of the efforts to keep the store alive, soliciting pledges from supporters to buy one book a month. The appeal was addressed to residents and friends of the Noe Valley neighborhood in which the store was located, and it emphasized the importance of neighborhood preservation:

> The return will not simply be saving the store, but creating a whole new sense of community around the store, with events planned for loyal supporters

to get to know one another and share in the meaning of saving the store, preserving our commitment to books and their value, and strengthening the character of 24th Street and the neighborhood as a whole.[23]

These efforts were thus not just about preserving a local institution, but were also seen as helping to solidify a local identity.

However, despite the support that initially pours out after these kinds of appeals, the bookstore-cum-charity often sees its fortunes slide again, and many (including some of those mentioned above) eventually go under. When people view their efforts as temporary philanthropy rather than as integrated into their everyday understandings of what it means to be a consumer, they soon drift back to giving their business to Amazon, Costco, and the like. On the other hand, what has probably been more significant for ensuring the survival of independents has been the direct opposition to chain stores that has surfaced in some communities. For instance, in Austin in 2003, independent retailers rallied a couple hundred residents to turn out at a community forum to oppose a proposed downtown development. The development, which was to feature a Borders, was to be built across the street from an established independent bookstore and independent record store. Residents not only directed their anger at developers, but at city officials who had provided financial incentives for the project. Borders later decided to pull out of the development, though it is unclear how much its decision was based on local opposition.[24] Similar protests against the establishment of a Borders or Barnes & Noble involving alliances of independents and residents have taken place in Burlington, Vermont, Oak Park, Illinois, and Bridgehampton, Long Island, among other locales.[25]

Occasionally, protests have taken more creative forms. An Austin group calling itself Friends United in Creative Knowledge of the Faceless Attitudes of Corporate Entities, affiliated with the independent/alternative bookstore FringeWare, organized Bag Day in 1998, calling on people around the country to attempt to enter a Barnes & Noble with paper bags over their heads. The action was meant to protest "corporate chains that invade neighborhoods and treat people as faceless entities." The action's anthem summed up much antichain sentiment, including a jab at routinized workers:

Sung to the tune of *If You're Going to San Francisco*

If you're going to Barnes and Noble,
be sure to wear a bag upon your head.

If you're going to Barnes & Noble
you're going to meet some robotic clerks in there.

All those who come to Barnes and Noble,
November 23rd will be a good time there.
In the aisles of Barnes and Noble,
angry people with bags upon their heads.

All across the nation, such a strange vibration,
corporate conglomeration,
there's a whole generation, with a new explanation,
who are sick and tired of disinformation.

All those who come to Barnes and Noble
be sure to wear some bags upon your head.
If you go to Barnes and Noble,
November 23rd will be a good time there.[26]

The action got a fair amount of publicity, but did not blunt the chain's momentum. FringeWare, on the other hand, went under in 1999.

In a few cases, resident opposition to chains has had concrete success, leading to public policy that restricts the superstores. In San Francisco in 1998, the city's planning commission reversed a vote of approval for a new Borders outlet after a neighborhood merchants association and neighborhood residents organized against the superstore. Rallying to defend the local independent bookstore, opponents of the Borders protested that the superstore would be several times larger than any existing business in the Union Street neighborhood and would not fit with the locale's character. The neighborhood had previously also been successful in keeping a Blockbuster Video outlet out of the area.[27]

A little to the south, residents of the town of Capitola also viewed the proposed entry of a Borders as unwelcome. Citizens protested that the superstore would harm the community's integrity as well as endanger local independents. Opponents of the Borders included the poet Adrienne Rich, who claimed that the building of such superstores went beyond competition:

The attempted malling of our coastal towns, the destruction of their livability and character, the wipe-out, by hugely capitalized chains, of small local enterprises, many of which had to survive the '89 quake and did, with community support — this isn't "competition." This is unbridled, unrestricted financial power against every other human consideration.[28]

Although the town planning commission approved the superstore's development, the city council subsequently voted to greatly restrict the store's size, thus effectively quashing the superstore's quest to enter Capitola.[29]

These sorts of actions are rare. Indeed, one can find almost as many examples of residents joining with city officials to ask a chain book superstore to settle in their communities. However, these actions are important for demonstrating how public policy can be utilized to explicitly support certain kinds of retailers and link them to particular definitions of quality of life. That is to say, they make consumption a matter of public deliberation rather than simply private choice. They therefore point the way to an approach to consumer issues that accepts the legitimacy of restricting choice in the name of some other social good.

While the focus on bookstores has some unique qualities, these campaigns do parallel antichain activity in other retail sectors.[30] Much of that activity has been spearheaded by independent retailers, for instance, local coffee stores' campaigns against Starbucks.[31] But in many cases, other constituents are equal or lead partners in opposition. Sometimes residents initiate campaigns against the chains' presence in their neighborhoods, as happened, for example, in fights against drugstores such as Thrifty, Rite Aid, and CVS.[32] Preservationists, often led by the National Trust for Historic Preservation, have played an active role in attempts to save "Main Streets" and stave off the effects of uncontrolled sprawl, while unions oppose the presence of retailers with notorious labor practices. Wal-Mart has been a particular target of these campaigns.[33] The most common method of preventing the establishment of big-box retailers is to pass regulations limiting the size of new retail businesses.[34] In other cases, ordinances subject a new retailer to design restrictions that mandate structures must be compatible with existing architecture. Citizens have also tried to eliminate the tax breaks and other financial incentives that are often given to chains thinking of setting up shop in a given locale. On occasion, communities have simply barred chains altogether. In each of these cases, local businesses and their supporters articulate the importance of smallness, the personalized touch, and independence. Whether it be Wal-Mart, Toys "R" Us, or Borders, these stores are seen by some residents as destroying the physical, social, and cultural landscape. And by viewing this issue with the eyes of citizens, residents feel the right and responsibility to do something about it.

All these campaigns, whether fund-raising for the local bookstore or protesting the construction of a superstore, take a great deal of organizational resources. This is one reason why they are not more common. However, there is another, more quiet kind of activity that similarly connects consumption to politics — those day-to-day individual decisions about where to shop and what to buy that take into account a broader set of outcomes than immediate personal fulfillment. One bookstore customer wrote,

> I imagine that most book lovers who shop at independent bookstores do so for political reasons. And so do I. I patronize independent grocery stores, photo shops, and clothiers. Those choices are political, and the politics are important.[35]

This writer is surely wrong in ascribing such motives to most patrons of independents. But her (perhaps disingenuous) assumption that this is so jars us into realizing that this approach to consumption can appear as natural to some people as an approach that values bargain-hunting does to others.

Books, Bookstores, and Imagining a Different World

Theoretical debates about consumer culture tend to center on the question of whether consumption is an instrument of oppression or a legitimate expression of popular pleasure.[36] This question has been at the heart of numerous studies that examine the manipulative powers of institutions of consumption or, alternatively, the abilities of people to use consumer goods to affirm identities and subvert the dominant meanings of popular culture. Important as these debates are, they tend to be less helpful for answering a different set of questions. As Mica Nava has argued, the theoretical split between those condemning and those defending consumption has diverted attention from the potential political power of consumerism.[37] Booksellers, both independent and chain, have surely worked to provide a setting that distracts customers from the cares of the world, and that seeks to reassure them that at least in this space, consumers call the shots. In this way, the bookstore does appear to situate itself in a privatized sphere of leisure separate from the public sphere of politics. But at the same time, independent booksellers, in their attacks on the chains (and indirectly, the patrons of chains), also present a critique of prevailing economic and consumer practices. This critique is intended to mobilize the public to action. Although this is not usually part of the intention, it can also help spur a vision of consumption that incorporates a political dimension.

The sphere of consumption includes a number of phenomena that observers might readily identify as embodying differential power relations. It is, after all, through the houses, vehicles, clothing, and other goods and services Americans purchase that they most publicly display economic inequalities. And the enormous variety of affordable consumer goods available to Americans is linked to a global system of production that gives manufacturers easy access to natural resources, and that depends on labor practices that keep many workers poorly paid and tightly controlled. Yet prevailing cultural models of consumption, the ways in which people understand what it means to engage in consumption, often exclude considerations about power relations — except for the contest between store owner and customer over prices. When shopping is seen as an expression of the sovereign consumer who is not constrained by the judgments of others, and when consumption is believed to be best realized when it provides personal satisfaction and entertainment, it is seemingly distanced from politics.

As I have explained, independent booksellers, like their chain counterparts, engage in many practices that promote these individualized ways of conceptualizing consumption. Similarly, today's independents reinforce other cultural ideals that were first mined by the chains. Numerous analysts have rightly noted that consumer culture emphasizes novelty: new products, new experiences, a new generation of youth on the cutting edge. This is a theme that booksellers embrace, as can be seen in their attention to frontlist books and their rejection of the staid elitism of the past in favor of a hip, happening image. But at the same time, there remains a persisting fondness for older retail forms. The independent finds a receptive audience among many Americans when decrying what the emphasis on innovation in retail appears to have produced — a packaged, standardized, and impersonal culture that crowds out the type of shop represented by the small, old-fashioned bookseller. Taking into account these somewhat contradictory messages, we might ask, then, How does the plight of the independent bookseller inspire a politicized understanding of consumption? What are the political and cultural implications of the kinds of retail-related activism I have described? And what are the limits of these movements?

Beginning in the 1960s, a chaotic, inefficient book distribution system gradually gave way to one that is far more orderly and uniform, but that is also less distinct from other consumer industries. Bookselling is now dominated by firms using sophisticated technology and managerial techniques to ensure a smooth flow of books and to control geographically far-flung operations. Extensive marketing is utilized to try to make sales more plentiful and more predictable. And this once highly decentralized sector has become increasingly concentrated in a few hands. The appearance within the book trade of large-scale, complex corporate entities relying on speedy transactions and standardized procedures is in one sense simply a delayed instance of a traditional commercial undertaking being turned into a rationalized business enterprise, a process that affected innumerable other industries long ago. However, not only was the book trade extremely late in embracing modern business techniques, but there has been unceasing ambivalence about these developments in book work. The loudest condemnation comes from those members of the industry who stand to lose the most — small firms and persons whose jobs are made redundant. But even book professionals actively engaged in promoting and implementing these changes tend to express some sadness about the transformation of their industry, with the disappearance of the independent bookseller symbolizing much that is seen as regrettable.

Sentiments that mourn the passing of organizational forms such as small businesses are often dismissed by academics as anachronistic nostalgia mired in an idealization of the past. And there surely is a hearty dose of romanticization attached to odes to the small bookseller. But we also need to take seriously those regrets about its passing. The independent bookstore's continued ability to generate affection, even among those book buyers and industry personnel whose actions end up undermining it, speaks to a certain amount of dissatisfaction with those social changes that render institutions such as the independent bookstore less viable. In the valorization of the independent bookseller, one hears distaste for a number of tendencies associated with capitalism and the process of rationalization, as well as a sense that books are exceptionally moral objects deserving of protection from these forces.

The critique of the chains articulated by independent booksellers, workers, and some citizens contains first, a lament for what is lost with the growing rationalization of everyday life. The chains' standardized efficiencies contribute to a world where commercial districts look increasingly alike, and where commercial experiences are thoroughly regulated, from the floor plan that steers patrons past potential impulse buys, to the scripted greeting of the sales clerk, to the discreetly placed video cameras that ensure no untoward behavior goes unnoticed. Along with this, the demise of the independent bookseller is a reminder of how large, impersonal, powerful institutions are controlling more and more aspects of our lives. But the denigration of the chains is also fed by resentment toward those aspects of capitalism summed up in the term "commercialism." The chains' commitment to growth and profits is viewed as producing ruthless competition and a valuation of books, workers, and customers only for the revenues they bring in, while the use of aggressive marketing methods is attacked by critics as representing one more arena in which consumers are harassed and manipulated, and as demeaning to the books being sold.

Together, commercialism and rationalization are perceived as quashing opportunities for first-time authors, or books likely to garner only a small audience, or bookstores that reflect a personalized vision. But organizations such as the chains are resented not just for engaging in such practices, but for creating the conditions in which others must follow their lead. In these circumstances, to defy considerations of cost-efficiency is to risk total economic failure. So book professionals find themselves, however reluctantly, acting in ways that further the very tendencies they condemn, from turning down books they believe are worthy but not marketable to undercutting the competition. The struggle to reconcile their ideals with the requirements of the market can be heard in the statement of a publisher:

> And if you insist on perceiving books that are meant to care for the soul, and the spirit, and the mind simply as, you know, commercial value, then it devalues our mind and our spirits and our civilization ultimately. And I don't know how, I mean capitalism is not designed to deal with these questions, right? So I don't know how to get out of that, I don't know how to solve that problem except to say that the booksellers and the publishers in some ways have to agree that there're going to be certain aspects of their business that don't have to be defined by the standard economic terms that the rest of the world runs on. And it's getting harder and harder for people to make those accommodations.

The publisher's concerns were echoed by a wholesaler:

> We have certain values that we hold dear to ourselves that we want to be able to hold onto and not lose. We are a company that's traditionally very value driven, and we probably haven't looked enough over the years at our bottom line. So we're kind of moving in that direction of being able to look at the bottom line and have an awareness of what it means. Different business equations and how they fit in. But we're really holding on dearly to those values that got us going in the first place. . . . We're in the process of being a very value-oriented business trying to get a bottom-line orientation but also keeping our values and trying to find the balance there between.

Such a balance is not easily found. This wholesaler's company subsequently went out of business.

Whether or not the past was in reality better is not really the issue here. The prechain era was not an especially golden age in terms of the diversity of books readily available to readers. Nor was the prechain era widely populated by warm, caring booksellers who welcomed all community members into their stores. And so those who seek to preserve the independent are probably guilty of nostalgia, of imagining an idyllic past that never existed. But that is not to say that they cannot accept change or are afraid of the future, for critics of the chains are also imagining a world that in some respects is preferable to the one that they presently occupy. And by doing so, they highlight problems with the present and open up possibilities for change. It is perhaps no accident that the bookstore is the catalyst for this. Bookstores are often represented as places to stir up dreams, with the books they offer providing material used to imagine different places, different people, different ideas, and a different existence. In imagination there is hope.

The dismay expressed at standardization, economies of scale, impersonality, extreme efficiency, and predictability in book retailing does sometimes translate into explicit opposition to those techniques so useful for becoming better capitalists. Opposition not just to commercialism, but to rationalization as well, then becomes a motivating force for tilting at contemporary capitalism. This is seen in attempts to reform core principles of the free market system such as the promotion of competition and the rewarding of efficiency. Those industry legal challenges against publishers who grant better terms to retailers placing bigger orders and those communities that ban large-scale retail facilities are implicitly saying that the strongest do not deserve to win.

Of course, the independents' critique of capitalism can only go so far. As small businesspeople, they are still intimately tied to the market, and their livelihood still depends on selling as many books as possible. Few, if any, of the book professionals I interviewed would explicitly call themselves anticapitalist. Indeed, the enthusiasm shown for the Book Sense marketing campaign indicates that there are parts of capitalist culture they are happy to embrace. Similarly, the kind of equal-opportunity argument represented by reference to the level playing field is in keeping with the small businessperson's traditional placement in the mainstream of American political culture. Nonetheless, these businesspeople find themselves articulating a position that is at times inadvertently radical. And a primary reason why this happens is because they sell books.

Books are widely considered to be a "different" kind of commodity, deserving of so much more respect than other commercial goods that even displaying them alongside such objects, or using marketing methods that appear to destroy their dignity, or treating one book as equivalent to another, generates concern and criticism. The book industry is among those occupational groups in the United States with a large number of people who see their work as a sort of calling; that is, they consider the intrinsic worth of disseminating books and literary values as equal to, if not more important than, simply earning money. The comments of a wholesaler typify this view:

> There are always going to be people who are very, very bottom-line oriented, and they want to make whatever enterprise they're with be economically successful. And to them, it's going to be like making a movie. You bring in the right stars, the right writers, the right producers, and all the right pieces in place, and there'll be a familiar version of an earlier movie. And it'll sell and there'll be thousands and thousands of dollars made at every showing. You know, like a *Terminator Five; Death Wish Number Seventeen;* Sylvester Stallone's, whatever he does, *Number Twelve*. And that happens in books a lot too. And then there's going to be people who are just purely involved in the work because they love it. Because they feel like they're involved in some essential human task that separates us from the other creatures. You know, we have an intellect, a spirit, and a soul. And they want to be involved in it. They regard it as, I think, being part of human evolution. And it shows in their work.

For people like this wholesaler, the work they do is especially meaningful because it engages their creativity and it contributes to the greater good. Both he and the publisher previously quoted use similar, quasi-religious language, speaking of the way that books nourish the human spirit and soul. In this sense, books are, to use Viviana Zelizer's phrase, sacred products.[38] The tendency to view books as a special kind of object is perhaps best seen in the reluctance to call books "products" at all. Among those book professionals I interviewed, only a few people unselfconsciously spoke of dealing in products rather than in books. In contrast, others noted an uneasy association between books and commodities. As a publisher at a major house said, "If you can divorce yourself from the emotion attached to it, you're just providing a product. But we really can't separate ourselves from the emotional part."

Just as books are believed to have particular moral worth, bookselling is viewed as an especially moral endeavor. When asked in what ways, if any, a bookstore is different from a grocery store, a small publisher reflected that the similarities were superficial, the differences profound:

> Well, I think in a certain way, of course, there's no difference in that the function of a store is to sell things and in enough volume to be able to stay open. So

on sort of that basic level, I'd say nothing. But what's being sold — For better or worse, there is a group of book lovers in this country who believe that a book, as an object, is worth more, is intrinsically more significant than blue jeans or just any store. And so, I happen to be one of those people who believe that. So therefore, you know, it's all the difference in the world. It functions, I think, really as a place to, in this society, to exchange ideas in a way that nothing else does.

An independent bookseller sounded a similar note:

I mean with this whole chain thing, I think a lot about what I think about these things — what I think about chains and how are books different than these other consumer products. You know, are we just all deluding ourselves to think that they are [*laughs*]. Because one thing that's really happening is a lot of idealistic booksellers I think are being made to come up against reality, against market reality. A lot sooner than they thought they would have to, maybe. How is it different, well . . . the basic difference is that a book really is a little piece of culture. Yeah, I guess I can't be more eloquent than that. That it has to do with our entire intellectual life, and with our progress, and with our quality of life, although a grocery store has to do with the quality of life as well. There's simply a bigger difference between, I would say, any two books and any two different brands of orange juice. It's just a *much* larger difference. And it's a much more important difference.

On the other hand, another independent reflected, perhaps booksellers are deluding themselves:

You know, in a lot of ways it isn't different from a grocery store. We're selling ideas. The product is different. But probably a lot of the things that I have to deal with on a day-to-day basis are not that different. I know all of us pseudo-intellectuals kind of cringe when we refer to what we're doing as selling product. But we are selling a product of a sort. And when we get down to that level, we're trying to do the same thing as they're doing. Trying to keep the products on the shelf that the customers want. You know, I spend about 95 percent of my time dealing with product as opposed to dealing with books and ideas. Which is what I want to do, but it's not what I do.

For many in the book industry (as in the larger society), equating the life of the mind to profane commodities with price tags attached is a hard — and perhaps unprincipled — thing to do. But as a sales rep observed, "No matter how you look at it, no matter how cerebral you want to be and say, 'Well, I'm a bookseller,' you're still a merchant. You're still a retailer."

Books have, of course, long been bought and sold on the market, as have other goods and services associated with the mind, such as education. But since the nineteenth century, there have been efforts by the book industry to treat this item as a different sort of commodity, as a noncommercial object of commerce. For booksellers, selecting titles because of their "intrinsic" worthiness rather than because they are easily sold has been a way to demonstrate and preserve their special status. By maintaining that no two books are reducible to one another, and by using aesthetic, moral, and personal (as well as commercial) criteria to stock their stores, booksellers have tried to keep books from becoming mere products. But these efforts have been severely undermined. Like the department stores, drugstores, and variety stores that preceded them, the mall chain bookstores that blatantly employed impersonal, commercial selection criteria were despised for so blithely ignoring the hard-achieved distinction between a book and a product. The chain superstores are perhaps even more threatening. Despite their explicit mandate to bring profits to their shareholders, and their reliance on centralized technology to determine the most salable goods, the superstores' offerings are not obviously different from those of their independent counterparts. The superstores are committed to trafficking in products, but to the public, these goods still look like books.

In most respects, books are not intrinsically different from other commodities. They can be bought, sold, displayed, thrown away, or burned like any other object. And despite their desire to treat books as special kinds of objects that are not products, by virtue of being in an industry operating in a capitalist system, book professionals are usually forced to base most of their decisions about producing, distributing, and selling books on what will earn the greatest profits. This is not likely to change anytime soon. The marketplace for books is not about to be dismantled in favor of some public or nonprofit solution. But on the other hand, the association of books and bookselling with the human mind and with humanity itself continues to militate against a purely instrumental approach to dealing in the printed word. And the concept of the book remains an important device for reflecting on and criticizing the contemporary social order, among both book professionals and the larger public. While the decline of the independent stationery shop or hardware store or drugstore causes the occasional wistfulness about a transformed world, the demise of the bookstore can provoke cries of "Is nothing sacred?" The criticisms of bigness, price-cutting, and standardization being made by booksellers are quite similar to those raised by other independent retailers. But these arguments have a greater likelihood of being heard when books are at issue.

Alternative Visions of Consumption

Contemporary images of the consumer are to a large degree modeled after the figure of the capitalist. Both are assumed to have similar orientations to the market, in that they compete with one another for advantage. And both are assumed to have similar understandings of advantage; the capitalist is motivated by the quest to keep costs low and profits high, and the consumer is motivated by the quest to obtain the most material goods at the lowest price. Consequently, just as the independent bookseller stands as a reproach to rationalized capitalism, she poses a challenge to consumers and ideas about consumption.

Certainly, the prevailing cultural models of consumption in the twenty-first-century United States do not posit consumers as the allies of those fighting capitalism. Taken together, these dominant visions of the consumer assume an individual who is self-interested and makes choices according to personal lifestyle or taste preferences. Furthermore, this consumer looks to consumption as an arena that, in contrast to so much else in life, is painless and fun to navigate. An orientation toward consumption that views it as an entertaining experience to be purchased (preferably at a bargain) is one that stresses individual fulfillment and conflict-free social interaction. From this perspective, consumption is an "oasis" from politics, and debates about which social interests are served by particular consumer institutions are foreclosed.

The recent history of bookselling in many ways exemplifies how these ideas about consumption have become so fixed in our society. Booksellers' reinvention of the bookstore as an entertaining establishment open to a nonelite audience has been a resounding success, with customers lining up for the author events, filling the cafés, and socializing in the store aisles. Book buyers have come to expect hassle-free shopping, and are irritated by those stores that do not offer plenty of parking and salespeople who offer opinions only when asked. Large numbers of Americans seem to accept the domination of bookselling by a few companies, with their standardized appearance and operations, as the price one pays for access to greater discounts. And in the end, these discounts are what appear to capture readers' hearts most successfully. Surrounded by marketing messages about the irrationality of paying more if there is someone willing to sell for less, consumers savor the victory of a book discount equivalent to the price of the mocha latte they purchase in the store café.

The logic of discounting encourages the idea that people have the right to get more for their dollar. On a per capita basis, Americans consume more of just about everything (though not books) than any other people in the world. Yet Americans continue to have rising expectations for the amount of material goods they should be able to own, and the frequency at which possessions should be replaced. Those who voluntarily buy less instead of more are viewed as an oddity — perhaps exceptionally virtuous, perhaps pointlessly ascetic, but still making a difficult sacrifice. And since most Americans do not renounce steady acquisition, but also find that they do not have the incomes to satisfy all their desires, bargain hunting does indeed appear to be rational behavior.

Some may point to such behavior as evidence that *Homo economicus* sums up humans' true nature. Yet the case of bookselling shows that even with the emphasis now placed on discounting, both retailers and consumers consistently employ noneconomic considerations when participating in the marketplace. They derive a variety of meanings from the environment, experiences, and relationships to be found at a bookstore, and these meanings influence their actions in ways that cannot be reduced to rational calculations of gains and losses. Nor is bookselling unique; numerous other sociological and anthropological studies have illustrated the ways in which culture always mediates economic transactions. Furthermore, the case of bookselling demonstrates that cultural meanings connected to consumption have changed over time and continue to remain in flux. One reason I have devoted so much attention to bookselling of the past is because history shows us that Americans have understood and practiced consumption in ways that are different from those we take for granted now. Sometimes this has included orientations to consumption that do not prioritize the individual's own material advantage or that do not see all retailers as morally equivalent. Beyond the antichain sentiment I have described, there is a long tradition in the United States of demonstrating social alliances through shopping behavior, such as membership in food cooperatives, the patronize-your-own campaigns of ethnic groups, or the practice of boycotting businesses as a form of political protest.[39]

T. H. Breen provides a particularly illuminating analysis of the relationship between consumption and politics in his discussion of the boycotts of British imports that preceded the American Revolution. Breen shows how American colonists developed a consciousness that their purchase or boycott of consumer goods could be a political act, and how this went hand in

hand with the development of discourse about rights and liberties more generally. Breen's insight is that making the choice of whether to forego goods
such as paper or tea could actually be a vehicle for politicizing a population.
And this in turn resulted in the further politicization of consumption:

> By mobilizing people ordinarily excluded from colonial politics, the non-
> consumption movement of this period greatly expanded the base of revolu-
> tionary activities. The Townshend boycott politicized even the most mun-
> dane items of the household economy and thereby politicized American
> women. Decisions about consumption could not be separated from decisions
> about politics.[40]

There have been other periods in American history when consumer activity
was widely understood to hold explicit political meanings; in the twentieth
century, this was perhaps strongest in the 1930s. But one can also identify
more recent cases, for example, when the purchase of grapes stood for the exploitation of farmworkers, the high sales of Japanese cars stood for the United
States' declining economic might, and the patronage of malls stood for standing up to terrorism. In each of these cases, one sees consumer goods charged
with political meaning. Yet none of them represent a fully politicized view of
consumption, as each remains limited to a focus on a single item or issue.

Contemporary cultural ideas about consumption are the result of a complex set of processes having to do with the growing industrial capacity of the
world, the effects of suburbanization on people's mobility patterns, women's
entry into the paid labor force, the coercive nature of work (and subsequent
fetishizing of leisure), the widespread dissemination of media images of commodities, and the practices of consumer institutions. While I have touched on
some of these other factors, I have been most interested in how the practices
of book professionals both reflect and further particular ideas about consumption. Those practices and associated ideas are not always straightforward. For instance, the decline of elitism in the book trade contributed to
new approaches to bookstore design, and the selection and marketing of
books, as well as to booksellers' promotion of an ideology of consumer sovereignty. But taking on a populist identity also helped remove independent
booksellers' diffidence about defining their problems in political terms and
engaging in political activity. Here, we see the emergence of booksellers'
challenge to consumers. At the same time as they promote shopping as an entertaining escape from the rat race, by publicizing their dispute with the
chains, independent booksellers remind patrons that consumption is not a
conflict-free arena after all. The largely unspoken implication is that no one

stays neutral; through their actions consumers inevitably take sides in these conflicts.[41]

The business press is filled with pronouncements that consumers today want it all — selection, convenience, good service, and low prices. Retailers are admonished that they will soon be left with empty stores if they do not deliver on these expectations. And indeed, much retailer marketing is focused on reassuring consumers that they are sovereign and can have it all. Yet to accept this notion means overlooking that our choices of where to shop, what to buy, and how much to consume do have consequences. They are not simply private acts that serve to enhance individual well-being. Rather, unlimited consumption creates enormous environmental strains. Choices about what businesses to patronize determine which companies, along with their commercial, labor, and aesthetic practices, will thrive and which will go out of business. Choices about what products to purchase also have consequences for workers in distant locales, since those goods are made by people working under varying conditions. And such choices have consequences for social relations as consumption can be used to flaunt inequality and to mark those who do not possess certain consumer items as deficient.

Choices about consumption can be treated as private and trivial or they can be viewed as a means to demonstrate commitments to particular values. Most contemporary orientations to consumption do not include a vision that calls for citizenship, that is, people's active participation in the processes that affect their locales and public affairs more generally. Yet an apolitical approach to consumption is not intrinsic to the nature of consumer activity. I am not trying to argue that consumption is simply a diversion from more serious forms of political engagement. Rather, in a consumer-oriented society and culture, it is necessary to understand how consumption can become an act of civic participation.[42]

As consumers who want the most for their money, readers may indeed be better served by the chains and other discount outlets. But to the extent that citizens have an interest in maintaining some control over their retail institutions and their cultural landscape, they may find themselves allied with independents. It is important to reiterate that no one is innocent here. Like the chains, independent booksellers often make selection decisions that favor bestsellers, pay their employees minimum wage, and regard marketing as a way to establish meaningful personal relationships with customers. Nonetheless, because of their size, resources, and clout, the chains have an ability to influence the dissemination of books, consumer practices, and the built environment in ways that are out of reach of the independents. In other words, one needs to consider the effects of differential power in this domain.

Most obviously, the power of the book chains, as well as other major book retailers such as Amazon.com, Costco, and Wal-Mart, gives them a great deal of influence over what Americans read. This is not a simple case of censorship; more books are available than ever before for those readers who know how to find them. But as the major retailers become the most accessible sources of books for the population, their selection decisions have the effect of determining which books are widely available. And maybe even more important, through their marketing decisions, these retailers play a large role in determining which books get the most attention. The major booksellers' selection and marketing methods are not necessarily worse than those of other retailers. But these methods represent only a limited number of ways to approach such decisions.

Beyond the issue of exposure to reading material, there are additional considerations that apply to any large chain, not just those that sell books. As I have discussed, large retailers have a great deal of power to define the contours of everyday commercial life. Whether it be habits connected to the mode of transportation used to travel to a store, the kinds of interactions one encounters in a store, or the extent to which the look and experience of a store differ from one region to the next, the ubiquity of chains and the resources they can put into marketing heavily influence consumers' expectations around consumption. Independent retailers are similarly affected; in order to compete, they often end up adopting the same practices.

Furthermore, as manufacturers (or in the case of the book industry, publishers) become increasingly dependent on a few retail clients, the balance of power within the system of production and distribution changes to favor such retailers. Fearful of losing their major customers, producers are compelled to supply goods at the prices and terms demanded by the retailers. In many sectors, clothing being one of the best examples, the organizational and labor practices of manufacturers stem from the intense competition to meet the demands of the major buyers for speed, flexibility, and low prices.

Similarly, large retailers hold a disproportionate amount of power in relations with local communities. Small enterprises tend not to be able to exercise the same kind of clout. While collectively small merchants may contribute significantly to the economic health of a locale, the lesser impact of any single establishment limits the influence that a merchant might have with planning boards, regulatory agencies, and so forth. Additionally, a locally owned and operated store is directly dependent on the goodwill of local residents and cannot risk alienating large parts of the community. And aside from any personal attachment to a locale, the store proprietor knows that the fate of her entire business is tied to the future of that community.

A corporate chain, on the other hand, faces different types of constraints. Managers are primarily responsible to shareholders, and make decisions about where to locate an outlet, when to pull out, and how to operate their businesses according to what will best benefit the company as a whole. Any single outlet is dispensable. Moreover, size brings with it considerable power in negotiations with local governments. Local officials become beholden to large retailers who provide, or hold out the promise of providing, tax monies and jobs. In the competition with other nearby locales for such retailers, governments frequently agree to cut through land use regulations, provide roads and other infrastructure, redeploy police, offer tax breaks, and in effect agree to undercut local independent retailers by denying them equivalent benefits. Catering to large retailers can be an expensive undertaking for a locale, but once these retailers are in place, few officials want to risk losing them.

Therefore, what distinguishes chains from independents is not simply a matter of different styles that might appeal to different tastes. Rather, retailers have different amounts of power that give them greater or lesser ability to control their relations with other economic actors and with the communities that host them. Recognizing how such power is acquired and utilized adds to an understanding, not only of the chains, but of the economic system that produced them and that pushes independents to follow in their footsteps. And with that understanding of how commerce works and how it shapes human action, citizens can interact with the market in a more politically conscious manner: weighing choices about when they are willing to make trade-offs and compromises in order to retain the benefits of the market, and when it is important to alter existing market arrangements in order to produce some other benefit.

While my position is clearly critical of chain retailers, whether chains or independents prevail is ultimately not the primary issue when thinking about consumption as citizenship. Rather, taking this approach to consumption is consequential in a couple different ways. First, it does not reduce consumption to a private activity oriented to self-interest, but makes consumer behavior a matter of public debate with a view toward determining what will most benefit the common good. As Neal Ryan notes, there are times when public interest should take precedence over individual desires; he gives the example of transportation systems where individuals may prefer private cars to public transit, but the social cost is too great.[43] In this view, consumer opportunities, and economic activity more generally, can be regulated by public policy. Second, to conceptualize consumption in terms of citizenship is to make those choices that are not subject to regulation a matter of individual conscience, that is, something that is consistent with an individual's principles as well as his wants. To say that a normative dimension applies to consumption does not preordain the choices people make. Especially in a society such as the United States where there are enormous differences in the values people hold, such choices will vary considerably. But for most people, the result will still sometimes mean making do with less: less convenience, fewer options, or a smaller quantity of goods. This approach would also prod consumers to consider the perspectives of producers, retailers, workers, and others who make consumption possible, and perhaps realize that the customer is not always right.

Despite the prevailing vision of consumption as something one simply does for oneself, consumption is inextricably political in that it can be related to the common good and has implications for the gains and losses faced by particular groups. Of course, within a society riven by various kinds of inequalities, it is not only businesses that compete and have different interests, but consumers too. Some may object that asking consumers to ignore discounts overlooks the interests of the poor. However, the problem of poverty is less about the cost of books and other discretionary goods, and more about a system that makes basic needs such as housing and health care so expensive. The Consumer Price Index shows that since 1980, the costs of food, apparel, and commodities have risen below the general rate of consumer goods and services inflation, while the costs of shelter and medical care have risen considerably higher.[44] Certainly, an understanding of the political nature of consumption includes thinking about how these latter necessities have been turned into luxuries. Wal-Mart is no salvation if your rent takes up half your income. Similarly, Amazon's discounts do not compensate for a decline in the reading material available in public libraries, or a foundering public education system. Low-income people tend to have limited choices in general, and consumption is no exception; many are forced to put aside both principles and preferences because of a lack of affordable (or sometimes any) alternatives in their neighborhoods. Nevertheless, the United States is a society where a large portion of the population is housed, fed, and clothed and does have choices about what, where, and how to buy.

To say that consumers have a responsibility to recognize shopping as an unavoidably political activity, and to be conscious of the outcomes of their choices, would appear to take some of the fun out of shopping. Perhaps that would be one result. But there are compensations — one being that consumers could discover they have more power than they realize. The idea that "money talks" is so accepted in American society that it has become a cliché, though one usually uttered with cynicism about the futility of getting people to act according to other criteria. But Americans neither have to accept the logic that humans only act according to economic self-interest nor dispense with whatever economic power they have. Alexandra Chasin has argued that the drive to make shopping an avenue for expressing one's values can have the effect of reducing politics to symbolic and economic phenomena.[45] However, by spending or withholding their money in order to support institutions or values they care about, Americans do much more than make a symbolic statement, they act in ways that have immediate effects on those enterprises seeking their business. Therefore, such behavior is not a substitute for political action, but provides a means to exercise influence in economic processes that generally appear beyond the control of ordinary people.

Those interested in social change are continuously confronting the problem of political ineffectiveness: how do people combat the major forces that seem so impervious to change, especially in the face of widespread indifference to mass political movements. Clearly, there is no single answer; effective political action occurs on many fronts. But in an era when politics is expected to be dramatic (and hence, often staged), from contests at the ballot box to protests on the streets, it is easy to forget the politics of mundane, routine life. Those regular activities that occur on a day-to-day basis are no less politically consequential than those demarcated as special occasions. There are multiple domains of social life where one plays one's part to keep the whole thing going — at work, at home, and as a consumer. By seeing oneself as a political being who can act in multiple spheres, politics becomes not just something one does in one's spare time but is integrated into everyday life. The politics of consumption may not be very spectacular, but it is not unimportant; one makes individual choices as a consumer that collectively have great impact.

All this may appear to have taken us far from the struggles and concerns of booksellers. But that is not actually the case, as booksellers and consumers face similar dilemmas arising from their participation in the market. Booksellers try to reconcile their devotion to books, those expressions of the life of the mind and the human condition, with their active involvement in the book's commodification. And as consumers, we try to reconcile the act of acquiring commodities for the self with a need to make meaning, which sometimes includes a commitment to bettering the human condition. The ironies are endless, but they do not need to stop us.

Ownership Histories of Major American Chain Bookstores

Barnes & Noble

1910	Doubleday bookstore opened by Doubleday, Page Publishers
1986	Doubleday sold to Bertelsmann
1990	Bertelsmann sells Doubleday Book Shops to BDB Corp.

1913	Charles Scribner's Sons opens first Scribner Book Store
1984	Scribner family sells Charles Scribner's Sons to Macmillan Inc.
1984	Scribner family sells Scribner Book Stores to Rizzoli International Bookstore
1989	BDB Corp. acquires Scribner's Costa Mesa bookstore and Scribner's name from Macmillan Publishing Co. and Rizzoli International

1982	Gary Hoover founds Bookstop
1989	Crown Books buys 41 percent interest in Bookstop Inc. from an investment group
1989	BDB Corp. buys 51 percent interest in Bookstop Inc.
1990	Crown agrees to sell stake in Bookstop; BDB Corp. achieves full control

1873	Charles Montgomery Barnes starts used book business in Wheaton, Illinois
1917	William Barnes, Charles's son, enters into partnership with George Clifford Noble in New York City as textbook jobber and retailer

1969	Barnes family sells Barnes & Noble to Amtel Corp.
1971	Leonard Riggio acquires Barnes & Noble from Amtel
1979	Barnes & Noble acquires Marboro Book Stores and mail-order operations
1979	Barnes & Noble acquires Bookmasters
1984	Vendex International acquires 30 percent stake in Barnes & Noble
1985	Barnes & Noble acquires College Stores Associates
1986	Barnes & Noble (Leonard Riggio and Vendex/Vendamerica) acquires B. Dalton, Bookseller, from Dayton Hudson; merger produces BDB Corp.

1966	Dayton Co. opens first B. Dalton, Bookseller, outlet in Edina, Minnesota
1968	Dayton Co. acquires Pickwick Book Shops
1969	Dayton Co. renamed Dayton Hudson
1982	B. Dalton launches Pickwick Discount Books
1986	Dayton Hudson sells B. Dalton to Barnes & Noble (Leonard Riggio and Vendamerica); merger produces BDB Corp.
1986	Pickwick Discount Books closed
1989	BDB Corp. acquires Scribner's Costa Mesa bookstore and Scribner's name from Macmillan Publishing Co. and Rizzoli International
1990	BDB Corp. acquires Doubleday Book Shops from Bertelsmann
1990	First Barnes & Noble superstore opened

1991	BDB Corp. name changed to Barnes & Noble
1993	Barnes & Noble goes public; Len Riggio retains private control of college bookstore division
1994	Vendex sells most of its shares in Barnes & Noble, leaving Len Riggio the single largest shareholder with 26 percent of the company's shares
1996	Barnes & Noble acquires 20 percent stake in Chapters, Canada's largest bookstore chain
1996	Barnes & Noble acquires 50 percent of Calendar Club
1997	Barnes & Noble launches an online Web site, Barnesandnoble.com
1998	Barnes & Noble sells 50 percent of Barnesandnoble.com to Bertelsmann
1999	Barnes & Noble College Stores launches Textbooks.com
1999	Barnes & Noble acquires Babbage's Etc. from Len Riggio (includes Babbage's, Software Etc., GameStop, Gamestop.com)
1999	Barnes & Noble acquires J. B. Fairfax International USA
1999	Barnes & Noble sells shares in Chapters, reducing its stake to 7 percent
1999	Barnes & Noble completes IPO of Barnesandnoble.com
2000	Barnes & Noble acquires 53 percent stake in MightyWords.com
2000	Barnesandnoble.com acquires 32 percent stake in Enews.com
2000	Barnes & Noble acquires Funco
2000	Barnes & Noble acquires Fatbrain.com

2000	Barnes & Noble reduces stake in iUniverse.com to 29 percent
2000	Barnes & Noble acquires 50 percent stake in *Book* magazine
2000	Barnes & Noble forms Silver Lining
2001	Barnesandnoble.com forms two digital imprints: Barnes & Noble Digital and World Digital Library
2001	Barnes & Noble acquires SparkNotes.com from Delias Corp.
2001	Barnesandnoble.com's stake in eNews at 47 percent; Barnes & Noble holds 53 percent
2001	Barnes & Noble sells EPVI to CPI
2001	Barnes & Noble reduces stake in Chapters to 2 percent
2001	Babbage's name changed to GameStop
2001	Barnes & Noble's stake in iUniverse reduced to 22 percent
2002	Barnes & Noble issues IPO for GameStop; retains two-thirds stake
2002	MightyWords.com shuts down
2002	eNews is closed down
2002	Barnes & Noble increases stake in Barnesandnoble.com to 38 percent; Bertelsmann increases stake to 36.9 percent
2002	Barnes & Noble acquires Sterling Publishing
2003	Barnes & Noble forms Barnes & Noble Classics
2003	Silver Lining renamed Barnes & Noble Basics
2003	Barnes & Noble acquires Bertelsmann's 37 percent stake in Barnesandnoble.com, raising its stake to 75 percent
2003	Barnes & Noble discontinues *Book* magazine
2004	Barnes & Noble completes reacquisition of Barnesandnoble.com
2004	Barnes & Noble fully spins off GameStop

Borders Group

1853	August Brentano founds Brentano's as a hotel newsstand
1933	Brentano family sells majority stake to Stanton Griffis
1962	Nixon Griffis, Stanton's son, and other shareholders sell Brentano's to Crowell-Collier Publishing Co.
1968	Brentano's acquires Paul Elder & Co. of San Francisco and Campbell's Book Store of Los Angeles
1973	Crowell-Collier, which merged with Macmillan in 1960, renamed Macmillan
1981	Macmillan sells Brentano's to Brentano's president, Paul Ohran, and vice presidents Peter Slater and Monica Hollander
1982	Brentano's files for Chapter 11 bankruptcy
1983	Brentano's acquired by Waldenbooks

| 1973 | Louis and Thomas Borders open first Borders Book Shop general bookstore in Ann Arbor |

1992	Borders Book Shops sold to Kmart
1933	Walden Book Co. founded as chain of rental libraries by Lawrence Hoyt and Melvin Kafka
1957	Kafka sells his interest to Hoyt
1960	Russell Hoyt, Lawrence's son, enters business
1962	First Walden Book Store established in Pittsburgh, Pennsylvania
1969	Hoyt sells Walden Book Co. to Broadway Hale Stores; name changed to Waldenbooks
1974	Broadway Hale becomes Carter Hawley Hale
1983	Waldenbooks acquires Brentano's
1984	Carter Hawley Hale sells Waldenbooks to Kmart
1984	Waldenbooks opens Reader's Market
1986	First Waldenbooks & More opened
1987	Waldenbooks acquires U.S. outlets of Coles
1990	Management of Reader's Market switched from Waldenbooks to Kmart
1992	Waldenbooks & More discontinued
1992	Kmart founds Basset Book Shops
1992	Kmart acquires Borders Book Shops
1993	Borders absorbs Basset Book Shops
1995	Waldenbooks discontinues Longmeadow Press
1994	Kmart combines operations of Waldenbooks and Borders to form the Borders-Waldenbooks Group
1994	Borders-Walden Group acquires CD Superstore Inc. which is then renamed Planet Music Inc.
1994	Borders-Walden Inc. renamed the Borders Group
1995	Borders Group goes public; Kmart sells its stake in the company
1997	Borders Group acquires the Library Ltd. of St. Louis
1997	Borders Group acquires Books Etc. of the United Kingdom
1999	Borders Group acquires 19.9 percent of Sprout Inc.
1999	Borders Group acquires All Wound Up
2001	Sprout is dissolved
2001	All Wound Up is discontinued
2003	Borders Group acquires stake in Echo
2003	Borders Group acquires Hawley-Cooke Booksellers of Louisville
2003	Borders forms Borders Classics (publishing)
2003	Borders changes name of State Street Classics to Borders Press
2004	Borders Group acquires 97 percent stake of Paperchase Products of the United Kingdom

Crown Books

1954	Herbert Haft opens first Dart Drug store
1977	Robert Haft, Herbert's son, founds Crown Books
1981	Thrifty Drug Stores buys 50 percent share of Crown Books
1983	Crown goes public
1984	Dart Group sells Dart Drug
1986	Thrifty sells stake in Crown; Dart Group is majority shareholder
1989	Super Crown Books Corp. organized as wholly owned subsidiary of Crown
1990	First Super Crown opened
1993	Herbert Haft removes Robert Haft from family businesses; Ronald Haft named Crown president
1995	Herbert and Ronald Haft removed from Crown management
1998	Dart Group (including Crown and other subsidiaries) sold to Richfood Holdings
1998	Crown files for Chapter 11 bankruptcy
1999	Crown emerges from bankruptcy
2001	Crown files for Chapter 11 bankruptcy again
2001	Crown files for liquidation

Books-A-Million

1917	Bookland founded
1987	Bookland Stores Inc. acquires Gateway
1988	First Books-A-Million superstore opened
1992	Books-A-Million acquires Book$mart, American Wholesale, and Anderson News Corp., all companies controlled by Books-A-Million's principal owners, the Anderson family
1992	Books-A-Million goes public
1994	Books-A-Million purchases Books & Co. of Ohio
1998	Anderson News Corp. acquires Aramark Magazine & Book Services
1998	Books-A-Million launches Joe Muggs Newsstand
1998	Books-A-Million acquires NetCentral

Lauriat's

1973	Encore Books founded
1984	Rite Aid Corp. acquires Encore Books from David Schlessinger
1992	Encore Books opens its first superstore
1994	Rite Aid sells Encore Books to Lauriat's

1872	Charles E. Lauriat opens first Lauriat's in Boston
1982	Lauriat's establishes Royal Discount Bookstores
1992	Royal Discount Bookstores acquires Buddenbrooks Booksmith of Boston
1994	ING Equity Partners helps finance purchase of Encore Books by Lauriat's/CMI Holding Corp.
1994	Lauriat's acquires Book Corner stores from Hudson County News Co.; Hudson retains right to Book Corner name for Hudson's airport outlets
1995	Lauriat's opens first superstore
1996	Thomas H. Lee Co. sells interest in CMI Holding Corp. to ING Equity Partners; ING becomes majority owner of CMI
1998	Lauriat's files Chapter 11 bankruptcy
1999	Lauriat's liquidates business

Chapter One

1. Edward Shils, "The Bookshop in America," in *The American Reading Public: What It Reads, Why It Reads,* ed. Roger H. Smith (New York: R. R. Bowker, 1963), pp. 138–39.

2. Ibid., pp. 148–49.

3. Charles Hix, "Crown's Jewels: A Super Crown Tour," *Publishers Weekly* 237 (50), December 14, 1990, pp. 39–40; Nancy Youman, "Wooing Back the Bookworms," *Adweek's Marketing Week* 31 (25), June 18, 1990, p. 17.

4. "With Sales Improving, Walden Looking for Better '90," *BP Report on the Business of Publishing* 15 (14), March 5, 1990, pp. 1–2.

5. John Mutter, "Barnes & Noble Goes on the Road," *Publishers Weekly* 237 (50), December 14, 1990, pp. 35–38; Maureen J. O'Brien, "Barnes & Noble Opens First 'Superstore,'" *Publishers Weekly* 237 (37), September 14, 1990, p. 8.

6. Nora Rawlinson, "They Look Like Libraries!" *Library Journal* 115 (20), November 15, 1990, p. 6. Nora Rawlinson, the author of this piece, soon moved to the position of editor-in-chief at *Publishers Weekly,* the primary periodical serving the book industry. She left that position in 2005.

7. Youman, "Wooing Back the Bookworms."

8. On the early development of the chain store, see Paul H. Nystrom, *Economics of Retailing: Retail Institutions and Trends,* 3rd revised and enlarged ed. (New York: Ronald Press, 1932), pp. 213–25; M. M. Zimmerman, *Super Market: Spectacular Exponent of Mass Distribution* (New York: Super Market Publishing Co., 1937); Godfrey M. Lebhar, *Chain Stores in America, 1859–1962,* 3rd ed. (New York: Chain Store Publishing Corp., 1963); James M. Mayo, *The American Grocery Store: The Business Evolution of an Architectural Space* (Westport, Conn.: Greenwood, 1993).

9. The most comprehensive examination of the contemporary book industry is Lewis A. Coser, Charles Kadushin, and Walter W. Powell, *Books: The Culture and Commerce of Publishing* (1982; Chicago: University of Chicago Press, 1985). Using an organizational perspective, Coser, Kadushin, and Powell describe how people within publishing do their jobs, as well as the major changes that have confronted publishing in recent years. While still valuable, this study is now quite dated. See also Walter W. Powell, "Whither the Local Bookstore?" *Daedalus* 112 (1), Winter 1983, pp. 51–64; here Powell noted the consequences of rationalizing bookselling in the early 1980s. Other sociological works on the twentieth-century book industry include Robert Escarpit, *The Book Revolution* (1965; London: George G. Harap & Co., 1966); Robert Escarpit, *Sociology of Literature*, 2nd ed. (London: Frank Cass & Co., 1971); Michael Lane with Jeremy Booth, *Books and Publishers: Commerce against Culture in Postwar Britain* (Lexington, Mass.: Lexington Books, 1980); Elizabeth Long, *The American Dream and the Popular Novel* (Boston: Routledge & Kegan Paul, 1985); Walter W. Powell, *Getting into Print: The Decision-Making Process in Scholarly Publishing* (Chicago: University of Chicago Press, 1985); Irving Louis Horowitz, *Communicating Ideas: The Politics of Scholarly Publishing,* 2nd expanded ed. (New Brunswick: Transaction, 1991); Eva Hemmungs Wirtén, *Global Infatuation: Explorations in Transnational Publishing and Texts: The Case of Harlequin Enterprises and Sweden* (Uppsala: Section for Sociology of Literature at the Department of Literature, Uppsala University, 1998); Patricia H. Thornton, *Markets from Culture: Institutional Logics and Organizational Decisions in Higher Education Publishing* (Stanford, Calif.: Stanford Business Books, 2004). For an account of different scholarly perspectives used to analyze book publishing, see Laura J. Miller, "Publishing as Medium," in *International Encyclopedia of the Social and Behavioral Sciences,* ed. Neil J. Smelser and Paul B. Baltes, pp. 12599–603 (Amsterdam: Pergamon, 2001).

10. Lane appears to have been the first to use this phrase. Michael Lane, "Shapers of Culture: The Editor in Book Publishing," *Annals of the American Academy of Political and Social Science* 421, September 1975, pp. 34–42.

11. Coser, Kadushin, and Powell, *Books,* p. 7.

12. Ibid., p. 35.

13. Two books, both written by industry veterans, that also argue that the most valuable books are now sacrificed to the quest for profits are André Schiffrin's *The Business of Books: How International Conglomerates Took Over Publishing and Changed the Way We Read* (London: Verso, 2000), and Jason Epstein's *Book Business: Publishing Past Present Future* (New York: W. W. Norton, 2001).

14. See Richard Ohmann, "The Shaping of a Canon: U.S. Fiction, 1960–1975," *Critical Inquiry* 10 (1), September 1983, pp. 199–223.

15. Raymond Williams, *Marxism and Literature* (Oxford: Oxford University Press, 1977).

16. Elizabeth Long, "The Cultural Meaning of Concentration in Publishing," *Book Research Quarterly* 1 (4), Winter 1985–86, pp. 3–27. See also Michael Lane, "Publishing Managers, Publishing House Organization and Role Conflict," *Sociology* 4 (3), September 1970, pp. 367–83; Lane, *Books and Publishers;* Ann Haugland, "Books

as Culture/Books as Commerce," *Journalism Quarterly* 71 (4), Winter 1994, pp. 787–99, for useful analyses of the culture-commerce distinction.

17. Janice Radway, "The Book-of-the-Month Club and the General Reader: On the Uses of 'Serious Fiction,'" in *Literature and Social Practice,* ed. Philippe Desan, Priscilla Parkhurst Ferguson, and Wendy Griswold (Chicago: University of Chicago Press, 1989), pp. 154–76; Janice Radway, "The Scandal of the Middlebrow: The Book-of-the-Month Club, Class Fracture, and Cultural Authority," *South Atlantic Quarterly* 89 (4), Fall 1990, pp. 703–36; Janice Radway, "Mail-Order Culture and Its Critics: The Book-of-the-Month Club, Commodification and Consumption, and the Problem of Cultural Authority," in *Cultural Studies,* ed. Lawrence Grossberg, Cary Nelson, and Paula A. Treichler (New York: Routledge, 1992), pp. 512–30; Janice Radway, *A Feeling for Books: The Book-of-the-Month Club, Literary Taste, and Middle-Class Desire* (Chapel Hill: University of North Carolina Press, 1997).

18. For instance, Herbert J. Gans, *Popular Culture and High Culture: An Analysis and Evaluation of Taste* (New York: Basic Books, 1974); Alan Swingewood, *The Myth of Mass Culture* (London: Macmillan, 1977).

19. Radway, "The Scandal of the Middlebrow," pp. 726–29.

20. Karl Marx and Friedrich Engels, "Manifesto of the Communist Party" (1848), in *The Marx-Engels Reader,* 2nd ed., ed. Robert C. Tucker (New York: W. W. Norton, 1978), pp. 469–500.

21. Karl Polanyi, *The Great Transformation* (1944; Boston: Beacon, 1957), p. 30; Karl Polanyi, "Our Obsolete Market Mentality: Civilization Must Find a New Thought Pattern" (1947), in *Economic Sociology,* ed. Richard Swedberg (Cheltenham: Edward Elgar Publishing, 1996), pp. 146–54.

22. Mark Granovetter, "Economic Action and Social Structure: The Problem of Embeddedness" (1985), in *The Sociology of Economic Life,* ed. Mark Granovetter and Richard Swedberg (Boulder: Westview Press, 1992), pp. 53–81; Mark Granovetter, "Economic Institutions as Social Constructions: A Framework for Analysis," *Acta Sociologica* 35 (1), March 1992, pp. 3–11.

23. Sharon Zukin and Paul DiMaggio, introduction to *Structures of Capital: The Social Organization of the Economy,* ed. Sharon Zukin and Paul DiMaggio (Cambridge: Cambridge University Press, 1990), p. 17. For additional statements on the role of culture in economics, see Kenneth E. Boulding, "Toward the Development of a Cultural Economics," in *The Idea of Culture in the Social Sciences,* ed. Louis Schneider and Charles M. Bonjean (London: Cambridge University Press, 1973), pp. 47–64; Paul DiMaggio, "Cultural Aspects of Economic Action and Organization," in *Beyond the Marketplace: Rethinking Economy and Society,* ed. Roger Friedland and A. F. Robertson (New York: Aldine de Gruyter, 1990), 113–36; Roger Friedland and Robert R. Alford, "Bringing Society Back In: Symbols, Practices, and Institutional Contradictions," in *The New Institutionalism in Organizational Analysis,* ed. Walter W. Powell and Paul J. DiMaggio (Chicago: University of Chicago Press, 1991), pp. 232–63; Frank R. Dobbin, "Cultural Models of Organization: The Social Construction of Rational Organizing Principles," in *The Sociology of Culture: Emerging Theoretical Perspectives,* ed. Diana Crane (Oxford: Blackwell, 1994), pp. 117–41.

24. Thornton, *Markets from Culture*.

25. Ibid., p. 139.

26. Don Slater, "Capturing Markets from the Economists," in *Cultural Economy: Cultural Analysis and Commercial Life*, ed. Paul du Gay and Michael Pryke (London: Sage, 2002), pp. 59, 60.

27. For example, Paul du Gay and Michael Pryke, "Cultural Economy: An Introduction," in du Gay and Pryke, *Cultural Economy*, pp. 1–19. See also Michel Callon, "The Embeddedness of Economic Markets in Economies," introduction to *The Laws of the Markets*, ed. Michel Callon (Oxford: Blackwell, 1998), pp. 1–57. Among American work that does discuss the constitutive role of culture in economics are Paul DiMaggio, "Culture and Economy," in *The Handbook of Economic Sociology*, ed. Neil J. Smelser and Richard Swedberg (Princeton: Princeton University Press, 1994), pp. 27–57; and Viviana A. Zelizer, *The Social Meaning of Money* (New York: Basic Books, 1994).

28. Max Weber, "Religious Rejections of the World and Their Directions" (1915), in *From Max Weber: Essays in Sociology*, ed. H. H. Gerth and C. Wright Mills (New York: Oxford University Press, 1946), pp. 323–59; Max Weber, *Economy and Society: An Outline of Interpretive Sociology* (Berkeley: University of California Press, 1978).

29. However, it needs to be underscored that both book publishing and bookselling, even by the major firms, are considerably less profitable than other entertainment industries. Additionally, the book industry, like other media industries, is less rationalized than most other consumer goods industries, in large part because the items offered for sale change frequently and substantially, and because consumer tastes in media products are difficult to predict. For a discussion of these problems, see Paul M. Hirsch, "Processing Fads and Fashions: An Organization-Set Analysis of Cultural Industry Systems" (1972), in Granovetter and Swedberg, *The Sociology of Economic Life*, pp. 363–83.

30. George Ritzer, *The McDonaldization of Society: An Investigation into the Changing Character of Contemporary Social Life*, revised ed. (Thousand Oaks, Calif.: Sage, 1996).

31. Ibid., pp. 131–36.

32. See Philip Slater, *The Pursuit of Loneliness: American Culture at the Breaking Point*, revised ed. (Boston: Beacon Press, 1976).

33. John H. Bunzel, *The American Small Businessman* (New York: Alfred A. Knopf, 1962); David E. Shi, *The Simple Life: Plain Living and High Thinking in American Culture* (New York: Oxford University Press, 1985); Norman Pollack, *The Humane Economy: Populism, Capitalism, and Democracy* (New Brunswick: Rutgers University Press, 1990).

34. For example, Rob Shields, ed., *Lifestyle Shopping: The Subject of Consumption* (London: Routledge, 1992); William Leach, *Land of Desire: Merchants, Power, and the Rise of a New American Culture* (New York: Vintage Books, 1993); Pasi Falk and Colin Campbell, eds., *The Shopping Experience* (London: Sage, 1997); Kim Humphrey, *Shelf Life: Supermarkets and the Changing Cultures of Consumption* (Cambridge: Cambridge University Press, 1998); Rachel Bowlby, *Carried Away: The Invention of Modern Shopping* (New York: Columbia University Press, 2001); Sharon Zukin, *Point of Purchase: How Shopping Changed American Culture* (New York: Routledge, 2004).

35. Rob Shields, "Spaces for the Subject of Consumption," in Shields, *Lifestyle Shopping,* p. 6.

36. Ibid.; see also Rob Shields, "The Individual, Consumption Cultures and the Fate of Community," in Shields, *Lifestyle Shopping,* pp. 99–113.

37. Gregory P. Stone, "City Shoppers and Urban Identification: Observations on the Social Psychology of City Life," *American Journal of Sociology* 60 (1), July 1954, pp. 38–40.

38. David Monod, *Store Wars: Shopkeepers and the Culture of Mass Marketing, 1890–1939* (Toronto: University of Toronto Press, 1996).

39. Karl Marx, *The Eighteenth Brumaire of Louis Bonaparte* (1869; New York: International Publishers, 1963), p. 50; Marx and Engels, "Manifesto of the Communist Party," p. 482.

40. Daniel J. Boorstin, *The Americans: The Democratic Experience* (1973; New York: Vintage Books, 1974), p. 111.

41. C. Wright Mills, *White Collar: The American Middle Classes* (New York: Oxford University Press, 1951), pp. 34–35.

42. Viviana A. Zelizer, "Human Values and the Market: The Case of Life Insurance and Death in 19th-Century America" (1978), in Granovetter and Swedberg, *The Sociology of Economic Life,* pp. 285–304.

43. Ann Swidler, "Culture in Action: Symbols and Strategies," *American Sociological Review* 51 (2), April 1986, pp. 273–86.

44. Christopher M. Dixon et al., "Latte Grande, No Sprinkles: An Exploratory Observational Study of Customer Behaviour at Chapters Bookstores," in *Beyond the Web: Technologies, Knowledge and People: Proceedings of the 29th Annual Conference of the Canadian Association for Information Science* (Quebec City, 2001), pp. 165–74.

45. See Coser, Kadushin, and Powell, *Books;* John P. Dessauer, *Book Publishing: The Basic Introduction,* new expanded ed. (New York: Continuum, 1993).

Chapter Two

1. Elizabeth L. Eisenstein, *The Printing Press as an Agent of Change: Communications and Cultural Transformations in Early-Modern Europe* (1979; Cambridge: Cambridge University Press, 1980); Lucien Febvre and Henri-Jean Martin, *The Coming of the Book: The Impact of Printing 1450–1800* (1958; London: Verso, 1990).

2. On the early American book trade, see Lawrence C. Wroth, "Book Production and Distribution from the Beginning to the American Revolution," in *The Book in America: A History of the Making and Selling of Books in the United States,* 2nd ed., by Hellmut Lehmann-Haupt, in collaboration with Lawrence C. Wroth and Rollo G. Silver (New York: R. R. Bowker, 1952), pp. 1–59; Charles A. Madison, *Book Publishing in America* (New York: McGraw-Hill, 1966); John Tebbel, *A History of Book Publishing in the United States,* vol. 1, *The Creation of an Industry, 1630–1865* (New York: R. R. Bowker, 1972); James Gilreath, "American Book Distribution," *Proceedings of the American Antiquarian Society* 95 (part 2), October 16, 1985, pp. 501–83; Henry Walcott Boynton, *Annals of American Bookselling, 1638–1850* (1932; New Castle: Oak

Knoll Books, 1991); Ronald J. Zboray, *A Fictive People: Antebellum Economic Development and the American Reading Public* (New York: Oxford University Press, 1993); Hugh Amory and David D. Hall, eds., *A History of the Book in America,* vol. 1, *The Colonial Book in the Atlantic World* (Cambridge: Cambridge University Press, 2000).

3. John Tebbel, *A History of Book Publishing in the United States,* vol. 2, *The Expansion of an Industry, 1865–1919* (New York: R. R. Bowker, 1975), p. 106; Joshua L. Rosenbloom, "Economics and the Emergence of Modern Publishing in the United States," *Publishing History* 29, 1991, pp. 59–61; Zboray, *A Fictive People.*

4. Alan Trachtenberg, *The Incorporation of America: Culture and Society in the Gilded Age* (New York: Hill & Wang, 1982), p. 143.

5. See, e.g., Hamilton Wright Mabie, *Books and Culture* (New York: Dodd, Mead and Company, 1896). The classic statement on this conception of culture is from Matthew Arnold, *Culture and Anarchy* (1932; Cambridge: Cambridge University Press, 1960). For analyses of the genteel culture of the Gilded Age, see also Raymond Williams, *Culture and Society, 1780–1950* (New York: Harper Torchbooks, 1958); Helen Lefkowitz Horowitz, *Culture and The City: Cultural Philanthropy in Chicago from the 1880s to 1917* (1976; Chicago: University of Chicago Press, 1989); Richard L. Bushman, *The Refinement of America: Persons, Houses, Cities* (New York: Vintage Books, 1993).

6. Michael Denning, *Mechanic Accents: Dime Novels and Working-Class Culture in America* (London: Verso, 1987); Nicola Beisel, "Constructing a Shifting Moral Boundary: Literature and Obscenity in Nineteenth-Century America," in *Cultivating Differences: Symbolic Boundaries and the Making of Inequality,* ed. Michèle Lamont and Marcel Fournier (Chicago: University of Chicago Press, 1992), pp. 104–28; Dee Garrison, *Apostles of Culture: The Public Librarian and American Society, 1876–1920* (1979; Madison: University of Wisconsin Press, 2003).

7. Paul DiMaggio, "Cultural Entrepreneurship in Nineteenth-Century Boston: The Creation of an Organizational Base for High Culture in America," in *Media, Culture and Society: A Critical Reader,* ed. Richard Collins et al. (London: Sage, 1986), pp. 194–211.

8. George P. Brett, "Book-Publishing and Its Present Tendencies," *Atlantic Monthly* 111, April 1913, p. 455.

9. O. H. Cheney, *Economic Survey of the Book Industry 1930–1931,* 1st ed. (New York: National Association of Book Publishers, 1931), p. 224. By "list-making," Cheney means the activities of acquisition and editing, the list being all those titles published by a particular house.

10. American Book Publishers Council, *The Situation and Outlook for the Book Trade* (New York: American Book Publishers Council, 1951).

11. See, for example, Henry I. Burr, *Observations on Trade Book Sales* ([New York]: American Book-Stratford Press, 1949); Charles F. Bound, *A Banker Looks at Book Publishing* (New York: R. R. Bowker, 1950); "Book Distribution Is Topic of Bookbuilders' Meetings," *Publishers Weekly* 164 (10), September 5, 1953, pp. 847–48; Frederic G. Melcher, "How Shall We Face the Whole Problem?" *Publishers Weekly* 166 (12), September 18, 1954, p. 1291; Frederic G. Melcher, "Publishers Concentrate on the Problems of Distribution," *Publishers Weekly* 169 (20), May 21, 1956, p. 2137; "Central

Role Is Distribution," *Publishers Weekly* 175 (24), June 15, 1959, p. 50; Chandler B. Grannis, "The ALA Bulletin Views Book Distribution," *Publishers Weekly* 183 (21), May 27, 1963, p. 42; Chandler B. Grannis, "Distribution and Other Problems for 1965," *Publishers Weekly* 186 (25), December 28, 1964, p. 55; "Authors, Booksellers, Publishers in Sharp Exchange at First PW Seminar," *Publishers Weekly* 203 (16), April 16, 1973, pp. 24–26; Benjamin M. Compaine, *Book Distribution and Marketing, 1976–1980* (White Plains, N.Y.: Knowledge Industry Publications, 1976); Arthur Andersen & Co., *Book Distribution in the United States: Issues and Perceptions* (New York: Book Industry Study Group, 1982); Leonard Shatzkin, *In Cold Type: Overcoming the Book Crisis* (Boston: Houghton Mifflin, 1982).

12. Rental libraries existed in the thousands during the first half of the twentieth century; sometimes the rental library was the only book outlet in a community. As well as standing on their own, rental libraries were placed in department stores and in regular bookshops, sometimes to be operated by the bookstore itself, sometimes by a rental chain. See R. L. Duffus, *Books: Their Place in a Democracy* (Boston: Houghton Mifflin, 1930), pp. 133–40; William West, "Selling More Books," *Bulletin of the National Retail Dry Goods Association* 20 (12), December 1938, pp. 52–53; Philip B. Eppard, "The Rental Library in Twentieth-Century America," *Journal of Library History* 21 (1), Winter 1986, pp. 240–52. For an account of the rental library during its later years, and shortly before it disappeared altogether, see Charles B. Anderson, "Portrait of a Rental Library," *Publishers Weekly* 194 (11), September 9, 1968, pp. 52–54.

13. Cheney, *Economic Survey*, pp. 234, 236.

14. William Miller, *The Book Industry* (New York: Columbia University Press, 1949), pp. 89, 147.

15. John P. Dessauer, "Book Industry Economics in 1984," in *The Book Publishing Annual*, (New York: R. R. Bowker, 1985), pp. 105–20. See also "Changes in Distribution Viewed at N.Y.U. Course," *Publishers Weekly* 172 (28), November 18, 1957, pp. 28–30.

16. Walter S. Hayward and Percival White, *Chain Stores: Their Management and Operation*, 2nd ed. (New York: McGraw Hill, 1925); Paul H. Nystrom, *Economics of Retailing: Retail Institutions and Trends*, 3rd revised and enlarged ed. (New York: Ronald Press, 1932); M. M. Zimmerman, *Super Market: Spectacular Exponent of Mass Distribution* (New York: Super Market Publishing Co., 1937); Godfrey M. Lebhar, *Chain Stores in America, 1859–1962*, 3rd ed. (New York: Chain Store Publishing Corp., 1963); Alfred D. Chandler, Jr., *The Visible Hand: The Managerial Revolution in American Business* (Cambridge, Mass.: Belknap Press, 1977).

17. Duffus, *Books*, pp. 124–25.

18. This industry publication first appeared in 1873 as *The Publishers' Weekly*. In the 1940s, the name was simplified to *Publishers' Weekly*, and then again in 1971, when it became *Publishers Weekly*. To avoid confusion, I have used the modern form of the name in all references.

19. Ruth Leigh, "Bookselling and Chain Store Methods," *Publishers Weekly* 117 (20), May 17, 1930, pp. 2514–16.

20. The book industry is somewhat unique in its tradition of returns. Retailers and wholesalers are generally allowed to return unsold books to publishers for credit.

This practice, first implemented in the United States in the mid-nineteenth century, was used sporadically until the 1930s, and became more or less institutionalized after Simon & Schuster offered a full returns privilege on Wendell Wilkie's *One World,* which it published in 1943. W. S. Tryon, "Book Distribution in Mid-Nineteenth Century America: Illustrated by the Publishing Records of Ticknor and Fields, Boston," *Papers of the Bibliographical Society of America* 41 (3), 1947, p. 226; Shatzkin, *In Cold Type,* pp. 97–99; Kenneth C. Davis, *Two-Bit Culture: The Paperbacking of America* (Boston: Houghton Mifflin, 1984), p. 161; John P. Dessauer, *Book Publishing: The Basic Introduction,* new expanded ed. (New York: Continuum, 1993), p. 127. Returns are yet another aspect of the "distribution problem" that has long stymied the publishing industry. Considered wasteful and expensive as they encourage publishers to oversell and retailers to overbuy, returns can cause financial chaos for a press that discovers months after books go out its doors that they were not really sold after all. For mass-market paperbacks, returns have been known to account for more than 50 percent of books originally shipped.

21. Chandler, *The Visible Hand;* Susan Strasser, *Satisfaction Guaranteed: The Making of the American Mass Market* (Washington: Smithsonian Institution Press, 1989).

22. Charles E. Brookes, "The Ohio Book Project — a Laboratory: The Wholesaler's Problem," *Publishers Weekly* 155 (23), June 4, 1949, p. 2291.

23. American Book Publishers Council, *The Situation and Outlook for the Book Trade,* p. 31.

24. Miller, *The Book Industry,* p. 90.

25. For more on the history of the book wholesaler, see Laura J. Miller, "The Rise and Not-Quite-Fall of the American Book Wholesaler," *Journal of Media Economics* 16 (2), 2003, pp. 97–120.

26. Duffus, *Books,* p. 63.

27. Coburn T. Wheeler, "The Position of the Wholesaler in the Book Trade," *Harvard Business Review* 11 (2), January 1933, p. 241.

28. One estimate held that during the decades between the Civil War and World War I, 90 percent of book sales in the United States came from channels other than bookstores. While Sheehan contends that this figure is most likely an exaggeration, he agrees that sales from bookshops probably comprised a minority of overall book sales. Donald Sheehan, *This Was Publishing: A Chronicle of the Book Trade in the Gilded Age* (Bloomington: Indiana University Press, 1952), pp. 152, 189.

29. "The modern subscription-book business, like its sister, the mail-order business, comes nearer the standardization and 'efficiency' of American business in general than do other branches of the book trade" (Duffus, *Books,* p. 73). For more on subscription and mail-order selling, see Sheehan, *This Was Publishing,* pp. 190–98.

30. As has been well documented, the success of the "paperback revolution" of the 1940s was dependent on the exploitation of newsstands as the principal channel of distribution. See Frank L. Schick, *The Paperbound Book in America: The History of Paperbacks and Their European Background* (New York: R. R. Bowker, 1958); Roger H. Smith, *Paperback Parnassus: The Birth, the Development, the Pending Crisis . . . of the Modern American Paperbound Book* (Boulder: Westview Press, 1976); Davis, *Two-Bit Culture.*

31. George P. Brett Jr., in *Publishers on Publishing,* ed. Gerald Gross (1930; New York: Grosset & Dunlap, 1961), pp. 127–28.

32. Quoted in Ruth I. Gordon, "Paul Elder: Bookseller-Publisher, 1897–1917: A Bay Area Reflection" (Ph.D. diss., University of California, Berkeley, 1977), p. 136.

33. Lawrence W. Levine, *Highbrow/Lowbrow: The Emergence of Cultural Hierarchy in America* (Cambridge: Harvard University Press, 1988).

34. For a piece that contains most of the criticisms directed at nonbook outlets, see Ellis Parker Butler, *Dollarature; or, The Drug-Store Book* (Boston: Houghton Mifflin, 1930). Butler excoriates drugstores for price-cutting, for catering to the common shopgirl, for mixing books with toiletries, for using uninformed clerks to sell books, and for furthering the standardization of literature.

35. Cheney, *Economic Survey,* p. 264.

36. "Better Bookselling for Department Stores," *Publishers Weekly* 135 (1), January 7, 1939, p. 27.

37. American Book Publishers Council, *The Situation and Outlook for the Book Trade,* p. 35.

38. Probably the best history of department stores and their place in American culture is William Leach, *Land of Desire: Merchants, Power, and the Rise of a New American Culture* (New York: Vintage Books, 1993). See also Gunther Barth, *City People: The Rise of Modern City Culture in Nineteenth-Century America* (Oxford: Oxford University Press, 1980); Peter Samson, "The Department Store, Its Past and Its Future: A Review Article," *Business History Review* 55 (1), Spring 1981, pp. 26–34; Susan Porter Benson, *Counter Cultures: Saleswomen, Managers, and Customers in American Department Stores, 1890–1940* (Urbana: University of Illinois Press, 1986).

39. Barth, *City People,* p. 127.

40. Ralph M. Hower, *History of Macy's of New York 1858–1919: Chapters in the Evolution of the Department Store* (Cambridge: Harvard University Press, 1943), pp. 102, 161.

41. John Wanamaker, *Golden Book of the Wanamaker Stores* (Philadelphia: John Wanamaker, 1911), p. 78; "Book Trade Turns Out to Honor Wanamaker's Joe McCleary," *Publishers Weekly* 172 (3), July 15, 1957, p. 30.

42. See, e.g., West, "Selling More Books," p. 42.

43. S. Holt McAloney, "Books Sell Other Merchandise," *Bulletin of the National Retail Dry Goods Association* 20 (12), December 1938, pp. 56–57.

44. Advertisement, *Dry Goods Economist,* no. 3965, July 3, 1920, p. 72. For a later example, see "The Pulling Power of Book Fairs," *Stores* 42 (10), November 1960, pp. 60–61.

45. "A Bargain-Counter Book Victory," *Literary Digest* 47 (24), December 13, 1913, pp. 1158–59.

46. For an analysis of American reading habits over time, see Helen Damon-Moore and Carl F. Kaestle, "Surveying American Readers," in *Literacy in the United States: Readers and Reading Since 1880,* ed. Carl F. Kaestle et al. (New Haven: Yale University Press, 1991), pp. 180–203. These authors find that higher levels of education since the 1940s probably did produce a slight increase in the proportion of the total population

who were regular book readers. Nevertheless, a college degree hardly guaranteed a reading habit. Between 1949 and 1984, only 30 to 52 percent of all college graduates were classified as regular book readers; in 1984, the figure was 37 percent (p. 194). The book industry has undoubtedly benefited from the growth of higher education, but a widespread culture of book reading has never materialized in the United States.

47. Laura J. Miller, "Selling the Product," in *A History of the Book in America*, vol. 5, *The Enduring Book: Print Culture in Postwar America*, ed. David Paul Nord, Joan Shelley Rubin, and Michael Schudson (New York: Cambridge University Press, forthcoming).

48. John K. Winkler, *Five and Ten: The Fabulous Life of F. W. Woolworth* (New York: Robert M. McBride, 1940); Lebhar, *Chain Stores in America;* Eugene Ferkauf, *Going into Business: How to Do It, by the Man Who Did It* (New York: Chelsea House Publishers, 1977). The company now known as Kmart has in its history spelled its name variously as K-mart, K mart, and Kmart.

49. See, e.g., U.S. Senate, Select Committee on Small Business, *Discount-House Operations: Hearings Before a Subcommittee of the Select Committee on Small Business, United States Senate, Eighty-Fifth Congress, Second Session on Competitive Impact of Discount-House Operations on Small Business [June 23, 24, and 25, 1958]* (Washington: United States Government Printing Office, 1958), p. 393; "Korvette's New Store Poses Threat to Philadelphia Bookstores," *Publishers Weekly* 176 (19), November 9, 1959, p. 32; "Profits between the Lines," *Discount Merchandiser* 2 (8), August 1962, pp. 40–41; "Books Make Profits," *Discount Merchandiser* 2 (10), October 1962, p. 45.

50. Lee Werblin, "Supermarkets and the Rack Jobber," *Publishers Weekly* 165 (25), June 19, 1954, pp. 2650–51; M. M. Zimmerman, *The Super Market: A Revolution in Distribution* (New York: McGraw-Hill, 1955), pp. 236–57; Business Week, "The Supermarket: Revolution in Retailing," in *Changing Patterns in Retailing: Readings on Current Trends,* ed. John W. Wingate and Arnold Corbin (Homewood, Ill.: Richard D. Irwin, 1956), pp. 75–90; Julian H. Handler, *How to Sell the Supermarkets: For Non-Food Manufacturers and Distributors,* 3rd ed. (New York: Fairchild Publications, 1966), pp. 42, 151–52.

51. Alan Dutscher, "The Book Business in America," *Contemporary Issues* 5 (17), April–May 1954, pp. 46–47.

52. On the conglomeratization of the publishing industry, see, e.g., Dan Lacy, "The Changing Face of Publishing," in *What Happens in Book Publishing,* 2nd ed., ed. Chandler B. Grannis (New York: Columbia University Press, 1967), pp. 423–37; Elin B. Christianson, "Mergers in the Publishing Industry, 1958–1970," *Journal of Library History* 7 (1), January 1972, pp. 5–32; James Chotas and Miriam Phelps, "Who Owns What," in *The Question of Size in the Book Industry Today: A Publishers Weekly Special Report,* ed. Judith Appelbaum (New York: R. R. Bowker, 1978), pp. 9–12; Walter W. Powell, "Competition versus Concentration in the Book Trade," *Journal of Communication* 30 (2), Spring 1980, pp. 89–97; Lewis A. Coser, Charles Kadushin, and Walter W. Powell, *Books: The Culture and Commerce of Publishing* (1982; Chicago: University of Chicago Press, 1985); Robert E. Baensch, "Consolidation in Publishing and Allied Industries," *Book Research Quarterly* 4 (4), Winter 1988–89, pp. 6–14; Albert N. Greco, "Mergers and Acquisitions in Publishing, 1984–1988: Some Public

Policy Issues," *Book Research Quarterly* 5 (3), Fall 1989, pp. 25–44; Dan Lacy, "From Family Enterprise to Global Conglomerate," *Media Studies Journal* 6 (3), Summer 1992, pp. 1–13; Beth Luey, "The Impact of Consolidation and Internationalization," introduction to *The Structure of International Publishing in the 1990s,* ed. Fred Kobrak and Beth Luey (New Brunswick: Transaction, 1992), pp. 1–22; Dessauer, *Book Publishing;* John F. Baker, "Reinventing the Book Business," *Publishers Weekly* 241 (11), March 14, 1994, pp. 36–40; Albert Greco, "Market Concentration Levels in the U.S. Consumer Book Industry: 1995–1996," *Journal of Cultural Economics* 24 (4), November 2000, pp. 321–36. For an outline of who owns whom in publishing, see Laura J. Miller "Major Publishers' Holdings" (http://people.brandeis.edu/~lamiller/publishers.html).

53. "Book Chains Do $35,000,000 Business," *Publishers Weekly* 121 (1), January 2, 1932, p. 48; "Government Census of Retailing," *Publishers Weekly* 121 (4), January 23, 1932, p. 375; Paul D. Doebler, "Areas of Major Change in the Book Industry Today," in *Book Industry Trends 1978,* by John P. Dessauer, Paul D. Doebler, and E. Wayne Nordberg (Darien, Conn.: Book Industry Study Group, 1978), p. 24.

54. On the origins and early years of Doubleday Book Shops, see Madison, *Book Publishing in America,* p. 279; F. N. Doubleday, *The Memoirs of a Publisher* (Garden City, N.Y.: Doubleday, 1972), pp. 177–79; John Tebbel, *A History of Book Publishing in the United States,* vol. 3, *The Golden Age between Two Wars, 1920–1940* (New York: R. R. Bowker, 1978), pp. 108–9.

55. On Brentano's early days, see "In and Out of the Corner Office," *Publishers Weekly* 123 (14), April 8, 1933, pp. 1212–13; "Brentano's Faces Crisis as Trustees Resign," *Publishers Weekly* 123 (13), April 1, 1933, pp. 1124–25; Farnsworth Fowle, "Crowell-Collier Buys Brentano's and Will Run It as Subsidiary," *New York Times,* April 5, 1962; Tom Mahoney and Leonard Sloane, *The Great Merchants: America's Foremost Retail Institutions and the People Who Made Them Great,* new and enlarged ed. (New York: Harper & Row, 1966).

56. Adolph Kroch held an interest in Brentano's during the 1930s. When Kroch severed his ties with the national chain, he was given the Chicago branch, which then became Kroch's & Brentano's.

57. *American Book Trade Directory,* 15th ed. (New York: R. R. Bowker, 1961).

58. "Record Number of Bookshops Were Opened in 1961," *Publishers Weekly* 181 (3), January 15, 1962, pp. 97–98.

59. Sidney Gross, "How to Stock," in *How to Run a Paperback Bookshop,* ed. Sidney Gross and Phyllis B. Stecklers (New York: R. R. Bowker, 1965), p. 58.

60. Kate Whouley, "Paperback Booksmith: The History and Legacy of an Industry Pioneer," *American Bookseller* 13 (5), January 1990, pp. 35–38; John Mutter, "Vision-Smith: Marshall Smith," *Publishers Weekly* 245 (18), May 4, 1998, p. 43.

61. John Mutter, "Managing a Revolution," Publishers Weekly 241 (18), May 2, 1994, pp. 51–55.

62. See, e.g., Lisa Belkin, "Discounter Purchases B. Dalton," *New York Times,* November 27, 1986, sec. D; "The Advent of the World Book," *Economist* 305 (7530–31), December 26, 1987, p. 110; Whouley, "Paperback Booksmith," p. 38.

63. See the appendix for chronologies of the merger and acquisition activity described below.

64. Doebler, "Areas of Major Change in the Book Industry Today," p. 24, and my own calculation based on figures from "B. Dalton Boosts Lead Over Waldenbooks in Bookstore Chain Ranking," *BP Report on the Business of Book Publishing* 8 (27), June 13, 1983, pp. 1–3, and U.S. Bureau of the Census, *1982 Census of Retail Trade: Preliminary Report Industry Series: Book Stores (Industry 5942)* (Washington, D.C.: U.S. Government Printing Office, 1984). It should be noted that these figures represent bookstore sales only, and do not include book sales from other kinds of outlets. When the latter are factored in, the market share of the chains would be reduced accordingly.

65. Broadway Hale changed its name to Carter Hawley Hale in 1974.

66. For this account of Waldenbooks' development, see, e.g., West, "Selling More Books," pp. 52–53; Miller, *The Book Industry,* p. 119; American Book Trade Directory, 1969–1970, 19th ed. (New York: R. R. Bowker, 1969); "Walden, Dalton Neck and Neck for Top Revenue Spot," *BP Report on the Business of Book Publishing* 6 (27), June 8, 1981, pp. 1–3; Jerome P. Frank, "Waldenbooks at 50: America's Biggest Book Chain Aims to Turn More Browsers into Buyers," *Publishers Weekly* 223 (17), April 29, 1983, pp. 36–41; John Mutter, "Bankruptcy Updates: Brentano's, Hastings, A&W," *Publishers Weekly* 224 (15), October 7, 1983, p. 16; "'K-books?' How Walden Could Help K mart," *Chain Store Age, General Merchandise Edition* 60, September 1984, pp. 88, 93; Earl C. Gottschalk, Jr., "Carter Hawley Says It Wouldn't Be Hurt by Selling Book Unit to General Cinema," *Wall Street Journal,* May 1, 1984; John Mutter, "Waldenbooks to Be Sold to K mart Chain," *Publishers Weekly* 226 (5), August 3, 1984, pp. 15–16; Stephen J. Sansweet, "Carter Hawley to Sell Walden Book Unit to K mart; General Cinema Ends Option," *Wall Street Journal,* July 23, 1984; Nancy Yoshihara, "Carter Hawley Committed to Sell Book Chain," *Los Angeles Times,* May 25, 1984, sec. 4; "Waldenbooks Agrees to Acquire Coles' U.S. Stores," *BP Report on the Business of Book Publishing* 12 (34), August 3, 1987, pp. 1, 9; The Reference Press and Publishers Group West, *Hoover's Guide to the Book Business* (Austin: Reference Press, 1993).

67. Following a 1969 merger, Dayton was renamed the Dayton Hudson Corporation.

68. On the development of B. Dalton, see "Minneapolis Department Store to Open String of Bookshops," *Publishers Weekly* 189 (19), May 9, 1966, p. 70; "B. Dalton, Bookseller Opens in a Suburb as Subsidiary of Dayton's," *Publishers Weekly* 190 (9), August 29, 1966, pp. 332–34; "B. Dalton, Bookseller Opens in St. Louis Area," *Publishers Weekly* 191 (8), February 20, 1967, pp. 137–38; "Dayton Corporation Acquires Pickwick Book Shops," *Publishers Weekly* 193 (18), April 29, 1968, p. 59; "Walden, Dalton Neck and Neck"; Stan Luxenberg, *Books in Chains: Chain Bookstores and Marketplace Censorship* (New York: National Writers Union, 1991).

69. Barnes & Noble's publishing operations were separately acquired that year by Harper & Row. But in 1991, Riggio's BDB Corporation reacquired the right to publish under the Barnes & Noble name.

70. Barnes & Noble Inc., Form S-3, *Initial Public Offering Prospectus,* September 28, 1994, p. 27.

71. On the development of Barnes & Noble and its merger with B. Dalton, see, e.g., "Sixty-Five Years of Bookselling," *College Store* 5 (7), April 1939, pp. 10 – 11, 34; "Barnes & Noble, Educational Bookstore, Celebrates 75 Years of Service," *Publishers Weekly* 155 (7), February 12, 1949, pp. 901– 4; Tebbel, *A History of Book Publishing in the United States*, vol. 3, pp. 220 –21; "Barnes & Noble Buys Marboro Book Chain," *BP Report on the Business of Book Publishing* 4 (46), October 29, 1979, p. 1; "Barnes & Noble in Joint Venture with Pathmark for Supermarket Book Depts.," *BP Report on the Business of Book Publishing* 6 (35), August 17, 1981, pp. 1, 7; Allene Symons, "Ad Club Members Hear Barnes & Noble's Plans," *Publishers Weekly* 224 (25), December 16, 1983, pp. 47– 49; "Dayton Hudson Puts Dalton on the Block," *BP Report on the Business of Book Publishing* 11 (43), October 6, 1986, pp. 1, 7; "Group Headed by Barnes & Noble to Acquire Dalton," *BP Report on the Business of Book Publishing* 12 (1), December 1, 1986, pp. 1, 7– 8; Martha Groves, "Dayton Hudson Places B. Dalton Up for Sale," *Los Angeles Times,* October 1, 1986, sec. 4; Michael McCarthy and Frank Allen, "Dayton Hudson Plans to Sell B. Dalton, Acknowledges Limited Outlook for Unit," *Wall Street Journal,* October 1, 1986; Bill Richards, "Dayton Hudson Agrees to Sell B. Dalton Unit," *Wall Street Journal,* November 28, 1986; Allene Symons, "Barnes & Noble to Buy B. Dalton; Will Become Largest Chain," *Publishers Weekly* 230 (24), December 12, 1986, pp. 17, 23; "Barnes & Noble Acquires Trademark from HarperCollins," *BP Report on the Business of Book Publishing* 16 (7), January 14, 1991, pp. 7– 8; "B&N Acquires Former Trademark, Changes Corporate Name," *Publishers Weekly* 238 (5), January 25, 1991, p. 14; John Mutter, "A Chat with Bookseller Len Riggio," *Publishers Weekly* 238 (20), May 3, 1991, pp. 33 –38; Stephanie Strom, "Barnes & Noble Goes Public: Vol. 2," *New York Times,* September 3, 1993, sec. D; The Reference Press and Publishers Group West, *Hoover's Guide to the Book Business;* Benn Hall Associates, "Fact Sheet: Department Store of Books, Barnes & Noble, Inc." (circa 1956), Lawrence B. Romaine Trade Catalog Collection (MSS 107), Booksellers Catalogs, box 5, University of California, Santa Barbara.

72. The Hafts sold Dart Drug in 1984, but by that time, the drugstore company was only one of several subsidiaries of the Dart Group. In addition to Crown Books, the Dart Group included Trak Auto, a discount auto parts chain, Shoppers Food Warehouse, a discount grocery chain, Total Beverage, a discount beverage chain, and various real estate holdings. A separate company, Combined Properties, owned major shopping centers in the Washington, D.C., area.

73. On the history of Crown, see, e.g., "D.C. Bookstore War Goes to Court," *BP Report on the Business of Book Publishing* 4(17), April 2, 1979, pp. 2 –3; "Dart, Thriftyway Jointly Open Chain of Stores," *BP Report on the Business of Book Publishing* 5 (34), July 28, 1980, p. 3; "Dalton Leads Walden in Chain Revenue Lineup," BP Report on the Business of Book Publishing 7 (26), June 7, 1982, pp. 1–3; Howard Fields, "Crown Books Offering Goes for $25 a Share," *Publishers Weekly* 224 (9), August 26, 1983, p. 287; Howard Fields, "Crown Chain in SEC Filing Reveals $3-Million Profits," *Publishers Weekly* 223 (23), June 10, 1983, pp. 26 –27; Charles Trueheart, "'You'll Never Pay Full Price Again': The Mushrooming of Crown Books," *Publishers Weekly* 223 (1), January 7, 1983, pp. 40 – 48; Dart Group, *Annual Report 1992;* Robin Goldwyn Blumenthal, "Dart Group Is Emerging from Its Recession-Era Shell," *Wall Street Journal,* sec. B, April 23, 1993; Bryan Burrough, "Divided Dynasty," *Vanity Fair* 56 (12), December 1993, pp.

182–88, 228–40; Karen De Witt, "In Feud over Retail Empire, Family Splits in Public View," *New York Times,* August 29, 1993; Robert A. Rosenblatt, "A Storybook Struggle," *Los Angeles Times,* sec. D, July 18, 1993,; Kara Swisher, "Father-Son Struggle Splinters Dynasty," *Washington Post,* sec. A, July 25, 1993,; Kara Swisher, "Rift in the Boardroom Leads to Family Purge," *Washington Post,* sec. A, July 26, 1993; Robert D. Hershey Jr., "A Reopening of Wounds in Haft Family Struggle," *New York Times,* sec. C, September 12, 1994; Kara Swisher, "The Tale of a House Divided," *Washington Post,* sec. W, May 23, 1994; "Management Changes at Crown," *Bookselling This Week* 2 (34), December 18, 1995, pp. 1, 3; "Haft Resigns from Crown, Chain Positions Itself for New Growth," *Bookselling This Week* 2 (26), October 23, 1995, pp. 1, 5; "Haft Lands Phar from Book World," *Publishers Weekly* 242 (38), September 18, 1995, p. 33; Crown Books Corporation, *Form 10-K for the Fiscal Year Ended January 28, 1995* (1995); Crown Books Corporation, *Form 10-K for the Fiscal Year Ended January 31, 1998* (1998); Dan Cullen, "Crown Files Chapter 11," *Bookselling This Week* 5 (12), July 20, 1998, pp. 1, 3; Jim Milliot, "'Substantial Doubt' about Crown Books' Future," *Publishers Weekly* 245 (19), May 11, 1998, p. 12; Jim Milliot, "Sale of Parent Puts Future of Crown Books in Question," *Publishers Weekly* 245 (16), April 20, 1998, p. 12; Jim Milliot, "Scaled-Down Crown Books Emerges from Bankruptcy," *Publishers Weekly* 246 (47), November 22, 1999, p. 9; John Mutter, "Crown Books Files for Bankruptcy Again," *Publishers Weekly* 248 (8), February 19, 2001, p. 9; Edward Nawotka, "BAM to Buy Crown Stores in D.C. and Chicago," *Publishers Weekly* 248 (11), March 12, 2001, p. 14. For more on the development of all these various chains, see Miller, "Selling the Product."

74. "Crown Sales Top $200 Million; Super Stores Planned," *BP Report on the Business of Book Publishing* 15 (23), May 7, 1990, pp. 1, 6; Charles Hix, "Crown's Jewels: A Super Crown Tour," *Publishers Weekly* 237 (50), December 14, 1990, pp. 39–40; Maureen J. O'Brien, "Barnes & Noble Opens First 'Superstore,'" *Publishers Weekly* 237 (37), September 14, 1990, p. 8; John Mutter, "Chain Chain Change," *Publishers Weekly* 241 (17), April 24, 1995, p. 23.

75. See, e.g., "Bookstop Expanding Presence in Texas Book-Selling Market," *BP Report on the Business of Book Publishing* 10 (36), August 19, 1985, pp. 2–3; "Supermarket Format Propels Bookstop," *Chain Store Age, General Merchandise Trends* 63, December 1987, pp. 57–60; "B&N/Dalton Buys Controlling Interest in Bookstop," *BP Report on the Business of Book Publishing* 14 (43), October 2, 1989, p. 1; "Crown Books Acquires Stake in Bookstop," *BP Report on the Business of Book Publishing* 14 (40), September 11, 1989, p. 1; Crown Books Corporation, *Annual Report 1992* (1992), p. 19; Joe Moreau, "Doing Business in the Age of the Superstore," *American Bookseller* 16 (2), October 1992, pp. 46–53.

76. "New Shops," *Publishers Weekly* 203 (11), March 12, 1973, p. 52; "Walden Emphasizes Non-Book Items in New Outlet," *BP Report on the Business of Book Publishing* 11 (7), January 20, 1986, p. 4; "Sales Up 7% at Walden: First Super Stores Set," *BP Report on the Business of Book Publishing* 17 (14), March 2, 1992, pp. 1, 5–7; John Mutter, "Borders Chain Plans to Expand and Experiment, Offering Filing Shows," *Publishers Weekly* 239 (38), August 24, 1992, pp. 8, 15–16; John Mutter and Maureen O'Brien, "Walden Parent Kmart Buys Borders Chain," *Publishers Weekly* 239 (45), October 12, 1992, p. 8;

"K Mart's Fast Move in Book Superstores," *Mergers and Acquisitions* 27 (4), January/February 1993, p. 48; John Mutter, "Beyond Borders: 'Trimming' Walden," *Publishers Weekly* 241 (6), February 7, 1994, pp. 28–32.

77. See, e.g., Stephanie Strom, "Kmart's Earnings Remedy: Sell Off Drugstore Chain," *New York Times,* sec. C, August 5, 1993; John Holusha, "Kmart to Sell Its Control of 3 Chains," *New York Times,* sec. C, August 17, 1994; Stephanie Strom, "Shareholders Stun Kmart with Defeat of Plan," *New York Times,* June 4, 1994.

78. "Independents Lose Market Share in 1995, Chains Gain," *Bookselling This Week* 3 (11), June 24, 1996, p. 1; NPD Group Inc. and Carol Meyer, *1997 Consumer Research Study on Book Purchasing* (New York: Book Industry Study Group, 1998). The annual surveys put out by the Book Industry Study Group track purchases of adult trade books in units sold. They define the category "chain" to mean the largest national bookstore chains; during the 1990s, that list went from including about a dozen companies down to four. Market share not accounted for by a chain or independent is made up of sales through used bookstores, book clubs, warehouse clubs, discount stores, food stores, drugstores, and other outlets.

79. "Opening '98 Bookstore Sales Down; Independents' '97 Market Share Drops," *Bookselling This Week* 4 (49), April 13, 1998, pp. 1, 4. Unlike the previous studies cited, this survey looks at dollar sales (rather than book units) in bookstores (rather than in all outlets).

80. "In Fact . . . ," *Bookselling This Week* 5 (4), May 11, 1998, p. 1; Richard Howorth, *Independent Bookselling and True Market Expansion* (Tarrytown, N.Y.: American Booksellers Association, 1999), p. 2. Once Crown and Lauriat's went out of business, the overall market share of the chains declined slightly, though Barnes & Noble and Borders solidified their hold on the bookstore market. In 2001, bookstore chains had a 23.4 percent share of adult books sold, while independents took 14.8 percent of the market. See Jim Milliot, "Bookstores, Clubs Gain Market Share in '01," *Publishers Weekly* 249 (15), April 15, 2002, p. 12.

81. Jim Milliot and John F. Baker, "Bertelsmann Pays $200 M for 50% Stake in B&N.com," *Publishers Weekly* 245 (41), October 12, 1998, p. 10.

82. Edward Nawotka, "Borders.com Relaunched under Amazon," *Publishers Weekly* 248 (32), August 6, 2001, p. 9; Calvin Reid, "Amazon.com in Pact to Take Over Borders.com," *Publishers Weekly* 248 (16), April 16, 2001, p. 9.

83. Adam L. Penenberg, "Crossing Amazon," *Forbes* 165 (9), April 17, 2000, pp. 168–70.

84. Milliot, "Bookstores, Clubs Gain Market Share in '01."

85. A 1983 survey showed that 19 percent of books read were borrowed from a public, school, or employer library. On the other hand, 49 percent of books read were purchased by the reader. An additional 29 percent were either received as a gift or borrowed from a friend or relative, and it can be safely assumed that most of these were at some point purchased. Market Facts Inc., *1983 Consumer Research Study on Reading and Book Purchasing: Focus on Adults* (New York: Book Industry Study Group, 1984), p. 168.

Chapter Three

1. For a general discussion of consumer sovereignty that shows how this ideal is connected to the tradition of liberalism, see Don Slater, *Consumer Culture and Modernity* (Cambridge: Polity, 1997).

2. Chandler B. Grannis, "Title Output and Average Prices," in *The Book Publishing Annual* (New York: R. R. Bowker, 1985), p. 127; *Books in Print, 2001–2002,* 54th ed. (New Providence, N.J.: R. R. Bowker, 2001).

3. "The Bookseller's Value to the Community," *Bookseller, Newsdealer, and Stationer,* May 1, 1914, quoted in U.S. House of Representatives, Committee on Interstate and Foreign Commerce, *Price Regulation for Trade-Marked Articles: Hearings on H.R. 11; A Bill to Clarify the Law, to Promote Equality Thereunder, to Encourage Competition in Production and Quality, to Prevent Injury to Good Will, and to Protect Trade-Mark Owners, Distributors, and the Public against Injurious and Uneconomic Practices in the Distribution of Articles of Standard Quality under a Distinguishing Trade-Mark, Name, or Brand [April 22 and 23, 1926]* (Washington: Government Printing Office, 1926), p. 221.

4. J. J. Estabrook, "Profitable Bookselling," *Bulletin of the National Retail Dry Goods Association* 20 (12), December 1938, p. 55.

5. Janice Radway, "The Scandal of the Middlebrow: The Book-of-the-Month Club, Class Fracture, and Cultural Authority," *South Atlantic Quarterly* 89 (4), Fall 1990, pp. 703–36; Janice Radway, "Mail-Order Culture and Its Critics: The Book-of-the-Month Club, Commodification and Consumption, and the Problem of Cultural Authority," in *Cultural Studies,* ed. Lawrence Grossberg, Cary Nelson, and Paula A. Treichler (New York: Routledge, 1992), pp. 512–30; Janice Radway, *A Feeling for Books: The Book-of-the-Month Club, Literary Taste, and Middle-Class Desire* (Chapel Hill: University of North Carolina Press, 1997).

6. "The Future of Bookselling," *Publishers Weekly* 149 (22), June 1, 1946, p. 2895.

7. James F. Albright, "What to Tell the Neophyte: Bookselling Is a Good Career," in *A Manual on Bookselling,* 1st ed., ed. Charles B. Anderson, Joseph A. Duffy, and Jocelyn D. Kahn (New York: American Booksellers Association, 1969), p. 49.

8. Michael Kammen, *American Culture, American Tastes: Social Change and the 20th Century* (New York: Basic Books, 1999).

9. Stan Luxenberg, *Books in Chains: Chain Bookstores and Marketplace Censorship* (New York: National Writers Union, 1991), p. 6.

10. Eliot Leonard, "Bookstore Chains," in *The Business of Book Publishing: Papers by Practitioners,* ed. Elizabeth A. Geiser, Arnold Dolin, with Gladys S. Topkis (Boulder: Westview Press, 1985), pp. 244–55.

11. For instance, in 1983, Crown stores offered up to 10,000 books, while the average Dalton carried 22,000 titles in 1985. Charles Trueheart, "'You'll Never Pay Full Price Again': The Mushrooming of Crown Books," *Publishers Weekly* 223 (1), January 7, 1983, p. 45; "Store Wars: The Chains Are Coming!" *Stores* 67 (4), April 1985, p. 53. Even after the transition to the superstore strategy, Crown remained committed to the type of mass merchandising perfected by the mall outlets. As the manager of a SuperCrown outlet told me, "When my company makes a buy, they are definitely

thinking about buying the kind of author that either has a track record, that appeals to the largest number of people, or is writing the kind of book that is currently hot, that appeals to the largest number of people."

12. Stewart McBride, "The Corner Bookstores Take on the Book Chains," *Christian Science Monitor,* September 30, 1982, sec. B.

13. C. Wright Mills, *White Collar: The American Middle Classes* (New York: Oxford University Press, 1951), pp. 182–88.

14. Radway, *A Feeling for Books,* p. 77.

15. William Leach, *Land of Desire: Merchants, Power, and the Rise of a New American Culture* (New York: Vintage Books, 1993).

16. John P. Dessauer, "Cultural Pluralism and the Book World," *Book Research Quarterly* 2 (3), Fall 1986, pp. 3–6. For a more extended defense of cultural pluralism, see Herbert J. Gans, *Popular Culture and High Culture: An Analysis and Evaluation of Taste* (New York: Basic Books, 1974).

17. For the argument that consumer choice is empowering, see John Fiske, *Reading the Popular* (1989; London: Routledge, 1991), p. 35; Debra Grodin, "The Interpreting Audience: The Therapeutics of Self-Help Book Reading," *Critical Studies in Mass Communication* 8 (4), December 1991, pp. 404–20.

18. Pierre Bourdieu, *Distinction: A Social Critique of the Judgement of Taste* (1979; Cambridge: Harvard University Press, 1984).

19. Laura J. Miller, "The Rise and Not-Quite-Fall of the American Book Wholesaler," *Journal of Media Economics* 16 (2), 2003, pp. 97–120. The terms "wholesaler" and "distributor" are employed with some inconsistency in the book industry. While these terms are often used interchangeably, over the past few decades they have also come to refer to different types of organizations. In such usage, the wholesaler is the one who purchases books from a large number of publishers (with the privilege of making returns) and resells them to retailers. On the other hand, the distributor, sometimes called a master or exclusive distributor, provides additional specialized services, including sales and marketing, to a limited number of client presses. The distributor then sells its clients' books both directly to retailers and to other wholesalers.

20. Michael J. Robinson and Ray Olszewski, "Books in the Marketplace of Ideas," *Journal of Communication* 30 (2), Spring 1980, pp. 81–88; John P. Dessauer, *Book Publishing: The Basic Introduction,* new expanded ed. (New York: Continuum, 1993); *Books in Print, 1994–95,* 47th ed. (New Providence, N.J.: R. R. Bowker, 1994); *Books in Print, 2001–2002.* These statistics are derived from the database of the R. R. Bowker Company, publisher of *Books in Print,* and thus reflect those American presses that have made their existence known to Bowker. In the 1970s, Bowker started to count certain presses that had previously been excluded from their tally, and so the earliest numbers are not entirely comparable to the later ones.

21. Some would put scholarly and university presses in this category too.

22. Miller, "The Rise and Not-Quite-Fall of the American Book Wholesaler," pp. 112–13.

23. Kay Putnam Dillon, "Dayton Hudson Is Bullish on Books," *Publishers Weekly* 204 (17), October 22, 1973, pp. 65–66; Paul D. Doebler, "The Computer in Book Distribution," *Publishers Weekly* 218 (11), September 12, 1980, pp. 25–41; Michael Friedman, "Waldenbooks' System Runs Distribution Cycle," *Chain Store Age Executive* 60, March 1984, pp. 94, 97.

24. Matthew Rose, "Selling Literature Like Dog Food Gives Club Buyer Real Bite," *Wall Street Journal,* April 10, 2002, sec. A; "Bookmarks," *Consumer Reports* 67 (1), January 2002, p. 25.

25. Lee A. Weber, "Managing a Branch Bookstore: Problems and Responsibilities," in Anderson, Duffy, and Kahn, *A Manual on Bookselling,* pp. 213–16.

26. Theodore Wilentz, "American Bookselling in the 1960's," in *The American Reading Public: What It Reads, Why It Reads,* ed. Roger H. Smith (New York: R. R. Bowker, 1963), p. 45.

27. See, e.g., Karen Jenkins Holt, "Book Superstores Take Cue from Supermarkets, as Borders Transforms Approach to Product Categories," *Book Publishing Report* 27 (14), April 8, 2002, pp. 1–2.; John Mutter, "Borders's Imperative: Reinvent the Company," *Publishers Weekly* 249 (27), July 8, 2002, pp. 14–15.

28. John Mutter, "Barnes & Noble Ready for More Expansion," *Publishers Weekly* 249 (23), June 10, 2002, p. 9.

29. Dillon, "Dayton Hudson Is Bullish on Books," p. 66.

30. Walter W. Powell, "Whither the Local Bookstore?" *Daedalus* 112 (1), Winter 1983, pp. 60–61.

31. Borders Group Inc., *Form 10-K for the Fiscal Year Ended January 26, 2003* (2003), p. 2; Barnes & Noble Inc., *Barnes & Noble Booksellers 2002 Annual Report* (2003), p. 9.

32. Barnes & Noble Inc., *Form 10-K for the Fiscal Year Ended February 3, 2001* (2001), p. 6; Karen Angel, "Are Independents Making a Comeback?" *Publishers Weekly* 245 (23), June 8, 1998, p. 25.

33. David D. Kirkpatrick, *Report to the Authors Guild Midlist Books Study Committee* (2000), p. 40.

34. Molly Shapiro, "The Secrets of Handselling Debut Authors," *American Bookseller* 20 (13), August 1997, p. 37.

35. Jay Conrad Levinson, "How to Be a Techno-Guerrilla," *American Bookseller* 21 (1), September 1997, p. 79.

36. See, e.g., Richard Cross and Janet Smith, "The ABC's of Database Marketing," *American Bookseller* 19 (2), October 1995, pp. 75–80; "1 to 1 with Martha Rogers," *Bookselling This Week* 5 (8), June 15, 1998, p. 6; Steven Weingrod, "Learning the Principles of Relationship Marketing: Begin by Building a Customer Database," *Bookselling This Week* 5 (13), July 27, 1998, p. 8. For further analysis of relationship marketing in bookselling, see Laura J. Miller, "Cultural Authority and the Use of New Technology in the Book Trade," *Journal of Arts Management, Law, and Society* 28 (4), Winter 1999, pp. 297–313.

37. David Mehegan, "Amazon Man," *Boston Globe,* May 20, 2003, sec. C; Jim Milliot and Karen Holt, "Media Growth Slows at Amazon," *Publishers Weekly* 251 (31), August 2, 2004, p. 6.

38. Christopher Lasch, *The Minimal Self: Psychic Survival in Troubled Times* (New York: W. W. Norton, 1984), pp. 36–38.

Chapter Four

1. Susan Strasser, *Satisfaction Guaranteed: The Making of the American Mass Market* (Washington, D.C.: Smithsonian Institution Press, 1989).

2. Walter S. Hayward and Percival White, *Chain Stores: Their Management and Operation,* 2nd ed. (New York: McGraw Hill, 1925), p. 6.

3. On the symbolism that has surrounded the small businessperson for much of American history, see John H. Bunzel, *The American Small Businessman* (New York: Alfred A. Knopf, 1962); Rowland Berthoff, "Independence and Enterprise: Small Business in the American Dream," in *Small Business in American Life,* ed. Stuart W. Bruchey (New York: Columbia University Press, 1980), pp. 28–48; Sandra M. Anglund, *Small Business Policy and the American Creed* (Westport, Conn.: Praeger, 2000).

4. Kent Macdonald, "The Commercial Strip: From Main Street to Television Road," *Landscape* 28 (2), 1985, p. 14.

5. For the history of shopping centers and malls, see Kenneth T. Jackson, *Crabgrass Frontier: The Suburbanization of the United States* (New York: Oxford University Press, 1985), pp. 257–61; William Severini Kowinski, *The Malling of America: An Inside Look at the Great Consumer Paradise* (New York: William Morrow, 1985); Lizabeth Cohen, "From Town Center to Shopping Center: The Reconfiguration of Community Marketplaces in Postwar America," *American Historical Review* 101 (4), October 1996, pp. 1050–81; Thomas W. Hanchett, "U.S. Tax Policy and the Shopping-Center Boom of the 1950s and 1960s," *American Historical Review* 101 (4), October 1996, pp. 1082–1110; Kenneth T. Jackson, "All the World's a Mall: Reflections on the Social and Economic Consequences of the American Shopping Center," *American Historical Review* 101 (4), October 1996, pp. 1111–21; Richard Longstreth, *City Center to Regional Mall: Architecture, the Automobile, and Retailing in Los Angeles, 1920–1950* (Cambridge: MIT Press, 1997).

6. Kowinski, *The Malling of America;* Margaret Crawford, "The World in a Shopping Mall," in *Variations on a Theme Park: The New American City and the End of Public Space,* ed. Michael Sorkin (New York: Noonday Press, 1992), pp. 3–30.

7. "Can More Booksellers Take Advantage of the Growing Suburban Market?" *Publishers Weekly* 158 (16), October 14, 1950, pp. 1769–71.

8. Ibid.

9. "Booksellers Haft and LeBaire Speak at Publishers Ad Club," *American Bookseller* 4 (5), January 1981, p. 35.

10. Clarence Wescott, "Aim of Bookstore Design: Mix Leisure with Excitement," *Publishers Weekley* 193 (15), April 8, 1968, pp. 40–41.

11. "B. Dalton, Bookseller, Opens in a Suburb as Subsidiary of Dayton's," *Publishers Weekly* 190 (9), August 29, 1966, pp. 332–34; "B. Dalton, Bookseller, Opens in St. Louis Area," *Publishers Weekly* 191 (8), February 20, 1967, pp. 137–38; "B. Dalton Chain Grows: Third Store Opened," *Publishers Weekly* 191 (18), May 1, 1967, pp. 49–50;

"B. Dalton Phoenix Store Is New, Spacious, and Fun," *Publishers Weekly* 192 (6), August 7, 1967, p. 45; "B. Dalton, Bookseller, Foresees Growing Chain of Stores," *Publishers Weekly* 194 (3), July 15, 1968, pp. 44–45; Kay Putnam Dillon, "Dayton Hudson Is Bullish on Books," *Publishers Weekly* 204 (17), October 22, 1973, pp. 65–66.

12. Marshal L. Oliver, "Is an Architect Necessary?" in *A Manual on Bookselling,* 1st ed., ed. Charles B. Anderson, Joseph A. Duffy, and Jocelyn D. Kahn (New York: American Booksellers Association, 1969), p. 22.

13. Eliot Leonard, "Bookstore Chains," in *The Business of Book Publishing: Papers by Practitioners,* ed. Elizabeth A. Geiser, Arnold Dolin, with Gladys S. Topkis, (Boulder: Westview Press, 1985), p. 245.

14. Jean F. Mercier, "HQ Is Still Back-of-the-Tracks But Walden Is Opening #200," *Publishers Weekly* 202 (14), October 2, 1972, pp. 22–23.

15. Jerome P. Frank, "Waldenbooks at 50: America's Biggest Book Chain Aims to Turn More Browsers into Buyers," *Publishers Weekly* 223 (17), April 29, 1983, p. 40.

16. Barnes & Noble Inc., *Form S-3, Initial Public Offering Prospectus* (September 28, 1994), p. 6.

17. Barnes & Noble Inc., *Barnes & Noble 1995 Annual Report* (1996), p. 2.

18. Tony Adler, "Quality and Quantity," *Chicago Tribune,* December 20, 1992.

19. See Charles Hix, "Crown's Jewels: A Super Crown Tour," *Publishers Weekly* 237 (50), December 14, 1990, pp. 39–40.

20. See Melissa Ryan, "Better Bookselling through Design," *American Bookseller* 18 (8), March 1995, pp. 79–83.

21. John Mutter, "The Coming of the Category Killers," *Bookseller,* no. 4557, April 23, 1993, p. 23.

22. John Mutter, "BAM's Birmingham Surprise: Retailer Opens a Books & Co.," *PW Daily for Booksellers* (electronic newsletter), March 11, 2002.

23. See the annual *Consumer Research Study on Book Purchasing* prepared by the NPD Group for the American Booksellers Association and the Book Industry Study Group.

24. NPD Group Inc. and Carol Meyer, *The 1999 Consumer Research Study on Book Purchasing* (New York: Book Industry Study Group, 2000), pp. 3.29–31.

25. Barnes & Noble Inc., *Barnes & Noble 1997 Annual Report* (1998), p. 13.

26. William Leach, "Strategists of Display and the Production of Desire," in *Consuming Visions: Accumulation and Display of Goods in America, 1889–1920,* ed. Simon J. Bronner (New York: W. W. Norton, 1989), pp. 99–132. On the cultural meanings of turn-of-the-century grocery store window displays, see Keith Walden, "Speaking Modern: Language, Culture, and Hegemony in Grocery Window Displays, 1887–1920," *Canadian Historical Review* 70 (3), September 1989, pp. 285–310.

27. Quoted in "Riggio Touts Value of Advertising in Book Selling," *BP Report on the Business of Book Publishing* 14 (50), November 20, 1989, p. 5. For the toothpaste analogy, see also Bonnie K. Predd, "Marketing Writes New Chapter in Bookselling History," *Marketing News,* September 14, 1984, p. 51.

28. For one study of book buyers' interactions with table displays, see M. Stokmans and M. Hendrickx, "The Attention Paid to New Book Releases on a Display Table," *Poetics* 22 (3), April 1994, pp. 185–97.

29. Predd, "Marketing Writes New Chapter."

30. Ken White and Frank White, *Display and Visual Merchandising* (Westwood, N.J.: St. Francis Press, 1996), p. 20.

31. N. R. Kleinfield, "The Supermarketer of Books," *New York Times Magazine*, November 9, 1986, p. 65.

32. "A New Prize," *Publishers Weekly* 241 (6), February 7, 1994, p. 32; Mary B. Tabor, "In Bookstore Chains, Display Space Is for Sale," *New York Times*, January 15, 1996, sec. A.

33. John Mutter, "One Size Doesn't Fit All," *Publishers Weekly* 244 (1), January 6, 1997, pp. 41–42.

34. Barnes & Noble Inc., *Form S-3, Initial Public Offering Prospectus*, p. 28.

35. John Mutter, "B&N's Special Terms," *Publishers Weekly* 241 (27), July 4, 1994, pp. 19–21; Bernie Rath, "Co-op Advertising: Breaking the Independent Bookstore Paradigm," *American Bookseller* 19 (10), May 1996, pp. 22–23.

36. Doreen Carvajal, "For Sale: On-Line Bookstore's Recommendations," *New York Times*, February 8, 1999, sec. A; Doreen Carvajal, "Amazon.com Plans to Revise Its Ad Program," *New York Times*, February 10, 1999, sec. C; Doreen Carvajal, "Amazon.com Site Tells Users of Book Promotion Payments," *New York Times*, March 2, 1999, sec. C; Steven M. Zeitchik, "Amazon.com Reveals All (Sort of)," *PW Daily for Booksellers* (electronic newsletter), March 2, 1999; Edward Nawotka, "Amazon Demands Payola for E-mail Promotion, Analyst Attacks Again," *PW Daily for Booksellers* (electronic newsletter), February 7, 2001.

37. Amazon.com, "Learn about Amazon.com's Co-op and Review Policy," http://www.amazon.com/exec/obidos/tg/stores/browse/co-op/-/4/ref=br_b_dis/104-8594436-1483939 (accessed June 2003).

38. Amazon.com, "Paid Placements" www.amazon.com/exec/obidos/subst/misc/co-op/small-vendor-info.html/104-8594436-1483939 (accessed June 2003); Edward Nawotka, "Amazon.com's New Juice: Sponsored Search Results," *PW Daily for Booksellers* (electronic newsletter), January 8, 2001; Steven Zeitchik, "Amazon's Sponsored Links: A Good Deal While It Lasted," *PW NewsLine* (electronic newsletter), March 26, 2002; Steven Zeitchik and Jim Milliot, "The Strangest Program You've Never Heard Of," *Publishers Weekly* 252 (14), April 4, 2005, pp. 5, 8.

39. Bob Geiger, "B. Dalton Spots Hit the 'Books,'" *Advertising Age* 58 (47), November 2, 1987, p. 102.

40. See [Jenner & Block], *The Fundamentals: Book Publishers' Obligations to Book Retailers under the Federal Antitrust Discrimination Law* (Tarrytown, N.Y.: American Booksellers Association, 1996).

41. "BookSense.com Testing New Publisher Co-Op Program," *Bookselling This Week* (electronic newsletter), March 20, 2003, pp. 5–6. See chapter 7 for a discussion of Book Sense.

42. Rath, "Co-op Advertising," p. 23.

43. Thorstein Veblen, *The Theory of Business Enterprise* (New York: Charles Scribner's Sons, 1904), pp. 8–13, 47.

44. Ibid., pp. 306–12. This obviously has much in common with Weber's account of the growth of rationality.

45. Montaville Flowers, *America Chained: A Discussion of "What's Wrong with the Chain Store"* (Pasadena: Montaville Flowers Publicists, 1931), p. 80.

46. Joseph H. Appel, "Does Chain Growth Tend Toward Standardization of Food? Is This Desirable?" (1929), in *Current, Conflicting Views on the Chain Store Controversy,* ed. T. H. Hall (Chicago: National Research Bureau, 1930), p. 86.

47. Daniel J. Boorstin, *The Americans: The Democratic Experience* (1973; New York: Vintage Books, 1974), pp. 109–12.

48. Janice Radway, *A Feeling for Books: The Book-of-the-Month Club, Literary Taste, and Middle-Class Desire* (Chapel Hill: University of North Carolina Press, 1997), pp. 202–210, 221.

49. See, e.g., Stuart Chase and F. J. Schlink, *Your Money's Worth: A Study in the Waste of the Consumer's Dollar* (New York: Macmillan, 1927), chaps. 9–10; E. C. Sams, "Is the Chain System Detrimental to Personal Opportunity and Initiative," (1929), in Hall, *Current, Conflicting Views on the Chain Store Controversy,* p. 46; Harold M. Haas, *Social and Economic Aspects of the Chain Store Movement* (1939; New York: Arno Press, 1979), pp. 39–40.

50. John P. Nichols, *The Chain Store Tells Its Story* (New York: Institute of Distribution, 1940), p. 207.

51. Daniel M. Bluestone, "Roadside Blight and the Reform of Commercial Architecture," in *Roadside America: The Automobile in Design and Culture,* ed. Jan Jennings (Ames: Iowa State University Press, 1990).

52. Jackson, *Crabgrass Frontier,* p. 240.

53. Blanche Lemco van Ginkel, "Aesthetic Considerations," in *Urban Problems: A Canadian Reader,* ed. Ralph R. Krueger and R. Charles Bryfogle (1961; Toronto: Holt, Rinehart and Winston of Canada, 1971), p. 48.

54. Jane Jacobs, *The Death and Life of Great American Cities* (1961; New York: Vintage Books, 1992), p. 4.

55. John A. Jakle, "Roadside Restaurants and Place-Product-Packaging," *Journal of Cultural Geography* 3, Fall/Winter 1982, pp. 76–93; Stan Luxenberg, *Roadside Empires: How the Chains Franchised America* (New York: Viking, 1985).

56. On the history and philosophy of historic preservation in the United States, see Kevin Lynch, *What Time Is This Place?* (Cambridge: MIT Press, 1972); Charles B. Hosmer Jr., *Preservation Comes of Age: From Williamsburg to the National Trust, 1926–1949* (Charlottesville: University Press of Virginia, 1981); James Marston Fitch, *Historic Preservation: Curatorial Management of the Built World* (1982; Charlottesville: University Press of Virginia, 1990); Diane Barthel, *Historic Preservation: Collective Memory and Historical Identity* (New Brunswick: Rutgers University Press, 1996). Barthel discusses American preservationists who possess a sense of cultural stewardship similar to that

of book professionals. She describes how preservationists also grew to understand the need to counter an elitist image, and tried to make their agenda more inclusive.

57. Barthel, *Historic Preservation,* p. 130.

58. Chester H. Liebs, "Remember Our Not-So-Distant Past?" *Historic Preservation* 30 (1), January–March 1978, pp. 30–35.

59. "Goals and Programs: A Summary of the Study Committee Report to the Board of Trustees, the National Trust for Historic Preservation, 1973," in *The History of the National Trust for Historic Preservation, 1963–1973,* ed. Elizabeth D. Mulloy (1973; Washington, D.C.: The Preservation Press, 1976), p. 281. See Richard V. Francaviglia, *Main Street Revisited: Time, Space, and Image Building in Small-Town America* (Iowa City: University of Iowa Press, 1996), for a contrary argument that nostalgia for older commercial architecture is misplaced since, he contends, the traditional small town main street was very much standardized across the United States.

60. Herbert J. Gans, *Popular Culture and High Culture: An Analysis and Evaluation of Taste* (New York: Basic Books, 1974). Gans is primarily discussing the mass media, but his argument has been influential for thinking about culture in general. See also Herbert J. Gans, *The Levittowners: Ways of Life and Politics in a New Suburban Community* (1967; New York: Columbia University Press, 1982).

61. See, e.g., Travel Myrtle Beach Shopping Guide, http://www.travelmyrtlebeach. com/attractions/shopping (accessed February 22, 2005); Sarah Kershaw, "For Blue-Collar Riviera, a Conflict over Identity," *New York Times,* September 7, 2002, sec. A.

62. In contrast to George Ritzer, for example, who implies that humans are naturally inclined to diversity, I would stress that this stance toward order is cultural rather than reflecting some kind of inborn preference for diversity. See George Ritzer, *The McDonaldization of Society: An Investigation into the Changing Character of Contemporary Social Life,* revised ed. (Thousand Oaks, Calif.: Sage, 1996), p. 136.

63. Robert Venturi, Denise Scott Brown, and Steven Izenour, *Learning from Las Vegas: The Forgotten Symbolism of Architectural Form,* rev. ed. (1972; Cambridge: MIT Press, 1977), p. 53.

64. E. Relph, *Place and Placelessness* (London: Pion, 1976), p. 109. For the connection between places and personal and cultural identity, see also Anne Buttimer, "Home, Reach, and the Sense of Place," in *The Human Experience of Space and Place,* ed. Anne Buttimer and David Seamon (New York: St. Martin's, 1980).

65. R. David Unowsky, "On My Mind," *Bookselling This Week* 1 (25), October 10, 1994, p. 4.

66. Borders Group Inc., *1995 Borders Group, Inc., Annual Report* (1996), p. 2.

67. Borders Group Inc., *Form 10-K for the Fiscal Year Ended January 27, 2002* (2002), p. 2.

68. See Stacey Mitchell, *The Home Town Advantage: How to Defend Your Main Street against Chain Stores . . . and Why It Matters* (Minneapolis: Institute for Local Self-Reliance, 2000); Thad Williamson, David Imbroscio, and Gar Alperovitz, *Making a Place for Community: Local Democracy in a Global Era* (New York: Routledge, 2002), chap. 7.

69. John Mutter, "Borders Group to Launch Franchise in Malaysia," *Publishers Weekly* 251 (44), 2004, p. 10.

70. Keith Acheson and Christopher Maule, *Much Ado about Culture: North American Trade Disputes* (Ann Arbor: University of Michigan Press, 1999), pp. 244–57.

71. For a brief account of some regulatory efforts to impede big-box retailing in Ontario, see Alan G. Hallsworth, Ken G. Jones, and Russell Muncaster, "The Planning Implications of New Retail Format Introductions in Canada and Britain," *Service Industries Journal* 15 (4), October 1995, pp. 148–63.

72. "New Chapter in Canadian College Bookselling," *PW Daily for Booksellers* (electronic newsletter), April 5, 1999.

73. "Flagging a Problem," *Quill and Quire* 66 (3), March 2000, p. 69.

74. Arthur Donner Consultants Inc. and Lazar and Associates, *The Competitive Challenges Facing Book Publishers in Canada* (Ottawa: Minister of Public Works and Government Services, 2000), p. 50.

75. "Amazon.com Takes on China," *Toronto Star,* August 20, 2004, sec. E.

76. See, e.g., Edward Nawotka, "Looking for Respect: SeekBooks.com Launches Enhanced Program," *PW Daily for Booksellers* (electronic newsletter), August 9, 2000; Judith Rosen, "BookSite Launches Partners Program," *Publishers Weekly* 248 (52), December 24, 2001, p. 21.

Chapter Five

1. Barnes & Noble Inc., *Form 10-K for the 52 Weeks Ended January 28, 1995* (1995), p. 64.

2. Quoted in Brad Zellar, "Border's 30th Anniversary," *Publishers Weekly* 248 (47), November 19, 2001, p. 30.

3. Joseph R. Gusfield, *Community: A Critical Response* (New York: Harper & Row, 1975), pp. xv–xvi.

4. Ibid.; Thomas Bender, *Community and Social Change in America* (1978; Baltimore: Johns Hopkins University Press, 1982).

5. See, e.g., Chandler B. Grannis, "The Bookseller in the Community," *Publishers Weekly* 193 (23), June 3, 1968, p. 105.

6. Avin Mark Domnitz, "Toward the New Year and Beyond: A Holiday Message from ABA President Avin Mark Domnitz," *Bookselling This Week* 2 (34), December 18, 1995, p. 3.

7. Gregory P. Stone, "City Shoppers and Urban Identification: Observations on the Social Psychology of City Life," *American Journal of Sociology* 60 (1) July 1954, pp. 37, 40.

8. Gaia, the bookstore mentioned here, closed in 2000. The following year, it was reopened as a living and cultural center.

9. See, e.g., Susan Korones, "Books and Food in Boston: Two Case Histories," *American Bookseller* 4 (6), February 1981, pp. 30–32; Barbara Livingston, "A View from Washington: Bill Kramer of Kramerbooks," *American Bookseller* 4 (6), February 1981, pp. 32–33.

10. See Ray Oldenburg, *The Great Good Place: Cafes, Coffee Shops, Community Centers, Beauty Parlors, General Stores, Bars, Hangouts and How They Get You through the Day* (New York: Paragon House, 1989); Mike Davis, *City of Quartz: Excavating the Future in Los Angeles* (1990; New York: Vintage Books, 1992); Michael Sorkin, ed., *Variations on a Theme Park: The New American City and the End of Public Space* (New York: Noonday Press, 1992); Sharon Zukin, *The Cultures of Cities* (Cambridge, Mass.: Blackwell, 1995).

11. Kate Whouley, "A Tomato-Juice Cure to a Bookselling Hangover," *American Bookseller* 19 (5), December 1995, p. 21. By "value migration," Whouley means the changing tastes and expectation of bookstore customers; she borrows the term from business consultant Adrian Slywotzky.

12. Borders Group Inc., *1995 Borders Group, Inc., Annual Report* (1996), p. 2.

13. Barnes & Noble Inc., *1996 Barnes & Noble Annual Report* (1997), pp. 3, 5.

14. John Mutter, Jim Milliot, and Edward Nawotka, "Borders Group Revamps Superstore Management," *Publishers Weekly* 248 (9), February 26, 2001, p. 9; Karen Holt, "B&N Cuts Community Reps; Has 2% Comp Rise," *Publishers Weekly* 250 (36), September 8, 2003, p. 9.

15. David Finkel, "Displeased to Seat You," *New York* 30 (42), November 3, 1997, p. 15.

16. Bryant Frazer, "In-store Cafés Provide Hangout for Book Lovers," *Bookselling This Week* 1 (16), August 8, 1994, p. 5.

17. Barnes & Noble Inc., *Form S-3, Initial Public Offering Prospectus* (September 28, 1994), p. 25.

18. Claire Kirch, "Book Cellar Uncorks Books and Wine," *Publishers Weekly* 251 (23), June 7, 2004, p. 17.

19. For these details, I refer to the following articles from the electronic newsletter *PW Daily for Booksellers*: Edward Nawotka, "Borders Takes a Tip from Bibelot, Adds Donna's Cafes," March 1, 2002; Edward Nawotka, "New Category at Borders: Alcohol Added to One Cafe Menu," July 2, 2002; "Hot Christmas Present: Borders to Offer Wi-Fi in All Stores by Year End," September 5, 2003; "Borders Gets New Bean Counters," August 12, 2004; "B&N Warms Up to Hot Spots," March 10, 2004.

20. Laura J. Miller, Lynne (E. F.) McKechnie, and Paulette M. Rothbauer, "The Clash Between Armchairs and Cash Registers: Customer Behavior and Corporate Strategies at Book Superstores" (paper presented at the Eleventh Annual Conference of the Society for the History of Authorship, Reading, and Publishing, Claremont, Calif., July 11, 2003).

21. Judith Rosen, "The Evolution of Author Tours," *Publishers Weekly* 245 (47), November 23, 1998, pp. 20–21.

22. Lloyd Wendt and Herman Kogan, *Give the Lady What She Wants! The Story of Marshall Field & Company* (Chicago: Rand McNally, 1952), p. 304.

23. Patricia Holt, "Ethel Stevenson: A Veteran Bookseller Talks about Reaching Nonreaders," *Publishers Weekly* 213 (12), March 20, 1978, p. 54.

24. Wendt and Kogan, *Give the Lady What She Wants,* p. 363.

25. Donna Martin, "Author Events Bring Silver Lining to Rainy Day Books," *Publishers Weekly* 246 (12), March 22, 1999, pp. 39–41.

26. Nomi Schwartz, "Special Events for Bookstores off the Author Tour Track," *Bookselling This Week* 6 (29), December 6, 1999, p. 2.

27. See Gunther Barth, *City People: The Rise of Modern City Culture in Nineteenth-Century America* (Oxford: Oxford University Press, 1980); Susan Porter Benson, *Counter Cultures: Saleswomen, Managers, and Customers in American Department Stores, 1890–1940* (Urbana: University of Illinois Press, 1986); William Leach, *Land of Desire: Merchants, Power, and the Rise of a New American Culture* (New York: Vintage Books, 1993).

28. Karen Angel, "Alaskan Store Becomes Culture Mart to Keep Chains at Bay," *Publishers Weekly* 245 (27), July 6, 1998, pp. 20–21; John Mutter, "PW's Bookseller of the Year: Elaine Petrocelli, Book Passage, Corte Madera, California," *Publishers Weekly* 244 (18), May 5, 1997, pp. 44–51.

29. John F. Kasson, *Amusing the Million: Coney Island at the Turn of the Century* (New York: Hill & Wang, 1978).

30. Sam Weller, "Customers Enliven Window Display," *Publishers Weekly* 247 (7), February 14, 2000, p. 89.

31. Patrick L. Phillips, "Merging Entertainment and Retailing," *Economic Development Review* 13 (2), Spring 1995, p. 14; Susan G. Davis, "Space Jam: Media Conglomerates Build the Entertainment City," *European Journal of Communication* 14 (4), December 1999, pp. 435–59.

32. Jim Milliot, "Disney Exec Named Prez of B&N Stores," *Publishers Weekly* 248 (9), February 26, 2001, p. 9.

33. While this tendency became accentuated in the late twentieth century, it had developed considerably earlier. See Martha Wolfenstein, "Fun Morality: An Analysis of Recent American Child-Training Literature," in *Childhood in Contemporary Cultures,* ed. Margaret Mead and Martha Wolfenstein (Chicago: University of Chicago Press, 1955), pp. 168–78.

34. Kasson, *Amusing the Million.* See also Kathy Peiss, *Cheap Amusements: Working Women and Leisure in Turn-of-the-Century New York* (Philadelphia: Temple University Press, 1986).

35. See Laura J. Miller, "Major Publishers' Holdings," http://people.brandeis.edu/~lamiller/publishers.html.

36. "Borders-Walden Buys Music Chain," *Publishers Weekly* 241 (37), September 12, 1994, p. 9; Jim Milliot, "B&N to Acquire Babbage's Video, Software Chain," *Publishers Weekly* 246 (41), October 11, 1999, p. 10.

37. Barnes & Noble Inc., *Spin-Off of Gamestop Corp. through the Distribution by Barnes & Noble, Inc., of Shares of Gamestop Corp. Class B Common Stock to Its Common Stockholders* (November 5, 2004).

38. "Chains Post 5-Year Sales Gain of 27%," *Publishers Weekly* 251 (12), March 22, 2004, p. 5.

39. Doreen Carvajal, "Borders Events to Go Digital in Deal with Net Start-Up," *New York Times,* December 7, 1999, sec. C; John Mutter, "B&N.com Opens BNTV,"

Publishers Weekly 247 (27), July 3, 2000, p. 11; Edward Nawotka, "Bamm.com Adds Downloadable Interviews," *Publishers Weekly* 249 (24), June 17, 2002, p. 16.

40. Susan G. Davis, "The Theme Park: Global Industry and Cultural Form," *Media, Culture and Society* 18 (3), July 1996, p. 407.

41. Neil Postman, *Amusing Ourselves to Death: Public Discourse in the Age of Show Business* (1985; New York: Penguin Books, 1986), pp. 43, 87, 92.

42. Robert Escarpit, *Sociology of Literature,* 2nd ed. (1958; London: Frank Cass & Co., 1971), p. 91.

43. David Riesman, "Bookworms and the Social Soil," in *Individualism Reconsidered and Other Essays* (Glencoe, Ill.: The Free Press, 1954), pp. 258–65.

44. For sales figures for this period, see Book Industry Study Group, Statistical Service Center, *Book Industry Trends 1993* (New York: Book Industry Study Group, 1993); Book Industry Study Group and Center for Communications and Media Management, *Book Industry Trends 2002* (Matawan, N.J.: Book Industry Study Group, 2002).

45. Veronis Suhler Stevenson, *Communications Industry Forecast and Report,* 17th ed. /21st ed. (New York: Veronis Suhler Stevenson, 2003), p. 49. The *Forecast* and the *Report* were originally published separately. After the two titles were merged, the publisher retained their individual edition numbers.

46. This perspective contradicts Fiske, who asserts an openness in television that enables viewers to derive their own meanings from what they watch. John Fiske, *Television Culture* (1987; London: Routledge, 1989).

Chapter Six

1. See Marshall Sahlins, *Stone Age Economics* (Chicago: Aldine Atherton, 1972).

2. "The Net Price System," *Publishers Weekly* 41 (19), May 7, 1892, pp. 708–9.

3. "A Fool's Paradise," *Publishers Weekly* 128 (17), October 26, 1935, pp. 1552–53.

4. "Sixty-Five Years of Bookselling," *College Store* 5 (7), April 1939, pp. 10–11, 34; Barnes & Noble, "A Tremendous Reservoir of Books to Meet Every Individual Need" (circa 1940s), Lawrence B. Romaine Trade Catalog Collection (MSS 107), Booksellers Catalogs, box 5, University of California, Santa Barbara.

5. U.S. Senate, Committee on Interstate and Foreign Commerce, *National Fair Trade Legislation — 1959: Hearings before a Special Subcommittee on Fair Trade on S. 1083; A Bill to Amend the Federal Trade Commission Act, as Amended, So As to Equalize Rights in the Distribution of Merchandise Identified by a Trademark, Brand, or Trade Name [June 15, 16, and July 10, 1959]* (Washington, D.C.: U.S. Government Printing Office, 1961), pp. 352–53.

6. See, e.g., Robert Reed, "How an Industry Is Getting Crowned," *Advertising Age* 54 (23), May 30, 1983, pp. M4–5; Charles Trueheart, "'You'll Never Pay Full Price Again': The Mushrooming of Crown Books," *Publishers Weekly* 223 (1), January 7, 1983, pp. 40–48.

7. "Dalton to Open Discount Stores," *BP Report on the Business of Book Publishing* 6 (42), October 5, 1981, pp. 1, 6–7; "Dalton to Launch Discount Stores?" *BP Report on the Business of Book Publishing* 6 (41), September 28, 1981, pp. 1, 8; "Pickwick to Establish

New Outlets in Minneapolis, Columbus," *BP Report on the Business of Book Publishing*
9 (31), July 9, 1984, p. 2; Brian Moran, "Pickwick Adds to Discount Book Threat,"
Advertising Age 55(46), July 30, 1984, p. 28; "Dayton Hudson Unit Closes Unprofitable
Discount Book Chain," *Wall Street Journal,* June 18, 1986; "Dalton Closes Pickwick
Discount Book Chain," *BP Report on the Business of Book Publishing* 11 (29), June 23, 1986,
pp. 1, 7–8.

8. "Walden to Match Dalton's 35% Discount on New Hardcover Releases," *BP
Report on the Business of Book Publishing* 8 (43), October 10, 1983, pp. 1, 6; "Waldenbooks
Launches Reader's Market, Discount Chain Subsidiary," *BP Report on the Business of
Book Publishing* 10 (1), December 3, 1984, pp. 1, 7; "K mart Acquires Waldenbooks,
Rite Aid Acquires Encore Books," *BP Report on the Business of Book Publishing* 9 (34),
August 6, 1984, pp. 1, 7; John Mutter, "Waldenbooks to Be Sold to K mart Chain,"
Publishers Weekly 226 (5), August 3, 1984, pp. 15–16; "Waldenbooks Goes Beyond Low
Prices," *Chain Store Age, General Merchandising Trends* 61, March 1985, pp. 21–22;
"Competition Causes Discounting 'Price Wars' among General Bookstore Chains,"
BP Report on the Business of Book Publishing 10 (47), November 4, 1985, pp. 1, 5–6;
Allene Symons and Sonja Bolle, "Issues in Bookselling, 1984," in *The Book Publishing
Annual* (New York: R. R. Bowker, 1985), pp. 185–92; "Kmart Shifts Responsibility for
Readers Market," *BP Report on the Business of Book Publishing* 16 (3), December 10, 1990,
pp. 7–8.

9. John Mutter, "B&N Outlines Strategies for Wall Street," *Publishers Weekly* 240
(39), September 27, 1993, p. 20.

10. See, e.g., Jim Milliot and John Mutter, "Sales Jump, but Online Efforts Result
in Loss," *Publishers Weekly* 246 (48), November 29, 1999, p. 22; David D. Kirkpatrick,
"Quietly, Booksellers Are Putting an End to the Discount Era," *New York Times,*
October 9, 2000, sec. A.

11. "'Phoenix' Sparks Amazon.com Gains," *Publishers Weekly* 250 (30), July 28, 2003,
p. 10.

12. See, e.g., Bob McCullough, "Booksellers in a Bind," *Publishers Weekly* 241 (41),
October 10, 1994, pp. 16–18; "'Order of the Phoenix' Debut Smashes Records," *Publishers Weekly* 250 (26), June 30, 2003, pp. 9, 15; Jim Milliot and Kevin Howell, "'Phoenix'
Sales Remain Strong in Most Channels," *Publishers Weekly* 250 (27), July 7, 2003, p. 10.

13. NPD Group Inc., *1991–1992 Consumer Research Study on Book Purchasing* (New
York: Book Industry Study Group, 1993), p. 26; Jim Milliot, "Bookstores, Clubs Gain
Market Share in '01," *Publishers Weekly* 249 (15), April 15, 2002, p. 12. While these figures apply to adult books, an even greater proportion of children's titles were purchased at such nonbook outlets.

14. See the annual surveys conducted by the NPD Group, which show warehouse
clubs in particular attracting book buyers of high income and education.

15. "In Fact . . . ," *Bookselling This Week* 5 (22), October 19, 1998, p. 1.

16. Ruth Leigh, "Mrs. Housewife, May We Present Mr. Chain Store," *Chain Store
Progress* 3 (1), January 1931, p. 5.

17. Donald R. Richberg, "Who Wants Chain Stores?" (1938), in *Chain Stores and
Legislation,* ed. Daniel Bloomfield (New York: H. W. Wilson, 1939), pp. 112–13.

18. "Shall We Curb the Chain Stores?" (1938), in Bloomfield, *Chain Stores and Legislation*, p. 32.

19. For example, U.S. House of Representatives, Committee on Interstate and Foreign Commerce, *Fair Trade, 1959: Hearings on H.R. 768, H.R. 1253, H.R. 2463, H.R. 2729, H.R. 3187, H.R. 5252, and H.R. 5602; Bills to Amend the Federal Trade Commission Act, as Amended, with Respect to Fair Trade [March 16–20, 23–25, 1959]* (Washington, D.C.: U.S. Government Printing Office, 1959), p. 748.

20. U.S. House of Representatives, Committee on the Judiciary, Antitrust Subcommittee, *Study of Monopoly Power: Hearings on Resale Price Maintenance, H.R. 4365, H.R. 4592, H.R. 4662, and H.R. 6367 [H.R. 6925] [February 13–15, 18, 20–22, 25, and 27, 1952]* (Washington, D.C.: Government Printing Office, 1952), p. 307.

21. U.S. Senate, Committee on Interstate and Foreign Commerce, *Fair Trade: Hearings on S. 3850; A Bill to Amend the Federal Trade Commission Act, as Amended, So as to Equalize Rights in the Distribution of Identified Merchandise [July 21 and 22, 1958]* (Washington, D.C.: United States Government Printing Office, 1958), p. 271.

22. While this was not the issue that received the most attention in early-twentieth-century attacks on price-cutting, it has become a much more salient problem with contemporary discounting. With the increase in global trade, retailers now have more possibilities for securing low-priced merchandise. This means falling prices (and wages) for domestic producers as well. Farmers and garment workers have been especially squeezed by consumers' expectations that cheap food and clothing will be available to them.

23. See, e.g., Montaville Flowers, *America Chained: A Discussion of "What's Wrong with the Chain Store"* (Pasadena: Montaville Flowers Publicists, 1931); Charles G. Daughters, *Wells of Discontent: A Study of the Economic, Social, and Political Aspects of the Chain Store* (New York: Charles G. Daughters, 1937). For a later example of these types of criticisms, see Walter Henry Nelson, *The Great Discount Delusion* (New York: David McKay, 1965).

24. Louis D. Brandeis, "Cutthroat Prices: The Competition That Kills," *Harper's Weekly* 58 (2969), November 15, 1913, pp. 10–12.

25. U.S. Senate, Committee on Interstate and Foreign Commerce, *Resale Price Fixing: Hearings on H.R. 5767, an Act to Amend the Federal Trade Commission Act with Respect to Certain Contracts and Agreements Which Establish Minimum or Stipulated Resale Prices and Which Are Extended by State Law to Persons Who Are Not Parties to Such Contracts and Agreements, and for Certain Other Purposes [June 2–5, 1952]* (Washington, D.C.: Government Printing Office, 1952), p. 666.

26. Price maintenance was not the only strategy for curtailing the power of price-cutting department stores and chains; there were also attempts during the early twentieth century to impose special taxes on such stores. However, since the book trade was not involved in these campaigns, I do not discuss them here. For accounts of such efforts, see Charles F. Phillips, "State Discriminatory Chain Store Taxation," *Harvard Business Review* 14 (3), Spring 1936, pp. 349–59; Maurice W. Lee, "Anti-Chain-Store Tax Legislation," *Journal of Business of the University of Chicago* 12 (3), July 1939, pp. 1–80; John P. Nichols, *The Chain Store Tells Its Story* (New York: Institute of

Distribution, 1940); Joseph Cornwall Palamountain Jr., *The Politics of Distribution* (1955; New York: Greenwood, 1968); Paul Ingram and Hayagreeva Rao, "Store Wars: The Enactment and Repeal of Anti-Chain-Store Legislation in America," *American Journal of Sociology* 110 (2), September 2004, pp. 446–87.

27. *Bobbs-Merrill Co. v. Straus et al.,* 139 Fed. 155, July 11, 1905.

28. Ralph M. Hower, *History of Macy's of New York 1858–1919: Chapters in the Evolution of the Department Store* (Cambridge: Harvard University Press, 1943), pp. 353–58; Donald Sheehan, *This Was Publishing: A Chronicle of the Book Trade in the Gilded Age* (Bloomington: Indiana University Press, 1952), pp. 225–37; Charles A. Madison, *Book Publishing in America* (New York: McGraw-Hill, 1966), pp. 158–60; John Tebbel, *A History of Book Publishing in the United States,* vol. 2, *The Expansion of an Industry 1865–1919* (New York: R. R. Bowker, 1975).

29. Most notably, the 1911 decision, *Dr. Miles Medical Co. v. John D. Park & Sons Co.,* 220 U.S. 373.

30. Charles Albert Pearce, *NRA Trade Practice Programs* (New York: Columbia University Press, 1939); Ewald T. Grether, *Price Control under Fair Trade Legislation* (1939; New York: Arno Press, 1976), p. 151.

31. "Macy's Starts Own Book Club," *Publishers Weekly* 133 (12), March 19, 1938, pp. 1273–75; "The Book Club War Is On," *Publishers Weekly* 133 (13), March 26, 1938, p. 1355; *ABA Almanac 1950* (New York: American Booksellers Association, 1950); Hellmut Lehmann-Haupt, "Book Production and Distribution from 1860 to the Present Day," in *The Book in America: A History of the Making and Selling of Books in the United States,* 2nd ed., by Hellmut Lehmann-Haupt, in collaboration with Lawrence C. Wroth and Rollo G. Silver (New York: R. R. Bowker, 1952), pp. 383–90; S. C. Hollander, "United States of America," in *Resale Price Maintenance,* ed. B. S. Yamey (Chicago: Aldine, 1966), pp. 65–100; U.S. House of Representatives, Subcommittee on Monopolies and Commercial Law, *Fair Trade: Hearings on H.R. 2384: Fair Trade Repeal [March 25 and April 10, 1975]* (Washington, D.C.: U.S. Government Printing Office, 1975); John Tebbel, *A History of Book Publishing in the United States,* vol. 3, *The Golden Age between Two Wars, 1920–1940* (New York: R. R. Bowker, 1978), pp. 459–69.

32. "House Hearings Close on Price Maintenance Law," *Publishers Weekly* 181 (26), June 25, 1962, p. 38.

33. U.S. Senate, *Act to Repeal Enabling Legislation for Fair Trade Laws: Report to Accompany H.R. 6971* (November 20, 1975).

34. Aside from their parallel attempts to encourage an approach to consumption that lies outside of a bargain mentality, the early fair trade movement bears little relation to the current movement that also goes by the name fair trade. Contemporary promoters of fair trade seek to encourage the purchase of globally traded goods at prices that allow living wages for the workers who produce those goods. Coffee has been the most visible fair-traded product, but others are involved as well. It is ironic that retailers such as Starbucks, the country's largest coffee house chain, call themselves participants in fair trade since the original fair trade movement was about opposition to the dominance of retail chains.

35. Max Weber, "Religious Rejections of the World and Their Directions" (1915), in *From Max Weber: Essays in Sociology,* ed. H. H. Gerth and C. Wright Mills (New York: Oxford University Press, 1946), pp. 323–59.

36. Jeannie Marshall, "Antiquariansaredoomed.com," *National Post,* September 30, 2000, sec. E.

37. Franklin D. Roosevelt Library, President's Personal File, 200Q (1937: Telegrams), container 232, "Miller-Tydings Bill (1937), Public Reactions to."

38. For example, "Too Much Concentrated Power," *Publishers Weekly* 131 (19), May 8, 1937, p. 1934.

39. Federal Trade Commission, Washington, D.C., "Miller-Tydings Bill and Act: Background and Economic Effects," April 3 [11], 1941, Franklin D. Roosevelt Library, Samuel I. Rosenman Collection, container 38, Miller-Tydings Bill and Act.

Chapter Seven

1. Barbara A. Bannon, "An Interview with Roysce Smith," *Publishers Weekly* 204 (2), July 9, 1973, p. 33.

2. "In Fact . . . ," *Bookselling This Week* 2 (45), March 11, 1996, p. 1; "In Fact . . . ," *Bookselling This Week* 4 (9), June 16, 1997, p. 1. Independent bookstores have continued to close at a faster rate than new stores have been established. Especially hard hit have been women's bookstores, though plenty of other specialized and general stores have failed. Chain competition is not always cited as the direct cause of a store's closing; in some cases, an owner has decided to retire. But the competitive climate has made it more difficult for a retiring owner to sell the store, and so makes it more likely that the store will shut down altogether.

3. For a study of a very different industry in which firms' owners are also frequently motivated by nonfinancial considerations, see Fiona M. Scott Morton and Joel M. Podolny, "Love or Money? The Effects of Owner Motivation in the California Wine Industry," *Journal of Industrial Economics* 50 (4), December 2002, pp. 431–56.

4. For one example of this kind of conflict, see Dan Cullen, "Small Presses Big at PNBA," *Bookselling This Week* 1 (23), September 26, 1994, p. 4.

5. "Milestones," *Bookselling This Week* 1 (36), December 26, 1994, p. 5.

6. Len Fulton, "Peopleship," in *The Whole COSMEP Catalog,* ed. Dick Higgins (Paradise, Calif.: Dustbooks, 1973), pp. 5–6.

7. Bill Henderson, "Independent Publishing: Today and Yesterday," *Annals of the American Academy of Political and Social Science* 421, September 1975, p. 103; Gary Todoroff, "Big," *Small Press,* Winter 1994, p. 22.

8. Jeffrey L. Perlah, "Small and Independent Presses Reach Maturity," *American Bookseller* 18 (1), Fall 1994, pp. iv–v.

9. See, e.g., Abe Peck, "From Underground to Alternative: Peace Signs and Dollar Signs," *Media Studies Journal* 12 (3), Fall 1998, pp. 156–62; David Hesmondhalgh, "Indie: The Institutional Politics and Aesthetics of a Popular Music Genre," *Cultural Studies* 13 (1), 1999, pp. 34–61; Chris Atton, "Reshaping Social Movement Media for a New Millennium," *Social Movement Studies* 2 (1), 2003, pp. 3–15.

10. For profiles of these two stores, see Pat and Fred Cody, *Cody's Books: The Life and Times of a Berkeley Bookstore, 1956 to 1977* (San Francisco: Chronicle Books, 1992); John Mutter, "Managing a Revolution," *Publishers Weekly* 241 (18), May 2, 1994, pp. 51–55.

11. U.S. Federal Trade Commission, *In the Matter of Harper & Row, Publishers, Inc.: Complaint Counsel's Memorandum in Opposition to Respondents' Motions for Summary Dismissal of the Section 2(d) and 2(e) Counts* (June 6, 1989).

12. See, e.g., Maxwell J. Lillienstein, "Concentration and Other Threats to the Book Industry," *American Bookseller* 4 (2), October 1980, p. 24; Len Vlahos, "In Plain Terms," *Bookselling This Week* 1 (21), September 12, 1994, p. 5.

13. "FTC Cites Five Publishers for Anti-Trust Violations," *Publishers Weekly* 176 (19), November 2, 1959, p. 29; "NYABA Votes Action on Mass Market Paperback Discounts," *Publishers Weekly* 176 (23), December 7, 1959, pp. 22–23; "FTC Issues More Decrees on Promotion Allowances," *Publishers Weekly* 182 (12), September 17, 1962, pp. 41–42; Kenneth C. Davis, *Two-Bit Culture: The Paperbacking of America* (Boston: Houghton Mifflin, 1984).

14. "Concern over Discount Discrepancies Troubles Book Publishers," *BP Report on the Business of Book Publishing* 2 (26), June 25, 1977, pp. 1, 3–4; Maxwell J. Lillienstein, "A Booksellers' Nightmare," *American Bookseller* 1 (7), March 1978, p. 11; "Lillienstein Article Alleges Discrimination in Mass Market Discounts," *BP Report on the Business of Book Publishing* 4 (26), June 4, 1979, pp. 1, 9; Maxwell J. Lillienstein, "'I Accuse . . . ,'" *American Bookseller* 2 (11), July 1979, pp. 30–34.

15. There is some evidence that the large wholesalers also granted the chains discounts that were not available to independents. See Jim Milliot, "B&T and the Case of the Errant Packing Slip," *Publishers Weekly* 242 (28), July 10, 1995, p. 8, for an incident where Baker & Taylor was caught granting a B. Dalton outlet a discount higher than advertised in Baker & Taylor's schedule of prices. In the 2001 trial against Barnes & Noble and Borders (discussed later in this chapter), the American Booksellers Association also charged Ingram with giving the chains better discounts along with other financial awards, such as granting full credit for returns, a privilege denied independents. See the transcript of the court trial: U.S. District Court for the Northern District of California, *American Booksellers Association, Inc., et al. vs. Barnes & Noble, Inc., et al.*, vol. 1 (2001), p. 16.

16. U.S. Federal Trade Commission, *In the Matter of Harper & Row, Publishers, Inc.: Nonbinding Statement of Complaint Counsel* (March 7, 1989), p. 13; U.S. District Court for the Northern District of California, *American Booksellers Association vs. Barnes & Noble*, pp. 23–25.

17. U.S. Federal Trade Commission, *In the Matter of Harper & Row: Nonbinding Statement of Complaint Counsel*, pp. 14–15.

18. Lila Freilicher, "ABA: The Convention Goes West," *Publishers Weekly* 204 (2), July 9, 1973, p. 20.

19. Allene Symons, "Growth, Innovation Mark the Regional Booksellers Movement," *Publishers Weekly* 223 (15), April 15, 1983, p. 26.

20. Allene Symons and Sonja Bolle, "Issues in Bookselling, 1984," in *The Book Publishing Annual* (New York: R. R. Bowker, 1985), p. 190. See also "Two Regionals

Stress Advantage of Independent Stores to Public," *American Bookseller* 4 (7), March 1981, p. 12.

21. "Independent Booksellers Mull Possibility of Forming Association," *BP Report on the Business of Book Publishing* 2 (12), February 28, 1977, p. 5; Roger H. Smith, "Independent Distributors," part 1, "The Controversy behind Their Retailing Efforts," *Publishers Weekly* 214 (22), November 27, 1978, p. 49; "News from Three Regionals in the Midwest," *American Bookseller* 4 (9), May 1981, p. 21; Ginger Curwen with Robert Mack, "A Guide to the Regional Associations," *American Bookseller* 5 (1), September 1981, pp. 60–61.

22. "Board of Directors' Meeting," *American Bookseller* 1 (8), April 1978, pp. 42–43; "News in Brief," *BP Report on the Business of Book Publishing* 4 (17), April 2, 1979, p. 7; "ABA Dissident Slate Wants More Independent Representation," *BP Report on the Business of Book Publishing* 4 (18), April 8, 1979, pp. 4–5; "ABA Officers, Directors Elected: Dissident Slate Gets 20% of Vote," *BP Report on the Business of Book Publishing* 4 (22), May 7, 1979, p. 6; G. Roysce Smith, "Talking to the Board," *American Bookseller* 2 (10), June 1979, p. 7.

23. Van A. Messner, "'I Accuse' Draws Flurry of Replies," *American Bookseller* 3 (1), September 1979, p. 14.

24. "ABA Board Actions," *American Bookseller* 4 (3), November 1980, p. 12; Robert D. Hale, "Survival Strategy: A Report," *American Bookseller* 4 (3), November 1980, pp. 9–11.

25. Lois Kempton, "Other Opinions on Litigation," *American Bookseller* 5 (10), June 1982, p. 10.

26. "ABA Members Voice Opinions on Association Services and Potential Litigation," *American Bookseller* 5 (10), June 1982, p. 14.

27. During the case's discovery phase, the NCBA found that these practices had been occurring since about 1972.

28. See, e.g., "ABA Board Passes Resolution Applauding NCBA Action," *ABA Newswire,* October 25, 1982, p. 1; "Report of the February Board Meeting," *American Bookseller* 5 (8), April 1982, pp. 11–12; "At the Membership Meeting," *American Bookseller* 5 (11), July 1982, p. 37; "Bookseller Apologizes to ABA Board for 'No Confidence' Resolution," *BP Report on the Business of Book Publishing* 7 (28), June 21, 1982, pp. 1–2; "California Booksellers File Suit against Avon Books, Alleging Illegal Discount," *BP Report on the Business of Book Publishing* 7 (19), April 19, 1982, pp. 1, 7; John F. Baker, "ABA at Anaheim: Upbeat, with Strong Notes of Dissent," *Publishers Weekly* 221 (24), June 11, 1982, pp. 14, 18; Ginger Curwen, "Record Attendance, High Spirits, and an Explosive General Membership Meeting Mark ABA Convention in Anaheim," *ABA Newswire,* June 14, 1982, p. 1; Ginger Curwen, "Antitrust Suit Filed against Avon Books by Northern California Booksellers Association, Cody's Books, and Bookplate," *ABA Newswire,* April 19, 1982, p. 1; Ginger Curwen, "Report of the May Board Meeting," *American Bookseller* 5 (11), July 1982, p. 10; Daisy Maryles, "A Buoyant Crowd . . . and Rumblings of Dissent," *Publishers Weekly* 221 (26), June 25, 1982, pp. 44–49; Andy Ross, "NCBA Explains Lawsuit, Seeks Funds," *American Bookseller* 5 (10), June 1982, pp. 9–10.

29. Donald Laing, "Facing the Future," *American Bookseller* 6 (1), September 1982, p. 23.

30. Andy Ross, "Northern California Booksellers Association Comments on September 'View,'" *American Bookseller* 6 (3), November 1982, pp. 7–8.

31. "At the Membership Meeting," *American Bookseller* 7 (11), July 1984, p. 33.

32. Theresa S. Lazo, "Bookseller Representation on the ABA Board," *American Bookseller* 7 (12), August 1984, p. 7.

33. "Twenty-five Booksellers Join to Solicit Independent Nominations to ABA Board," *ABA Newswire*, October 17, 1983, p. 1; Lisa See, "Independents Seek ABA Board Representation," *Publishers Weekly* 224 (20), November 11, 1983, p. 33; "Independent Committee Offers Alternate Slate in Upcoming ABA Election," *BP Report on the Business of Book Publishing* 9 (15), March 19, 1984, pp. 3–4; "ABA Expecting Improved Attendance for 84th Convention," *BP Report on the Business of Book Publishing* 9 (24), May 21, 1984, pp. 1–2; "Independent Committee to Run Alternate ABA Slate," *ABA Newswire*, March 12, 1984, p. 1; "ABA Board Votes to Allocate Funds for Analysis of Avon Cost Study," *BP Report on the Business of Book Publishing* 9 (47), November 5, 1984, pp. 1–2; Bernie Rath, "An Open Letter to the ABA Membership from ABA Executive Director Bernie Rath," *ABA Newswire*, April 2, 1984, p. 1; Symons and Bolle, "Issues in Bookselling, 1984."

34. "NCBA Wins Opening Round Victory in Lawsuit against Avon," special report in *BP Report on the Business of Book Publishing* 11 (48), November 10, 1986, pp. 1, 7–8.

35. On the NCBA case, see, e.g., "Bantam Named as Co-Defendant in NCBA Suit over Bookseller Discounts," *BP Report on the Business of Book Publishing* 7 (50), November 29, 1982, pp. 1, 3; "NCBA Adds Bantam as Co-Defendant in Antitrust Suit," *ABA Newswire*, November 29, 1982, p. 1; "Avon Documents in NCBA Suit Show Discounts Offered to Bookstore Chains," *BP Report on the Business of Book Publishing* 7 (35), August 16, 1982, pp. 1, 7; "Bantam Admits It Offers 'Incentive' Bonuses to Chains in NCBA Suit Filing," *BP Report on the Business of Book Publishing* 8 (9), February 7, 1983, pp. 1, 5–6; "Avon to End Direct Service to over 1700 Accounts," *BP Report on the Business of Book Publishing* 10 (4), December 24, 1984, p. 1; "Independent Booksellers Cry Foul over Dalton Insert in Rolling Stone," *BP Report on the Business of Book Publishing* 9 (35), August 13, 1984, pp. 1–2; "NCBA Adds Advertising Discrimination Charge to Complaint against Avon," *BP Report on the Business of Book Publishing* 9 (38), September 3, 1984, p. 2; "Avon Responds to NCBA Charges," *BP Report on the Business of Book Publishing* 10 (6), January 14, 1985, p. 2; "Anger, Disappointment Greet Avon Decision Ending Some Direct Bookstore Service," *BP Report on the Business of Book Publishing* 10 (5), January 7, 1985, pp. 1, 8; "NCBA Wins Opening Round"; "Northern California Booksellers Association Files Suit against Major Chains," *BP Report on the Business of Book Publishing* 12 (9), February 2, 1987, pp. 1, 6–7; "Crown Files Countersuit against NCBA," *BP Report on the Business of Book Publishing* 12 (13), March 2, 1987, pp. 2–3; "NCBA, Bookstore Chains Agree to Dismiss Suits," *BP Report on the Business of Book Publishing* 12 (43), October 5, 1987, pp. 1, 8–9; "Avon Adopts New Incentive Plan; Suit with NCBA to Be Dismissed," *BP Report on the Business of Book Publishing* 12 (47), November 2, 1987, pp. 1, 5–6; Katherine Bishop, "The Battle of the Booksellers,"

New York Times, March 17, 1987, sec. D; Caroline E. Mayer, "N. California Booksellers Charge Chains with Collusion," *Washington Post,* January 30, 1987, sec. F; Madalynne Reuter, "NCBA Sues Three Chains for 'Inducing' Unfair Discounts," *Publishers Weekly* 231 (5), February 6, 1987, p. 16.

36. U.S. Federal Trade Commission, *In the Matter of Harper & Row: Nonbinding Statement of Complaint Counsel,* p. 65.

37. U.S. Federal Trade Commission, *In the Matter of Harper & Row, Publishers, Inc.: Nonbinding Statement of Harper & Row, Publishers, Inc.* (March 14, 1989), p. 8.

38. U.S. Federal Trade Commission, *In the Matter of Harper & Row: Nonbinding Statement of Complaint Counsel,* pp. 3, 25.

39. Murray Forseter, "FTC Complaint Demands Action," *Chain Store Age Executive* 65 (2), February 1989, p. 6.

40. On the FTC investigation, see, e.g., "FTC Begins Investigation of Six Major Publishers," *Publishers Weekly* 233 (24), June 17, 1988, p. 11; U.S. Federal Trade Commission, *In the Matter of Harper & Row, Publishers, Inc.: Complaint* (December 20, 1988); "FTC Complaint Says Chains 'Induced' Discriminatory Prices from Publishers," *BP Report on the Business of Book Publishing* 14 (18), April 3, 1989, pp. 1, 4–6; Rhonda Razzano, "FTC Decision May Affect Price-Breaks, Take-Backs," *Chain Store Age Executive* 65 (2), February 1989, pp. 18–20; "Initial Agreement Reached in FTC Publishing Investigation," *BP Report on the Business of Book Publishing* 17 (3), December 7, 1992, pp. 1, 6; Calvin Reid, "'Agreements' in FTC Publishers Investigation," *Publishers Weekly* 239 (54), December 14, 1992, p. 9; U.S. Federal Trade Commission, *In the Matter of Harper & Row, Publishers, Inc.: Order Withdrawing Matter from Adjudication* (November 12, 1992); "Robinson-Patman Update," *FTC: Watch,* no. 397, September 20, 1993, p. 11; "Former BDD Counsel Nominated to Chair FTC," *Bookselling This Week* 1 (40), January 30, 1995, p. 1; "FTC Drops Antitrust Case against Publishers," *Bookselling This Week* 3 (23), September 30, 1996, pp. 1, 3; Doreen Carvajal, "F.T.C. Drops Case against Big Publishers," *New York Times,* September 21, 1996; Jim Milliot, "FTC Dismisses Pricing Case against Six Publishers," *Publishers Weekly* 243 (40), September 30, 1996, pp. 10, 22.

41. "Competition, Not Equality, Is the Goal of the FTC, Booksellers Told," *BP Report on the Business of Book Publishing* 18 (8), January 18, 1993, pp. 1–2.

42. Along with the Northern California Independent Booksellers Association, these included the Mountain & Plains Booksellers Association, Pacific Northwest Booksellers Association, and Intermountain Independent Booksellers Association.

43. The New Atlantic Independent Booksellers Association, Mid-South Independent Booksellers Association, and Upper Midwest Booksellers Association.

44. The Oregon Independent Booksellers Association, Independent Booksellers of Sonoma County, Houston Area Independent Booksellers Association, Unchained Booksellers of the Piedmont, Independent Booksellers of Chicago, Independent Booksellers of Washington, Omaha Independent Booksellers Association, Madison Area Independent Booksellers Association, and Connecticut Independent Booksellers Association.

45. See Shannon Maughan, "Vote on Name Change Energizes NCBA," *Publishers Weekly* 240 (40), October 4, 1993, pp. 19–20; John Mutter, "NCBA Stresses

Independence in Name," *Publishers Weekly* 240 (45), November 8, 1993, p. 16; "Houston to Celebrate Independents in January," *Bookselling This Week* 1 (35), December 19, 1994, p. 1; "Intermountain Show Accents Independent," *Bookselling This Week* 1 (27), October 24, 1994, p. 5; Cullen, "Small Presses Big at PNBA"; Bridget Kinsella, "Intermountain Group Goes Independent," *Publishers Weekly* 241 (44), October 31, 1994, p. 20; Jim Milliot, "MPBA to Limit Membership," *Publishers Weekly* 241 (38), September 19, 1994, p. 18; John Mutter, "Oregon Booksellers Form Independent Association," *Publishers Weekly* 241 (6), February 7, 1994, p. 32; Martin Pedersen, "Booksellers Band Together for Survival," *Publishers Weekly* 241 (36), September 5, 1994, pp. 22–23; Nora Rawlinson, "PNBA Grows with an Expanding Market," *Publishers Weekly* 241 (42), October 17, 1994, pp. 25–26; Richard Scott, "Bylaws Changes Underscore New Business at MPBA," *Bookselling This Week* 1 (24), October 3, 1994, p. 7; Lisa See, "Sonoma Indies Form Association," *Publishers Weekly* 241 (49), December 5, 1994, p. 26; "IIBA Advances Independent Agenda," *Bookselling This Week* 2 (28), November 6, 1995, p. 1; "Once WIBA, IBOW Bows," *Publishers Weekly* 242 (20), May 15, 1995, p. 20; "Indie Ideas," *Publishers Weekly* 242 (14), April 3, 1995, p. 23; Karen Angel, "Omaha Indies Take Defensive Action," *Publishers Weekly* 242 (29), July 17, 1995, p. 130; Karen Angel, "HABA Declares Independence," *Publishers Weekly* 242 (4), January 23, 1995, p. 24; Bridget Kinsella, "Chicago Area Indies Unite," *Publishers Weekly* 242 (15), April 10, 1995, p. 19; John Mutter, "Washington Indies Form Association," *Publishers Weekly* 242 (5), January 30, 1995, p. 32; "NY/NJBA, MABA to Merge," *Bookselling This Week* 3 (25), October 14, 1996, pp. 1, 5; Elizabeth Bernstein, "NY/NJ and Mid-Atlantic Bookseller Groups Merge," *Publishers Weekly* 243 (42), October 14, 1996, p. 12; "UMBA Show Bonds Booksellers," *Bookselling This Week* 4 (24), October 6, 1997, pp. 1, 5; "Mid-South Show Features Independents," *Bookselling This Week* 4 (21), September 15, 1997, pp. 1, 4; Karen Angel, "UMBA to Vote on Adding 'Independent' to Name," *Publishers Weekly* 244 (36), September 1, 1997, p. 24; Elizabeth Bernstein, "UMBA: 'A Worthwhile and Productive Show,'" *Publishers Weekly* 244 (43), October 20, 1997, pp. 21–22. It is interesting to note that the entire "independent" movement in the book industry appears to be strongest in the western part of the United States. Certainly, the northern California booksellers have been at the forefront of organizing against the chains and against conglomeratization in general. But on top of that, each of the others in the first group of major regional associations to declare themselves "independent" lay west of the Rockies. Similarly, northern California has the greatest concentration of those presses calling themselves independent. On the other hand, the mainstream of the book industry, including the big publishing houses and the bookstore chains, is commonly referred to by the shorthand "New York."

46. "Booksellers Express Discontent at ABA Annual Meeting," *BP Report on the Business of Book Publishing* 18 (27), June 7, 1993, pp. 1, 7–8; John Mutter with Jim Milliot, "ABA Members Fighting for 'Level Playing Field,'" *Publishers Weekly* 240 (23), June 7, 1993, pp. 7, 11–12.

47. The publishers were: Houghton Mifflin, Penguin U.S.A., St. Martin's Press, Rutledge Hill Press, and Hugh Lauter Levin Associates. Aside from Penguin, these were not the country's largest presses. This was because the ABA deliberately excluded those publishers that were then still under FTC investigation. However, in 1996, the

ABA added FTC respondent Random House as a defendant, arguing that Random House was among the worst offenders in terms of unequal treatment of book retailers. Random House also proved to be the most recalcitrant about agreeing to a settlement with the ABA.

48. This account of the 1994 membership meetings is based on personal observation.

49. Nora Rawlinson, "The Show Must Go On," *Publishers Weekly* 243 (28), July 8, 1996, p. 11.

50. Quoted in John Mutter, "Publishers Sued by ABA Take Offensive," *Publishers Weekly* 242 (7), February 13, 1995, pp. 21–22.

51. On the ABA suit, see, e.g., "More Bookseller Discrimination?" *FTC: Watch,* no. 414, June 6, 1994, pp. 10–11; "ABA Lawsuit Charges Booksellers Are 'Harmed by Unlawfully Favorable Deals,'" *ABA Show Daily,* May 28, 1994, p. 49; John Mutter and Maureen O'Brien, "ABA Sues Five Publishers," *ABA Show Daily,* May 28, 1994, pp. 1, 46; "ABA Reaches Settlement with Penguin USA," *Bookselling This Week* 2 (29), November 13, 1995, pp. 1, 3; "ABA Reaches Settlement with Houghton Mifflin," *Bookselling This Week* 2 (27), October 30, 1995, pp. 1, 3; "Settlement Reached with Publisher in ABA Suit," *Bookselling This Week* 1 (42), February 13, 1995, pp. 1, 3; Karen Angel and John F. Baker, "ABA Settles with Hugh Lauter Levin in Price Suit," *Publishers Weekly* 242 (7), February 13, 1995, p. 10; John F. Baker, "Penguin Settles with ABA on Terms Similar to HM's," *Publishers Weekly* 242 (46), November 13, 1995, p. 12; John F. Baker, "Houghton Reaches Accord with ABA on Price Suit," *Publishers Weekly* 242 (44), October 30, 1995, p. 8; "Random House Settles with ABA," *Bookselling This Week* 3 (31), November 25, 1996, pp. 1, 3; "ABA Settles with St. Martin's; Random House Suit Proceeds," *Bookselling This Week* 3 (17), August 19, 1996, pp. 1, 3; "ABA Settles with Rutledge Hill," *Bookselling This Week* 3 (16), August 5, 1996, pp. 1, 3; "ABA Sues Random House," *Bookselling This Week* 2 (37), January 15, 1996, pp. 1, 3; John F. Baker, "ABA Sues Random on Pricing," *Publishers Weekly* 243 (2), January 8, 1996, p. 10; Jim Milliot, "Random House and ABA Settle Antitrust Lawsuit," *Publishers Weekly* 243 (48), November 25, 1996, p. 10; Jim Milliot, "St. Martin's Settles with ABA," *Publishers Weekly* 243 (24), August 19, 1996, p. 11; Jim Milliot, "ABA Settles with Rutledge Hill," *Publishers Weekly* 243 (32), August 5, 1996, p. 276; Jim Milliot, "Random House Withdraws from the ABA Convention," *Publishers Weekly* 243 (3), January 15, 1996, p. 310.

52. "ABA/Penguin Settlement May Set Antitrust Precedent," *Bookselling This Week* 4 (25), October 13, 1997, pp. 1, 3; "Penguin to Make $25 Million Payment to Independent Booksellers, ABA," *Bookselling This Week,* special edition, October 4, 1997, p. 1; "Penguin Discovers Improper Discounting," *Bookselling This Week* 3 (42), February 17, 1997, pp. 1, 5; Jim Milliot, "Penguin in Multi-Million Dollar Settlement with ABA," *Publishers Weekly* 244 (41), October 6, 1997, p. 10; Jim Milliot, "Galatro Points Finger at Superior in Penguin Discounting Scheme," *Publishers Weekly* 244 (35), August 25, 1997, p. 13; Jim Milliot, "ABA Monitoring Penguin Discount Probe," *Publishers Weekly* 244 (8), February 24, 1997, p. 10; Jim Milliot and John Mutter, "Penguin to Pay ABA $25 Million in Settlement," *Publishers Weekly* 244 (42), October 13, 1997, p. 10.

53. "Local Communities Support Bookseller Plaintiffs," *Bookselling This Week* 4 (48), April 6, 1998, pp. 1, 7; "ABA/Bookseller Lawsuit Grabs Nation's Attention," *Bookselling This Week* 4 (46), March 23, 1998, p. 1; "ABA, Independent Bookstores Sue Barnes & Noble and Borders," *Bookselling This Week,* special edition, March 18, 1998, p. 1; "A Word from the Wings: Riggio Lashes Out at ABA," *Publishers Weekly* 245 (23), June 8, 1998, p. 10; John F. Baker, "ABA Is Suing Borders, Barnes & Noble," *Publishers Weekly* 245 (12), March 23, 1998, pp. 16, 24; U.S. District Court for the Northern District of California, *American Booksellers Assn., Inc., v. Barnes & Noble, Inc.; Borders Group, Inc.; Borders, Inc.; and Walden Book Company, Inc.: Amended Complaint* (April 1998).

54. U.S. District Court for the Northern District of California, *American Booksellers Association, Inc., et al. vs. Barnes & Noble, Inc., et al.: Settlement Agreement* (April 19, 2001).

55. "FTC Receives More Petitions Opposing Proposed Ingram Acquisition," *Bookselling This Week* 6 (3), May 24, 1999, p. 1.

56. Doreen Carvajal, "Book Chain's Bid to Acquire Big Distributor Is under Fire," *New York Times,* April 5, 1999, sec. C; Dan Cullen, "Phone Bill 'Stuffers' Urge Opposition to B&N Merger," *Bookselling This Week* 5 (40), March 1, 1999, pp. 1, 4.

57. "Protect Independent Booksellers from Barnes & Noble" (Working Assets Long Distance telephone bill, February 1999).

58. Doreen Carvajal, "Book Retailer Ends Bid for Wholesaler," *New York Times,* June 3, 1999, sec. C; Dan Cullen, "*BTW* Gets Inside Story from FTC Chair," *Bookselling This Week* 6 (6), June 14, 1999, pp. 1, 4; Jim Milliot and Steven Zeitchik, "Barnes & Noble, Ingram Deal Scuttled by FTC Objections," *Publishers Weekly* 246 (23), June 7, 1999, pp. 10, 22.

59. "NCIBA Showcases Sales, Seminars," *Bookselling This Week* 4 (26), October 20, 1997, p. 5.

60. "Harry Potter and the Goblet of Crossfire?" *PW Daily for Booksellers* (electronic newsletter), June 28, 2000; "Harry Potter IV: Two Retailers Jump the Gun; Jacobs Writes Domnitz," *PW Daily for Booksellers* (electronic newsletter), July 5, 2000; "ABA Board Decries Breach of Potter Laydown Agreement," *Bookselling This Week* 7 (8), June 26, 2000, pp. 1–2; Shannon Maughan and Jim Milliot, "'Goblet of Fire' Sparks Controversy," *Publishers Weekly* 247 (27), July 3, 2000, p. 9.

61. "ABA Launches Sales Tax Action Initiative," *Bookselling This Week* 6 (13), August 23, 1999, pp. 1, 3.

62. "ABA Board Approves Vision Statement," *Bookselling This Week* 4 (15), August 4, 1997, p. 4.

63. "American Booksellers Association Strategic Plan," *Bookselling This Week* 4 (27), November 3, 1997, p. 3.

64. Elizabeth Bernstein, "It's Unanimous: NIBW Is Better in July," *Publishers Weekly* 243 (34), August 19, 1996, pp. 22–24; Jill Perlstein, "Getting a Jump on National Independent Bookstore Week, July 20–27," *American Bookseller* 19 (11), June 1996, p. 91.

65. "ABA Hires Marketing Honcho," *PW Daily for Booksellers* (electronic newsletter), September 28, 1998; "Carol Miles to Leave ABA," *Bookselling This Week* 5 (28), November 30, 1998, p. 2; "Miles Leaving ABA," *Publishers Weekly* 245 (49), December 7,

1998, p. 19; "Hoynes Joins ABA Staff," *Bookselling This Week* 5 (20), October 5, 1998, p. 3.

66. Quoted in Judith Rosen, "ABA Cuts Membership Department," *Publishers Weekly* 248 (49), December 3, 2001, p. 23.

67. See, e.g., "Book Sense Ready to Roll Nationally," *Bookselling This Week* 5 (37), February 8, 1999, pp. 1, 3; Avin Mark Domnitz, "Why Book Sense?" *Bookselling This Week* 6 (18), September 20, 1999, p. 3; Richard T. Scott, "Book Sense Campaign Is Launched," *Bookselling This Week* 5 (40), March 1, 1999, pp. 1, 3.

68. American Booksellers Association, "Marketing Program Letter of Agreement," April 2000.

69. Laura J. Miller, "The Best-Seller List as Marketing Tool and Historical Fiction," *Book History* 3, 2000, pp. 286–304.

70. "Important News about Book Sense," *Bookselling This Week* (electronic newsletter), March 25, 2004, p. 1.

71. "BookSense.com Welcomes New Member Stores," *Bookselling This Week* (electronic newsletter), October 31, 2002, p. 2.

72. "The Latest Book Cash News," *Bookselling This Week* 8 (24), November 5, 2001, pp. 1, 7; Rosemary Hawkins, "Book Sense Stores to Participate in Book Cash Promotion," *Bookselling This Week* 8 (14), August 20, 2001, pp. 1–2; Nomi Schwartz, "Stores Look Forward to Book Cash," *Bookselling This Week* 8 (17), September 10, 2001, pp. 1–2.

73. "Physician-Assisted Literacy — Prescription for Reading Program Gains Momentum," *Bookselling This Week* (electronic newsletter), April 24, 2002; "Prescription for Reading Program to Expand," *Bookselling This Week* (electronic newsletter), September 5, 2002, p. 4; "Book Cash Headed to Consumers with the *New York Times*," *Bookselling This Week* (electronic newsletter), July 18, 2002, pp. 6–7.

74. "ABA Members Get an Update and Share Views at BEA," *Bookselling This Week* (electronic newsletter), June 5, 2003, p. 4; "2003 Booksellers Forum Season Ends in New England," *Bookselling This Week* (electronic newsletter), May 8, 2003, pp. 1–2; John Mutter, "ABA Meetings: All Goes According to Plan," *Publishers Weekly* 250 (23), June 9, 2003, p. 11.

75. "Book Sense This Week," *Bookselling This Week* 6 (25), November 8, 1999, p. 5; Carl Lennertz, "Book Sense Advertising Update," *Bookselling This Week* 6 (10), July 19, 1999, p. 8; "Book Sense Coming to NPR," *Bookselling This Week* 7 (5), May 29, 2000, p. 5.

76. John Mutter, "ABA Reports Major Losses on Major Investments," *Publishers Weekly* 249 (19), May 13, 2002, p. 12.

77. Steven M. Zeitchik, "While the Biggies Merge . . . Book Sense Brands On," *PW Daily for Booksellers* (electronic newsletter), January 10, 2000; "Speak Up! Now's the Time to Nominate Your Favorite Titles for the Book Sense Book of the Year," *Bookselling This Week* (electronic newsletter), January 9, 2003, pp. 3–4.

78. John Mutter, "ABA Members 'Guardedly Optimistic' about Future," *Publishers Weekly* 248 (24), June 11, 2001, p. 10; "Independent Bookstores with Book Sense Continue with Sales Increases," *Bookselling This Week* (electronic newsletter), March 7, 2002.

79. William Leach, *Land of Desire: Merchants, Power, and the Rise of a New American Culture* (New York: Vintage Books, 1993), pp. 81–84.

80. American Booksellers Association, "Book Sense Fact Sheet" (2000).

81. Russ Lawrence, "Welcome, Indie-Mart Shoppers?" *Bookselling This Week* 6 (26), November 15, 1999, p. 6; Carl Lennertz, "A Campaign, Not a Chain," *Bookselling This Week* 6 (26), November 15, 1999, pp. 6, 8.

82. Dan Cullen, "ABA Town Hall and Annual Meeting Focus on the Settlement and Moving Ahead," *Bookselling This Week* 8 (6), June 18, 2001, p. 2; "2000 a Solid Year for Book Sense," *Bookselling This Week* 7 (31), January 8, 2001, pp. 1, 3.

83. Carl Lennertz, "Bonding and Branding," *Bookselling This Week* 7 (7), June 19, 2000, p. 5.

84. Philip Kotler, *Marketing Management,* 11th ed. (Upper Saddle River, N.J.: Prentice Hall, 2003), p. 420.

85. The goal "Promote the value of independent booksellers as a group through Book Sense and other cooperative activities" ranked third, whereas "Serve as the voice of independent professional booksellers and advocate on their behalf on issues such as trade practices, free expression, and literacy" ranked second. The first-ranked goal was "Provide independent professional booksellers with access to the information and skills they need to succeed in a changing world." The most explicitly activist goal was ranked fifth: "Support community activism and help create alliances that promote independent bookselling and other independent businesses" ("ABA Strategic Planning Committee Receives Members' Ranking of Draft Strategic Goals," *Bookselling This Week* [electronic newsletter], May 23, 2002, p. 1).

86. Carl Lennertz, "Book Sense Regional Bestseller Lists to Change Names in Order to Increase Publisher and Media Awareness," *Bookselling This Week* (electronic newsletter), April 11, 2002.

87. "Publishing 2002: Where the Buck Stops," *Publishers Weekly* 249 (1), January 7, 2002, p. 31.

88. David Monod, *Store Wars: Shopkeepers and the Culture of Mass Marketing, 1890–1939* (Toronto: University of Toronto Press, 1996), p. 66.

89. See, e.g., Harold D. Lasswell, *Propaganda Technique in World War I* (1927; Cambridge: MIT Press, 1971); Jacques Ellul, *Propaganda: The Formation of Men's Attitudes* (1965; New York: Vintage Books, 1973); Randal Marlin, *Propaganda and the Ethics of Persuasion* (Peterborough, Ontario: Broadview, 2002).

90. Jean-Jacques Rousseau, *The Social Contract and Discourse on the Origin of Inequality* (New York: Washington Square Press, 1967); Aristotle, *The Politics* (Harmondsworth: Penguin, 1981); Jürgen Habermas, *The Structural Transformation of the Public Sphere: An Inquiry into a Category of Bourgeois Society* (1962; Cambridge: MIT Press, 1989); Jürgen Habermas, *Moral Consciousness and Communicative Action* (Cambridge: MIT Press, 1990).

91. Emile Durkheim, *Moral Education: A Study in the Theory and Application of the Sociology of Education* (1925; New York: Free Press, 1973), pp. 57, 59.

92. Nancy Fraser, "Rethinking the Public Sphere: A Contribution to the Critique of Actually Existing Democracy," in *Habermas and the Public Sphere,* ed. Craig Calhoun (Cambridge: MIT Press, 1992), p. 131.

Chapter Eight

1. "Bookselling Daybook," *Publishers Weekly* 240 (21), May 24, 1993, p. 38.

2. Borders Group Inc., *Form 10-K for the Fiscal Year Ended January 27, 2002* (2002), p. 6. These figures include employees working in warehouses and corporate offices as well as in individual outlets.

3. The chains have tried to keep labor costs under control in back room tasks as well. Sometimes, they have shown great creativity in this area. For instance, B. Dalton was able to cut costs by using data-entry laborers at a Minnesota women's prison in the early 1980s. Karen E. Debats, "Training Alliance," *Personnel Journal* 61 (4), April 1982, p. 249.

4. See, e.g., Martin Oppenheimer, "Small-Minded," *Dollars and Sense,* no. 196, November/December 1994, pp. 20–21, 39–40.

5. "B. Dalton's Home-Made CCTV, VCR: To Catch a Thief," *Stores* 70 (6), June 1988, pp. 88–89.

6. See Borders Group Inc., *1995 Borders Group, Inc., Annual Report* (1996), p. 9.

7. In the past, at least two Doubleday outlets were unionized, though only one still was by the time Borders workers were organizing in early 1997. There are also a few large independents that are unionized.

8. "UFCW Targets Borders, Encore," *Bookselling This Week* 3 (33), December 9, 1996, pp. 1, 3; "City Council to Borders: Re-Hire Union Supporter," *Bookselling This Week* 3 (34), December 16, 1996, pp. 1, 5; Bridget Kinsella, "Borders Faces Union Protest, National Boycott Over Firing," *Publishers Weekly* 243 (50), December 9, 1996, p. 14; Bridget Kinsella, "Union Drive Grows at Borders — with Push from Author Moore," *Publishers Weekly* 243 (48), November 25, 1996, p. 12; Michael Moore, "Banned by Borders," *Nation* 263 (18), December 2, 1996, p. 10; Michael Wines, "An Odd Rift Develops between an Author and a Chain Promoting His Latest Book," *New York Times,* November 18, 1996, sec. C; Christien Gholson, "Union Organization as Performance Art," *Eight Ball,* April 1997, [pp. 15–17]; Shannon Matthews, *Borders Books and Union Stuff,* http://www.dolphin.upenn.edu/~amatth13/ (accessed June 6, 1997). See also the 1997 Michael Moore film *The Big One,* though this movie gives a more prominent role to Moore in the bookstore unionizing efforts portrayed than is probably justified.

9. The current manifestation of the IWW, a much smaller version of its famous ancestor, stated that it did not have the resources to organize on a national level, and so supported the UFCW's efforts among bookstore clerks ("Two Unions Target Borders," *Bookselling This Week* 3 [13], July 15, 1996, pp. 1, 7). The IWW does retain a focus on trying to organize retail workers.

10. Kathleen Anderson, "Why I Am in Favor of a Union," *Eight Ball,* [no. 4, 1997], p. 4.

11. Matthews, *Borders Books and Union Stuff.*

12. Greg Popek, "Hello, I Must Be Going," *Eight Ball,* April 1997, [p. 3].

13. Jason Chappell, "A Tale of Two Markets," *Eight Ball,* [no. 3, 1997, p. 6].

14. Edward Nawotka, "Borders and Minneapolis Union Still in Contract Negotiations," *PW Daily for Booksellers* (electronic newsletter), April 4, 2003. See also Laura Billings, "Gen X Catching on to the Benefits of Unionization," *Pioneer Press* (St. Paul), September 19, 2002, sec. B; Edward Nawotka, "New Union Efforts at Borders Group," *Publishers Weekly* 249 (45), November 11, 2002, p. 12; Mike Hughlett, "Borders Union Nixes Contract," *Pioneer Press* (St. Paul), September 26, 2003, sec. C; Edward Nawotka, "Borders Home Office Lays Off 12; Ann Arbor Store to Strike," *PW Daily for Booksellers* (electronic newsletter), November 7, 2003; Edward Nawotka, "First Union Contract at Borders? Not Quite," *PW Daily for Booksellers* (electronic newsletter), January 23, 2004; Robyn Repya, "Uptown Borders Employees Ratify Union Contract," *Borders Union,* http://www.bordersunion.org/node/142 (accessed November 16, 2004).

15. Washington Alliance of Technology Workers, *Day2@Amazon.com/WashTech Mission Statement,* http://www.washtech.org/amazon/111700_mission.php3 (accessed December 8, 2000).

16. See John Mutter, "Low Salaries and Wages Present Problems for Bookstores," *Publishers Weekly* 234 (12), September 16, 1988, pp. 34–36.

17. For one account of working in a Barnes & Noble superstore that mixes cynicism about a position "no one at the store . . . regards as a real job" with pleasure at being around books, see Peter Schwendener, "Reflections of a Bookstore Type," *American Bookseller* 19 (9), April 1996, pp. 89–93.

18. Stephen Strausbaugh, "Control through Costly Policy," *Bridges (ILWO Local 5),* February 2001, p. 2.

19. "Net Result: Powell's Shakes Up Section Head Approach," *PW Daily for Booksellers* (electronic newsletter), November 2, 1998; Dan Cullen, "Powell's Votes to Unionize," *Bookselling This Week* 6 (1), May 10, 1999, pp. 1, 3; Roxanne Farmanfarmaian, "Powell's Employees Vote to Unionize; Negotiations Begin," *Publishers Weekly* 246 (20), May 17, 1999, p. 14; Gail Kinsey, "Powell's Nears Vote on Union," *Oregonian* (Portland), April 18, 1999; "Love's Labor Lost: Powell's and Union Found to Violate Law," *PW Daily for Booksellers* (electronic newsletter), July 13, 2000; Kevin Howell and Roxanne Farmanfarmaian, "Booksellers Walk Out at Powell's," *Publishers Weekly* 247 (9), February 28, 2000, p. 28; Barbara Roether, "Powell's Pact Approved; Union Ratifies Contract," *PW Daily for Booksellers* (electronic newsletter), August 11, 2000; Edward Nawotka, "Strike Two: Unionized Powell's Workers Hold One Day Walk-out," *PW Daily for Booksellers* (electronic newsletter), November 17, 2003; "Contract Compact: Powell's and Union Settle Up," *PW Daily for Booksellers* (electronic newsletter), April 2, 2004.

20. Nomi Schwartz, "Concord Bookshop Embroiled in Controversy," *Bookselling This Week* (electronic newsletter), December 31, 2003, pp. 1–2; Judith Rosen, "Discord at Concord Bookshop," *Publishers Weekly* 251 (2), January 12, 2004, p. 19. Some of the employees who left the Concord Bookshop went on to found a new bookstore in Cambridge, Porter Square Books.

21. For studies of how service workers are compelled to communicate good cheer, see Arlie Russell Hochschild, *The Managed Heart: Commercialization of Human Feeling* (Berkeley and Los Angeles: University of California Press, 1983); Robin Leidner, *Fast Food, Fast Talk: Service Work and the Routinization of Everyday Life* (Berkeley and Los Angeles: University of California Press, 1993); The Project on Disney, *Inside the Mouse: Work and Play at Disney World* (Durham: Duke University Press, 1995).

22. See, e.g., Todd Gitlin, *Inside Prime Time* (New York: Pantheon Books, 1985), p. 189.

23. "The Campaign to Save Cover to Cover Booksellers" (flyer, 2003). See also Kevin Howell, "Customers Raising Cash to Save Cover to Cover," *Publishers Weekly* 250 (29), July 21, 2003, p. 76; Edward Nawotka, "Cover to Cover Booksellers and Foundry Bookstores to Close," *PW Daily for Booksellers* (electronic newsletter), June 25, 2003; Karen Schechner, "Customers Make Cover to Cover's Future Bright," *Bookselling This Week* (electronic newsletter), July 10, 2003, p. 3.

24. David Grogan, "Austin Residents Won't Be Boxed In," *Bookselling This Week* (electronic newsletter), January 23, 2003, pp. 4–5; David Grogan, "Borders Pulls Out of Austin Development," *Bookselling This Week* (electronic newsletter), April 24, 2003, pp. 3–4; Edward Nawotka, "BookPeople Helps Organize Protest against Chains," *Publishers Weekly* 250 (4), January 27, 2003, p. 121; Edward Nawotka, "Austin Still Weird; Borders Drops Plans for Downtown Store," *PW Daily for Booksellers* (electronic newsletter), April 24, 2003.

25. Shay Totten, "Border Battle," *Vermont Times* (Chittenden County), June 25, 1997; Nomi Schwartz, "Oak Park Retailers to Government: No Tax Breaks for Chains," *Bookselling This Week* 6 (7), June 21, 1999, p. 3; "A High Price to Pay: Bridgehampton B&N May Meet Resistance from Locals," *PW Daily for Booksellers* (electronic newsletter), March 7, 2003.

26. *Friends United in Creative Knowledge of the Faceless Attitudes of Corporate Entities,* http://fringeware.com/friends/ (accessed 1998); RTMARK, "Nationwide Protest against Barnes & Noble" (press release, November 10, 1998).

27. Ken Garcia, "Residents Lose Out to Superstores in San Francisco," *San Francisco Chronicle,* September 26, 1998, sec. A; John High, "Borders Permit Denied in San Francisco," *Publishers Weekly* 245 (46), November 16, 1998, p. 23.

28. Adrienne Rich, "Letter to *Santa Cruz County Sentinel,*" *Bookselling This Week* 5 (37), February 8, 1999, p. 9.

29. Dan Cullen, "Capitola Community Argues against 'Big Box' Expansion," *Bookselling This Week* 5 (36), February 1, 1999, p. 3; Dan Cullen, "Capitola City Council Votes to Limit Size of Incoming Borders," *Bookselling This Week* 5 (40), March 1, 1999, p. 3; Dan Cullen, "Capitola Shopping Center Blocked," *Bookselling This Week* 5 (45), April 5, 1999, p. 4; Dan Cullen and Jane Allison Havsy, "Borders Nixes Capitola Store Unless City Council Reverses Space Limitation," *Bookselling This Week* 5 (41), March 8, 1999, pp. 1, 3.

30. Curiously, booksellers made few alliances with antichain groups outside of the book industry until the early 2000s.

31. See, e.g., Frederic M. Biddle, "A Brewing Battle," *Boston Globe,* January 2, 1994, Business section; Pia Hinckle, "The 'Starbucks Legislation,'" *San Francisco Bay*

Guardian, July 20, 1994; Julie Solomon, "Not in My Backyard," *Newsweek,* September 16, 1996, pp. 65–66.

32. See, e.g., Craig McLaughlin and Jim Balderston, "When the Chains Go Marching In," *San Francisco Bay Guardian,* July 20, 1994; Tracie Rozhon, "Group Says New Drugstores Are a Menace to Main Street," *New York Times,* June 14, 1999, sec. B; "Hudson Valley Communities Fight CVS," *Home Town Advantage Bulletin,* no. 6 (electronic newsletter), August 2001.

33. For reports on some anti-Wal-Mart campaigns, see Sprawl-Busters, *Victorious Secret,* http://www.sprawl-busters.com/victoryz.html; Constance E. Beaumont, *How Superstore Sprawl Can Harm Communities, and What Citizens Can Do about It* (Washington, D.C.: National Trust for Historic Preservation, 1994); Ben Bennett and Gail McCormack, *Guelph against Goliath: A Community Stands Up to Wal-Mart and Other Big Box Stores* (Guelph: Ben Bennett Communications, 2001); Stephen Eugene Halebsky, "Small Towns and Big Stores: Local Controversies over the Siting of Superstores" (Ph.D. diss., University of Wisconsin, 2001).

34. For examples of this, see New Rules Project, *Physical Size Caps on Retail Businesses,* http://www.newrules.org/retail/size.html.

35. Julie Bach, "Hungry Minds Speak," *American Bookseller* 19 (6), January 1996, p. 12.

36. Exemplars include Herbert Marcuse, *One-Dimensional Man: Studies in the Ideology of Advanced Industrial Society* (Boston: Beacon Press, 1964); John Fiske, *Understanding Popular Culture* (London: Routledge, 1989).

37. Mica Nava, "Consumerism Reconsidered: Buying and Power," *Cultural Studies* 5 (1), January 1991, pp. 157–73.

38. Viviana A. Zelizer, "Human Values and the Market: The Case of Life Insurance and Death in 19th-Century America" (1978), in *The Sociology of Economic Life,* ed. Mark Granovetter and Richard Swedberg (Boulder: Westview Press, 1992), pp. 285–304.

39. See, e.g., Eugene R. Beem, "The Beginnings of the Consumer Movement," in *New Consumerism: Selected Readings,* ed. William T. Kelley (Columbus: Grid, 1973), pp. 13–25; Robert N. Mayer, *The Consumer Movement: Guardians of the Marketplace* (Boston: Twayne, 1989), p. 81; Dana Frank, "'Food Wins All Struggles': Seattle Labor and the Politicization of Consumption," *Radical History Review* (51), Fall 1991, pp. 65–89; Monroe Friedman, *Consumer Boycotts: Effecting Change through the Marketplace and the Media* (New York: Routledge, 1999); Jennifer Lee, *Civility in the City: Blacks, Jews, and Koreans in Urban America* (Cambridge: Harvard University Press, 2002), p. 24.

40. T. H. Breen, "'Baubles of Britain': The American and Consumer Revolutions of the Eighteenth Century," *Past and Present,* no. 119, May 1988, p. 93.

41. Individual consumers are not alone in taking sides through their decisions about which retailers to patronize. Independent booksellers frequently contact organizations that espouse a commitment to the public interest in order to protest their alliances with the major booksellers, especially online retailers. These arrangements can include an organization directing supporters to purchase a book the group is promoting by providing an Internet link to a major e-tailer, as MoveOn did in 2004, or agreements to donate a portion of an e-tailer purchase to a group, as in a 2004

arrangement between Amazon and Amnesty International. See "E-InBox: MoveOn Moves on Book Sense Link," *PW Daily for Booksellers* (electronic newsletter), April 6, 2004; Amazon.com, "Shop with a Purpose This Holiday Season" (promotional flyer, 2004).

42. Similar arguments have been made by Robert N. Bellah et al., *The Good Society* (1991; New York: Vintage Books, 1992), pp. 107–9; Naomi Klein, *No Logo: Taking Aim at the Brand Bullies* (Toronto: Vintage Canada, 2000), pp. 439–46.

43. Neal Ryan, "Reconstructing Citizens as Consumers: Implications for New Modes of Governance," *Australian Journal of Public Administration* 60 (3) September 2001, p. 105.

44. U.S. Department of Commerce, U.S. Census Bureau, *Statistical Abstract of the United States, 2004–2005,* 124th ed. (Washington, D.C.: U.S. Government Printing Office, 2004), p. 463.

45. Alexandra Chasin, *Selling Out: The Gay and Lesbian Movement Goes to Market* (New York: St. Martin's, 2000), p. 43.

ABA Almanac, 1950. 1950. New York: American Booksellers Association.

Acheson, Keith, and Christopher Maule. 1999. *Much Ado about Culture: North American Trade Disputes.* Ann Arbor: University of Michigan Press.

Albright, James F. 1969. "What to Tell the Neophyte: Bookselling Is a Good Career." In *A Manual on Bookselling,* 1st ed., ed. Charles B. Anderson, Joseph A. Duffy, and Jocelyn D. Kahn, pp. 47–50. New York: American Booksellers Association.

American Book Publishers Council. 1951. *The Situation and Outlook for the Book Trade.* New York: American Book Publishers Council.

American Book Trade Directory. 1961. 15th ed. New York: R. R. Bowker.

American Book Trade Directory, 1969–1970. 1969. 19th ed. New York: R. R. Bowker.

Amory, Hugh, and David D. Hall, eds. 2000. *A History of the Book in America.* Vol. 1, *The Colonial Book in the Atlantic World.* Cambridge: Cambridge University Press.

Anglund, Sandra M. 2000. *Small Business Policy and the American Creed.* Westport, Conn.: Praeger.

Appel, Joseph H. [1929] 1930. "Does Chain Growth Tend Toward Standardization of Food? Is This Desirable?" In *Current, Conflicting Views on the Chain Store Controversy,* ed. T. H. Hall, p. 86. Chicago: National Research Bureau.

Aristotle. 1981. *The Politics.* Harmondsworth: Penguin.

Arnold, Matthew. [1932] 1960. *Culture and Anarchy.* Cambridge: Cambridge University Press.

Arthur Andersen & Co. 1982. *Book Distribution in the United States: Issues and Perceptions.* New York: Book Industry Study Group.

Arthur Donner Consultants Inc. and Lazar and Associates. 2000. *The Competitive Challenges Facing Book Publishers in Canada.* Ottawa: Minister of Public Works and Government Services.

Atton, Chris. 2003. "Reshaping Social Movement Media for a New Millennium." *Social Movement Studies* 2 (1), pp. 3–15.

Baensch, Robert E. 1988–89. "Consolidation in Publishing and Allied Industries." *Book Research Quarterly* 4 (4), pp. 6–14.

Barth, Gunther. 1980. *City People: The Rise of Modern City Culture in Nineteenth-Century America.* Oxford: Oxford University Press.

Barthel, Diane. 1996. *Historic Preservation: Collective Memory and Historical Identity.* New Brunswick: Rutgers University Press.

Beaumont, Constance E. 1994. *How Superstore Sprawl Can Harm Communities, and What Citizens Can Do about It.* Washington, D.C.: National Trust for Historic Preservation.

Beem, Eugene R. 1973. "The Beginnings of the Consumer Movement." In *New Consumerism: Selected Readings,* ed. William T. Kelley, pp. 13–25. Columbus: Grid.

Beisel, Nicola. 1992. "Constructing a Shifting Moral Boundary: Literature and Obscenity in Nineteenth-Century America." In *Cultivating Differences: Symbolic Boundaries and the Making of Inequality,* ed. Michèle Lamont and Marcel Fournier, pp. 104–28. Chicago: University of Chicago Press.

Bellah, Robert N., Richard Madsen, William M. Sullivan, Ann Swidler, and Steven M. Tipton. [1991] 1992. *The Good Society.* New York: Vintage Books.

Bender, Thomas. [1978] 1982. *Community and Social Change in America.* Baltimore: Johns Hopkins University Press.

Bennett, Ben, and Gail McCormack. 2001. *Guelph against Goliath: A Community Stands Up to Wal-Mart and Other Big Box Stores.* Guelph: Ben Bennett Communications.

Benson, Susan Porter. 1986. *Counter Cultures: Saleswomen, Managers, and Customers in American Department Stores, 1890–1940.* Urbana: University of Illinois Press.

Berthoff, Rowland. 1980. "Independence and Enterprise: Small Business in the American Dream." In *Small Business in American Life,* ed. Stuart W. Bruchey, pp. 28–48. New York: Columbia University Press.

Bluestone, Daniel M. 1990. "Roadside Blight and the Reform of Commercial Architecture." In *Roadside America: The Automobile in Design and Culture,* ed. Jan Jennings, pp. 170–84. Ames: Iowa State University Press.

Book Industry Study Group and Center for Communications and Media Management. 2002. *Book Industry Trends 2002.* Matawan, N.J.: Book Industry Study Group.

Book Industry Study Group, Statistical Service Center. 1993. *Book Industry Trends 1993.* New York: Book Industry Study Group.

Books in Print, 1994–95. 1994. 47th ed. Vol. 1. New Providence, N.J.: R. R. Bowker.

Books in Print, 2001–2002. 2001. 54th ed. Vol. 1. New Providence, N.J.: R. R. Bowker.

Boorstin, Daniel J. [1973] 1974. *The Americans: The Democratic Experience.* New York: Vintage Books.

Boulding, Kenneth E. 1973. "Toward the Development of a Cultural Economics." In *The Idea of Culture in the Social Sciences,* ed. Louis Schneider and Charles M. Bonjean, pp. 47–64. London: Cambridge University Press.

Bound, Charles F. 1950. *A Banker Looks at Book Publishing.* New York: R. R. Bowker.

Bourdieu, Pierre. [1979] 1984. *Distinction: A Social Critique of the Judgement of Taste.* Cambridge: Harvard University Press.

Bowlby, Rachel. 2001. *Carried Away: The Invention of Modern Shopping.* New York: Columbia University Press.

Boynton, Henry Walcott. [1932] 1991. *Annals of American Bookselling, 1638–1850.* New Castle: Oak Knoll Books.

Brandeis, Louis D. 1913. "Cutthroat Prices: The Competition That Kills." *Harper's Weekly* 58 (2969), November 15, pp. 10–12.

Breen, T. H. 1988. "'Baubles of Britain': The American and Consumer Revolutions of the Eighteenth Century." *Past and Present,* no. 119, pp. 73–104.

Brett, George P. 1913. "Book-Publishing and Its Present Tendencies." *Atlantic Monthly* 111, pp. 454–62.

Brett, George P., Jr. [1930] 1961. Contribution to *Publishers on Publishing,* ed. Gerald Gross, pp. 125–28. New York: Grosset & Dunlap.

Bunzel, John H. 1962. *The American Small Businessman.* New York: Alfred A. Knopf.

Burr, Henry I. 1949. *Observations on Trade Book Sales.* [New York]: American Book–Stratford Press.

Bushman, Richard L. 1993. *The Refinement of America: Persons, Houses, Cities.* New York: Vintage Books.

Business Week. 1956. "The Supermarket: Revolution in Retailing." In *Changing Patterns in Retailing: Readings on Current Trends,* ed. John W. Wingate and Arnold Corbin, pp. 75–90. Homewood, Ill.: Richard D. Irwin.

Butler, Ellis Parker. 1930. *Dollarature; or, The Drug-Store Book.* Boston: Houghton Mifflin.

Buttimer, Anne. 1980. "Home, Reach, and the Sense of Place." In *The Human Experience of Space and Place,* ed. Anne Buttimer and David Seamon, pp. 166–87. New York: St. Martin's.

Callon, Michel. 1998. "The Embeddedness of Economic Markets in Economies." Introduction to *The Laws of the Markets,* ed. Michel Callon, pp. 1–57. Oxford: Blackwell.

Chandler, Alfred D., Jr. 1977. *The Visible Hand: The Managerial Revolution in American Business.* Cambridge, Mass: Belknap Press.

Chase, Stuart, and F. J. Schlink. 1927. *Your Money's Worth: A Study in the Waste of the Consumer's Dollar.* New York: Macmillan.

Chasin, Alexandra. 2000. *Selling Out: The Gay and Lesbian Movement Goes to Market.* New York: St. Martin's.

Cheney, O. H. 1931. *Economic Survey of the Book Industry, 1930–1931.* 1st ed. New York: National Association of Book Publishers.

Chotas, James, and Miriam Phelps. 1978. "Who Owns What." In *The Question of Size in the Book Industry Today: A Publishers Weekly Special Report,* ed. Judith Appelbaum, pp. 9–12. New York: R. R. Bowker.

Christianson, Elin B. 1972. "Mergers in the Publishing Industry, 1958–1970." *Journal of Library History* 7 (1), pp. 5–32.

Cody, Pat, and Fred Cody. 1992. *Cody's Books: The Life and Times of a Berkeley Bookstore, 1956 to 1977.* San Francisco: Chronicle Books.

Cohen, Lizabeth. 1996. "From Town Center to Shopping Center: The Reconfiguration of Community Marketplaces in Postwar America." *American Historical Review* 101 (4), pp. 1050–1081.

Compaine, Benjamin M. 1976. *Book Distribution and Marketing, 1976–1980.* White Plains, N.Y.: Knowledge Industry Publications.

Coser, Lewis A., Charles Kadushin, and Walter W. Powell. [1982] 1985. *Books: The Culture and Commerce of Publishing.* Chicago: University of Chicago Press.

Crawford, Margaret. 1992. "The World in a Shopping Mall." In *Variations on a Theme Park: The New American City and the End of Public Space,* ed. Michael Sorkin, pp. 3–30. New York: Noonday Press.

Damon-Moore, Helen, and Carl F. Kaestle. 1991. "Surveying American Readers." In *Literacy in the United States: Readers and Reading Since 1880,* ed. Carl F. Kaestle, Helen Damon-Moore, Lawrence C. Stedman, Katherine Tinsley, and William Vance Trollinger Jr., pp. 180–203. New Haven: Yale University Press.

Daughters, Charles G. 1937. *Wells of Discontent: A Study of the Economic, Social, and Political Aspects of the Chain Store.* New York: Charles G. Daughters.

Davis, Kenneth C. 1984. *Two-Bit Culture: The Paperbacking of America.* Boston: Houghton Mifflin.

Davis, Mike. [1990] 1992. *City of Quartz: Excavating the Future in Los Angeles.* New York: Vintage Books.

Davis, Susan G. 1996. "The Theme Park: Global Industry and Cultural Form." *Media, Culture and Society* 18 (3), pp. 399–422.

———. 1999. "Space Jam: Media Conglomerates Build the Entertainment City." *European Journal of Communication* 14 (4), pp. 435–59.

Denning, Michael. 1987. *Mechanic Accents: Dime Novels and Working-Class Culture in America.* London: Verso.

Dessauer, John P. 1985. "Book Industry Economics in 1984." In *The Book Publishing Annual,* pp. 105–20. New York: R. R. Bowker.

———. 1986. "Cultural Pluralism and the Book World." *Book Research Quarterly* 2 (3), pp. 3–6.

———. 1993. *Book Publishing: The Basic Introduction.* New expanded ed. New York: Continuum.

DiMaggio, Paul. 1986. "Cultural Entrepreneurship in Nineteenth-Century Boston: The Creation of an Organizational Base for High Culture in America." In *Media, Culture and Society: A Critical Reader,* ed. Richard Collins, James Curran, Nicholas Garnham, Paddy Scannell, Philip Schlesinger, and Colin Sparks, pp. 194–211. London: Sage.

———. 1990. "Cultural Aspects of Economic Action and Organization." In *Beyond the Marketplace: Rethinking Economy and Society,* ed. Roger Friedland and A. F. Robertson, pp. 113–36. New York: Aldine de Gruyter.

———. 1994. "Culture and Economy." In *The Handbook of Economic Sociology,* ed. Neil J. Smelser and Richard Swedberg, pp. 27–57. Princeton: Princeton University Press.

Dixon, Christopher M., Lynne (E. F.) McKechnie, Laura J. Miller, and Paulette M. Rothbauer. 2001. "Latte Grande, No Sprinkles: An Exploratory Observational

Study of Customer Behaviour at Chapters Bookstores." In *Beyond the Web: Technologies, Knowledge and People: Proceedings of the 29th Annual Conference of the Canadian Association for Information Science [Université Laval, Québec, May 27–29]*, pp. 165–74. Toronto: Canadian Association for Information Science.

Dobbin, Frank R. 1994. "Cultural Models of Organization: The Social Construction of Rational Organizing Principles." In *The Sociology of Culture: Emerging Theoretical Perspectives*, ed. Diana Crane, pp. 117–41. Oxford: Blackwell.

Doebler, Paul D. 1978. "Areas of Major Change in the Book Industry Today." In *Book Industry Trends, 1978*, ed. John P. Dessauer, Paul D. Doebler, and E. Wayne Nordberg, pp. 7–58. Darien, Conn.: Book Industry Study Group.

Doubleday, F. N. 1972. *The Memoirs of a Publisher*. Garden City, N.Y.: Doubleday.

Du Gay, Paul, and Michael Pryke. 2002. "Cultural Economy: An Introduction." In *Cultural Economy: Cultural Analysis and Commercial Life*, ed. Paul du Gay and Michael Pryke, pp. 1–19. London: Sage.

Duffus, R. L. 1930. *Books: Their Place in a Democracy*. Boston: Houghton Mifflin.

Durkheim, Emile. [1925] 1973. *Moral Education: A Study in the Theory and Application of the Sociology of Education*. New York: Free Press.

Dutscher, Alan. 1954. "The Book Business in America." *Contemporary Issues* 5 (17), pp. 38–58.

Eisenstein, Elizabeth L. [1979] 1980. *The Printing Press as an Agent of Change: Communications and Cultural Transformations in Early-Modern Europe*. 2 vols. in 1. Cambridge: Cambridge University Press.

Ellul, Jacques. [1965] 1973. *Propaganda: The Formation of Men's Attitudes*. New York: Vintage Books.

Eppard, Philip B. 1986. "The Rental Library in Twentieth-Century America." *Journal of Library History* 21 (1), pp. 240–52.

Epstein, Jason. 2001. *Book Business: Publishing Past, Present, and Future*. New York: W. W. Norton.

Escarpit, Robert. [1965] 1966. *The Book Revolution*. London: George G. Harap & Co.

———. [1958] 1971. *Sociology of Literature*. 2nd ed. London: Frank Cass & Co.

Falk, Pasi, and Colin Campbell, eds. 1997. *The Shopping Experience*. London: Sage.

Febvre, Lucien, and Henri-Jean Martin. [1958] 1990. *The Coming of the Book: The Impact of Printing, 1450–1800*. London: Verso.

Ferkauf, Eugene. 1977. *Going into Business: How to Do It, by the Man Who Did It*. New York: Chelsea House Publishers.

Fiske, John. [1987] 1989. *Television Culture*. London: Routledge.

———. 1989. *Understanding Popular Culture*. London: Routledge.

———. [1989] 1991. *Reading the Popular*. London: Routledge.

Fitch, James Marston. [1982] 1990. *Historic Preservation: Curatorial Management of the Built World*. Charlottesville: University Press of Virginia.

Flowers, Montaville. 1931. *America Chained: A Discussion of "What's Wrong with the Chain Store."* Pasadena: Montaville Flowers Publicists.

Francaviglia, Richard V. 1996. *Main Street Revisited: Time, Space, and Image Building in Small-Town America.* Iowa City: University of Iowa Press.

Frank, Dana. 1991. "'Food Wins All Struggles': Seattle Labor and the Politicization of Consumption." *Radical History Review,* no. 51, pp. 65–89.

Fraser, Nancy. 1992. "Rethinking the Public Sphere: A Contribution to the Critique of Actually Existing Democracy." In *Habermas and the Public Sphere,* ed. Craig Calhoun, pp. 109–142. Cambridge: MIT Press.

Friedland, Roger, and Robert R. Alford. 1991. "Bringing Society Back In: Symbols, Practices, and Institutional Contradictions." In *The New Institutionalism in Organizational Analysis,* ed. Walter W. Powell and Paul J. DiMaggio, pp. 232–63. Chicago: University of Chicago Press.

Friedman, Monroe. 1999. *Consumer Boycotts: Effecting Change through the Marketplace and the Media.* New York: Routledge.

Fulton, Len. 1973. "Peopleship." In *The Whole COSMEP Catalog,* ed. Dick Higgins, pp. 5–6. Paradise, Calif.: Dustbooks.

Gans, Herbert J. 1974. *Popular Culture and High Culture: An Analysis and Evaluation of Taste.* New York: Basic Books.

———. [1967] 1982. *The Levittowners: Ways of Life and Politics in a New Suburban Community.* New York: Columbia University Press.

Garrison, Dee. [1979] 2003. *Apostles of Culture: The Public Librarian and American Society, 1876–1920.* Madison: University of Wisconsin Press.

Gilreath, James. 1985. "American Book Distribution." *Proceedings of the American Antiquarian Society* 95, part 2, pp. 501–83.

Gitlin, Todd. 1985. *Inside Prime Time.* New York: Pantheon Books.

"Goals and Programs: A Summary of the Study Committee Report to the Board of Trustees, the National Trust for Historic Preservation, 1973." [1973] 1976. In *The History of the National Trust for Historic Preservation, 1963–1973,* ed. Elizabeth D. Mulloy, pp. 280–85. Washington, D.C.: Preservation Press.

Gordon, Ruth I. 1977. "Paul Elder: Bookseller-Publisher, 1897–1917: A Bay Area Reflection." Ph.D. diss., University of California, Berkeley.

Grannis, Chandler B. 1985. "Title Output and Average Prices." In *The Book Publishing Annual,* pp. 121–29. New York: R. R. Bowker.

Granovetter, Mark. [1985] 1992. "Economic Action and Social Structure: The Problem of Embeddedness." In *The Sociology of Economic Life,* ed. Mark Granovetter and Richard Swedberg, pp. 53–81. Boulder: Westview Press.

———. 1992. "Economic Institutions as Social Constructions: A Framework for Analysis." *Acta Sociologica* 35 (1), pp. 3–11.

Greco, Albert. 2000. "Market Concentration Levels in the U.S. Consumer Book Industry, 1995–1996." *Journal of Cultural Economics* 24 (4), pp. 321–336.

Greco, Albert N. 1989. "Mergers and Acquisitions in Publishing, 1984–1988: Some Public Policy Issues." *Book Research Quarterly* 5 (3), pp. 25–44.

Grether, Ewald T. [1939] 1976. *Price Control under Fair Trade Legislation.* New York: Arno Press.

Grodin, Debra. 1991. "The Interpreting Audience: The Therapeutics of Self-Help Book Reading." *Critical Studies in Mass Communication* 8 (4), pp. 404–20.

Gross, Sidney. 1965. "How to Stock." In *How to Run a Paperback Bookshop*, ed. Sidney Gross and Phyllis B. Steckler, pp. 52–64. New York: R. R. Bowker.

Gusfield, Joseph R. 1975. *Community: A Critical Response.* New York: Harper & Row.

Haas, Harold M. [1939] 1979. *Social and Economic Aspects of the Chain Store Movement.* New York: Arno Press.

Habermas, Jürgen. [1962] 1989. *The Structural Transformation of the Public Sphere: An Inquiry into a Category of Bourgeois Society.* Cambridge: MIT Press.

———. 1990. *Moral Consciousness and Communicative Action.* Cambridge: MIT Press.

Halebsky, Stephen Eugene. 2001. "Small Towns and Big Stores: Local Controversies over the Siting of Superstores." Ph.D. diss., University of Wisconsin, Madison.

Hallsworth, Alan G., Ken G. Jones, and Russell Muncaster. 1995. "The Planning Implications of New Retail Format Introductions in Canada and Britain." *Service Industries Journal* (4), pp. 148–63.

Hanchett, Thomas W. 1996. "U.S. Tax Policy and the Shopping-Center Boom of the 1950s and 1960s." *American Historical Review* 101 (4), pp. 1082–1110.

Handler, Julian H. 1966. *How to Sell the Supermarkets: For Non-Food Manufacturers and Distributors.* 3rd ed. New York: Fairchild Publications.

Haugland, Ann. 1994. "Books as Culture/Books as Commerce." *Journalism Quarterly* 71 (4), pp. 787–99.

Hayward, Walter S., and Percival White. 1925. *Chain Stores: Their Management and Operation.* 2nd ed. New York: McGraw Hill.

Henderson, Bill. 1975. "Independent Publishing: Today and Yesterday." *Annals of the American Academy of Political and Social Science* 421, pp. 93–105.

Hesmondhalgh, David. 1999. "Indie: The Institutional Politics and Aesthetics of a Popular Music Genre." *Cultural Studies* 13 (1), pp. 34–61.

Hirsch, Paul M. [1972] 1992. "Processing Fads and Fashions: An Organization-Set Analysis of Cultural Industry Systems." In *The Sociology of Economic Life*, ed. Mark Granovetter and Richard Swedberg, pp. 363–83. Boulder: Westview Press.

Hochschild, Arlie Russell. 1983. *The Managed Heart: Commercialization of Human Feeling.* Berkeley and Los Angeles: University of California Press.

Hollander, S. C. 1966. "United States of America." In *Resale Price Maintenance*, ed. B. S. Yamey, pp. 65–100. Chicago: Aldine.

Horowitz, Helen Lefkowitz. [1976] 1989. *Culture and the City: Cultural Philanthropy in Chicago from the 1880s to 1917.* Chicago: University of Chicago Press.

Horowitz, Irving Louis. 1991. *Communicating Ideas: The Politics of Scholarly Publishing.* 2nd expanded ed. New Brunswick: Transaction.

Hosmer, Charles B. Jr. 1981. *Preservation Comes of Age: From Williamsburg to the National Trust, 1926–1949.* 2 vols. Charlottesville: University Press of Virginia.

Hower, Ralph M. 1943. *History of Macy's of New York, 1858–1919: Chapters in the Evolution of the Department Store.* Cambridge: Harvard University Press.

Humphrey, Kim. 1998. *Shelf Life: Supermarkets and the Changing Cultures of Consumption.* Cambridge: Cambridge University Press.

Ingram, Paul, and Hayagreeva Rao. 2004. "Store Wars: The Enactment and Repeal of Anti-Chain-Store Legislation in America." *American Journal of Sociology* 110 (2), pp. 446–87.

Jackson, Kenneth T. 1985. *Crabgrass Frontier: The Suburbanization of the United States.* New York: Oxford University Press.

———. 1996. "All the World's a Mall: Reflections on the Social and Economic Consequences of the American Shopping Center." *American Historical Review* 101 (4), pp. 1111–21.

Jacobs, Jane. [1961] 1992. *The Death and Life of Great American Cities.* New York: Vintage Books.

Jakle, John A. 1982. "Roadside Restaurants and Place-Product-Packaging." *Journal of Cultural Geography* 3, pp. 76–93.

Kammen, Michael. 1999. *American Cultures American Tastes: Social Change and the 20th Century.* New York: Basic Books.

Kasson, John F. 1978. *Amusing the Million: Coney Island at the Turn of the Century.* New York: Hill & Wang.

Kirkpatrick, David D. 2000. *Report to the Authors Guild Midlist Books Study Committee.* Authors Guild and Open Society Institute.

Klein, Naomi. 2000. *No Logo: Taking Aim at the Brand Bullies.* Toronto: Vintage Canada.

Kotler, Philip. 2003. *Marketing Management.* 11th ed. Upper Saddle River, N.J.: Prentice Hall.

Kowinski, William Severini. 1985. *The Malling of America: An Inside Look at the Great Consumer Paradise.* New York: William Morrow.

Lacy, Dan. 1967. "The Changing Face of Publishing." In *What Happens in Book Publishing,* 2nd ed., ed. Chandler B. Grannis, pp. 423–37. New York: Columbia University Press.

———. 1992. "From Family Enterprise to Global Conglomerate." *Media Studies Journal* 6 (3), pp. 1–13.

Lane, Michael. 1970. "Publishing Managers, Publishing House Organization and Role Conflict." *Sociology* 4 (3), pp. 367–83.

———. 1975. "Shapers of Culture: The Editor in Book Publishing." *Annals of the American Academy of Political and Social Science* 421, pp. 34–42.

Lane, Michael, with Jeremy Booth. 1980. *Books and Publishers: Commerce against Culture in Postwar Britain.* Lexington, Mass.: Lexington Books.

Lasch, Christopher. 1984. *The Minimal Self: Psychic Survival in Troubled Times.* New York: W. W. Norton.

Lasswell, Harold D. [1927] 1971. *Propaganda Technique in World War I.* Cambridge: MIT Press.

Leach, William. 1989. "Strategists of Display and the Production of Desire." In *Consuming Visions: Accumulation and Display of Goods in America, 1889–1920,* ed. Simon J. Bronner, pp. 99–132. New York: W. W. Norton.

————. 1993. *Land of Desire: Merchants, Power, and the Rise of a New American Culture.* New York: Vintage Books.

Lebhar, Godfrey M. 1963. *Chain Stores in America, 1859–1962.* 3rd ed. New York: Chain Store Publishing Corporation.

Lee, Jennifer. 2002. *Civility in the City: Blacks, Jews, and Koreans in Urban America.* Cambridge, Mass.: Harvard University Press.

Lee, Maurice W. 1939. "Anti-Chain-Store Tax Legislation." *Journal of Business of the University of Chicago* 12 (3), pp. 1–80.

Lehmann-Haupt, Hellmut. 1952. "Book Production and Distribution from 1860 to the Present Day." In *The Book in America: A History of the Making and Selling of Books in the United States,* 2nd ed., by Hellmut Lehmann-Haupt, in collaboration with Lawrence C. Wroth and Rollo G. Silver, pp. 137–419. New York: R. R. Bowker.

Leidner, Robin. 1993. *Fast Food, Fast Talk: Service Work and the Routinization of Everyday Life.* Berkeley and Los Angeles: University of California Press.

Leonard, Eliot. 1985. "Bookstore Chains." In *The Business of Book Publishing: Papers by Practitioners,* ed. Elizabeth A. Geiser, Arnold Dolin, with Gladys S. Topkis, pp. 244–55. Boulder: Westview Press.

Levine, Lawrence W. 1988. *Highbrow/Lowbrow: The Emergence of Cultural Hierarchy in America.* Cambridge: Harvard University Press.

Liebs, Chester H. 1978. "Remember Our Not-So-Distant Past?" *Historic Preservation* 30 (1), pp. 30–35.

Long, Elizabeth. 1985. *The American Dream and the Popular Novel.* Boston: Routledge & Kegan Paul.

————. 1985–86. "The Cultural Meaning of Concentration in Publishing." *Book Research Quarterly* 1 (4), pp. 3–27.

Longstreth, Richard. 1997. *City Center to Regional Mall: Architecture, the Automobile, and Retailing in Los Angeles, 1920–1950.* Cambridge: MIT Press.

Luey, Beth. 1992. "The Impact of Consolidation and Internationalization." Introduction to *The Structure of International Publishing in the 1990s,* ed. Fred Kobrak and Beth Luey, pp. 1–22. New Brunswick: Transaction.

Luxenberg, Stan. 1985. *Roadside Empires: How the Chains Franchised America.* New York: Viking.

————. 1991. *Books in Chains: Chain Bookstores and Marketplace Censorship.* New York: National Writers Union.

Lynch, Kevin. 1972. *What Time Is This Place?* Cambridge: MIT Press.

Mabie, Hamilton Wright. 1896. *Books and Culture.* New York: Dodd, Mead and Company.

Macdonald, Kent. 1985. "The Commercial Strip: From Main Street to Television Road." *Landscape* 28 (2), pp. 12–19.

Madison, Charles A. 1966. *Book Publishing in America.* New York: McGraw-Hill.

Mahoney, Tom, and Leonard Sloane. 1966. *The Great Merchants: America's Foremost Retail Institutions and the People Who Made Them Great.* New and enlarged ed. New York: Harper & Row.

Marcuse, Herbert. 1964. *One-Dimensional Man: Studies in the Ideology of Advanced Industrial Society.* Boston: Beacon Press.

Market Facts Inc. 1984. *1983 Consumer Research Study on Reading and Book Purchasing: Focus on Adults.* New York: Book Industry Study Group.

Marlin, Randal. 2002. *Propaganda and the Ethics of Persuasion.* Peterborough, Ontario: Broadview.

Marx, Karl. [1869] 1963. *The Eighteenth Brumaire of Louis Bonaparte.* New York: International Publishers.

Marx, Karl, and Friedrich Engels. [1848] 1978. "Manifesto of the Communist Party." In *The Marx-Engels Reader,* 2nd ed., ed. Robert C. Tucker, pp. 469–500. New York: W. W. Norton.

Mayer, Robert. N. 1989. *The Consumer Movement: Guardians of the Marketplace.* Boston: Twayne.

Mayo, James M. 1993. *The American Grocery Store: The Business Evolution of an Architectural Space.* Westport, Conn.: Greenwood.

Miller, Laura J. 1999. "Cultural Authority and the Use of New Technology in the Book Trade." *Journal of Arts Management, Law, and Society* 28 (4), pp. 297–313.

———. 2000. "The Best-Seller List as Marketing Tool and Historical Fiction." *Book History* 3, pp. 286–304.

———. 2001. "Publishing as Medium." In *International Encyclopedia of the Social and Behavioral Sciences,* ed. Neil J. Smelser and Paul B. Baltes, pp. 12599–603. Amsterdam: Pergamon.

———. 2003. "The Rise and Not-Quite-Fall of the American Book Wholesaler." *Journal of Media Economics* 16 (2), pp. 97–120.

———. Forthcoming. "Selling the Product." In *A History of the Book in America.* Vol. 5, *The Enduring Book: Print Culture in Postwar America,* ed. David Paul Nord, Joan Shelley Rubin, and Michael Schudson. New York: Cambridge University Press.

Miller, Laura J., Lynne (E. F.) McKechnie, and Paulette M. Rothbauer. 2003. "The Clash between Armchairs and Cash Registers: Customer Behavior and Corporate Strategies at Book Superstores." Paper presented at the Eleventh Annual Conference of the Society for the History of Authorship, Reading and Publishing, Claremont, Calif., July 11.

Miller, William. 1949. *The Book Industry.* New York: Columbia University Press.

Mills, C. Wright. 1951. *White Collar: The American Middle Classes.* New York: Oxford University Press.

Mitchell, Stacey. 2000. *The Home Town Advantage: How to Defend Your Main Street against Chain Stores . . . and Why It Matters.* Minneapolis: Institute for Local Self-Reliance.

Monod, David. 1996. *Store Wars: Shopkeepers and the Culture of Mass Marketing, 1890–1939.* Toronto: University of Toronto Press.

Morton, Fiona M. Scott, and Joel M. Podolny. 2002. "Love or Money? The Effects of Owner Motivation in the California Wine Industry." *Journal of Industrial Economics* 50 (4), pp. 431–56.

Nava, Mica. 1991. "Consumerism Reconsidered: Buying and Power." *Cultural Studies* 5 (1), pp. 157–73.

Nelson, Walter Henry. 1965. *The Great Discount Delusion*. New York: David McKay.

Nichols, John P. 1940. *The Chain Store Tells Its Story*. New York: Institute of Distribution.

NPD Group Inc. 1993. *1991–1992 Consumer Research Study on Book Purchasing*. New York: Book Industry Study Group.

NPD Group Inc., and Carol Meyer. 1998. *1997 Consumer Research Study on Book Purchasing*. New York: Book Industry Study Group.

———. 2000. *The 1999 Consumer Research Study on Book Purchasing*. New York: Book Industry Study Group.

Nystrom, Paul H. 1932. *Economics of Retailing: Retail Institutions and Trends*. 3rd revised and enlarged ed. New York: Ronald Press.

Ohmann, Richard. 1983. "The Shaping of a Canon: U.S. Fiction, 1960–1975." *Critical Inquiry* 10 (1), pp. 199–223.

Oldenburg, Ray. 1989. *The Great Good Place: Cafes, Coffee Shops, Community Centers, Beauty Parlors, General Stores, Bars, Hangouts and How They Get You through the Day*. New York: Paragon House.

Oliver, Marshal L. 1969. "Is an Architect Necessary?" In *A Manual on Bookselling*, 1st ed., ed. Charles B. Anderson, Joseph A. Duffy, and Jocelyn D. Kahn, pp. 19–24. New York: American Booksellers Association.

Oppenheimer, Martin. 1994. "Small-Minded." *Dollars and Sense*, no. 196, November/December, pp. 20–21, 39–40.

Palamountain, Joseph Cornwall Jr. [1955] 1968. *The Politics of Distribution*. New York: Greenwood.

Pearce, Charles Albert. 1939. *NRA Trade Practice Programs*. New York: Columbia University Press.

Peck, Abe. 1998. "From Underground to Alternative: Peace Signs and Dollar Signs." *Media Studies Journal* 12 (3), pp. 156–162.

Peiss, Kathy. 1986. *Cheap Amusements: Working Women and Leisure in Turn-of-the-Century New York*. Philadelphia: Temple University Press.

Phillips, Charles F. 1936. "State Discriminatory Chain Store Taxation." *Harvard Business Review* 14 (3), pp. 349–59.

Phillips, Patrick L. 1995. "Merging Entertainment and Retailing." *Economic Development Review* 13 (2), pp. 13–15.

Polanyi, Karl. [1944] 1957. *The Great Transformation*. Boston: Beacon.

———. [1947] 1996. "Our Obsolete Market Mentality: Civilization Must Find a New Thought Pattern." In *Economic Sociology*, ed. Richard Swedberg, pp. 146–54. Cheltenham: Edward Elgar Publishing.

Pollack, Norman. 1990. *The Humane Economy: Populism, Capitalism, and Democracy*. New Brunswick: Rutgers University Press.

Postman, Neil. [1985] 1986. *Amusing Ourselves to Death: Public Discourse in the Age of Show Business*. New York: Penguin Books.

Powell, Walter W. 1980. "Competition versus Concentration in the Book Trade." *Journal of Communication* 30 (2), pp. 89–97.

———. 1983. "Whither the Local Bookstore?" *Daedalus* 112 (1), pp. 51–64.

———. 1985. *Getting into Print: The Decision-Making Process in Scholarly Publishing.* Chicago: University of Chicago Press.

The Project on Disney. 1995. *Inside the Mouse: Work and Play at Disney World.* Durham: Duke University Press.

Radway, Janice. 1989. "The Book-of-the-Month Club and the General Reader: On the Uses of 'Serious Fiction.'" In *Literature and Social Practice,* ed. Philippe Desan, Priscilla Parkhurst Ferguson, and Wendy Griswold, pp. 154–76. Chicago: University of Chicago Press.

———. 1990. "The Scandal of the Middlebrow: The Book-of-the-Month Club, Class Fracture, and Cultural Authority." *South Atlantic Quarterly* 89 (4), pp. 703–36.

———. 1992. "Mail-Order Culture and Its Critics: The Book-of-the-Month Club, Commodification and Consumption, and the Problem of Cultural Authority." In *Cultural Studies,* ed. Lawrence Grossberg, Cary Nelson, and Paula A. Treichler, pp. 512–30. New York: Routledge.

———. 1997. *A Feeling for Books: The Book-of-the-Month Club, Literary Taste, and Middle-Class Desire.* Chapel Hill: University of North Carolina Press.

Reference Press and Publishers Group West. 1993. *Hoover's Guide to the Book Business.* Austin: Reference Press.

Relph, E. 1976. *Place and Placelessness.* London: Pion.

Richberg, Donald R. [1938] 1939. "Who Wants Chain Stores?" In *Chain Stores and Legislation,* ed. Daniel Bloomfield, pp. 110–15. New York: H. W. Wilson.

Riesman, David. 1954. "Bookworms and the Social Soil." In *Individualism Reconsidered and Other Essays,* pp. 258–65. Glencoe, Ill.: Free Press.

Ritzer, George. 1996. *The McDonaldization of Society: An Investigation into the Changing Character of Contemporary Social Life,* revised ed. Thousand Oaks, Calif.: Sage.

Robinson, Michael J., and Ray Olszewski. 1980. "Books in the Marketplace of Ideas." *Journal of Communication* 30 (2), pp. 81–88.

Rosenbloom, Joshua L. 1991. "Economics and the Emergence of Modern Publishing in the United States." *Publishing History* 29, pp. 47–68.

Rousseau, Jean-Jacques. 1967. *The Social Contract and Discourse on the Origin of Inequality.* New York: Washington Square Press.

Ryan, Neal. 2001. "Reconstructing Citizens as Consumers: Implications for New Modes of Governance." *Australian Journal of Public Administration* 60 (3), pp. 104–9.

Sahlins, Marshall. 1972. *Stone Age Economics.* Chicago: Aldine Atherton.

Sams, E. C. [1929] 1930. "Is the Chain System Detrimental to Personal Opportunity and Initiative." In *Current, Conflicting Views on the Chain Store Controversy,* ed. T. H. Hall, p. 46. Chicago: National Research Bureau.

Samson, Peter. 1981. "The Department Store, Its Past and Its Future: A Review Article." *Business History Review* 55 (1), pp. 26–34.

Schick, Frank L. 1958. *The Paperbound Book in America: The History of Paperbacks and Their European Background.* New York: R. R. Bowker.

Schiffrin, André. 2000. *The Business of Books: How International Conglomerates Took Over Publishing and Changed the Way We Read.* London: Verso.

"Shall We Curb the Chain Stores?" [1938] 1939. In *Chain Stores and Legislation,* ed. Daniel Bloomfield, pp. 28–35. New York: H. W. Wilson.

Shatzkin, Leonard. 1982. *In Cold Type: Overcoming the Book Crisis.* Boston: Houghton Mifflin.

Sheehan, Donald. 1952. *This Was Publishing: A Chronicle of the Book Trade in the Gilded Age.* Bloomington: Indiana University Press.

Shi, David E. 1985. *The Simple Life: Plain Living and High Thinking in American Culture.* New York: Oxford University Press.

Shields, Rob. 1992. "The Individual, Consumption Cultures and the Fate of Community." In *Lifestyle Shopping: The Subject of Consumption,* ed. Rob Shields, pp. 99–113. London: Routledge.

———. 1992. "Spaces for the Subject of Consumption." In *Lifestyle Shopping: The Subject of Consumption,* ed. Rob Shields, pp. 1–20. London: Routledge.

———, ed. 1992. *Lifestyle Shopping: The Subject of Consumption.* London: Routledge.

Shils, Edward. 1963. "The Bookshop in America." In *The American Reading Public: What It Reads, Why It Reads,* ed. Roger H. Smith, pp. 138–50. New York: R. R. Bowker.

Slater, Don. 1997. *Consumer Culture and Modernity.* Cambridge: Polity.

———. 2002. "Capturing Markets from the Economists." In *Cultural Economy: Cultural Analysis and Commercial Life,* ed. Paul du Gay and Michael Pryke, pp. 59–77. London: Sage.

Slater, Philip. [1970] 1976. *The Pursuit of Loneliness: American Culture at the Breaking Point.* Revised ed. Boston: Beacon Press.

Smith, Roger H. 1976. *Paperback Parnassus: The Birth, the Development, the Pending Crisis . . . of the Modern American Paperbound Book.* Boulder: Westview Press.

Sorkin, Michael, ed. 1992. *Variations on a Theme Park: The New American City and the End of Public Space.* New York: Noonday Press.

Stokmans, M., and M. Hendrickx. 1994. "The Attention Paid to New Book Releases on a Display Table." *Poetics* 22 (3), pp. 185–97.

Stone, Gregory P. 1954. "City Shoppers and Urban Identification: Observations on the Social Psychology of City Life." *American Journal of Sociology* 60 (1), pp. 36–45.

Strasser, Susan. 1989. *Satisfaction Guaranteed: The Making of the American Mass Market.* Washington, D.C.: Smithsonian Institution Press.

Swidler, Ann 1986. "Culture in Action: Symbols and Strategies." *American Sociological Review* 51 (2), pp. 273–86.

Swingewood, Alan. 1977. *The Myth of Mass Culture.* London: Macmillan.

Symons, Allene, and Sonja Bolle. 1985. "Issues in Bookselling, 1984." In *The Book Publishing Annual,* pp. 185–92. New York: R. R. Bowker.

Tebbel, John. 1972. *A History of Book Publishing in the United States.* Vol. 1, *The Creation of an Industry, 1630–1865.* New York: R. R. Bowker.

———. 1975. *A History of Book Publishing in the United States.* Vol. 2, *The Expansion of an Industry, 1865–1919.* New York: R. R. Bowker.

———. 1978. *A History of Book Publishing in the United States.* Vol. 3, *The Golden Age between Two Wars, 1920–1940.* New York: R. R. Bowker.

Thornton, Patricia H. 2004. *Markets from Culture: Institutional Logics and Organizational Decisions in Higher Education Publishing.* Stanford: Stanford Business Books.

Trachtenberg, Alan. 1982. *The Incorporation of America: Culture and Society in the Gilded Age.* New York: Hill & Wang.

Tryon, W. S. 1947. "Book Distribution in Mid-Nineteenth Century America: Illustrated by the Publishing Records of Ticknor and Fields, Boston." *Papers of the Bibliographical Society of America* 41 (3), pp. 210–30.

Van Ginkel, Blanche Lemco. [1961] 1971. "Aesthetic Considerations." In *Urban Problems: A Canadian Reader,* ed. Ralph R. Krueger and R. Charles Bryfogle, pp. 46–50. Toronto: Holt, Rinehart and Winston of Canada.

Veblen, Thorstein. 1904. *The Theory of Business Enterprise.* New York: Charles Scribner's Sons.

Venturi, Robert, Denise Scott Brown, and Steven Izenour. [1972] 1977. *Learning from Las Vegas: The Forgotten Symbolism of Architectural Form.* Revised ed. Cambridge: MIT Press.

Veronis Suhler Stevenson. 2003. *Communications Industry Forecast and Report.* 17th ed./ 21st ed. New York: Veronis Suhler Stevenson.

Walden, Keith. 1989. "Speaking Modern: Language, Culture, and Hegemony in Grocery Window Displays, 1887–1920." *Canadian Historical Review* 70 (3), pp. 285–310.

Wanamaker, John. 1911. *Golden Book of the Wanamaker Stores.* Philadelphia: John Wanamaker.

Weber, Lee A. 1969. "Managing a Branch Bookstore: Problems and Responsibilities." In *A Manual on Bookselling,* 1st ed., ed. Charles B. Anderson, Joseph A. Duffy, and Jocelyn D. Kahn, pp. 213–16. New York: American Booksellers Association.

Weber, Max. [1915] 1946. "Religious Rejections of the World and Their Directions." In *From Max Weber: Essays in Sociology,* ed. H. H. Gerth and C. Wright Mills, pp. 323–59. New York: Oxford University Press.

———. 1978. *Economy and Society: An Outline of Interpretive Sociology.* Vol. 1. Berkeley: University of California Press.

Wendt, Lloyd, and Herman Kogan. 1952. *Give the Lady What She Wants! The Story of Marshall Field & Company.* Chicago: Rand McNally.

Wheeler, Coburn T. 1933. "The Position of the Wholesaler in the Book Trade." *Harvard Business Review* 11 (2), pp. 237–43.

White, Ken, and Frank White. 1996. *Display and Visual Merchandising.* Westwood, N.J.: St. Francis Press.

Wilentz, Theodore. 1963. "American Bookselling in the 1960's." In *The American Reading Public: What It Reads, Why It Reads,* ed. Roger H. Smith, pp. 151–66. New York: R. R. Bowker.

Williams, Raymond. 1958. *Culture and Society, 1780–1950.* New York: Harper Torchbooks.

———. 1977. *Marxism and Literature.* Oxford: Oxford University Press.

Williamson, Thad, David Imbroscio, and Gar Alperovitz. 2002. *Making a Place for Community: Local Democracy in a Global Era.* New York: Routledge.

Winkler, John K. 1940. *Five and Ten: The Fabulous Life of F. W. Woolworth.* New York: Robert M. McBride.

Wirtén, Eva Hemmungs. 1998. *Global Infatuation: Explorations in Transnational Publishing and Texts: The Case of Harlequin Enterprises and Sweden.* Uppsala: Section for Sociology of Literature at the Department of Literature, Uppsala University.

Wolfenstein, Martha. 1955. "Fun Morality: An Analysis of Recent American Child-Training Literature." In *Childhood in Contemporary Cultures,* ed. Margaret Mead and Martha Wolfenstein, pp. 168–78. Chicago: University of Chicago Press.

Wroth, Lawrence C. 1952. "Book Production and Distribution from the Beginning to the American Revolution." In *The Book in America: A History of the Making and Selling of Books in the United States,* 2nd ed., by Hellmut Lehmann-Haupt, in collaboration with Lawrence C. Wroth, and Rollo G. Silver, pp. 1–59. New York: R. R. Bowker.

Zboray, Ronald J. 1993. *A Fictive People: Antebellum Economic Development and the American Reading Public.* New York: Oxford University Press.

Zelizer, Viviana A. [1978] 1992. "Human Values and the Market: The Case of Life Insurance and Death in 19th-Century America." In *The Sociology of Economic Life,* ed. Mark Granovetter and Richard Swedberg, pp. 285–304. Boulder: Westview Press.

———. 1994. *The Social Meaning of Money.* New York: Basic Books.

Zimmerman, M. M. 1937. *Super Market: Spectacular Exponent of Mass Distribution.* New York: Super Market Publishing Co.

———. 1955. *The Super Market: A Revolution in Distribution.* New York: McGraw-Hill.

Zukin, Sharon. 1995. *The Cultures of Cities.* Cambridge, Mass.: Blackwell.

———. 2004. *Point of Purchase: How Shopping Changed American Culture.* New York: Routledge.

Zukin, Sharon, and Paul DiMaggio. 1990. Introduction to *Structures of Capital: The Social Organization of the Economy,* ed. Sharon Zukin and Paul DiMaggio, pp. 1–36. Cambridge: Cambridge University Press.

ABA. *See* American Booksellers Association (ABA)
ABBY awards, 186–87
ABC network, 134
About Books (television program), 133
accounting systems, 31–32
activism: bigness vs. capitalism in, 191–95; branding juxtaposed to, 184, 188–91; collective identity and, 162; context of, 161–63, 198–99; definitions in, 164–67; limits of, 12, 191, 192–93; against merger of Ingram and Barnes & Noble, 181–82; mergers/acquisitions as influence on, 178; moral justification for, 163, 179, 181, 192, 194–95; public relations campaigns as, 183–87; of trade associations, 169–74, 177–81, 271n.45; understandings of consumption in, 200. *See also* anti–chain store movements; legal actions
added value concept, 142
advertising: of Book Sense, 186; co-op practices and, 99–105, 149, 167–68, 185; of discounts, 96, 144–45, 146, 149; entertainment as/as entertainment, 134–35; media publicity and, 133–34
aesthetics, 109–10
agents, 5

Albuquerque (N.M.): bookstores in, 128, 163
alcoholic drinks: in cafés, 126; cross-promotion of, 186
alienation: identity and standardization juxtaposed to, 110; of staff, 15
alternative presses. *See* independent presses; small presses
Amazon.com: book talk (entertainment) on, 134; branding of, 189; as chain equivalent, 182–83; co-op practices of, 101; discounting practices of, 147, 148, 228; emergence and growth of, 52, 114; links to, 280n.41; power of, 226; reviews on, 80–81; unionization efforts at, 207
American Book Publishers Council, 29–30, 155
American Bookseller (periodical), 170
American Booksellers Association (ABA): chain-independent conflict in, 170–74; on community service, 121, 123; convention of, 20, 178; co-op practices and, 102–3; on discounting practices, 145, 153–54; on failing bookstores, 162; finances of, 186; lawsuit against chain bookstores, 180–81, 268n.15; lawsuit against publishers, 102, 177–80;